CRIMINA N EUROPE

Every managerial decision is risky, at least to some extent. Conducting business is impossible without venturing into new territories and even the most ordinary daily choices could turn out to be failures. Excessive risk, however, can be very detrimental, as was starkly illustrated by the most recent financial crisis. By criminalising managers' excessive risk-taking, criminal law enters a sphere which is at the core of the activity it affects. At the same time it provides for criminal punishment for courses of conduct that, without doubt, can be extremely harmful. This book examines existing criminalisation of excessive risk-taking and analyses whether such criminalisation is desirable and under which conditions.

Volume 8 in the series Hart Studies in European Criminal Law

Hart Studies in European Criminal Law

Series Editors: Professor Katalin Ligeti, University of Luxembourg;
Professor Valsamis Mitsilegas, Queen Mary University of London;
Professor Anne Weyembergh, Brussels Free University

Since the Lisbon Treaty, European criminal law has become an increasingly important field of research and debate. Working with the European Criminal Law Academic Network (ECLAN), the series will publish works of the highest intellectual rigour and cutting edge scholarship which will be required reading for all European criminal lawyers.

The series is happy to consider both edited and single authored titles. The series defines 'European' and 'criminal law' in the broadest sense, so books on European criminal law, justice and policy will be considered. The series also welcomes books which offer different methodological approaches.

Volume 1: *EU Criminal Law after Lisbon: Rights, Trust and the Transformation of Justice in Europe*
by Valsamis Mitsilegas

Volume 2: *Challenges in the Field of Economic and Financial Crime in Europe and the US*
Edited by Vanessa Franssen and Katalin Ligeti

Volume 3: *Chasing Criminal Money: Challenges and Perspectives On Asset Recovery in the EU*
Edited by Katalin Ligeti and Michele Simonato

Volume 4: *Limits to EU Powers: A Case Study of EU Regulatory Criminal Law*
by Jacob Öberg

Volume 5: *The Needed Balances in EU Criminal Law: Past, Present and Future*
Edited by Chloé Brière and Anne Weyembergh

Volume 6: *Redefining Organised Crime: A Challenge for the European Union?*
Edited by Stefania Carnevale, Serena Forlati and Orsetta Giolo

Volume 7: *White Collar Crime: A Comparative Perspective*
Edited by Katalin Ligeti and Stanisław Tosza

Criminal Liability of Managers in Europe

Punishing Excessive Risk

Stanisław Tosza

•HART•
OXFORD • LONDON • NEW YORK • NEW DELHI • SYDNEY

HART PUBLISHING
Bloomsbury Publishing Plc
Kemp House, Chawley Park, Cumnor Hill, Oxford, OX2 9PH, UK

HART PUBLISHING, the Hart/Stag logo, BLOOMSBURY and the Diana logo are trademarks of Bloomsbury Publishing Plc
First published in Great Britain 2019

First published in hardback, 2019
Paperback edition, 2020

A catalogue record for this book is available from the British Library.

Library of Congress Cataloging-in-Publication Data

Names: Tosza, Stanisław, author.

Title: Criminal liability of managers in Europe : punishing excessive risk / Stanisław Tosza.

Description: Oxford, UK ; Portland, Oregon : Hart Publishing, 2019. | Based on author's thesis (doctoral – University of Luxembourg and Utrecht University, 2016). | Includes bibliographical references and index.

Identifiers: LCCN 2018030886 (print) | LCCN 2018040560 (ebook) | ISBN 9781509914982 (Epub) | ISBN 9781509914975 (hardback)

Subjects: LCSH: Corporate governance—Law and legislation—England—Criminal provisions. | Risk management—Law and legislation—England—Criminal provisions. | Executives—Legal status, laws, etc.—England—Criminal provisions. | Corporate governance—Law and legislation—France—Criminal provisions. | Risk management—Law and legislation—France—Criminal provisions. | Executives—Legal status, laws, etc.—France—Criminal provisions. | Corporate governance—Law and legislation—Germany—Criminal provisions. | Risk management—Law and legislation—Germany—Criminal provisions. | Executives—Legal status, laws, etc.—Germany—Criminal provisions.

Classification: LCC KJC2635.5 (ebook) | LCC KJC2635.5 .T67 2018 (print) | DDC 345.4/0268—dc23

LC record available at https://lccn.loc.gov/2018030886

ISBN: HB: 978-1-50991-497-5
PB: 978-1-50994-495-8
ePDF: 978-1-50991-496-8
ePub: 978-1-50991-498-2

Typeset by Compuscript Ltd, Shannon

ACKNOWLEDGEMENTS

While preparing this book, I received enormous support, inspiration and guidance from people to whom I remain extremely grateful.

My warmest thanks go to Professor Katalin Ligeti, Professor John Vervaele, and Professor Ferry de Jong. While I am responsible for the shortcomings of this book, it owes its quality to their caring, demanding and tireless guidance.

I am particularly grateful to Professor Ligeti, who has been an exceptional and engaging guide into the world of academia.

I would also like to thank Professor John Spencer and Professor Thomas Weigend for their remarks on the entire book and in particular on the English and the German chapters respectively. Dr Juliette Tricot and Dr Yvonne Muller-Lagarde made extremely useful comments on the French chapter. Stuart Alford from the Serious Fraud Office helped me understand the nuances of the practical side of the English law of fraud. The accuracy of the national chapters owes a great amount to the generous help of all of those mentioned here; I remain responsible for all mistakes therein. I am also very grateful to Professor Silvia Allegrezza, Professor Michiel Luchtman, Professor François Kristen and Dr Lawrence Siry for their remarks on different versions of this book.

I express my gratitude towards Professor Włodzimierz Wróbel, who through his passion inspired me to become a scholar in criminal law and taught me the basics of reflection in this field.

During the preparation of this book, I was generously funded by the Luxembourg National Research Fund as well as the Max Planck Society, DAAD, GFPS, the French Embassy, and Utrecht University. I am particularly grateful to Professor Ulrich Sieber for his support, which enabled research into the German legal system. Dr Ewa Weigend was a uniquely warm host in Freiburg.

Many friends supported me while I was working on this book. Two of them have become particularly close, as we shared many moments of hope and despair in our parallel endeavours: Gavin Robinson and Michele Simonato. I am very happy we were there together. Very special thanks go to Gavin, who tirelessly corrected my shortcomings in mastering the language of Joseph Conrad, while giving me plenty of remarks on the content of the book.

To my parents I am grateful for all the love they have given me, for all their support in becoming who I am and for being a constant source of inspiration.

The book was supposed to be finished before she was born, but as I did not manage to wrap it up in time, Helenka has become part of the last stage of its preparations, affording me less time to read, but more to reflect. That was invaluable.

The most important person comes at the end. I am infinitely grateful to my wife Kasia for boundless love and constant tender support. I dedicate the book to her.

CONTENTS

TABLE OF CASES AND LEGISLATION

England

Cases

Legislation

France

Cases

Legislation

Germany

Cases

Legislation

General

Cases

EU and International Instruments

LIST OF ABBREVIATIONS

Abs	Absatz (subsection)
AG	Aktiengesellschaft
AktG	Aktiengesetz
All ER	All England Law Reports
art	article
Bafin	Bundesanstalt für Finanzdienstleistungsaufsicht
BayObLG	Bayerisches Oberstes Landesgericht
BeckRS	Beck online Rechtsprechung (CH Beck)
BGB	Bürgerliches Gesetzbuch
BGH	Bundesgerichtshof
Bull crim	Bulletin des arrêts de la Cour de cassation (chambre criminelle)
BVerfG	Bundesverfassungsgericht
Cass crim	Cour de cassation, chambre criminelle
CEO	Chief Executive Officer
ch	chapter
CP	French Penal Code (Code Pénal)
CPS	Crown Prosecution Service
Cr App R	Criminal Appeal Reports
ECHR	European Convention on Human Rights
ECtHR	European Court of Human Rights
EWCA Crim	England and Wales Court of Appeal Criminal Division
GmbH	Gesellschaften mit beschränkter Haftung
GmbHG	Gesetz betreffend die Gesellschaften mit beschränkter Haftung
HC	House of Commons
HGB	Handelsgesetzbuch

HL	House of Lords
KB	King's Bench
KritV	Kritische Vierteljahresschrift für Gesetzgebung und Rechtswissenschaft
KWG	Gesetz über das Kreditwesen
Law Com	Law Commission
LG	Landgericht
LIBOR	London Interbank Offered Rate
MDR	Monatsschrift für Deutsches Recht
NJW	Neue Juristische Wochenschrift
NStZ	Neue Zeitschrift für Strafrecht
NStZ-RR	Neue Zeitschrift für Strafrecht Rechtsprechungs-Report
OLG	Oberlandesgericht
QB	Queen's Bench
RGSt	Entscheidungen des Reichsgerichtes in Strafsachen
s	section
SA	Société anonyme
SARL	Société à responsabilité limitée
SAS	Société par actions simplifiée (simplified joint-stock company)
SCA	Société en commandite par actions (partnership limited by shares)
SFO	Serious Fraud Office
StGB	Strafgesetzbuch
StPO	Strafprozeßordnung
StV	Strafverteidiger
TFEU	Treaty on the Functioning of the European Union
VAG	Gesetz über die Beaufsichtigung der Versicherungsunternehmen
wistra	Zeitschrift für Wirtschafts- und Steuerstrafrecht
WLR	Weekly Law Reports
ZStW	Zeitschrift für die gesamte Strafrechtswissenschaft

'Of all injustice, none is more grave than that of the people who, when they are most false, conduct their affairs as if they were good men.'

Cicero, *On Duties*

'Fraud against the trusting fails to heed not only natural love but the added bond of faith, which forms a special kind of trust. Therefore, in the tightest circle, the centre of the universe and seat of Dis, all traitors are consumed eternally.'

Dante, *Inferno*, canto 11

'In retrospect, many firms … took on too much risk and did not have sufficient resources to manage those risks effectively in a rapidly changing environment.'

John J. Mack, Chairman, *Written Submission of Morgan Stanley to the Financial Crisis Inquiry Commission*

1

Introduction

In the first weeks of January 2008, a trader of the Société Générale Jérôme Kerviel caused losses amounting to approximately €4.9 billion and almost brought one of the most important French banks to bankruptcy. This was the last act of otherwise very successful, however highly risky, strain of transactions spanning between 2005–2007. Kerviel's task was to bet on market tendencies in such a way that while he put the money on a certain trend, he would also bet on its opposite (a technique called hedging). In theory these investments should bring the same amount of win and loss, but market inefficiencies result in small differences from which one can make the profit if one invests huge sums of money. The mechanism entailed low risk, but the wins were also limited. In order to increase the wins, Kerviel stopped hedging his transactions, which he concealed from the bank by introducing fictitious transactions into the bank computer system. These transactions allowed him to make enormous profit, but at the same time exposed the bank to very high risk of loss and breached applicable regulations.[1] Although some red flags were waved he was not caught until his last – unsuccessful – bet.[2] Kerviel assumed that the financial crisis, which was unravelling at the time, would be just a temporary turbulence and that the market would soon start to recover. As this was not the case, the bet resulted in a huge loss, and eventually in a criminal conviction for Kerviel.[3]

Every managerial decision is risky, at least to some extent. Conducting business is impossible without venturing into new territories and even the most ordinary daily choices could end in failure. Excessive risk, however, can be very detrimental, as we were grimly reminded by the most recent financial crisis. It could bring large and reputable companies or even whole economic systems to the brink of collapse. By criminalising managers' excessive risk-taking criminal law enters a sphere which is at the core of the activity it affects. At the same time, it provides for criminal punishment for courses of conduct which, without

[1] In particular concerning the requirement regarding the Cooke ratio, which is the ratio of capital the bank should keep in order to balance the risk of its investments.

[2] It is the subject of legal battle between the bank and the trader whether there was some tacit acceptance of his actions.

[3] The case is still subject to legal procedures and both parties (Société Générale and Jérôme Kerviel) have presented different versions of the facts. The author takes no position in this regard and presented the case according to available sources, including court judgments. For judgments, see Jugement du tribunal de grande instance de Paris (chambre 11-3), 5 October 2010 (first instance); Cour d'Appel de Paris (no. 11/404), 24 October 2012 (appeal); Cass crim 19 March 2014, Bull crim no 86.

doubt, can be extremely harmful. The objective of this book is to examine existing criminalisation of excessive risk-taking, as well as to analyse whether such criminalisation is desirable, and if so, under which conditions.

The *Kerviel* case illustrates crucial issues which will be at the centre of the reflection in this book. In the first place, it shows the gravity of excessive risk-taking. Each of the unhedged bets was excessively risky and could potentially damage the bank significantly. In this sense, all of these transactions deserved a sanction in the same way as the last one, which turned out to be unlucky. Would (and should) Kerviel have been punished, had he been caught when still on a winning streak? Secondly, Kerviel did not take any money for himself. All the profits he generated over the years were for the Société Générale only. His only motivation was a sort of star status he acquired within the bank and the bonus calculated in view of his performance. Is it fair to require such motivation from a manager and punish him for it only when things go wrong?

1. Financial Crisis and Excessive Risk

The *Kerviel* case is a good exemplification of an excessively risky rogue trader. However, the problem is not limited to cases of 'black sheep'. The detrimental character of excessively risky policies led to the collapse of such banks as the Royal Bank of Scotland in the United Kingdom and Hypo Real Estate in Germany, which then needed to be nationalised, engaging large sums of public money.[4] John J Mack, the CEO of Morgan Stanley at the time when the financial crisis of 2007–2008 started, explained that what triggered the financial crisis was that:

> In retrospect, many firms ... took on too much risk and did not have sufficient resources to manage those risks effectively in a rapidly changing environment.[5]

It is an almost universal opinion that the essential cause of the crisis was 'the combination of a credit boom and a housing bubble',[6] in particular linked with extending credit to borrowers, whose credit ratings were low.[7] This was coupled

[4] Financial Services Authority, *The Failure of the Royal Bank of Scotland, Financial Services Authority Board Report* (December 2011), available at www.fsa.gov.uk/pubs/other/rbs.pdf; Matthäus Buder, Max Lienemeyer, Marcel Magnus, Bert Smits and Karl Soukup, 'The Rescue and Restructuring of Hypo Real Estate' (2011) 3 *Competition Policy Newsletter* 41.

[5] Written Submission of Morgan Stanley to the Financial Crisis Inquiry Commission, John J Mack, Chairman (January 2010), available at http://fcic-static.law.stanford.edu/cdn_media/fcic-testimony/2010-0113-Mack.pdf.

[6] Viral Acharya, Thomas Philippon, Matthew Richardson and Nouriel Roubini, 'The Financial Crisis of 2007–2009: Causes and Remedies' (2009) 18(2) *Financial Markets, Institutions and Instruments* 89, 98.

[7] Tobias F Rötheli, 'Causes of the Financial Crisis: Risk Misperception, Policy Mistakes, and Banks' Bounded Rationality' (2010) 39 *Journal of Socio-Economics* 119. There is vast literature analysing the causes of the financial crisis, stemming from public institutions, non-governmental and academic institutions. Besides publications cited in this section, see, eg the following publications: *The Financial*

with financial market innovation and the practice of rating agencies of granting excellent ratings to financial assets based on underlying credit claims, turning them into very attractive investments in view of their risk-return profiles.[8]

While the crisis began in the United States with the collapse of the Lehman Brothers Bank, it spilled into Europe as European banks had also invested intensively in the American mortgage market. Moreover, European markets and institutions were affected by distressed financial markets in the United States and the resulting limited access to capital.[9] This evolved into a sovereign debt crisis due to the costs of the efforts of governments to rescue systemically important financial institutions together with already existing high government debts and in view of the deterioration of the lending climate in general.[10]

When discussing the causes of the financial crisis, excessive risk-taking is mentioned in various contexts, which include external market factors and internal business culture factors. The following reasons were named: imprudent mortgage lending;[11] amassing of vast highly correlated housing risks;[12] problems regarding sophisticated credit derivatives instruments;[13] failure of risk management systems,[14] in particular '[g]reedy and potentially incompetent executives

Crisis Inquiry Report, Final Report of the National Commission on the Causes of the Financial and Economic Crisis in the United States (January 2011), available at http://fcic.law.stanford.edu/report; International Organisation of Supreme Audit Institutions, *The Causes of the Global Financial Crisis and Their Implications for Supreme Audit Institutions* (INTOSAI, October 2010), available at /www.intosai.org/uploads/gaohq4709242v1finalsubgroup1paper.pdf; Carmen M Reinhart and Kenneth S Rogoff, *This Time is Different: Eight Centuries of Financial Folly* (Princeton, NJ and Oxford: Princeton University Press, 2009); Stephany Griffith-Jones, José Antonio Ocampo and Joseph E Stiglitz (eds), *Time for a Visible Hand: Lessons from the 2008 World Financial Crisis* (Oxford University Press, 2010); Stijn Claessens, M Ayhan Kose, Luc Laeven and Fabián Valencia (eds), *Financial Crises: Causes, Consequences, and Policy Responses* (International Monetary Fund, 2014).

[8] Rötheli, 'Causes of the Financial Crisis' (n 7) 119; See also Martin F Hellwig, 'Systemic Risk in the Financial Sector: An Analysis of the Subprime-Mortgage Financial Crisis' (2009) 157(2) *De Economist* 129, 166; Adair Turner, *The Turner Review: A Regulatory Response to the Global Banking Crisis* (Financial Services Authority, March 2009) 13 et seq, available at www.fsa.gov.uk/pubs/other/turner_review.pdf.

[9] INTOSAI, *The Causes of the Global Financial Crisis and Their Implications for Supreme Audit Institutions* (n 7) 15, para [49].

[10] Ibid; DG Economic and Financial Affairs, 'Why Did the Crisis Happen?', available at http://ec.europa.eu/economy_finance/explained/the_financial_and_economic_crisis/why_did_the_crisis_happen/index_en.htm; see also DG Economic and Financial Affairs, *Economic Crisis in Europe: Causes, Consequences and Responses* (European Economy 7, 2009), available at http://ec.europa.eu/economy_finance/publications/pages/publication15887_en.pdf.

[11] Mark Jickling, *Causes of the Financial Crisis*, Report for Congress (Congressional Research Service, 29 January 2009) 5.

[12] Dissenting Statement of Commissioner Keith Hennessey, Commissioner Douglas Holtz-Eakin and Vice Chairman Bill Thomas in *The Financial Crisis Inquiry Report, Final Report of the National Commission on the Causes of the Financial and Economic Crisis in the United States* (January 2011), 'The Ten Essential Causes of the Financial and Economic Crisis', 418, available at http://fcic.law.stanford.edu/report.

[13] Jongho Kim, 'From Vanilla Swaps to Exotic Credit Derivatives: How to Approach the Interpretation of Credit Events' (2008) 13(5) *Fordham Journal of Corporate and Financial Law* 705, 708.

[14] Simon Ashby, *The 2007–09 Financial Crisis: Learning the Risk Management Lessons*, Research Report (Centre for Risk, Banking and Financial Services, University of Nottingham, January 2010)

and senior managers, who have been blamed for encouraging or at best turning a blind eye to excessive risk taking';[15] homogenisation of assumptions about risk among financial actors;[16] limited information on risk exposure as regards over-the-counter derivatives;[17] short-term incentives in the form of annual bonuses; while risky strategies may become failures in the much longer run.[18] Another factor is connected with the longevity of the economic boom. In general, the longer it lasts, the more there are persons in decision-making positions not having experienced a serious downturn and thus showing a tendency to favour riskier strategies.[19] Some of these risks were linked with individual decisions; some are more systemic.

Whilst the consequences of excessive risk-taking are not solely linked to the most recent or any other financial crisis, it powerfully highlighted the potentially disastrous results when this phenomenon gets out of hand. Moreover, excessive risk-taking is not limited to the financial market as managerial decisions in any domain of business may be overly daring. An example of the disastrous consequences of careless management has been recently provided by the collapse of British Home Stores (BHS), which gravely affected not only its existing, but also former employees. Therefore, although the financial crisis was an inspiration for this monograph, the problems presented here are not limited to the times or aftermaths of financial crunches.

2. Business Decisions and Excessive Risk-Taking

Risk-taking is at the very beginning and at the very core of business activity. Since time immemorial, one of the typical business activities has been bringing merchandise from one region to another. Once arrived at their destination, the goods were sold at a higher price than that for which they were acquired. This surplus was the merchant's gain and at the same time his compensation for the risk he took while transporting the goods, which was the risk of being robbed by brigands or pirates or having the merchandise destroyed by a natural disaster. It is a truism that today's much more sophisticated businesses also carry an element of risk. An investment can always turn into a financial disaster, be it because of the action of others (criminal or legal) or because of unexpected events (eg change of

12–13, available at www.nottingham.ac.uk/business/businesscentres/crbfs/research/researchreports.aspx; Jickling, *Causes of the Financial Crisis* (n 11) 8.

[15] Ashby, *The 2007–09 Financial Crisis* (n 14) 13.

[16] Andrew G Haldane and Robert M May, 'Systemic Risk in Banking Ecosystems' (2011) 469 *Nature* 351; Robert Skidelsky, 'What the Wolves of Wall Street can teach us about risk', Project Syndicate, *The Guardian*, 24 March 2014, available at www.theguardian.com.

[17] Jickling, *Causes of the Financial Crisis* (n 11) 9.

[18] Association of Chartered Certified Accountants, *Corporate Governance and the Credit Crunch*, Discussion Paper (London, 2008), available at www.accaglobal.com/gb/en/technical-activities/technical-resources-search/2008/november/corporate-governance-and-the-credit-crunch.html.

[19] Rötheli, 'Causes of the Financial Crisis' (n 7) 120.

prices or natural catastrophes), or simply because of miscalculations (as to costs, demand, supply, etc). Many successful businessmen make bad investments and one can say that failure is as much a part of business as is success.*

The nature and level of risk can vary. It can be very limited if one invests in government bonds, although it is not impossible that the government goes bankrupt. The risk can be much higher if one invests in sophisticated financial instruments. One may risk less by investing in the production of commodities that are in common use, while investing in commercial scientific research carries the risk because it can bring no result or not be useful in practice. Even investments that look at first instance bound to be successful may turn out to be failures. In one of his short stories, the Hungarian writer Sándor Márai writes of an investment that appeared to guarantee a success and for no explicable reason failed. A waiter, tired of his profession, acquires a restaurant that had always attracted clients. Although he makes no particular mistake, from the moment he takes over the restaurant, clients stop coming without any rational explanation and at the end he is forced to sell the place. When the new owner reopens it, the flow of clients begins immediately.[20]

While Márai's is a work of fiction, it points out that an element of luck is inevitably present in every investment. When contemplating the criminalisation of excessively risky decisions by managers, one has to bear in mind that risk is always present in business and doing business is a question of measuring, accommodating and preventing risk according to the rules of the domain in question. However, even when done properly, there will always be a margin of unknown factors and their appreciation and how to evade them is left to those who take the decisions. Furthermore, risk, regardless of whether its source is natural or human created, is a social phenomenon, ie depending on dynamic factors (cultural, economic, legal, etc). The answer to the question of whether risk is excessive depends on a variety of factors and perception thereof and will thus be subject to change over time.[21]

In their pursuit of profit for the company, managers could go as far as committing acts which could turn out to be administrative irregularities or even criminal offences. In the middle of 2015 it has been revealed that, for many years, Volkswagen had been manipulating tests as regards the emission of polluting substances in various Diesel models of its cars. The manipulation consisted in furnishing the cars with software able to detect whether the car was being tested and alter its performance and pollution in comparison to situations of normal driving. The case can be understood as an exemplary case of excessive

* Note on gender-neutral formulation: Throughout this book, all gender-specific terms are to be considered to refer to both the feminine and the masculine form – except when referring to a particular person.

[20] Sándor Márai, 'Three Swans' in *Magia* (a collection of his short stories, in the Polish translation published by Czytelnik, Warszawa, 2008) 103–13.

[21] This aspect is also reflected in the changes of the standards in domains where risk is more comprehensively regulated, such as banking (eg the evolution of Basel Accords I, II, III). See Laurent Balthazar, *From Basel 1 to Basel 3. The Integration of State of the Art Risk Modelling in Banking Regulation* (Palgrave Macmillan, 2006). Similarly, the FATF Recommendations evolved over time (see www.fatf-gafi.org/topics/fatfrecommendations/documents/review-and-history-of-fatf-standards.html).

risk-taking. The managers of Volkswagen, apparently, took a decision to install the software altering the results of the tests and permitting the company to sell concerned models, while presenting them as less polluting and more powerful. However, this decision exposed the company to various risks in case the manipulation was discovered, in particular, the costs of a variety of sanctions, costs of calling back the cars and making necessary changes, as well as the damage to reputation. All these risks could be considered excessive.

In an older scandal concerning the German industrial giant Siemens, the managers were found to have paid bribes in order for Siemens to obtain lucrative contracts. Although the contracts were potentially beneficial for the company, they carried a risk that, once corruption is uncovered, it may result in significant reputational damage and in substantive losses due to fines (as well as in other expenses such litigation costs, etc). Regardless of the liability for the offence of bribery, the managers were also prosecuted for abuse of trust in managing the assets of the company. In a controversial court battle which included judgments of the Federal Court of Justice (BGH), the accusation was based on the creation and use of slush funds (which served to pay the bribes), which assets were hidden and therefore not correctly entered into the company's books.[22] According to the BGH, the company would no longer be able to use such funds,[23] an argument only theoretically plausible according to commentators, as it was the management of Siemens who controlled the slush funds.[24] This case demonstrates a similar problem to the one in *Kerviel*: the difficulty faced by the courts in addressing in a straightforward way the problem of excessive risk-taking. The essence of the problem was not so much in the hiding of the funds, but in the dilemma whether exposing the company to the risk of negative consequences by committing acts infringing the law (including criminal), but undertaken for the benefit of the company, should be assimilated to other abuses of trust in managing the company's assets.

3. Excessive Risk-Taking and Criminal Liability

The crucial context in which criminal liability for excessive risk-taking comes into play is the divide between capital and management, which is the common model of limited companies. Investors entrust their money to professionals who are supposed to manage the company's affairs in a way that brings profit. The relationship between the company (and the shareholders) and the managers

[22] BGH (29 August 2008) NStZ 2009, 95, 97, para [37].

[23] Ibid para [43].

[24] Jürgen Seier, 'Untreue' in Hans Achenbach and Andreas Ransiek (eds), *Handbuch Wirtschaftsstrafrecht*, 3rd edn (Heidelberg, München, Landsberg, Frechen, Hamburg: CF Müller, 2012) marginal no 407 et seq.

relies on trust in that the managers are expected to use the assets in the best interests of the company. Managers to whom the company assets have been entrusted are accountable vis-à-vis the investors according to rules provided for by company law, their contracts and a plethora of other rules regulating the particular domain of business.

For the most serious breaches of law, managers may be held criminally liable. However, there is a consensus (at least in the three legal orders under investigation in this book) that criminal conviction is not the appropriate response to business decisions which were simply risky and turned out to be disadvantageous. At the same time, all three legal orders (as well as many others, if not all) criminalise misappropriation of company assets by its managers or the use of assets contrary to the interests of the company, or to relevant rules, in a way that results in a loss.

The problem of criminalisation of excessively risky decisions is located between these opposite positions. While most commonly managers who act contrary to the company interests or breach relevant rules would be subject to criminal liability when they cause loss to the company, the question of the need to punish excessively risky decisions can appear in three situations. First, and most typically, it would be the case where an act of mismanagement was detected, but no loss occurred. Secondly the prosecution may also be inclined to look for a possibility to punish excessively risky management, if it is impossible to prove the loss according to the relevant standard of proof or, thirdly, where it is impossible to link it to the manager's act.

These cases will remain at the borderline between causing a loss to the company because of wilful misuse of the company assets and decisions, which were technically correct and taken without breaching any applicable rules, but turned out to be failures, which resulted in a loss for the company. The excessively risky decision in this context does not cause loss (at least not yet), but there is a need to demonstrate that the risk was excessive, thus its analysis must significantly enter into the sphere of the quality of the business decision.

In order to examine criminalisation of excessive risk-taking, three legal orders will be examined: England and Wales,[25] France and Germany. There are three main reasons for selecting these jurisdictions. First and foremost, these systems offer very different approaches to the criminalisation of excessive risk-taking and thus allow the reader to survey a panorama of existing legal solutions and to make a meaningful comparative analysis. Secondly, they represent fairly different systems of criminal law, and have a tradition of inspiring other legislators. Thirdly, Germany, the United Kingdom and France are the three biggest economies in Europe, and the biggest globally after the United States, China and Japan.[26]

[25] For the sake of brevity further references to the legal system of England and Wales will only use 'England' or 'English'.

[26] According to the Gross Domestic Product 2014 as provided by the World Bank: http://data.worldbank.org/data-catalog/GDP-ranking-table.

As to the first, England, the Fraud Act 2006, in particular fraud by abuse of position provided for in section 4, provides a possibility to punish a manager who dishonestly abuses his position by exposing the company to excessive risk. The French offence of *abus de biens sociaux* (provided mainly by article L241-3 4° and 5° as well as article L242-6 3° and 4° of the Commercial Code (*Code de commerce*)) punishes high-level managers for acting against the company's interests. Exposing the company to excessive risk is one of the forms of acting against these interests. The offence of *Untreue* in German law (section 266 of the Criminal Code, StGB) punishes improper conduct in relation to entrusted property if the conduct results in damage. However, the theory of '*schadensgleiche Vermögensgefährdung*' associates, under certain conditions, endangerment with damage and thus excessive risk-taking is also incriminated.

In none of the chosen countries is taking excessive risk criminalised as such, but rather remains one of the possibilities of committing the offence mainly targeting acts causing effective loss. It is therefore highly relevant to shed light on this type of managerial misconduct in existing law and to evaluate whether it should be criminalised, and if so, under which conditions and to what extent.[27]

4. Scope and Structure

This book studies the problem of mismanagement of company assets by exposing them to excessive risk and thus harming the financial interests of the company, and of different categories of actors whose financial interests are linked with the company (shareholders, stakeholders).[28] The problem will be examined in the existing law in three jurisdictions and then analysed in light of the question whether it is legitimate and justified to criminalise such acts and, if so, how to design criminalisation of such acts. Such a proposal may serve the national legislator as well as potentially the European one.[29]

[27] Interestingly, the BHS scandal triggered more calls to strip Sir Philip Green of his knighthood than for criminal prosecution, in particular for fraud by abuse of position.

[28] Certain issues which might be associated with the topic of risk are not treated in this book: criminal liability linked to protection of environment or safety of employees; liability for dangerous products; corporate criminal liability (as the company is rather a victim in this context). The book also does not analyse offences which criminalise breaches of very concrete rules of diligence. It concentrates on the issues of substantive criminal law, as questions about the choice of sanction and procedural law issues naturally only come afterwards and require another body of research. For preliminary reflections on the topic see Stanisław Tosza, 'La responsabilidad por los actos riesgosos de gestión en las sociedades de capital: Un estudio de derecho comparado' (2010) 26 *La Revista Penal* 177.

[29] For instance, by virtue of art. 83(2) of the Treaty on the Functioning of the European Union (TFEU), if criminalisation of excessive risk-taking or more broadly managerial misconduct becomes 'essential to ensure the effective implementation of a Union policy'. It is important to stress that this book does not examine the question whether criminalisation of excessive risk-taking should be made at the EU level or what role the EU should play in tackling this problem. In order to ask this question, it would be necessary to perform a complex analysis including issues related to the EU legal system, which would go beyond the ambitions of this book.

Three terms used throughout this book require brief explanation: 'risk', 'excessive' and 'manager'. The word 'risk' is understood here as the probability of a negative consequence.[30] Risk is a different concept from danger or hazard. The notion of risk indicates an ambition to control the future.[31] This implies a possibility to either control or at least predict the risk. Hence one can speak about its excessiveness.

The answer to the question whether the risk taken by the manager was excessive is crucial for criminal liability for offences, which punish this kind of decision. It is, however, impossible to provide it *in abstracto*. This answer will depend on a plethora of factors and standards applicable to particular commercial activities, concrete businesses or deals and contexts. An abstract definition for excessiveness of risk cannot take all these particularities into account. Therefore it is submitted here that criminal law cannot provide for such a definition. This is also linked with the function that criminal law should play among other branches of law in the protection of legal interests. While these other branches (civil or administrative) are tasked with the overall protection of such interests, criminal law should only intervene as regards selected, particularly serious infringements and thus may rely on the regulation of a particular domain provided for by other branches of law or non-legal tools. Criminal liability examined here enters the scene on the condition that risk was excessive according to the applicable standards (ie the relevant domain of law, the relevant type of business or deal, etc).[32]

This approach is similar to the one a criminal judge would need to take in many cases, where it would be necessary to call an expert witness in order to analyse whether the risk was excessive or was it normal risk that the manager was allowed to take.[33] At the same time, such assessments are no stranger to the everyday business of companies.[34] Where it is impossible to determine whether the risk was excessive or not, ultimately the *in dubio pro reo* rule will have to

[30] The term 'risk' is used in many different contexts and with different meanings. Furthermore, risk is painstakingly categorised in particular in the literature on risk management. It can be differentiated as downside risk (pure risk), which includes only the possibility of a negative outcome; or two-way risk (speculative risk) implying that the outcome may be better or worse in comparison to what is expected. It can be classified as to its type: business risk; non-business risk; financial risk; operational risk; and event risk. It can also be classified as to its source, as coming from the physical, social, political, legal, general economic or operational environment(s). For both classifications, see Brian Coyle, *Risk Awareness and Corporate Governance* (Financial World Publishing, 2002) 5–8. There is no need throughout this book to differentiate between different types or sources of risk, as the relevant question is whether it is excessive or not (which might or might not be linked to the type of risk in concrete situations). Moreover, as the question of liability makes sense only in the case of (at least potentially) negative consequences, risk will be understood here only as downside risk.

[31] Anthony Giddens, 'Risk and Responsibility' (1999) 62(1) *Modern Law Review*, 1, 3.

[32] Of course, this will need to be proved in the criminal process, depending on the concrete requirements of the offence in question.

[33] See also an interesting study on biases as regards risk among judges: W Kip Viscusi, 'How Do Judges Think about Risk?' (1999) 1(1) *American Law and Economics Review* 26.

[34] See, eg, the reflection of the German Constitutional Court (Bundesverfassungsgericht) in the judgment assessing the conformity of the offence of *Untreue* with the German Constitution: BVerfG (23 June 2010) NJW 2010, 3209, 3220, para [146].

be applied.[35] Another relevant question is related to the perception of risk as excessive or normal in the given circumstances.[36] While it is necessary to establish that the transaction was objectively abnormal, its perception as such will be the question of the manager's *mens rea*.

The understanding of the term 'manager' in this monograph is functional. It will mean a company official at any level, who is empowered to take decisions (alone or with other persons) affecting the assets of the company and who, while taking these decisions, enjoys a certain level of discretion. The latter condition is necessary to exclude persons who perform only mechanical tasks within the company. The approach adopted does not automatically imply that there is or there should be no difference between different categories of managers. The focus of the book is on managers of companies, which have legal personality and their own assets. While the legal framework of company law may differ significantly between national systems, the typical models for such companies are the limited liability company (*société à responsabilité limitée, Gesellschaft mit beschränkter Haftung*) and the public limited company (*société anonyme, Aktiengesellschaft*).[37]

The first three chapters will analyse the criminalisation of excessive risk-taking in the three national legal systems (Chapter 2, England and Wales, Chapter 3, France and Chapter 4, Germany). The function of these chapters is twofold: on the one hand, they should analyse the existing law in view of excessive risk-taking, which is particularly important as regards the English and the French legal systems, where such analysis is scarce. On the other hand, they should set the scene for the comparative analysis. In order to achieve a common platform and facilitate the comparison, the three national chapters are laid out according to the same structure.

Having analysed the possibilities to criminalise excessive risk-taking and setting the common ground for comparison, Chapter 5 will then provide the comparative analysis of the three national systems in accordance with the functional approach.[38] The aim of this chapter is to establish the models of criminalisation of excessive risk-taking by managers and the crucial factors determining criminal liability and distinguishing characteristics in each of these

[35] Ibid para [151].

[36] As to differences in attitude towards risk among managers, see Les Coleman, *Why Managers and Companies Take Risks* (Heidelberg: Physica-Verlag, 2006), in particular ch 7 'Why Managers Take Risks'.

[37] For a comparative analysis of these types of companies in the English, French and German legal systems, inter alia, see Mads Andenas and Frank Wooldridge, *European Comparative Company Law* (Cambridge University Press, 2009); Andreas Cahn and David C. Donald, *Comparative Company Law* (Cambridge University Press, 2010), the latter only as regards Germany, the United Kingdom and the United States.

[38] It requires that legal rules must be 'seen purely in the light of their function, as an attempt to satisfy a particular legal need'. Konrad Zweigert and Hein Kötz, *An Introduction to Comparative Law*, 3rd edn (Oxford: Clarendon Press, 1998) 44. See also the critique of this approach in Maurice Adams and John Griffiths, 'Against Comparative Method' in Maurice Adams and Jacco Bomhoff (eds), *Practice and Theory in Comparative Law* (Cambridge University Press, 2012) 283 et seq.

systems. The result of this analysis will provide inspiration for the normative part of the analysis and for critical evaluation at the end of Chapter 7.

The ultimate aim of the book is to find a better/best solution of the problem, to which the second part of the book will be dedicated (Chapters 6 and 7). For this purpose a legal framework will be built consisting of an analysis of reasons that trigger the introduction of criminal liability (such as protection against harm or protection of legal interests), together with an analysis of ethical aspects of excessive risk-taking, which will be completed by examining principles limiting the use of criminal law, such as the principle of proportionality and the legality principle (the fair warning principle).[39] This framework will first be analysed theoretically and then in the context of excessive risk-taking by company managers (Chapter 6). The outcome of this analysis should prepare the ground for answering the question whether and to what extent it is legitimate and justified to criminalise excessive risk-taking by managers. This result will then be used to elaborate a model of criminalisation of excessive risk-taking, as well as to evaluate the approach taken in each of the three examined legal orders (Chapter 7).

Five sample cases will be used throughout the whole study in order to put more flesh onto the theoretical analysis. At each stage of the examination in this book (analysis of national systems, comparison, designing the blueprint for criminalisation), the sample cases will be used as a tool in order to examine how they would be solved in a given legal framework. This tool is intended not only to bring the sometimes quite abstract reflection more to life, but also to test the criminal law solutions evoking the characteristics crucial for determining liability. Each of the chapters on national systems will contain at its end a section where the five cases are resolved according to the law of this system. The solutions given in the three examined legal systems will be compared in Chapter 5. Furthermore, the model of criminalisation proposed in the concluding chapter will also be tested in light of these cases.

The inspiration for these sample cases came in the first place from real-life situations, including the ones described above (Kerviel and banking crises, including sub-prime mortgages issues, 'Dieselgate' and Siemens). However, the situations were simplified for the reader not to be distracted by issues that would have limited relevance for the analysed problems (eg evidentiary problems or non-criminal law issues). The role of these cases is to serve as sort of a litmus paper, which when applied to a concrete criminal law solution should reveal its actual characteristics.

The five cases have in common that the perpetrator is a manager responsible for safeguarding the company's financial interests, but manages the entrusted assets in a way that exposes the company to an important risk of loss. Although the manager knows of the risk and accepts to take it, he does not want the company to suffer the loss, or hopes that it will not occur, or even on the contrary, he wishes for

[39] A more detailed explanation of this framework is provided in the introduction to Chapter 6.

the company to profit. The sample cases remain purposefully unclear on certain issues in order to leave some flexibility, making it possible to point out which variables determine criminal liability. The cases are as follows:

I A bank manager grants a credit to a client knowing that the guarantee offered by the client (eg mortgage) for securing the credit would be insufficient in the case of non-payment by the client. The manager nevertheless hopes that the client will be able to repay the credit.

II A top manager of the bank instructs lower-level managers to grant credits which are not fully secured (see above) in order to increase the bank's turnover. The top manager conceives of the possibility that some of these credits may not be repaid; however, he hopes that the overall beneficial economic situation will allow enough of these problematic clients to repay their loans so that the bank will profit. Simultaneously, he is convinced of his successful business strategy and hopes to be rewarded with a bonus and to leave the bank before any trouble might begin to occur.

III A director of a construction company realises that he has a significant surplus of money due to a very successful sale of apartments. The company needs to pay for materials and work to subcontractors, but the first creditors have to be paid in only three months' time. Instead of keeping the money in the bank account, he decides to gamble with it on the stock exchange (ie invest it in a fairly aggressive way).

IV The perpetrator is a director of a department responsible for new projects within a car manufacturing company. For the past three years the department has been working mainly on a new luxury SUV model. The model is ready, but the director is aware of a problem with the sound system integrated into the car, which is supposed to be a great asset of the car. For some reason it is not possible to eliminate interference with the on-board computer which might cause unpleasant sound. This does not put the passengers in danger, but if many models have this problem, the company might need to recall sold cars in order to repair the system. In order to resolve the problem, a full reprogramming is necessary. At the same time the executives of the company are pressing to finalise the work, since the set deadline for presenting the new model is approaching. The director decides not to disclose the problem to the executives.

V A manager becomes aware of a possibility to obtain a lucrative contract for his company from the Ministry of Infrastructure. The contract is worth several million euros. Knowing that his company is not the most competitive on the market, he decides to increase its chances by arranging a meeting with the public official responsible for this issue and offers him an envelope with €50,000, which were assigned from the company's budget. The public official accepts the money. Eventually the company is awarded the contract. The manager is aware that if this becomes known to the competent authorities, the company may be stripped of the contract, banned from participating in public bidding and fined, but he hopes that these consequences will not materialise.

As to the last case, although it is about corruption, which most probably would be punished as such, the focus of the analysis will be different. This case illustrates the questions which may arise if the illegal act of the manager risks exposing the company to sanctions (and consequences linked to them) even if the manager acted (at least in part) in the interests of the company. Here we see an example where the same act infringes different types of legal interests, both public, as regards corruption, and private, as regards the company's exposure to risk.[40]

These scenarios can also be modified so that the perpetrator acts negligently (and not intentionally). As to the first case, the manager would not know that the guarantee is insufficient, but he should have and could have known that, had he correctly verified the details of the guarantee offered. In case II, the manager did not order the employees to grant not fully secured credits, but they were doing so on their own initiative because of their concerns for the bank's turnover and in view of the bonuses linked to their success. However, the manager failed in his supervision duties and did not prevent his employees from allowing the loans under such conditions. Finally, in case IV, the manager was not aware of the failure of the sound system, but it was his duty to verify it, which he failed to fulfil.

[40] The practical relevance of this sample case has also been linked with the rules on the limitation period which may result in a shorter period for corruption than for the offence protecting the company interests, as is the case in the French legal system (see further Chapter 3, 3.1.3(ii)). An issue linked with this case is how to treat acts which fulfil the definitions of two (or more) offences.

2

England and Wales

1. Introduction and History

English law offers various possibilities of incriminating excessive risk-taking by managers. Although not an object of express criminalisation, it has been subject to criminal punishment by way of the common law offence of conspiracy to defraud, which was confirmed by three major judgments (*Sinclair*, *Allsop* and *Wai Yu-Tsang*). The recent Fraud Act 2006 expressly included exposure to risk in the provisions. While English law provides these and many other offences which could be applied to situations of interest for this book, its use may be countered by the requirement of dishonesty and its particularities.

Before the Fraud Act entered into force, actions and omissions which this Act incriminates were covered, although to a limited extent, mainly by two Theft Acts dating from 1968 and from 1978. Besides the definition of theft they contained eight so-called 'offences of deception'.[1] These offences were not useful in cases of excessive risk-taking since they required a transfer of property to the perpetrator or a gain on his side in another way (eg obtaining of services).

In order to address these issues, English law made use of the common law offence of conspiracy to defraud, which consisted of being 'party to an agreement with the common intention to defraud one or more of the persons'.[2] The particularity of this conspiracy is that the act, to which the defendants conspire, need not constitute an offence.[3] Its application to excessive risk-taking by managers has been confirmed by three major judgments (*Sinclair*, *Allsop* and *Wai Yu-Tsang*).

[1] These eight offences were committed by a person who dishonestly and by deception would: obtain property belonging to another, with the intention of permanently depriving the other of it (Theft Act 1968, s 15); obtain a money transfer (Theft Act 1968, s 15A); obtain services (Theft Act 1978, s 1); secure the remission of an existing liability to make a payment (Theft Act 1978, s 2(1)(a)); induce a creditor to wait for payment or to forgo payment with intent to permanently default on the debt (Theft Act 1978, s 2(1)(b)); obtain an exemption from or abatement of liability to make a payment Theft Act 1978, s 2(1)(c); obtain a pecuniary advantage (Theft Act 1968, s 16); procure the execution of a valuable security (Theft Act 1968, s 20(2).) See Law Commission, *Fraud: Report on a Reference under Section 3(1)(e) of the Law Commissions Act 1965*, Law Com No 276 (July 2002) 7.

[2] *Wai Yu-Tsang v R* [1992] 1 AC 269.

[3] Kenneth Cambell, 'The Fraud Act 2006' (2007) 18 *King's Law Journal* 337, 346.

The Criminal Law Act 1977 introduced a statutory form of conspiracy (section 1), which, in contrast, required that the perpetrator foresee the commission of an offence. The 1977 Act abolished many types of conspiracies existing at the time at common law, but spared conspiracy to defraud.[4]

Not only in the context of the punishment for excessive risk-taking, which has a marginal place in the English debate, but also with regard to the general solution to the problem of the offences related to deception and fraud, there was a consensus that the state of the law was unsatisfactory,[5] which prompted the Government to refer the issue to the Law Commission. The latter produced a report criticising both the common law offence of conspiracy to defraud for the extreme width of its scope, and the statutory offences for being too narrow.[6] Particularly as regards the offence of conspiracy to defraud, the Commission recommended its abolition,[7] an unsurprising suggestion in the context of a general trend to abandon common law offences. Conspiracy to defraud was also criticised in the literature for insufficient compatibility with the principle of legality, in particular the fulfilment of the requirement of legal certainty contained in Article 7 of the European Convention on Human Rights (ECHR).[8]

The conclusions of the report of the Law Commission formed the basis for the Fraud Act, which was eventually enacted in 2006. The Act abolished most of the offences of deception[9] and provided for a new general offence of fraud[10] including three ways of committing it:

(a) by false representation (section 2);

[4] AP Simester, JR Spencer, GR Sullivan and GJ Virgo, *Simester and Sullivan's Criminal Law: Theory and Doctrine*, 5th edn (Oxford and Portland: Hart Publishing, 2013) 310.

[5] Simester et al, *Simester and Sullivan's Criminal Law* (n 4) 609.

[6] Law Com No 276 (n 1) 13. The Law Commission referred mainly to the two Theft Acts (1968 and 1978), but gave examples of other Acts providing for provisions punishing fraudulent acts, eg fraudulent trading (Companies Act 1985, s 458), insider dealing (Criminal Justice Act 1993, s 52), and misleading statements and practices in the context of the financial markets (Financial Services Act 1986, s 47), ibid 15.

[7] Ibid Recommendation 5.

[8] David Ormerod and David Huw Williams, *Smith's Law of Theft*, 9th edn (Oxford University Press, 2007) 132.

[9] Simester et al, *Simester and Sullivan's Criminal Law* (n 4) 609, note 19: obtaining property by deception (Theft Act 1968, s 15); obtaining a money transfer by deception (Theft Act 1968, s 15A); obtaining a pecuniary advantage by deception (Theft Act 1968, s 16); procuring the execution of a valuable security by deception (Theft Act 1968, s 20); obtaining services by deception (Theft Act 1978, s 1); evading liability by deception (Theft Act 1978, s 2).

[10] According to Fraud Act 2006, s 1(3), a person guilty of fraud is liable: (a) on summary conviction, to imprisonment for a term not exceeding 12 months or to a fine not exceeding the statutory maximum (or to both); (b) on conviction on indictment, to imprisonment for a term not exceeding 10 years or to a fine (or to both). The Sentencing Guidelines Council issued also guidelines for sentencing for this offence: Sentencing for Fraud: Statutory Offences, Definitive Guideline (October 2009) and then Fraud, Bribery and Money Laundering Offences. Definitive Guideline effective from 1 October 2014, available at www.sentencingcouncil.org.uk/wp-content/uploads/Fraud_bribery_and_money_laundering_offences_-_Definitive_guideline.pdf. As fraud is an offence triable either way, no time limitation for prosecution applies.

(b) by failing to disclose information (section 3); and
(c) by abuse of position (section 4).

Fraud by false representation (section 2) consists of dishonestly making a false representation with an intention to make a gain for oneself or another or to cause loss to another or expose him to a risk of loss. Fraud by failing to disclose information consists of (dishonestly) failing to disclose to another person information which the perpetrator is under a legal obligation to disclose with the same intention as above: to make a gain for himself or another or to cause loss to another or expose him to a risk of loss.[11] For the commission of fraud by abuse of position, the Fraud Act 2006 requires that the perpetrator occupy a position in which he is expected to safeguard, or to not act against, the financial interests of another person and he (dishonestly) abuses that position with the same intention as in the two previous modalities.[12] The abuse might also be committed by omission.[13]

The Fraud Act 2006 was praised for its legislative technique because of its clarity. The new law is simpler and more accessible than the previous legislation, which left much uncertainty as to its scope. The 'inchoate mode' of approaching fraud has, however, been criticised for allowing very broad criminalisation, which is linked with the major difference between the new offence of fraud and the old offences of deception provided by the Theft Acts.[14] It lies in the fact that fraud is a conduct crime, whereas the old offences required proof of result consisting in the defendant obtaining something from the victim (by deception).[15] According to the new design, fraud, on the contrary, does not require the proof of result.[16] The removal of this element was compensated by the *mens rea* element of intention to make a gain, cause a loss or expose to a risk of loss. It is therefore not the actual result but the result foreseen by the perpetrator which will be important for the offence. Similarly, the proof of causation lost its importance, but also reappeared in the *mens rea*, since the perpetrator must have the intention that through his action the foreseen result occurs.

This change is of extreme importance since it broadens the scope of the provision significantly. This brought one author to talk about the 'inchoate mode' in which fraud has been defined,[17] since there is no need to prove any actual harm to the victim. Inchoate offences criminalise courses of conduct coming close to the commission of an offence, but without requiring that the actual offence be committed.[18] To say that fraud was drafted in the 'inchoate mode' suggests that

[11] Fraud Act 2006, s 3.
[12] Ibid s 4(1).
[13] Ibid s 4(2).
[14] Simester et al, *Simester and Sullivan's Criminal Law* (n 4) 610.
[15] Ibid 609.
[16] Attorney General: 'The Bill has been drafted on the basis that it focuses on the conduct of the defendant rather than on the consequences of the defendant's acts'. Hansard, HL, 19 July 2005, vol 673, col 1414.
[17] Simester et al, *Simester and Sullivan's Criminal Law* (n 4) 610.
[18] Ibid 291.

the offence is able to catch the perpetrator even before he manages to actually harm the victim.[19] The scope of the offence thus extends already to grounds which are normally occupied by preparation and attempt, without excluding the application of the two latter offences as well. Fraud is not the only offence which has been widened in this way (the scope of the offences created by the Terrorism Act 2006 could make another example), thus giving larger room for manoeuvre for the prosecutor and raising doubts in relation to the harm principle.[20] The difference between the old and the new approaches can be shown with reference to the recent case of *Jeevarajah*, in which two defendants, who ran a shop where lottery tickets were sold, falsely informed their client that his ticket had lost whereas in reality it was a winning one. The defendants later tried to claim the money, but were unsuccessful.[21] Although their conduct would have constituted an attempt under the Theft Act, they were convicted for accomplished fraud under the new law.[22]

Another important difference compared to the old law is that fraud is currently one offence (created by section 1) with three different ways of committing it. This implies important procedural consequences. If the prosecutor bases his accusation on section 4, but fails to prove its *actus reus*, it is still possible to convict the accused on the basis of sections 2 or 3 in the same trial, if it is possible to prove the *actus reus* of one of these modalities. This rule will however be limited by the guarantee of fair trial as enshrined in Article 6 of the ECHR. Therefore, it will not be possible to convict a defendant for a different modality of fraud, if he had no chance to contest the allegation based on this modality.[23]

Despite the recommendation of the Law Commission report,[24] the Government refrained from abolishing the common law offence of conspiracy to defraud, for fear that there may be situations in which it might still be useful to prosecute for this offence, instead of fraud or other offences, for instance in situations of 'multiple offences or large serious fraud offences'.[25] Therefore, it remains possible for the prosecutor to file charges in relation to this offence. However, in order to avoid excessive use of the common law conspiracy, the Attorney General has issued 'guidelines for prosecutors on the use of the common law offence of conspiracy to defraud', limiting situations in which it may be used.[26]

[19] Cambell, 'The Fraud Act 2006' (n 3) 341.

[20] Simester et al, *Simester and Sullivan's Criminal Law* (n 4) 610.

[21] *R v Jeevarajah* [2012] EWCA Crim 1299.

[22] Simester et al, *Simester and Sullivan's Criminal Law* (n 4) 610.

[23] Ibid 609, who cites the following case as an example of the application of this rule: *R v Falconer-Atlee* (1974) 58 Cr App R 348.

[24] Law Com No 276 (n 1) Recommendation 5.

[25] Clare Montgomery and David Ormerod (eds), *Montgomery and Ormerod on Fraud: Criminal Law and Procedure* (Oxford University Press, Release 9, December 2012) D-7008 et seq.

[26] Attorney General's Guidelines for Prosecutors on the Use of the Common Law Offence of Conspiracy to Defraud (First published 2007, Updated version 29 November 2012).

The debate on the criminalisation of excessive risk-taking in English law is rather limited and focuses mainly on two cases of conspiracy to defraud (*R v Allsop*[27] and *Wai Yu-Tsang*).[28] Despite certain clarifications given by the Fraud Act 2006, many questions of interpretation of fraud in the context of risk-taking remain open, in particular in view of the scarce jurisprudence so far produced. In particular, it remains to be seen if the directions given in the judgments mentioned above, which were issued in cases of conspiracy to defraud, remain a valid guidance under the new law. Whilst some aspects of these judgments are taken as inspiration, the analysis is not based solely thereupon; they are subject to detailed analysis under the section on common law conspiracy to defraud (see 4.5 below).

In addition, the Financial Services (Banking Reform) Act 2013 introduced the offence of reckless misconduct in the management of a financial institution. While its application is limited to senior managers in the financial sector, it addresses the problem of excessively risky management in financial institutions and complements the picture of the English system. This offence will be analysed in a separate section (see 7 below).

2. Protected Legal Interests

Fraud is considered to be one of the property offences and it certainly focuses on protecting private property.[29] The law naturally protects the owner of the assets in question, but is not limited to them. In the case of companies, it is not only the company which can be the victim of the abuse of position, but it is considered that other persons can become victims, for instance 'existing and potential shareholders, creditors and depositors'.[30] Since the offence does not require any result, it may be considered a victimless crime and it is theoretically possible to convict a person without the victim giving evidence.[31]

It is important to note that the English criminal procedure does not grant the victim any special status within criminal procedure (like eg the French *partie civile*).[32] The judge, however, may grant compensation to any person who suffered from the offence.[33] This category is very broad and it is for the judge to decide whom he considered prejudiced by the crime.[34] On the other hand, any person,

[27] *R v Allsop* (1977) 64 Cr App R 29.

[28] *Wai Yu-Tsang* (n 2).

[29] Simester et al, *Simester and Sullivan's Criminal Law* (n 4) 608.

[30] *Wai Yu-Tsang* (n 2).

[31] Montgomery and Ormerod, *Montgomery and Ormerod on Fraud* (n 25) D-2024/D.2.114–D.2.115.

[32] John Spencer, 'The Victim and the Prosecutor' in Anthony Bottoms and Julian V. Roberts (eds), *Hearing the Victim: Adversarial Justice, Crime Victims and the State* (Cullompton: Willan Publishing, 2010) 143. For the historical evaluation of the position of the victim in English criminal law, see ibid 141 et seq.

[33] Powers of Criminal Courts (Sentencing) Act 2000, s 130.

[34] *Chappell* (1985) 80 Cr App R 31. According to this judgment the judge may grant compensation regardless of whether the victim would have an independent civil claim against the offender.

including the victim, may start a private prosecution for the offence. The practical implications make the possibilities to make use of this right rather limited.[35]

Simester and Sullivan pointed out that the reason for criminalisation extends also to considerable psychological distress associated with victimisation in cases of property offences. 'In each case, the conduct prohibited can be seen as an attack upon the victim's entitlement to dispose of his property by his own full and informed choice.'[36] In that view, fraud by abuse of position, which is the most relevant modality of fraud from the perspective of company management, 'is a crime partly because it entails the manipulation or exploitation of another'.[37] In this sense, fraud protects the victim's free will and autonomy as well as the freedom to control his own material situation. Furthermore, this modality of fraud protects the important value of trust, thanks to which the perpetrator is allowed to have access to assets and customers and he should use it to the benefit of the person who entrusted them to him.[38] The mere dishonest abuse of such a position, without causing any harm but exposing a person to risk of loss, can victimise a person whose trust is abused (eg the shareholders). Moreover, one can claim that exposing assets to a risk of loss creates a harm to their owner, which is further corroborated, if it is admitted, as the Court of Appeal did in *Allsop*, that assets exposed to risk are worth less than they would be worth in the absence of any such exposure.[39]

Since there are different ways of committing fraud, one could ask what is the core moral wrong that the offence of fraud is aiming to address. The element, which is repeated in all three modalities of fraud (and also in conspiracy to defraud), is dishonesty, ie acting dishonestly. In this interpretation, fraud would amount to being dishonest in one of the specific contexts described by sections 2–4 of the Fraud Act or of conspiracy to defraud, which add an element (conduct) making dishonesty worthy of criminal punishment. In view of the broad terminology used to describe the *actus reus*, its role ought not to be overestimated, leaving the focus on the question of dishonesty. As Ormerod and Williams put it: 'the morally dubious conduct additional to dishonesty seems hard to identify, it could be something as innocuous as failing to work for an employer as hard as one might'.[40]

While the English doctrine does not use the concept of protected interests, as is the case, for instance, in the German scholarship, it seems fair to conclude that the offence focuses mainly on protecting property and reprimanding dishonesty in situations described by the offence.

See also David Ormerod and Anthony Hooper (gen eds), *Blackstone's Criminal Practice 2013* (Oxford University Press, 2012) E16.1–E16.4/ 2278–79.

[35] For a thorough analysis of this right see Spencer, 'The Victim and the Prosecutor' (n 32) 145 et seq.

[36] Simester et al, *Simester and Sullivan's Criminal Law* (n 4) 608.

[37] Ibid 608.

[38] Simon Farrell, Nicholas Yeo and Guy Ladenburg, *Blackstone's Guide to the Fraud Act 2006* (Oxford University Press, 2007) 31 et seq.

[39] *Allsop* (n 27) 32.

[40] Ormerod and Williams, *Smith's Law of Theft* (n 8) 133.

3. Main Offences

3.1. Common Elements

All three sections describing the modalities of fraud contain two common requirements, which need to be proven, namely dishonesty and special intention. The special intention complements the *mens rea* requirements, in addition to the *mens rea* required for each of the three modalities. However, the design of the special intention requirement is very broad, hence it will not play an important role in shaping the scope of application of the offence. To the contrary, dishonesty will play a much more important role, and will make the conduct described in the *actus reus*, which is not blameworthy per se, worthy of criminal punishment. These two common elements will be described here in turn before embarking on the analysis of the particularities of each of the modalities of fraud.

3.1.1. *Dishonesty*

The Fraud Act 2006 does not provide any definition of or guidance as to how to understand the element of dishonesty. The problem how to understand dishonesty existed already under the previous law and was subject to extensive debates and jurisprudence.[41] According to the judgment in *Feely*,[42] dishonesty should be taken as an ordinary word and the jury should be asked whether they found the conduct of the defendant to be dishonest. In a subsequent judgment in *Ghosh*,[43] the Court of Appeal decided to introduce a two-elements test for dishonesty which, despite certain criticisms, was widely accepted,[44] until a very recent judgment in *Ivey* shortened it by eliminating its second part.[45]

According to *Ghosh*, in order to establish that the defendant acted dishonestly the jurors needed to answer positively the following two questions:

(1) Was what was done dishonest according to the ordinary standards of reasonable and honest people?

(2) Must the defendant himself have realised that what he was doing would be regarded as dishonest by the standards of reasonable and honest people?[46]

[41] For the evolution of the understanding of dishonesty see, eg Jacques Parry, Anthony Arlidge, Joanne Hacking and Josepha Jacobson, *Arlidge and Parry on Fraud*, 3rd edn (London: Sweet & Maxwell, 2007) 6 et seq;

[42] *R v Feely* [1973] 2 WLR 201; [1973] QB 530, 537–38.

[43] *R v Ghosh* [1982] QB 1053.

[44] Law Com No 276 (n 1) 43/5.18. See, eg *R v Benjamin Jason Cornelius* [2012] EWCA Crim 500, where the Court of Appeal said: 'We wish therefore to make clear that the decision in Ghosh remains good law'.

[45] *Ivey v Genting Casinos (UK) Ltd t/a Crockfords* [2017] UKSC 67, para [74].

[46] *R v Ghosh* [1982] QB 1053, 1064.

This was a mixed – objective and subjective – approach to dishonesty. The objective part, which remains valid, belongs to the *actus reus* of the offence and requires that the tribunal of facts evaluates whether the conduct was dishonest according to the standard of reasonable and honest people.[47] The deleted subjective part, belonging to the *mens rea*, required that the jury would establish that the defendant was aware that his act was dishonest according to this standard.[48] The question whether he considered his act dishonest was irrelevant. The division between the *actus reus* and *mens rea* aspect of dishonesty was not very strict, since the objective part of the test could also take into account the cognitive aspects of the manager's mental state.

The test was criticised for its various shortcomings.[49] The criticism focused in particular on the second part of the test for granting too much importance to the subjective element of the defendant's vision as to people's morality. It was through this sort of consideration that the judgment in *Ivey* eliminated that element. Under *Ghosh*, the defendant could theoretically evoke in his defence that 'everybody does that'.[50] It was this kind of reasoning that was used, although unsuccessfully, when in the course of the trials of members of the House of Lords for false accounting regarding the use of their official expenses, the defendants tried to assert the claim that their behaviour was part of the 'office culture'.[51] However, such excuse had its limitations, since it was not the personal conviction of the defendant that was the basis of the subjective part, but his awareness of the fact that a reasonable and honest person would consider such behaviour to be dishonest.[52]

The objective part of the test was not spared criticism either, although it remains good law. This part assumes that the members of the jury, who would evaluate the occurrence of this element, have consistent values, whereas in practice they rather vary to an important extent both in cultural and socio-economic aspects.[53] This leads to the danger of differing convictions as to the standard of dishonesty, and an impossibility for a reasonable person to predict if his conduct

[47] Ormerod and Hooper, *Blackstone's Criminal Practice 2013* (n 34) B4.54/ 408.

[48] Ibid 15/2.05–2.07; Parry et al, *Arlidge and Parry on Fraud* (n 41) 9/2-013.

[49] Simester et al, *Simester and Sullivan's Criminal Law* (n 4) 549. For analysis of the deficiencies of Ghosh, see, eg Montgomery and Ormerod, *Montgomery and Ormerod on Fraud* (n 25) D-1006 et seq; David Ormerod, 'The Fraud Act 2006: Criminalising Lying?' (2007) *Criminal Law Review* 193, 200 et seq.

[50] Simester et al, *Simester and Sullivan's Criminal Law* (n 4) 549.

[51] Simester et al, *Simester and Sullivan's Criminal Law* (n 4) 550.

[52] This reasoning was also confirmed in the recent case concerning the LIBOR scandal, where the Court of Appeal restated that the standard to be applied is the one of honest and reasonable people generally and not the one of honest and reasonable bankers: *R v Hayes* [2015] EWCA Crim 1944, see especially para [32].

[53] Simester et al, *Simester and Sullivan's Criminal Law* (n 4) 548. Similarly, the members of the jury may have also a discrepant code of values in comparison to the defendant due to various factors (sex, age, background, etc); this problem is not limited to the offence of fraud, but concerns all offences, where a test of reasonable person is applied; for a detailed analysis see Mayo Moran, *Rethinking the Reasonable Person: An Egalitarian Reconstruction of the Objective Standard* (Oxford University Press, 2003).

should be regarded as dishonest or not. In view of the defendant's inability to foresee whether his conduct constitutes an offence, questions as to the contravention of Article 7 of the ECHR can be raised.[54] It is important to point out that the jury should not take into account whether people usually do something or not (eg commit small tax evasions or abuse the system of compensation of costs), but whether they regard it as dishonest.[55]

There are a number of procedural aspects that influence the implications of dishonesty. Fraud is an offence which is 'triable either way', meaning that it can be tried either in a magistrates' court or in the Crown Court, depending mainly on the defendant's decision to plead guilty or not guilty and on the seriousness of the offence. If the defendant pleads not guilty, he has the right to elect trial by jury.[56] It was argued that the vagueness of the test for dishonesty may encourage a larger number of defendants to 'try their luck' before a jury, where they risk much higher punishment, if convicted.[57] In any case the prosecution must be prepared to be able to demonstrate dishonesty before a jury.[58]

The dynamics of the jury system will shape to a large extent the practice of application of the offence of fraud.[59] The involvement of juries in fraud trials was subject to criticism in two major reports[60] and a Bill which provided the possibility to exclude them from these trials.[61] However, the Bill failed and so far there has been no new proposal in this regard.[62]

[54] Simester et al, *Simester and Sullivan's Criminal Law* (n 4) 549; Law Commission, *Legislating the Criminal Code: Fraud and Deception*, Consultation Paper No 155 (1999) elaborates on this problem (at 5.33 et seq).

[55] Parry et al, *Arlidge and Parry on Fraud* (n 41) 12/2-020.

[56] Andrew Ashworth, *Principles of Criminal Law*, 6th edn (Oxford University Press, 2009) 7.

[57] Montgomery and Ormerod, *Montgomery and Ormerod on Fraud* (n 25) D-1009.

[58] For two reasons this chapter (as well as the rest of the book when discussing the English legal system) will refer to the jury instead of using a more neutral expression 'the tribunal of fact'. First, the English model of criminalisation of excessive risk-taking will be particularly shaped by the involvement of the juries and result in distinct characteristics in comparison to the two other legal systems. The reference to the jury should point out this particularity. Secondly, cases of fraud tried in the magistrates' courts are of lesser gravity than those tried in the Crown Court. It is, however, important to bear in mind that cases where the jury will not be involved are not excluded.

[59] More generally on jury trials, see, eg Andrew Ashworth and Mike Redmayne, *The Criminal Process*, 4th edn (Oxford University Press, 2010) 323 et seq.

[60] Fraud Trials Committee (Roskill Committee), *Fraud Trials Committee Report* (London: HMSO, 1986); see also Lord Devlin, 'Trial by Jury for Fraud' (1986) *Oxford Journal of Legal Studies* 311; Lord Justice Auld, *Review of the Criminal Courts of England and Wales* (London: Stationery Office, 2001), in particular ch 5 para [173] et seq. See also Ormerod and Williams, *Smith's Law of Theft* (n 8) 398 et seq; Michael Levi, 'The Roskill Fraud Commission Revisited: An Assessment' (2003) 11(1) *Journal of Financial Crime* (July) 38.

[61] Criminal Justice Act 2003, s 43, allows applications for trial in the Crown Court to be conducted without a jury. However, in order to be applied for fraud it requires further legislation. The Fraud (Trials Without a Jury) Bill, introduced in 2007, was meant to provide such legislation for serious fraud, but was blocked by the House of Lords: Ashworth and Redmayne, *The Criminal Process* (n 59) 330. In the meantime, Criminal Justice Act 2003, s 43 was repealed by Protection of Freedoms Act 2012, Sch 10 Part 10).

[62] Ashworth and Redmayne, *The Criminal Process* (n 59) 330; see also:Miriam Peck, *The Fraud (Trials Without a Jury) Bill 2006–07*, House of Commons Research Paper 06/57 (23 November 2006).

Although the fact that the trial involves the jury will influence all the aspects of the process, as regards the offence of fraud, it will have particular impact on the test of dishonesty; namely, it will be applied by twelve laymen with different backgrounds and most probably without experience in business.[63] Moreover, the verdict of the jury is limited to pronouncing the defendant 'guilty' or 'not guilty' and no reasons are given for the decision.[64] The jury deliberates in private and it is a criminal offence 'to obtain, disclose or solicit any particulars of statements made, opinions expressed, arguments advanced or votes cast by members of a jury in the course of their deliberations'.[65] Therefore, there is no possibility to establish the reasons which convinced the jury in a concrete case that the defendant was or was not dishonest. In view of that, there is no systematised doctrine which would allow us to precisely foresee which conduct will be considered dishonest and which will not, as it will be assessed on a case-by-case basis.

From the viewpoint of the liability of managers, it is essential to establish when excessive risk-taking committed by them can be considered dishonest. After the judgment in *Ivey*, the jury will analyse only the objective part of the old *Ghosh* test, ie whether an honest and reasonable person would consider what the manager in question did as dishonest. One can ask whether the standard should be the one of an honest and reasonable (ordinary) person or of a manager of such qualities. *Ghosh* did not introduce any differentiation in this regard, suggesting that an ordinary person should be taken as a model.[66] It seems plausible to claim that the assessment will be made for a reasonable and honest person in such a position, meaning the manager.[67]

The judgment in the case of *Sinclair* addressed the problem of what is the importance of the quality of the decision for the assessment of dishonesty, in particular whether the risk taken by a company director was dishonest.[68] The Court of Appeal in its nuanced opinion stated that the defendant's counsel was wrong in asserting that 'the test to distinguish between conduct which is fraudulent, and conduct which is not, is whether the transaction is a normal transaction'.[69] The question of honesty cannot be replaced by the test of the normality of the transaction. The Court of Appeal aligned itself with the following formulation:

> For the Crown it is contended that it is fraudulent to take a risk to the prejudice of another's rights, which risk is known to be one which there is no right to take, and that

[63] Andrew Sanders, Richard Young and Mandy Burton, *Criminal Justice*, 4th edn (Oxford University Press, 2010) 559.

[64] Mark Coen and Jonathan Doak, 'Embedding Explained Jury Verdicts in the English Criminal Trial' (2017) 37(4) *Legal Studies* 786. See also Gillian Daly, 'Jury Secrecy: R v. Mirza; R v. Connor and Rollock' (2004) 8 *International Journal of Evidence and Proof* 186.

[65] Juries Act 1974, s 20D.

[66] Parry et al, *Arlidge and Parry on Fraud* (n 41) 16.

[67] The judgment in *Sinclair* seems to suggest it: [1968] 1 WLR 1246, 1251.

[68] Ibid.

[69] Ibid 1249 and 1251.

> if such a risk is taken it is no defence to say that the person taking the risk had an honest belief that no prejudice but only benefit would result.[70]

From this judgment, it follows that the fact that the transaction was abnormal does not in itself imply that the defendant acted dishonestly.

A more troublesome question is how the jury will evaluate the (dis)honesty of a defendant. In view of this judgment in *Ghosh*, the jury will be confronted with the question whether an honest and reasonable person in such situation would not take the risk the manager took. The fact that the defendant honestly believed that 'no prejudice but only benefit would result'[71] does not as such render his act honest. According to Parry:

> a defendant who takes even a slight risk with another's property, knowing that the other would not allow that risk to be taken if he knew the true position, will almost inevitably be found to have acted dishonestly. His belief that the risk would not materialise ought not to be a defence.[72]

While the above interpretation would generally allow the incrimination of managers who knowingly take excessive risk, it seems that it might be far-fetched. Since the jury needs to infer dishonesty from the evidence, the sole fact that the manager took excessive risk, in particular if he intended the company eventually to benefit from it, may be insufficient for the prosecution to decide to proceed with the case. It can be assumed that some additional circumstances would be needed to render the manager's act more reprehensible. In particular, two factors may contribute to his dishonesty. First, it may be the fact the he acted mainly for his own personal interest, eg in view of increased commission for the transaction, provided that there is some direct tangible gain.[73] Secondly, some additional factors might demonstrate lack of integrity, eg colluding with the client who provides incorrect information in the process of obtaining a loan, or knowingly and intentionally breaching one of the rules regulating the execution of his duties.[74] The sole fact that he breached one of these rules does not render him dishonest, as he may plausibly claim that he did so by mistake. Additional difficulty will be linked with the fact that a business decision may be taken within a complex structure and after a decision-making process, within which it is difficult to precisely attribute one person's influence. Where the motivation is only to prove himself to be a successful manager (by increasing the company's turnover), or to please higher management, may not be sufficient to convince the jury that the manager was dishonest. Ultimately, the particularities of the case will decide whether or not the prosecution see the prospect of conviction as sufficient to proceed with the case.[75]

[70] Ibid 1251.
[71] Ibid 1251.
[72] Parry et al, *Arlidge and Parry on Fraud* (n 41) 13/2-024.
[73] *Allsop* (n 27).
[74] *Wai Yu-Tsang* (n 2) 269–72.
[75] This section is mainly based on the interview conducted at the Serious Fraud Office.

3.1.2. Special Intention

The second common element is the requirement of *mens rea*. According to this requirement, the perpetrator must not only have the required intention to commit what the *actus reus* described. He must also intend by his actions either:

- to make a gain (for himself or another);
- to cause loss to another; or
- to expose another to a risk of loss.

The previous offences of deception required that the perpetrator obtain something as a result of his conduct. The new offence does not require this result, but moves the objective guiding the defendant's actions to the *mens rea* part.[76] Such a broad description of *mens rea* gives the prosecution various possibilities to charge the defendant for fraud, focusing the evidence only on the intention to cause loss or expose to a risk of loss in cases where it is impossible to prove his gain or the intention to achieve any such gain.[77]

With respect to intent as required for fraud, managers can be held liable for exposing their companies to a risk of loss in two different configurations. In the first one, exposing the company to a risk of loss is the manager's true intention. In these cases the manager will most often not wish to cause any damage; on the contrary, he hopes that the company will benefit in the end, or that his actions will save the company from difficulties.[78] The manager may have additional motivation to act in this way, which might be seeking his own benefit, eg development of his career as a successful manager, or else in the form of financial gratification (a bonus or an increase in the company's value of which he owns shares).

As to the second configuration, it will be possible to convict a manager for effectively exposing his company to the risk of loss, while his intention was directed at other objectives. It will be obvious that, if the defendant acted with intention to cause prejudice, his state of mind comprised also the intention to expose to a risk of loss. The flexibility of the formulation shows itself fully in cases where it is impossible to prove that the defendant wanted to expose the company to a risk of loss (or to cause loss), if the prosecution can prove that he effectively did expose it to this, while seeking personal or another's gain.

The first aspect of the requirement of intention is the very meaning of the verb 'to intend', by which the perpetrator's state of mind is described in Fraud Act 2006, sections 2–4. It certainly covers situations in which the defendant wants something to happen.[79] Therefore, all the situations, according to the configurations described above, where managers willingly expose their companies to a risk of loss

[76] Farrell et al, *Blackstone's Guide to the Fraud Act 2006* (n 38) 17.

[77] Ibid 19.

[78] Two cases described further in this chapter can exemplify such situations: *Allsop* as to the first one and *Wai Yu-Tsang* (see 4.5 below).

[79] Parry et al, *Arlidge and Parry on Fraud* (n 41) 19.

or have this intention without achieving it, are covered by this limb. The question is whether it is possible to extend liability for situations where there is no intention in the sense described above, but, while acting, the perpetrator was nevertheless aware of the fact that his decision may put the company at risk of loss.

The question of the extension of intent was discussed in *Woollin*, where the House of Lords defined it in the following way:

> (1) The result is intended when it is the actor's purpose to cause it.
>
> (2) A court or jury may also find that a result is intended, though it is not the actor's purpose to cause it, when:
>
> (a) the result is a virtually certain consequence of that act, and
> (b) the actor knows that it is a virtually certain consequence.[80]

Different authors seem to agree that this definition extends also to fraud,[81] although it was not formulated in a fraud case.[82] This means that where a manager does not want to cause loss or expose the company to the risk of loss, but it is virtually certain that the company will be exposed to the risk of loss and he is aware of it, the jury may still find him guilty of fraud, if other elements are fulfilled. If the defendant's state of mind does not amount to one of those described in *Woollin*, he must be acquitted (eg if it would be possible to prove that he acted recklessly, but not intentionally).

As to the expression 'virtually', one could argue that it is very often not possible to say with full certainty that one act will be followed by another, it is thus safer to speak about a 'virtually' certain result. What is meant here is that the defendant is aware that his action in the 'normal course of events'[83] will cause the risk of loss and he decides to pursue it anyway.[84] It cannot exempt the defendant from liability that he was not sure whether he would be successful with his plan or not.[85] The use of the expression 'may' in the *Woollin* definition of the second type of intention suggests that juries, while deciding upon the defendant's liability, are free to attribute liability to him considering his blameworthiness with respect to all the circumstances.[86]

The extension of the understanding of intention granted some degree of flexibility to juries, which might contribute to achieving justice in particular cases.[87] However, this solution has been criticised for providing space for

[80] *Woollin* [1998] AC 82, 83, the formulation here after Farrell et al, *Blackstone's Guide to the Fraud Act 2006* (n 38) 19.

[81] Farrell et al, *Blackstone's Guide to the Fraud Act 2006* (n 38) 19; Ormerod and Williams, *Smith's Law of Theft* (n 8) at 136; Parry et al, *Arlidge and Parry on Fraud* (n 41) 54.

[82] Montgomery and Ormerod, *Montgomery and Ormerod on Fraud* (n 25) D-1025.

[83] As the Attorney-General formulated in the course of discussions preceding the enacting of the Fraud Act: Hansard, HL, 19 July 2005, vol 673, col 1414.

[84] Montgomery and Ormerod, *Montgomery and Ormerod on Fraud* (n 25) D-1025 et seq.

[85] Parry et al, *Arlidge and Parry on Fraud* (n 41) 55.

[86] Alan W. Norre, 'After *Woollin*' (1999) *Criminal Law Review*, 532, 537.

[87] Montgomery and Ormerod, *Montgomery and Ormerod on Fraud* (n 25) D-1026.

uncertainty and inconsistency in application of the law. This solution has been also blamed for confusing the boundaries of substantive law and the law of evidence and rendering the scope of liability undefined.[88]

An interesting question is whether the intention to make a gain for another is fulfilled if this other person is at the same time the victim of the offence through being exposed to risk of loss. This question will touch upon situations, already mentioned above, when the defendant exposes another to the risk of loss while willing that the victim benefits or at least avoids loss (which, as will be seen below, can also include 'keeping what one has'[89]). In two cases of conspiracy to defraud which will be subject to more detailed analysis below (*Allsop* and *Wai Yu-Tsang*),[90] the Court of Appeal and the Privy Council confirmed that although the ultimate motive of the defendant was beneficial for the victim, he did in fact intend (at least) to expose the victim to the risk of loss. In view of the phrasing of intent, even if the defendant does not seek his own gain, but the victim's gain, and even if he does not intend to cause loss to the victim or expose him to the risk of loss, he will possibly still be held liable. Hence, liability for fraud is possible when the defendant exposes the company to the risk of loss recklessly even though his intention aims at the gain of the latter. The only possible way to correct this far-reaching result would be through the idea of dishonesty, and it is not certain that the jury would find a reckless director of a bank to be dishonest.

The second issue to be analysed with regard to the requirement of intention is its object (to make a gain, to cause loss to another or to expose another to a risk of loss). As to the understanding of these terms, the Fraud Act provides for some clarification in section 5:

> (2) 'Gain' and 'loss'—
>
> (a) extend only to gain or loss in money or other property;
>
> (b) include any such gain or loss whether temporary or permanent; and 'property' means any property whether real or personal (including things in action and other intangible property).
>
> (3) 'Gain' includes a gain by keeping what one has, as well as a gain by getting what one does not have.
>
> (4) 'Loss' includes a loss by not getting what one might get, as well as a loss by parting with what one has.

The key element of these definitions is the word 'property', which is understood very broadly. According to section 5(2)(b), it can be any property, also real, including things in action (also called choses, which corresponds to legal right to sue, eg debts)[91] and intangible property (property which has no physical substance,

[88] Ibid D-1026.
[89] Fraud Act 2006, s 5(3).
[90] See 4.5 below.
[91] *Oxford Dictionary of Law*, 3rd edn (Oxford University Press, 1996).

eg copyrights, patents or trademarks).[92] Thus, the definition comprises intellectual property, although the Explanatory Notes point out that it is 'rarely "gained" or "lost"'.[93] This remark might be true in the context of typical fraudulent situations, however intellectual property rights might be lost, if they are not safeguarded properly. It would be possible, for instance, to envisage liability of a manager responsible for taking care of patent applications who fails to file such an application in time, because he has interests in a rival company which will benefit from a failure.

According to the judgment in *Oxford v Moss*,[94] confidential information is not covered by the definition of property. Although discussed in the parliamentary debates, the extension of the definition of property was rejected,[95] which means that trade secrets cannot be the object of fraud. However, it could be argued that even if the perpetrator's objective is that the company risks losing some confidential information (where losing would necessarily mean that this information is made public), it is virtually certain that this at least exposes the company to a risk of loss in pecuniary terms. Hence, such a situation could also be covered by this provision.

The terms 'gain' and 'loss' are also understood broadly, by including also keeping what one has, in the case of the former, and not getting what one might get, as to the latter. As to the risk of loss, there exists no definition of the word 'risk' and it should probably be taken as an ordinary English word referring to 'loss', which is defined in section 5. Even before the enactment of the Fraud Act 2006, the Court of Appeal held in *Allsop* that '[i]nterests which are imperilled are less valuable in terms of money than those same interests when they are secure and protected'.[96] If understood this way, it could be claimed that the fact of being exposed to risk of loss is enough to declare that an actual loss has taken place. As Parry points out, the phrase 'or to expose another to a risk of loss' might not in fact extend the scope of criminalisation, but simplify the explanations with which the jury should be provided.[97]

The third problem regarding the requirement of intention concerns intended causation. All three forms of fraud require such a link between the *actus reus* and the intent to make gain, cause loss or expose to a risk of loss. According to all three sections, the defendant must intend to achieve his objective 'by means of' making false representation, by failing to disclose information or by abusing his position.[98] It is important to point out that this problem of causation belongs to the *mens rea* and not to the *actus reus*, since fraud does not require a result. It will be necessary

[92] Ibid.
[93] Home Office, *Explanatory Notes: Fraud Act 2006* (8 November 2006) recital 24.
[94] *Oxford v Moss* (1979) 68 Cr App R 183.
[95] Hansard, HL, 19 July 2005, cols 1435–36.
[96] *Allsop* (n 27) 32.
[97] Parry et al, *Arlidge and Parry on Fraud* (n 41) 53.
[98] Fraud Act 2006, ss 2–4.

for the jury to establish whether it was part of the perpetrator's intention that a gain, a loss or a risk of loss is caused by his act.[99]

Under the previous law (Theft Acts 1968 and 1978), the courts faced the problem of causation (and remoteness) within the analysis of the *actus reus*, since the law required a proof of result.[100] It was necessary to establish whether the action of the defendant had resulted in the latter obtaining something from the victim and whether the chain of events was not too remote. The courts tended to deny causality, if the act in question was not a 'direct and immediate cause of the obtaining'.[101] In a case for obtaining winnings by false pretences, a man managed to bet on a horse by telling lies. The horse eventually won. The court held that the gain's immediate cause was the horse's win and not the false pretences, thus dismissing the case.[102]

3.2. Fraud by Abuse of Position

The way of committing fraud that is most relevant from the perspective of punishing excessive risk is described in Fraud Act 2006, section 4 (fraud by abuse of position):

> (1) A person is in breach of this section if he—
> (a) occupies a position in which he is expected to safeguard, or not to act against, the financial interests of another person,
> (b) dishonestly abuses that position, and
> (c) intends, by means of the abuse of that position—
> (i) to make a gain for himself or another, or
> (ii) to cause loss to another or to expose another to a risk of loss.

The offence has already been criticised in Parliament as a 'catch all provision that will be a nightmare of judicial interpretation … and help to bring the law into disrepute',[103] and the definition of position, seen as the most problematic element, was described as 'woolly'.[104]

It contains the same two elements of *mens rea* as other types of fraud – dishonesty and intention – and the *actus reus* is described in a rather 'minimalist' way.[105] It comprises only two elements: the description of the perpetrator by means of a position of trust and the description of his action, which consists in abusing this position. As will be shown below, the way the provision is drafted

[99] *Gilbert* [2012] EWCA Crim 2392, 29; Simester et al, *Simester and Sullivan's Criminal Law* (n 4) 614.
[100] Simester et al, *Simester and Sullivan's Criminal Law* (n 4) 613.
[101] Ibid 613.
[102] *Rex v Clucas* [1949] 2 KB 226.
[103] Standing Committee B, 20 June 2006, col 25.
[104] Hansard, HC, 12 June 2006, vol 447, col 549.
[105] Simester et al, *Simester and Sullivan's Criminal Law* (n 4) 609.

allows the inclusion of a plethora of relationships into its scope (see 3.2.1 below on manager as perpetrator). The question of whether the defendant abused his position will often be intertwined with the question of dishonesty, and thus is of little help to shape the contours of the offence (see 3.2.2 below on abuse). The question whether it is possible to require an additional element of *mens rea* will be discussed at 3.2.3 below.

3.2.1. Manager as Perpetrator

The offence described in Fraud Act 2006, section 4 can be committed only by a person who 'occupies a position in which he is expected to safeguard, or not to act against, the financial interests of another person'. The key element of this definition is the word 'position', which is described in the law as 'the position in which he is expected to safeguard, or not to act against, the financial interests of another person'. The Act does not specify any further how to understand this expression, which has given rise to intensive doctrinal debates.[106] Managers will undoubtedly fall into the scope of this provision. The relationships between director and company and between employer and employee are expressly mentioned in the Explanatory Notes.[107] Directors' duties to the company are described in the Companies Act 2006,[108] and they are in a fiduciary relationship with the company.[109] Employees are also in such a relationship under certain conditions.[110] But even without entering the murky waters of fiduciary duties,[111] it is clear that managers fulfil this limb of section 4. The Law Commission explained that the 'expectation to safeguard or power to damage may arise, for example, because the defendant is given authority to exercise a discretion on the victim's behalf, or is given access to the victim's assets, premises, equipment or customers'.[112] Managers effectively exercise discretion on behalf of the company and are given access to the property of the company that they are supposed to use for its benefit. Even employees that are given some managerial power, but with very limited discretion, will most likely be expected not to act against the financial interests of the company. If they were ordered to pursue the policy which encourages them to take excessively risky decisions, their acquittal will depend on the success of the defence that they acted under the orders of superiors.[113]

[106] See. eg Montgomery and Ormerod, *Montgomery and Ormerod on Fraud* (n 25) 2103; Parry et al, *Arlidge and Parry on Fraud* (n 41) 143 et seq.
[107] Home Office, *Explanatory Notes: Fraud Act 2006* (n 93) recital 20.
[108] Companies Act 2006, ss 170–77, in particular s 172 (duty to promote the success of the company) and s 174 (duty to exercise reasonable care, skill and diligence).
[109] For discussion of fiduciary duties of directors and employees, see Andrew Stafford and Stuart Ritchie, *Fiduciary Duties: Directors and Employees* (Bristol: Jordans, 2008) 5 et seq.
[110] Ibid 83 et seq.
[111] Ibid 8. See also Standing Committee B (n 103) col 18 et seq, col 21.
[112] Law Com No 276 (n 1) marginal no 7.37.
[113] See 6.2 below.

The second key element of the definition in section 4 is the term 'occupies', which implies that abuse of position should be committed while the perpetrator is occupying this position. A problem with this notion arises in cases of duties that go beyond the timeframe of the manager's contract. In this sense he can still abuse his position after he ceases to perform his functions.[114] Moreover, the CPS instructed in the guidelines that if the offence was planned while in office, and the perpetrator undertook some action at that time (eg he collected some information that he used after leaving office), the offence was committed while he was still in office and thus he can be prosecuted.[115]

The above problem will have limited impact on the liability of managers for excessive risk-taking. The situations where time-delay will play a role in that context are when managers take decisions which expose the company to a risk of loss, although this risk will foreseeably materialise, if at all, after they leave office. Often risky decisions boost the company's performance in the short term and managers get higher bonuses. The consequences might only arrive after they have left their positions. However, in English law it would not be a problem to consider such conduct as fraud. If the decision exposing the company to the risk of loss can be considered as abusive and taken dishonestly, and if the intention to gain is clear, the problem of the late occurrence of the result (or lack of its materialisation) does not preclude the manager's criminal liability.

3.2.2. Abuse

A person occupying a position described in the previous paragraph commits fraud described in Fraud Act 2006, section 4 if he 'abuses that position'. Similarly to 'position', the term 'abuse' was not defined by the Act. According to the Explanatory Notes: '[t]he term "abuse" is not limited by a definition, because it is intended to cover a wide range of conduct'.[116] Among the examples given by the Home Office, the following is the most relevant:

> Another example covered by this section is where a person who is employed to care for an elderly or disabled person has access to that person's bank account and abuses his position by transferring funds to invest in a high-risk business venture of his own.[117]

The term 'abuse' should be taken as an ordinary English word and it will be for the jury to decide on a case-by-case basis whether it took place or not.[118] Certainly, it should not be limited to breaches of fiduciary duties.[119] Abuse does not have to

[114] Montgomery and Ormerod, *Montgomery and Ormerod on Fraud* (n 25) D-2108.

[115] Crown Prosecution Service, *The Fraud Act 2006: Legal Guidance*, available at www.cps.gov.uk/legal/d_to_g/fraud_act/.

[116] Home Office, *Explanatory Notes: Fraud Act 2006*(n 93) recital 21.

[117] Ibid recital 23.

[118] Montgomery and Ormerod, *Montgomery and Ormerod on Fraud* (n 25) D-2109. See also the CPS in their *Legal Guidance* (n 115).

[119] *Regina v Valujevs and another* [2014] EWCA 2888.

be a legal act and need not have an impact on the company's obligations vis-à-vis third parties.[120] According to section 4(2), an abuse of position may be performed by omission.

A fictitious case proposed by one author shows possible excessive criminalisation provided by section 4. A compliance officer, instead of monitoring the bank's risk, plays card games on his computer. 'He is in a position of trust and by his omission he is abusing his position and exposing the bank to the risk of financial loss. Provided the jury find that he is dishonest, he is in breach of the section and guilty of fraud.'[121] One might add that playing cards during work time can hardly be considered honest. This case suggests that breaching professional duties could be punished under certain conditions as fraud. A situation of pure carelessness would probably encounter problems to meet the *mens rea* requirement, since it is an intentional offence. But if the defendant has intentionally breached his professional duty, it will not be too difficult to qualify his act as dishonest.

The initial idea of the Law Commission that in order to be criminal the abuse should be performed secretly, intended to add an element of blameworthiness, was abandoned.[122] It is indeed difficult to imagine why a secretly performed abuse of position should be criminal while abuse about which the victim is informed, but that he cannot prevent, should escape criminal sanction.[123] The Crown Prosecution Service (CPS) gave the following examples of abuse of position:

- an employee who fails to take up the chance of a crucial contract in order that an associate or rival company can take it up instead;
- a director of a company who dishonestly makes use of knowledge gained as a director to make a personal gain;
- an employee who abuses his position in order to grant contracts or discounts to friends, relatives and associates;
- a waiter who sells his own bottles of wine passing them off as belonging to the restaurant (*R v Doukas* [1978] 1 All ER 1071).[124]

Furthermore, the CPS expressed the view that:

> [p]rosecutors should guard against the criminal law being used as a debt collection agency or to protect the commercial interests of companies and organisations. However, prosecutors should also remain alert to the fact that such organisations can become the focus of serious and organised criminal offending.[125]

[120] Antje du Bois-Pedain, 'Die Strafbarkeit untreueartigen Verhaltens im englischen Recht: "Fraud by abuse of position" und andere einschlägige Strafvorschriften' (2010) 122(2) *Zeitschrift für die gesamte Strafrechtswissenschaft* 325, 344.

[121] Farrell et al, *Blackstone's Guide to the Fraud Act 2006* (n 38) 34.

[122] Law Com No 276 (n 1) marginal no 7.40.

[123] Parry et al, *Arlidge and Parry on Fraud* (n 41) 143.

[124] CPS, *Legal Guidance* (n 115).

[125] Ibid.

One can simply argue, in view of the description of the perpetrator, that an abuse of position consists in not safeguarding or in acting against the financial interests of another person. However, the fact that the Act did not use this expression might not only be considered a stylistic choice, but also a deliberate differentiation suggesting that an abuse is something more. The dictionary meaning of the word 'to abuse' is 'to use wrongly or improperly'.[126] If a person is not safeguarding the financial interests of a person he is supposed to safeguard or is acting against these interests and is doing it dishonestly, it will be hard to say that he is not abusing his position.[127] This reasoning shows that eventually it will be dishonesty that will be the crucial element deciding on the defendant's liability, despite the intention of the Law Commission not to let dishonesty 'do all the work'.[128]

In their daily work, managers take decisions that can expose their company to a risk of loss. That is natural, otherwise they could not take any decision, since each of them can potentially result in a loss. This corresponds to the correct or the right use of entrusted assets. The level of risk that a manager is allowed to take can be prescribed or can depend on practices in certain types of business. By not respecting these rules the manager might be in breach of his duties and thus abusing his position. This would be the case when the defendant is in breach of a rule governing his management duties.[129] But it can be argued that even if these duties are not formulated concretely, as is the case for directors in sections 171–177 of the Companies Act 2006 or any other rules, a manager is in any event supposed to make proper use of the assets of the company. If the manager takes a risk which is excessive to the type of business he is pursuing or to the type of transaction in question, he is improperly using his position, hence he is abusing his position. A decision can expose the company to excessive risk, but also passiveness of the manager can have such results. In view of Fraud Act 2006, section 4(2), the position can be also abused by omission.

It was said in *Sinclair* in the context of conspiracy to defraud that '[f]or the Crown it is contended that it is fraudulent to take a risk to the prejudice of another's rights, which risk is known to be one which there is no right to take'.[130] If the defendant took risks there was no right to take, he arguably abused his position. As already mentioned, the decision to consider the manager's behaviour to be an abuse will most probably be intertwined with the verdict on his honesty. A risk which can be considered honest according to the standard of honest and reasonable

[126] *Webster's College Dictionary* (2010). According to Lesley Brown (ed), *The New Shorter Oxford English Dictionary on Historical Principles* (Oxford: Clarendon Press, 1993) vol 1, the noun 'abuse' means 'an improper usage', while the verb 'abuse' means 'misuse; make a bad use of'.

[127] Parry et al, *Arlidge and Parry on Fraud* (n 41) 161.

[128] Law Com No 276 (n 1) marginal no 7.3.

[129] Arguably the behaviour of Wai Yu-Tsang in concealing information about dishonoured cheques which he was supposed to report could be considered an abuse in the sense of Fraud Act 2006, s 4: *Wai Yu-Tsang* (n 2) 273. For details on this case, see 4.5 below.

[130] *Sinclair* (n 67) 1251.

people will probably not be abusive, while if it is considered to be dishonest, it will tend also to be considered abusive. This reasoning might appear to be the fallacy of *petitio principi*,[131] although it is in fact not the case. A use becomes an abuse when it is incorrect according to certain rules, which apply in the context in question (eg allowing the manager to expose the assets to a certain level of risk). The reasoning on dishonesty will evaluate if an honest and reasonable person would consider this act dishonest. It is likely that, if it is considered that the manager knowingly used the assets in an incorrect way (committing an abuse), the jury would find that reasonable and honest people would consider it dishonest. And vice versa, if the conduct of the manager appears dishonest, it is more likely that they will consider it an abuse, not forgetting that it is to be understood as an ordinary English word and not a technical term.[132] Hence, it is not so much a case of circular reasoning, but rather evidence of the broad terms used in its design.

3.2.3. Mens Rea

Apart from dishonesty and intention, Fraud Act 2006, section 4 does not provide for any other *mens rea* requirement. In particular there is no requirement that the perpetrator be aware of the fact that he is expected to safeguard, or not to act against, the financial interests of another person. In two landmark decisions, the House of Lords held that even in lack of an explicit formulation of the *mens rea* requirement, the existence of such requirement is presumed in English criminal law.[133] It is hard to say how this rule will apply to section 4 or whether the courts will opt for strict liability in respect of this element. In any case, the defendant may claim that he did not act dishonestly, if he was not aware of his duties.[134]

3.3. Other Offences

In addition to fraud by abuse of position, a manager exposing his company to excessive risk might potentially commit other offences available in the English criminal law, in particular two other types of fraud, fraud by false representation (3.3.1 below) and fraud by failing to disclose information (3.3.2 below), as well as the offence of theft (3.3.3 below). The common requirements of dishonesty as well as special intention apply to these modalities as well.

[131] A dishonest use of assets is an abuse, while an abuse is defined as use which is not honest.
[132] Montgomery and Ormerod, *Montgomery and Ormerod on Fraud* (n 25) D-2109/D.2.338.
[133] *B v Dpp* [2000] 2 AC 428; *R v K* [2002] 1 AC 462.
[134] Montgomery and Ormerod, *Montgomery and Ormerod on Fraud* (n. 25) D-2101.

3.3.1. *Fraud by False Representation*

Fraud by false representation (Fraud Act 2006, section 2) is the most classical form of fraud, which can be associated with what continental criminal law would understand under this term.[135] According to section 2:

> (1) A person is in breach of this section if he—
> (a) dishonestly makes a false representation, and
> (b) intends, by making the representation—
> (i) to make a gain for himself or another, or
> (ii) to cause loss to another or to expose another to a risk of loss.

Fraud described in this section might be applied in particular to managers who elicited approval of their decisions, eg from shareholders or more senior managers, or persuaded such persons to take the decisions based on the managers' recommendations. It is possible that such conduct would be considered as an abuse of position and could be charged under section 4. This section does not require proof of the position in which the defendant is expected to safeguard the financial interests of the company. Moreover, in particular cases, it might better reflect the wrongdoing of the perpetrator.

According to section 2(3):

> 'representation' means any representation as to fact or law, including a representation as to the state of mind of—
> (a) the person making the representation, or
> (b) any other person.

In most cases the representation will concern facts. The law is explicit about the inclusion of states of mind in this category.[136] That allows also incorporating statements concerning future events in the sense that it includes statements as to what the perpetrator or another person (in the view of the perpetrator) is intending to do.[137] As to the statements of opinions, they can also be considered as representations as to the state of mind. The fact that they are wrong does not make them false in terms of section 2, but if the perpetrator presents an opinion as his own, while in fact thinking something else or presenting somebody else's opinion (knowing that it is not true), it can count as false representation (provided that the prosecution is able to prove it).[138] This category will comprise all types of statements made by managers, including their own opinions on the prospective results of this decision, as well as the quoted opinions of others (eg experts).

[135] Similar to eg *Escroquerie* (French Penal Code, art 313-1) or *Betrug* (German Penal Code (Strafgesetzbuch, StGB), s 263).

[136] It was necessary in view of the decision in *Dent*, which excluded such an interpretation under the previous law, see *R v Dent* [1955] 2 QB 590.

[137] Montgomery and Ormerod, *Montgomery and Ormerod on Fraud* (n 25) D-2038/1.

[138] Ibid D-2039 et seq.

False representation can be relative to law as well. This category will comprise, for instance, situations when a manager deliberately wrongly presented the legal effects of a legal act. However, if the law is unclear, an interpretation, which stays within the reasonable boundaries of the law, cannot count as false even if it is not commonly accepted, unless it is presented as such.[139]

As to the question of falsity, according to section 2(2):

> A representation is false if—
>
> (a) it is untrue or misleading, and
> (b) the person making it knows that it is, or might be, untrue or misleading.

In fact this subsection clarifies two aspects of the definition of fraud by false representation. One is the scope of understanding of the term false (a); the second provides for an additional element of the *mens rea* (b).[140]

The term 'untrue' should be understood in its ordinary meaning and the juries should be instructed to use it in this sense.[141] The representation need not be entirely false. It is enough that some statements are false, provided that it is through these statements that the defendant intended to make a gain, cause loss or expose to the risk of loss.[142]

In order to be false, it is enough that the representation is misleading. According to the Home Office a representation is misleading when it is 'less than wholly true and capable of an interpretation to the detriment of the victim'.[143] The classic example of misleading representation is when the perpetrator discloses true information to the victim in a credible way, while not giving information, which, if provided, would significantly alter the interpretation of this information.[144] Similarly, the perpetrator might be using ambiguous language.[145] By extending the understanding of false to misleading, the scope of criminalisation has become very broad. It is noteworthy that while civil law limits its applicability by introducing the *caveat emptor* rule, the Fraud Act 2006 makes no such distinction.[146] However, the CPS instructed that the prosecutor should bear in mind the existence of this rule. Moreover, also for the sake of consistency and in order to limit the already broad scope of the provision, the prosecution should be guided by the

[139] Ibid D-2038/1 et seq.

[140] Parry et al, *Arlidge and Parry on Fraud* (n 41) 90.

[141] Montgomery and Ormerod, *Montgomery and Ormerod on Fraud* (n 25) D-2041.

[142] Ibid D-2041.

[143] Home Office, 'Government Response to Consultation', *Fraud Law Reform: The Consultation Exercise* (2005) para 19, available at http://webarchive.nationalarchives.gov.uk/20130128103514/http://www.homeoffice.gov.uk/documents/cons-fraud-law-reform/Government_response.pdf?view=Binary.

[144] Simester et al, *Simester and Sullivan's Criminal Law* (n 4) 618.

[145] Montgomery and Ormerod, *Montgomery and Ormerod on Fraud* (n 25) D-2042.

[146] Simester et al, *Simester and Sullivan's Criminal Law* (n 4) at 618; Montgomery and Ormerod, *Montgomery and Ormerod on Fraud* (n 25) D-2042. *Caveat emptor* (Latin for buyer beware), is a 'common-law maxim warning a purchaser that he could not claim that his purchases were defective unless he protected himself by obtaining express guarantees from the vendor' (*Oxford Dictionary of Law* (n 91)).

caveat emptor rule.[147] In any case, this rule will not exclude the liability of a director who deliberately presents information in ambiguous terms or hides important information.

In spite of the legislative technique which confuses falsity with the *mens rea*, adding the passage that the person making the representation must know that it is, or might be, untrue or misleading has important consequences. It guarantees that the criminalisation extends to situations in which the defendant knew that the representation was false, but also to situations when he knew that it might be so.[148] Absolute certainty about facts or their interpretation is rare and thus a slight doubt should stop a person from using the representation. It thus appears that the crucial and only limit to extensive criminalisation will be dishonesty, which will prevent liability for false statements made with good intentions.[149] It is important to stress that this provision excludes liability for recklessness in the sense of situations where the perpetrator might and should have known that the representation is or might be untrue or misleading.

According to section 2(4) '[a] representation may be express or implied'. The Law Commission explained that representation is an assertion, which may be 'express, implicit in written or spoken words, or implicit in non-verbal conduct'.[150] Another problem is the question when one can say that the representation is actually made, in other words, at what moment the offence is committed. It is suggested that the representation is made in the moment when it is pronounced in the case of oral representation, posted in the case of mail, and sent in the case of email.[151] There is no need for the representation to be made directly to the person to whom it is intended to arrive or to any concrete addressee.[152]

There exists doubt as to whether the representation can be made by omission, in particular in view of the offence described in section 3. It is argued that this section does not apply in cases where a person did nothing other than fail to correct the erroneous conviction of another victim, while having no duty to do so.[153]

But under certain conditions a representation can be made by omission. If the perpetrator is asked to provide certain information and omits an important element, he might be liable for fraud.[154] Furthermore, under the previous law the

[147] Montgomery and Ormerod, *Montgomery and Ormerod on Fraud* (n 25) D-2035.

[148] Before the enactment of the Fraud Act 2006, the definition of deception used the term 'recklessness' (Theft Act 1968, s 15(4)), which was considered confusing by the Law Commission (Law Com No 276 (n 1) marginal no 7.17, note 9) and was avoided in the Fraud Act 2006.

[149] This position was taken also by the Attorney General (Hansard, HL, 19 July 2005, vol 673, col 1415–16). Similarly Parry et al, *Arlidge and Parry on Fraud* (n 41) 92 et seq; Farrell et al, *Blackstone's Guide to the Fraud Act 2006* (n 38) 26; Montgomery and Ormerod, *Montgomery and Ormerod on Fraud* (n 25) D-2045.

[150] Law Com No 276 (n 1) 61.

[151] Simester et al, *Simester and Sullivan's Criminal Law* (n 4) 619; Montgomery and Ormerod, *Montgomery and Ormerod on Fraud* (n 25) D-2026.

[152] Montgomery and Ormerod, *Montgomery and Ormerod on Fraud* (n 25) D-2025 et seq.

[153] Ibid D-2033.

[154] Ibid D-2032.

concept of 'continuing representation' was developed in *DPP v Ray*.[155] It applies to situations where the perpetrator by his action constantly makes a representation as to the existence of a certain situation. In the cited case, it was established that if one enters a restaurant and orders a meal, one continuously, by the act of remaining in the restaurant and having the meal, makes the representation as to one's intention to pay the bill at the end of the meal. Hence, the lack of action is in fact considered to be a positive representation.[156] A different variation of this case would relate to a situation where the perpetrator makes a true statement but he becomes aware of facts that make it false or the change of circumstances makes them so, but his behaviour suggests that such a change did not take place. Even if it would be considered as representation, it is necessary to prove dishonesty at this later stage as well.[157]

These rules might find application in cases where managers sought approval of their decision and omitted to present information they had, eg where the level of risk of an investment was raised because of new events or new information and, by omitting to mention it, they implied that the conditions remained as before. It is, however, difficult to predict whether the mere fact of non-communication of the new information or facts and proceeding with the investment would be considered as false representation. The situation might be different if the manager during this process communicated with those giving the agreement in a way that suggested that no change occurred. This could in fact constitute a new representation, without the necessity to use the concept of 'continuing representation'.[158] If this would be the case, dishonesty must be proved at the moment of the new representation.

3.3.2. Fraud by Failing to Disclose Information

Fraud by failing to disclose information described in section 3 of the Fraud Act 2006 criminalises situations where a person dishonestly fails to disclose to another person information, which he is obliged by a legal duty to disclose to that person, and he does so with the same intention as in other types of fraud.[159]

This provision could be of application in situations in which the manager dishonestly conceals information when he is obliged to disclose it, and he does so with the intention of making a gain or causing loss to the company or exposing it to a risk of loss. Such situation might occur in various contexts; for instance, a manager conceals information that he is obliged to disclose while seeking approval of his decision by a competent person or body while the information concerns the

155 *DPP v Ray* [1974] AC 370.

156 Montgomery and Ormerod, *Montgomery and Ormerod on Fraud* (n 25) D-2034.

157 Ibid D-2034.

158 Ibid D-2034.

159 '3. *Fraud by failing to disclose information*: A person is in breach of this section if he – (a) dishonestly fails to disclose to another person information which he is under a legal duty to disclose, and (b) intends, by failing to disclose the information – (i) to make a gain for himself or another, or (ii) to cause loss to another or to expose another to a risk of loss.'

exposure of the company to risk of loss or a higher level of such risk. Secondly, a manager could have information about a possible risk, which concerns the activity of the company or its products and does not disclose it, which might result, if the risk materialises, in loss. In the third scenario, a manager has the duty to disclose certain information and by the fact of not doing so he exposes the company to the risk of loss. It is not excluded that criminalisation under this section will overlap with section 2 or 4.[160]

In order to verify the manager's liability under section 3, it is necessary to examine whether he had the legal duty to disclose information and whether he failed to disclose it. Section 3 does not provide detailed information as to the requirement of the duty. It is considered that managers may fall into the scope of criminalisation of this provision, if they are under a legal duty to disclose information. Such an obligation might be statutory, contractual, be deduced from the fiduciary relationship or be part of general practices or customary rules.[161]

The offence described in this section is committed by omission consisting in the non-disclosure of the information as required under the duty described above. It can consist of the non-disclosure of any type of information and need not concern all the information in question in a certain context. It is enough that the defendant is partially silent or omits one detail of an issue.[162] The possibly absurd results of such a broad scope will be corrected by the fact that the problem of how much information was concealed will be reflected in the assessment of dishonesty.[163]

It is obviously necessary that the perpetrator fail to disclose the information to the person towards whom he is bound by the duty.[164] But the wording of section 3 does not express the need that the person to whom the information is not disclosed is the same as the one who can be exposed to the risk of loss. It is thus possible to envisage liability of a company director for breaching an information duty towards the company while the shareholders are exposed to the risk of loss.[165]

With the exception of the requirements of dishonesty and intention, common to all sections, section 3 contains no express provision on the *mens rea* requirement as to the knowledge of the defendant about his duty or the circumstances concerning it. Arguably this element of *mens rea* might be presumed, in particular in view of the judgments in *DPP v B* and *R v K*.[166] The CPS in its guidelines

[160] Montgomery and Ormerod, *Montgomery and Ormerod on Fraud* (n 25) D-2048.

[161] Home Office, *Explanatory Notes: Fraud Act 2006* (n 93) recital 18.

[162] Parry et al, *Arlidge and Parry on Fraud* (n 41) 138.

[163] Montgomery and Ormerod, *Montgomery and Ormerod on Fraud* (n 25) D-2050–D-2100. As the CPS points out in its guidelines: 'If a Defendant disclosed 90% of what he was under a legal duty to disclose but failed to disclose the (possibly unimportant) remaining 10%, the *actus reus* of the offence could be complete. Under such circumstances the Defendant would have to rely on the absence of dishonesty. Such cases can be prosecuted under the Act if the public interest requires it, though such cases will be unusual.' CPS, *Legal Guidance* (n 115).

[164] Parry et al, *Arlidge and Parry on Fraud* (n 41) 138.

[165] Montgomery and Ormerod, *Montgomery and Ormerod on Fraud* (n 25) D-2101.

[166] Simester et al, *Simester and Sullivan's Criminal Law* (n 4) 623; Montgomery and Ormerod, *Montgomery and Ormerod on Fraud* (n 25) D-2101.

considers section 3 to be a strict liability offence in this respect.[167] Even if the position of the CPS is accepted, the lack of knowledge concerning the duty will most probably exclude criminal liability for lack of dishonesty.[168] This will be of particular importance depending on the source of the duty. It is submitted that the question will be treated differently if the duty was enshrined in statutory law and thus should have been known by everybody, or if it was a question of some customary rules or general practices, the knowledge of which might not be full in case of newly appointed managers.

The above-described requirements are fairly broad. As it is the case for the other modalities of fraud, the requirement of dishonesty will play the crucial role in determining the perpetrator's criminal liability.

3.3.3. *Theft*

The offence of theft may also be the legal basis for prosecuting excessive risk-taking committed by managers against the interests of their companies. It has been used against directors who misapply the assets of their companies, as was notably done in the *Guinness* case.[169] The definition of this offence is provided for in section 1(1) of the Theft Act 1968, according to which:

> A person is guilty of theft if he dishonestly appropriates property belonging to another with the intention of permanently depriving the other of it.

The property of the company is to be considered property belonging to another, even if the manager is acting with the consent of the owner, provided that he was dishonest.[170] According to section 3 of the Theft Act 1968 '[a]ny assumption by a person of the rights of an owner amounts to an appropriation'. The very broad understanding of appropriation which the jurisprudence has given to the requirement of appropriation allows including any usurpation of the rights of the owner to be considered theft.[171] In this sense, a wrongful use of the property, ie exposing it to non-permitted risk, can also be considered an assumption of the rights of the owner.

[167] CPS, *Legal Guidance* (n 115) 'Failure to disclose information'.

[168] Ormerod, 'The Fraud Act 2006: Criminalising Lying?' (n 49) 206. The CPS guidelines also highlight the role of dishonesty in this context.

[169] *R v Saunders* (1996) 1 Cr App R 463. The CEO of Guinness at the time of the offence, Ernest Saunders, was the main defendant in the case where various defendants 'were convicted on a number of counts in relation to their dishonest conduct in a share support operation during Guinness Plc's takeover bid for the Distillers Company Plc' (at 463). The defendants made use of funds belonging to Guinness consisting in making payments to purchasers of Guinness shares, which was supposed to boost their value and enable the takeover. One of the offences for which Saunders was convicted (as well as other defendants) was theft, since the payments were not authorised by the Guinness board.

[170] David Ormerod, *Smith and Hogan's Criminal Law*, 13th edn (Oxford University Press, 2011) 819.

[171] Simester et al, *Simester and Sullivan's Criminal Law* (n 4) 523 et seq; Ormerod, *Smith and Hogan's Criminal Law* (n 170) 780 et seq.

Similarly, the *mens rea* requirement of intention to deprive has been very broadly construed in the jurisprudence. In particular, it is considered that, if the defendant took an amount of money with intention to return the same amount, he is still guilty of theft, because he cannot hand back the same coins and notes.[172] Moreover, Theft Act 1968, section 6(1), provides that:

> A person appropriating property belonging to another without meaning the other permanently to lose the thing itself is nevertheless to be regarded as having the intention of permanently depriving the other of it if his intention is to treat the thing as his own to dispose of regardless of the other's rights.

Despite the use of the expression 'dispose of', which would suggest parting with it, there is jurisprudence which extends its meaning to situations where the defendant wanted to treat the thing as his own in the sense of dealing with it and not disposing of it in the strict sense, thus not really meaning that the owner loses his property.[173] In particular, in *Fernandes*, the court held that:

> section 6 may apply to a person in possession or control of another's property who, dishonestly and for his own purpose, deals with that property in such a manner that he knows he is risking its loss.[174]

Finally, the offence of theft requires proof of dishonesty. In view of the broad design of the other elements of this offence, this element will be decisive for determining criminal liability of the defendant.[175]

4. Inchoate Offences

The scope of criminalisation is extended by means of a variety of inchoate offences which will be succinctly presented in this section. These are: certain preparatory acts (possession etc of articles for use in fraud; making or supplying articles for use in fraud); encouraging and assisting an offence; attempt and conspiracy (statutory conspiracy and common law conspiracy to defraud). As to the latter category, within the current state of English law, there exist two types of liability for conspiracy to commit an offence. The main option, common to all offences, is the statutory conspiracy provided for by the Criminal Law Act 1977 (see 4.4 below). Although the old common law offences of conspiracy were to a large extent abolished, some remains of the old law persist. It notably includes the offence of conspiracy to defraud, which is highly relevant as the crucial judgments on excessive risk-taking

[172] Simester et al, *Simester and Sullivan's Criminal Law* (n 4) 539; Montgomery and Ormerod, *Montgomery and Ormerod on Fraud* (n 25) D-3020/D.3.137.

[173] Simester et al,*Simester and Sullivan's Criminal Law* (n 4) 543.

[174] *Fernandes* (1996) 1 Cr App R 175.

[175] See also Law Commission, *Legislating the Criminal Code: Fraud and Deception*, Consultation Paper No 155 (1999) para 3.24.

were issued in relation to this offence, and is also in constant use, as was recently demonstrated in the LIBOR case (see 4.5 below).

4.1. Preparatory Acts

There exists no general law criminalising preparatory acts in England and Wales, as exists for attempt. However, the Fraud Act 2006 contains two provisions making punishable certain acts committed in preparation for fraud: possession etc of articles for use in fraud (section 6)[176] and making or supplying articles for use in fraud (section 7).[177] They constitute offences *sui generis* and do not require that the main offence of fraud be even attempted.[178]

Sections 6 and 7 may find only limited but potentially significant application to cases of excessive risk-taking. In this context it is first necessary to verify whether an item in question can be considered an 'article' under these sections and whether there is the necessary connection with excessive risk-taking constituting fraud by abuse of position or any other type of fraud or conspiracy to defraud, if this possibility is accepted.[179] In view of the broad interpretation of 'article', practically any item can fall into the scope of this term and it will depend on the modality whether it must effectively be designed or adapted for use in the course of or in connection with fraud or whether it will be enough that the perpetrator's intention is so, although the item is not apt for such use.[180] In the former case, the required *mens rea* will be limited to the knowledge of the article's character.

As to articles that could be considered in the context of excessive risk-taking, these will be mainly documents or electronic data.[181] However, other items cannot be excluded. Case 4 described in Chapter 1 (see 4.4. Sample cases) concerning the new car model could be altered so that the manager prepares the model car in such a way that the problem with the sound system does not appear. If the situation

[176] 'A person is guilty of an offence if he has in his possession or under his control any article for use in the course of or in connection with any fraud.'

[177] 'A person is guilty of an offence if he makes, adapts, supplies or offers to supply any article—

(a) knowing that it is designed or adapted for use in the course of or in connection with fraud, or
(b) intending it to be used to commit, or assist in the commission of, fraud.'

[178] The punishment for making or supplying articles for use in frauds (Fraud Act 2006, s 7) is the same as for the offence of fraud. As to possession etc of articles for use in frauds (s 6), the punishment provided for is of the same type, with the only exception that the maximum imprisonment cannot exceed five years.

[179] It is unclear how to interpret the expression 'any fraud' in the context of the plethora of offences incriminating fraudulent activities. This expression certainly includes fraud described in Fraud Act 2006, ss 2–4. The question remains open in particular in relation to the common law offence of conspiracy to defraud. For more detailed analysis, see Montgomery and Ormerod, *Montgomery and Ormerod on Fraud* (n 25) D-2122/1 et seq.

[180] Ibid D-2116.

[181] Farrell et al, *Blackstone's Guide to the Fraud Act 2006* (n 38) 66. Fraud Act 2006, s 8(1)(b) provides that '"article" includes any program or data held in electronic form'.

from that case can be considered fraud by abuse of position, the car could be seen as an article to be used for fraud and the perpetrator's conduct would be to adapt it for use in fraud.

The courses of conduct foreseen by sections 6 and 7 comprise possessing or having under control, making, adapting, supplying or offering to supply, thus covering virtually any kind of possible preparatory activity. Hence, the extensiveness of these two sections results in the fact that once the foreseen conduct can amount to fraud, then any kind of activity with any item, which could be used in connection with this offence or even possession of it, could become criminal, if the perpetrator has the required knowledge or intention.

The article in question may be prepared or designed per se only for the use in fraud. This will be the case of documents that were prepared in order to use them in the process of taking a decision, which would expose the company to excessive risk, eg an expert opinion wrongly assessing such risk, if the perpetrator is aware of its inaccuracy. However, also documents which contain correct information could be considered as articles according to these sections, if the person who has them in his possession or under his control, or the person producing, adapting or supplying them, intends that they are used in the course of or in connection with fraud. Since the person who makes, adapts or supplies necessarily has the articles in his possession for a certain time, the scope of liability can be stretched to cases where the articles served to prepare or to cover up the offence.[182] Not only documents can fall into the scope of these sections, but also software, eg a program used while preparing risk analysis, altered in a way so that it gives more optimistic results.

Both sections may be of application for two categories of perpetrators. First, they can be used to punish managers who were caught while preparing a decision exposing the company to excessive risk, which would constitute an abuse of position or other modality of fraud. They could also be held liable if such articles are used to cover up deficiencies in the process of taking such a decision (eg providing inaccurate economic justification).

Secondly, other persons who cooperate with managers could be held liable for possessing or preparing such documents or software provided that they have the required *mens rea*. An assistant who prepares (makes, adapts or supplies) documents or software for a manager knowing for which purpose the manager will use it can be held liable, even if he does not intend that the offence is committed. These provisions can be used to charge those who participate in a process of excessive risk-taking but with regard to whom there exist difficulties to prove that they have the position described in section 4. Notably, these offences do not require a proof of dishonesty of their perpetrator, but only certain knowledge or intention as to the possible or foreseen use of the articles, in a context where the eventual perpetrator of fraud needs to have been dishonest.[183]

[182] Montgomery and Ormerod, *Montgomery and Ormerod on Fraud* (n 25) D-2122/1.
[183] Ormerod and Williams, *Smith's Law of Theft* (n 8) 294.

4.2. Encouraging and Assisting Crime

Shortly after the Fraud Act 2006 was enacted, another piece of legislation, the Serious Crime Act 2007, introduced criminal liability for an inchoate offence of encouraging and assisting crime.[184] So far it does not seem that these provisions are being used on an important scale. However, if a decision is made to intensively tackle excessive risk-taking, this offence might potentially find broader application as regards assisting or encouraging the commission of fraud.[185]

Sections 44–46 of the Serious Crime Act 2007 provide for liability for two different types of conduct: encouraging and assisting. The important advantage of charging the offence under one of either type of conduct in this section is that there is no need to prove any connection with the main offence or any influence on the latter, which might be found by prosecutors as a convenient alternative to complicity (see 5.1 below). The act must be capable of encouraging or assisting the offence, but need not effectively encourage or assist. As far as the encouragement is concerned, this can also be aimed at a variety of addressees, eg in a journal article.[186] There is no defence of withdrawal or revocation that applies to assistance and encouragement.[187]

The *mens rea* is the most complicated element in the design of the offence of assistance and encouragement and requires that the defendant either intends to encourage or assist the commission of an offence (Serious Crime Act 2007, section 44) or believes that an offence will be committed and that his act will encourage or assist its commission (sections 44 and 45).

Two types of conduct may be considered here. First, conduct that would help a manager commit the above offence. This could be done through any kind of positive action and nothing seems to preclude assisting by omission. A person may provide the main perpetrator with documents, organise an expert analysis (not necessarily accurate, eg blurring the perspective of risk) or draft it by himself etc. By omission, the main perpetrator may be assisted by higher management who voluntarily disregard the fact that the former is taking excessively risky decisions. Other persons in the company may provide such help by eg not executing their control functions. Furthermore, a manager may be assisted also by a person external to the company, eg an expert who will incorrectly (and knowingly) assess the risk of a transaction.

[184] This subsection examines only encouragement and assistance to managers in the context of their decisions exposing their company to excessive risk. For further analysis of this type of liability see Simester et al, *Simester and Sullivan's Criminal Law* (n 4) 293 et seq; Ashworth, *Principles of Criminal Law* (n 56) 458 et seq.

[185] According to Serious Crime Act 2007, s 58(3), for the inchoate offence of encouraging and assisting, the perpetrator is liable to any penalty for which he would be liable on conviction of the anticipated or reference offence. The offence of encouraging and assisting does not apply to conspiracy to defraud, which is expressly excluded by the Act (Serious Crime Act 2007, Sch 3, para 39).

[186] Simester et al, *Simester and Sullivan's Criminal Law* (n 4) 295; *Jones* [2007] EWCA Crim 1118.

[187] Simester et al, *Simester and Sullivan's Criminal Law* (n 4) 306.

Secondly, encouraging might be done also by senior management who may effectively inspire, embolden or even pressurise managers to take decisions that by normal standards in the business would be considered too risky. They could also do this by omission in not reacting to such behaviour, if it could be clearly proved that they knew about it and that their silence was sending a clear signal of acceptance. Also, other employees could be held liable for encouraging as well as persons outside the company. Since encouragement need not have a precise addressee, an author of an article in a journal or a newspaper in which he emboldens managers to take excessively risky decisions could be held liable, if the *mens rea* requirement is fulfilled.

Moreover, liability for encouraging or assisting is also possible even if the main perpetrator does not act with the *mens rea* described in Fraud Act 2006, sections 2–4, ie he does not act dishonestly or/and without the intent, if the person assisting or encouraging would have the required *mens rea* if the perpetrator were to act.[188]

These rules could find application in cases where a person encouraged a manager and the latter believed that it was correct to take the risk, which in fact was excessive, thus not fulfilling the limb of dishonesty. In view of these rules, a person assisting or encouraging could be held liable either when he was reckless about the state of mind of the perpetrator, or if he was himself dishonest and acted with the intent of exposing the company to a risk of loss, or with the intent that the manager exposing the company to the risk will make a gain for the person encouraging or assisting or for another person foreseen by him.

4.3. Attempt

An attempt to commit fraud may also lead to a criminal conviction. The legal basis for such criminalisation used to be at common law, but became statutory with the adoption of the Criminal Attempts Act 1981.[189]

The *actus reus* of this offence requires that the perpetrator does an act which is more than merely preparatory to the commission of the offence.[190] While attempt was still a common law offence, the main difficulty was to decide when the

[188] According to Serious Crime Act 2007, s 47(5): 'In proving for the purposes of this section whether an act is one which, if done, would amount to the commission of an offence – (a) if the offence is one requiring proof of fault, it must be proved that – (i) D believed that, were the act to be done, it would be done with that fault; (ii) D was reckless as to whether or not it would be done with that fault; or (iii) D's state of mind was such that, were he to do it, it would be done with that fault'.

[189] Criminal Attempts Act 1981, s 1(1) provides that: 'If, with intent to commit an offence to which this section applies, a person does an act which is more than merely preparatory to the commission of the offence, he is guilty of attempting to commit the offence'. See also Simester et al, *Simester and Sullivan's Criminal Law* (n 4) 339. The perpetrator is liable to any penalty for which he would be liable on conviction of the attempted offence (Criminal Attempts Act 1981, s 4(1)).

[190] The expression 'does an act' generally indicates the legislators' intent to exclude liability for omission. Simester et al, *Simester and Sullivan's Criminal Law* (n 4) 344.

conduct was sufficiently close to the commission of the offence, which resulted in the development of the tests of proximity, such as the 'last act' test, the 'substantial step' test and the 'unequivocal act' test. The lack of a definition in the Criminal Attempts Act 1981 of what is more than merely preparatory ensured the continued prevalence of this discussion. The issue will be a question of fact, thus it will be for the jury to decide whether what the perpetrator did amounted to more than mere preparation.[191]

The requirement of *mens rea* is defined as 'intent to commit an offence', where the word 'offence' refers to the offence, which *actus reus* the perpetrator attempts to fulfil.

Fraud is an offence to which section 1 of the Criminal Attempts Act 1981 applies (section 1(4)).[192] What can be examined is the extent to which the *actus reus* of Fraud Act 2006, sections 2–4 can remain unfulfilled. Because of the 'inchoate mode'[193] in which this offence was drafted, the possibility of committing an attempted fraud will be limited and very often the perpetrator will enter into the phase of the commission of fraud.[194] Without entering into discussions on the *mens rea* of attempt in various configurations of *mens rea* of the main offence,[195] one can argue that it is not possible to convict for attempted fraud, if dishonesty and intention to make gain or cause loss or expose to loss could not be proved.

As to fraud by abuse of position only incomplete attempt is possible, since this offence requires no result.[196] For instance, a manager could be held liable for attempted fraud by abuse of position, if he prepared a contract that exposes the company to a risk which he was not allowed to take and he is about to sign it. As to fraud by false representation, criminal liability will mainly be possible in case of mistake of fact or failures of communication.[197] For the representation that is made by mail or email, one could argue that an attempt is made if the letter or email containing it was prepared for sending, but was not sent (eg the perpetrator was arrested on the way to the post office).[198] As for oral representation, one could imagine a case where a video message of a director was made, but not yet presented to the shareholders, which would fulfil this condition.

In view of the fact that attempt is excluded in cases of omission, there will be no possibility to punish fraud by abuse of position in this form. For the same reason, it will not be possible to commit attempted fraud by failing to disclose information.

[191] Ibid 340 et seq.

[192] According to Criminal Attempts Act 1981, s 1(4), liability for attempt is excluded in case of conspiracy (common law or statutory), aiding, abetting, counselling, procuring or suborning the commission of an offence.

[193] See section 1 above.

[194] Parry et al, *Arlidge and Parry on Fraud* (n 41) 474.

[195] Simester et al, *Simester and Sullivan's Criminal Law* (n 4) 346 et seq.

[196] On complete and incomplete attempt see: Ashworth, *Principles of Criminal Law* (n 56) 439.

[197] Farrell et al, *Blackstone's Guide to the Fraud Act 2006* (n 38) 63.

[198] Mongomery and Ormerod, *Montgomery and Ormerod on Fraud* (n 25) D-2030.

4.4. Statutory Conspiracy

According to Criminal Law Act 1977, section 1,[199] the *actus reus* of statutory conspiracy consists in an agreement with at least one more person to perform a course of conduct which would include the commission of an offence by at least one party to the agreement.[200] In view of section 1(b), the impossibility of committing the offence does not exclude liability for conspiracy.[201] Although conspiracies that did not go beyond mere agreement rarely find their way to court,[202] cases of conspiracy to commit fraud in a corporate environment might be more suitable for prosecution if relevant evidence is available (eg emails).

Due to the fact that the three modalities of fraud constitute one offence created by section 1 of the Fraud Act 2006, conspiracy to commit it need not refer to a precise modality, which might help to formulate a charge when it is impossible to decide under which modality of fraud the agreed course of conduct can be subsumed.[203] However, in view of the requirement of an agreement and of the *mens rea*, it is necessary that the conspiring persons agree to the relevant circumstances, eg that they (or one of them) will make a false representation or abuse their position.[204]

Statutory conspiracy can be used to punish excessive risk-taking in cases in which two or more persons agreed on a course of conduct, which according to their plan will expose their company to an excessive risk of loss, in circumstances which will qualify this main act as an offence of fraud, ie at least one of the conspirators will abuse his position, make false representation or fail to disclose information acting dishonestly and with the required intention. The other conspirators do not need to have the same intention or to act dishonestly, but they must know that the main perpetrator will fulfil this requirement or intend that he does so.[205] Since the conspirators must intend that the agreement be carried out, it is difficult to claim that they are not dishonest or that they have no intention to expose another to a risk of loss. However, it is not necessary for all of them to occupy the position required in section 4, be under an obligation to disclose as in section 3, or to make the representation as in section 2.

[199] 'If a person agrees with any other person or persons that a course of conduct will be pursued which, if the agreement is carried out in accordance with their intentions, either – (a) will necessarily amount to or involve the commission of any offence or offences by one or more parties to the agreement, or (b) would do so but for the existence of facts which render the commission of the offence or any offences impossible, he is guilty of conspiracy to commit the offence or offences in question.'

[200] The punishment for the statutory conspiracy should not exceed the maximum which is provided for the main offence (Criminal Law Act 1977, s 3): Farrell et al, *Blackstone's Guide to the Fraud Act 2006* (n 38) 44.

[201] For the analysis on the general aspects of conspiracy to defraud, see Ashworth, *Principles of Criminal Law* (n 56) 455; Simester et al, *Simester and Sullivan's Criminal Law* (n 4) 310 et seq.

[202] Simester et al, *Simester and Sullivan's Criminal Law* (n 4) 337.

[203] Farrell et al, *Blackstone's Guide to the Fraud Act 2006* (n 38) 40 et seq.

[204] Simester et al, *Simester and Sullivan's Criminal Law* (n 4) 331.

[205] For details on the *mens rea* requirement of the offence of conspiracy, see Simester et al, *Simester and Sullivan's Criminal Law* (n 4) 331.

The conspirators need not know that what they plan will amount to fraud, since ignorance of the law is not a defence,[206] but they need to know about the circumstances necessary for the commission of the agreed offence or intend or know that 'any such fact or circumstance will exist at the time the offence takes place'.[207] Therefore they need to know either that the conspirator who, according to the plan, will be the main perpetrator has the legal duty to disclose in case of section 3 fraud, or that he occupies the position of trust described in section 4, or they must intend that at the moment when the offence would take place, he has this duty or occupies this position.

Statutory conspiracy may be used to punish managers intending to expose their company to excessive risk if the actual fraud did not take place, either because the perpetrators abandoned their plan or the plot was discovered before the perpetrators entered the phase of attempt. It can also find its application in cases where fraud was actually committed by one of the conspirators, but for different reasons it is impossible or impractical to charge for the actual offence (eg there is not enough proof in respect of one of the perpetrators). It might be useful in such cases to charge all of the perpetrators with conspiracy, instead of charging only some of them for fraud and leaving others unpunished or charging them with conspiracy. In this way, statutory conspiracy might be used to punish collaboration in excessive risk-taking. This possibility is attractive inasmuch as it allows for sentencing the perpetrator to a punishment of the same severity as for the main offence of fraud.

4.5. Common Law Conspiracy to Defraud

The origins of conspiracy as a common law offence date back to the Middle Ages.[208] The Criminal Law Act 1977 which introduced the statutory law of conspiracy abolished most of the common law offences of conspiracy, except, inter alia, conspiracy to defraud. Around the same period as the enactment of this statute, a general feeling started to grow that conspiracy to defraud should be abolished. Lord Diplock was a notably vocal critic, expressing the shortcomings of conspiracy to defraud as an offence being based in common law and because of the extreme broadness of its design, in particular allowing the punishment of conspiring to commit acts that would not, if committed, constitute in themselves a substantive offence.[209] Various reports were produced that in some cases recommended limitation of the scope of conspiracy to defraud, while always recognising the practical

[206] Ibid 691.

[207] Ibid 331.

[208] For details on the history of conspiracy to defraud, see Montgomery and Ormerod, *Montgomery and Ormerod on Fraud* (n 25) D-7002 et seq, with sources referenced there.

[209] Ibid D-7007 et seq. For the criticism of Lord Diplock, see, eg the judgment in *Withers* [1974] 3 WLR 751, [1975] AC 842, 861–62.

need for maintaining the offence.[210] Finally, the report that led to the adoption of the Fraud Act 2006 recommended its entire abolition.[211] However, the consultation on the project led the government to withdraw the proposed abolition and at present the common law conspiracy to defraud is valid law.[212]

There is still an ongoing debate on the use of the common law offences.[213] As to the conspiracy to defraud, a certain reluctance to use this offence may be observed also among the judges.[214] Moreover, it is the rule that, if a conduct fulfils the conditions for a statutory offence, it should be prosecuted as such unless 'there is good reason for doing otherwise'.[215] Hence, the provisions of the Fraud Act 2006 should be used in the first place to charge in relation to offences described there. The Attorney General issued Guidelines for Prosecutors on the Use of the Common Law Offence of Conspiracy to Defraud,[216] according to which prosecution for conspiracy to defraud should be preferred over statutory fraud in two categories of situations: (a) if the conduct can more effectively be prosecuted as conspiracy to defraud; (b) if the conduct can only be prosecuted as conspiracy to defraud, with examples given for both of them. As to the first category of situations, the prosecutor might find it more effective to prosecute for conspiracy to defraud rather than fraud if the cases are complicated, because, for instance, various different offences are alleged, several jurisdictions are involved or the variety of types of victims who suffered from the offence.[217] Cases falling under the second category will mostly concern situations where it was intended that the main offence be committed by a person who is not part of the conspiracy.

The current definition of conspiracy to defraud comes from the speech of Viscount Dilhorne in the judgment of the House of Lords in *Scott v Metropolitan Police Commissioner*:[218]

> it is clearly the law that an agreement by two or more by dishonesty to deprive a person of something which is his or to which he is or would be or might be entitled and an agreement by two or more by dishonesty to injure some proprietary right of his, suffices to constitute the offence of conspiracy to defraud.[219]

[210] Law Commission, *Criminal Law: Conspiracy to Defraud*, Working Paper No 56 (1974); Law Commission, *Report on Conspiracy and Criminal Law Reform*, Law Com No 76 (1976); Law Commission, *Conspiracy to Defraud*, Working Paper No 104 (1987); Law Commission, *Conspiracy to Defraud*, Law Com No 228 (1994).

[211] Law Com No 276 (n 1) para 9.6.

[212] Montgomery and Ormerod, *Montgomery and Ormerod on Fraud* (n 25) D-7008 et seq. Before the legislative intervention, conspiracy to defraud at common law was subject to imprisonment at large. See Montgomery and Ormerod, *Montgomery and Ormerod on Fraud* (n 25) D-7027/D.7126. Criminal Justice Act 1987, s 12 limits the punishment for this type of conspiracy to a maximum of 10 years' imprisonment and/or an unlimited fine.

[213] See, eg Farrell et al, *Blackstone's Guide to the Fraud Act 2006* (n 38) 48 et seq.

[214] See, eg the analysis of Hickinbottom J in *R v. Evans and others* [2014] 1 WLR 2817.

[215] Farrell et al, *Blackstone's Guide to the Fraud Act 2006* (n 38) 51.

[216] Attorney General's *Guidelines for Prosecutors on the Use of the Common Law Offence of Conspiracy to Defraud* (First published 2007; Updated version 29 November 2012).

[217] Ibid.

[218] *Scott v Metropolitan Police Commissioner* [1975] AC 819.

[219] Ibid 840.

In view of this definition, conspiracy to defraud may occur in two ways: 'either by agreeing to prejudice a person's economic interests or by agreeing to prejudice a person's right properly to discharge his duty'.[220] The second option is relevant for cases where a person is misled in exercising his public duty, so it is only the first one that is of interest here. In the words of the judge in the *Wai Yu-Tsang* case, conspiracy to defraud in this case means to 'be party to an agreement with the common intention to defraud one or more of the persons named in the indictment'.[221]

As for the *actus reus*, there must in the first place be an agreement between two or more parties to prejudice another person's interests. There must be a common understanding between the conspirers as to how these interests would be prejudiced. Withdrawal from the agreement does not preclude criminal liability, similarly as in the case of statutory conspiracy and contrary to what might be possible for complicity.[222] It can only influence the level of punishment.[223] In particular, two rules concerning the agreement are different to the one in the statutory conspiracy and result in the broader scope of application of this common law offence. First, the agreement need not foresee the commission of a concrete substantive (statutory or common law) offence.[224] This provision will be relevant when the parties to the agreement agreed to prejudice the economic interests of another, but it is impossible, for different reasons, to prove all the elements of fraud. Secondly, there is no need, according to the agreement, that the main offence be performed by a member of the conspiracy.[225]

The agreement in question must foresee prejudice to the economic interests of another person. The agreement might not contain the plan to cause loss, but it is enough that the economic interests of the victim are put at risk.[226] The defendant cannot escape liability by claiming that they believed that the victim would profit or even that the victim effectively took profit from their activity.[227] The nuances of this issue where subject to the case law that will be analysed below.

An interesting territorial limitation might be relevant in cases of international companies pursuing business in different territories. The general rule is that an agreement which was made in England or Wales, but foresees commission of fraud outside this jurisdiction, cannot be prosecuted as conspiracy to defraud in England and Wales.[228]

[220] Montgomery and Ormerod, *Montgomery and Ormerod on Fraud* (n 25) D-7009.
[221] *Wai Yu-Tsang* (n 2) 269.
[222] Simester et al, *Simester and Sullivan's Criminal Law* (n 4) 259–61.
[223] Farrell et al, *Blackstone's Guide to the Fraud Act 2006* (n 38) 206.
[224] Ibid 206.
[225] Montgomery and Ormerod, *Montgomery and Ormerod on Fraud* (n 25) D-7014.
[226] Farrell et al, *Blackstone's Guide to the Fraud Act 2006* (n 38) 209.
[227] Ibid 209.
[228] The exceptions to this rule are stated in Criminal Justice Act 1993, s 5(3), according to which: 'A person may be guilty of conspiracy to defraud if – (a) a party to the agreement constituting the conspiracy, or a party's agent, did anything in England and Wales in relation to the agreement before its formation, or (b) a party to it became a party in England and Wales (by joining it either in person or through an agent), or (c) a party to it, or a party's agent, did or omitted anything in England and Wales

Similarly to fraud, there are two *mens rea* requirements for the conspiracy to defraud: dishonesty and intention to defraud. Dishonesty is understood in the same way as described for the offence of fraud, and certain judgments cited there were in fact given in relation to conspiracy to defraud. Conspiracy to defraud is triable only on indictment,[229] which means that the Crown Court has exclusive jurisdiction over it.[230] Hence, the remarks on the specificity of jury trials and its implications apply also to this offence. As to the managers who agreed to expose the company to excessive risk, but in their perception acted for its benefit, the same reservation as already described above will apply. Therefore, in order to consider the manager as dishonest, it will most probably be necessary that he was either motivated by direct and tangible personal interest or that he acted without integrity or knowingly and intentionally breached rules governing the execution of his duties. However, it will be for the jury to decide in a concrete case whether they found the perpetrator dishonest.

Ormerod and Williams make clear reference to situations of excessive risk-taking:

> In theft, D is not dishonest if he believes he has a right to do the act in question and this must also apply in conspiracy. If, however, he knows for example, that no 'ordinary decent company director' would take the risk in question, then he knows that the risk is an unjustifiable one and it is dishonest for him to take it.

And further:

> If no director could have believed the risk was justified, it follows that the defendant did not; but it would seem right that the jury be directed that they must find this is so.[231]

This understanding is also in agreement with the judgment in *Sinclair*.[232]

Conspiracy to defraud contains the requirement of intention formulated as 'intention to defraud'. In the words of Ormerod and Williams:

> If the conspirators know that the effect of carrying out the agreement will be to put V's property at risk, then they intend prejudice to V and, if they are dishonest, they are guilty of conspiracy to defraud him. This is so notwithstanding that it turns out that V's property is unimpaired, or even that he makes a profit out of the transaction.[233]

The understanding of these elements was the subject of two cases: *Allsop* and *Wai Yu-Tsang*. In view of their importance for the scope of criminalisation of excessive risk-taking they will be given a more in-depth analysis. In two important cases, the English courts confirmed that the excessive risk-taking could constitute conspiracy to defraud.

in pursuance of it, and the conspiracy would be triable in England and Wales but for the fraud which the parties to it had in view not being intended to take place in England and Wales'.

229 Ormerod and Hooper, *Blackstone's Criminal Practice 2013* (n 34) A5.63/ 102.

230 Ibid D3.13/ 1296.

231 Ormerod and Williams, *Smith's Law of Theft* (n 8) 208.

232 See 3.1.1 above.

233 Ormerod and Williams, *Smith's Law of Theft* (n 8) 210.

In *Allsop*,[234] the appellant questioned his conviction for conspiracy to defraud. The facts can be summarised according to the judgment as follows. *Allsop* was a 'sub-broker' for a hire-purchase finance company Prestige Finance Corporation. 'His function was to introduce business to Prestige in the shape of prospective hire-purchasers who wished to acquire motor cars.'[235] Part of this function was the filling-in of application forms containing details of the transaction, which in some cases would be entered falsely:

> For example, the price of the car concerned would be inflated so as to allow an illusory deposit to be shown as having been paid by the intending hire-purchaser; or the value of a car taken in part exchange would be stated at more than the true figure.[236]

It was clear that on none of these occasions did Allsop want to cause damage to Prestige:

> What he sought to bring about was an increase in the business he took to Prestige. He expected and believed that the transactions he introduced would in the end be duly completed so that Prestige would achieve their contemplated profit to the ultimate advantage of all concerned – including the appellant who got his commission.[237]

For these actions *Allsop* was convicted of conspiracy to defraud (he acted in collusion with other persons[238]) and in his appeal he questioned his conviction, arguing that the jury had been instructed incorrectly, since the judge had indicated that the prejudice of the company did not necessarily need to amount to the loss of money.

The case allowed the Court of Appeal to tackle two issues: the *mens rea* of conspiracy to defraud (and indirectly of fraud) and the meaning of 'prejudice' in the context of this offence. The main question of this judgment concerned the mental state of the defendant. The questioned judgment was based on the understanding that 'the appellant realised that the making of the false statements was likely to lead to the detriment or prejudice of the hire-purchase company in the sense of economic loss, but not necessarily the loss of money',[239] while the appellant argued that 'the jury should have been directed that they must be satisfied that the appellant intended to cause economic loss to the hire-purchase company'.[240] The Court of Appeal opted for the first interpretation, thus stating that the *mens rea* requirement for conspiracy to defraud is fulfilled if the defendant:

> intends by deceit to induce a course of conduct in another which puts that other's economic interests in jeopardy … even though he does not intend that actual loss should ultimately be suffered by that other.[241]

[234] *Allsop* (n 27).
[235] Ibid 29.
[236] Ibid 30.
[237] Ibid 30.
[238] Ibid 30.
[239] Ibid 29.
[240] Ibid 29.
[241] Ibid 29.

For the purpose of explaining why the Court adopted this view, Lord Justice Shaw went into a deeper analysis of the offence of fraud and its *mens rea* requirement stating:

> Generally the primary objective of fraudsmen is to advantage themselves. The detriment that results to their victims is secondary to that purpose and incidental. It is 'intended' only in the sense that it is a contemplated outcome of the fraud that is perpetrated.[242]

In order to reinforce this statement, he also elaborated on the meaning of loss:

> "Economic loss" may be ephemeral and not lasting, or potential and not actual; but even a threat of financial prejudice while it exists may be measured in terms of money.[243]

And further:

> Interests which are imperilled are less valuable in terms of money than those same interests when they are secure and protected.[244]

In this way, the Court justified the extension of criminalisation to exposing to a risk of loss, while claiming that in fact a risk of loss is a loss already suffered. If this understanding of loss were to be admitted, it would probably not be necessary to add exposing to the risk of loss to the definition of intent in the offence of fraud, since the term 'loss' would already comprise such a possibility. However, while defining this offence for the purpose of the new Fraud Act, it was preferred not to rely on this broad understanding of the meaning of loss and, at least for the sake of clarity, the intention to expose to a risk of loss as an alternative to the intention to cause a loss was expressly added.

A similar problem arose in the case of *Wai Yu-Tsang*.[245] The defendant in this case was the chief accountant of a bank who:

> failed to cause to be recorded in the bank's computerised ledgers the dishonour of United States cheques totalling US$124m., which the bank had purchased. Instead details were recorded in private ledgers, and entries giving a false impression were made in the bank's accounts.[246]

The chief accountant was convicted of:

> conspiring with the managing director, the general manager and others to defraud the bank and its existing and potential shareholders, creditors and depositors, by dishonestly concealing in the accounts of the bank the dishonouring of those cheques.[247]

[242] Ibid 31.
[243] Ibid 31.
[244] Ibid 32.
[245] *Wai Yu-Tsang* (n 2).
[246] Ibid 269.
[247] Ibid 269.

He was tried alone and convicted for conspiracy to defraud. Similarly to the *Allsop* case, the judge directed the jury that:

> imperilling the economic or proprietary interests of such person or persons was sufficient to constitute fraud even if no loss was suffered and the defendant did not desire that any loss should be caused.[248]

This was questioned by the defendant in his appeal, which was dismissed and the Privy Council was to pronounce its opinion in the case. This case is even more interesting in that it was not proven (at least until the decision in the case was taken) that any effective loss was suffered by the bank or its clients.[249] Arguably, the defendant was acting in the interest of the bank, since he wanted to prevent a run on the bank, which would otherwise occur. Therefore he wanted to prevent the actual loss the bank and his clients would most probably have suffered, if the run had taken place. At the same time, concealing the information about cheques put the bank and its clients at risk.

Similarly to the *Allsop* case, the debate focused on the *mens rea*. The defence argued that the defendant did not intend to put the bank at risk, but rather to save it, and suggested that if he did the former, it amounted to no more than recklessness.[250] The prosecution claimed that the objective of the defendant was to conceal information while saving the bank was only his motive.[251]

First of all, the Privy Council addressed the previous jurisprudence on the matter, in particular expressing its agreement with the reasoning presented in *Allsop*. The Privy Council agreed that in that case, it could be argued (as put forward in *Smith and Hogan Criminal Law*)[252] that there was an intention on the part of the defendant that the company pay for the cars, which the company would not have done but for the defendant's acts, although it suffered no loss in the end.[253]

The Privy Council decided to uphold the interpretation expressed in *Allsop*:

> [I]t is enough for example that, as in *R v. Allsop* and in the present case, the conspirators have dishonestly agreed to bring about a state of affairs which they realise will or may deceive the victim into so acting, or failing to act, that he will suffer economic loss or his economic interests will be put at risk. It is however important in such a case, as the Court of Appeal stressed in *R v. Allsop*, to distinguish a conspirator's intention (or immediate purpose) dishonestly to bring about such a state of affairs from his motive (or underlying purpose). The latter may be benign to the extent that he does not wish the victim or potential victim to suffer harm; but the mere fact that it is benign will not of itself prevent the agreement from constituting a conspiracy to defraud.[254]

[248] Ibid 269.
[249] Ibid 272.
[250] Ibid 271 et seq.
[251] Ibid 272.
[252] The judgment refers to John Smith, *Smith and Hogan Criminal Law*, 6th edn (Lexis Law Publishing, 1988) 273.
[253] *Wai Yu-Tsang* (n 2) 279.
[254] Ibid 280.

The decision in *Wai Yu-Tsang* confirms (which might have been doubtful in view of the facts in *Allsop*) that despite the fact that the motive of the defendant is to bring a positive result for the company, it is the immediate intention which counts for the fulfilment of the *mens rea* requirement.

To sum up the analysis of the two cases, one can argue that the case of *Allsop* need not necessarily be about risk-taking, since the victim actually suffered loss, as the company 'paid too much for cars worth less than their pretended value; and … relied upon the creditworthiness of hire-purchasers as measured by the deposit stated to have been paid when none had been paid'.[255] However, because of the way the judge instructed the jury in the case, the Court of Appeal was faced with the question, whether *mens rea* is fulfilled if D's action 'was likely to lead to the detriment or prejudice',[256] and responded positively.[257] Moreover, the case shows how the understanding of exposure to risk as actual loss can lead to punishment for conspiracy to defraud in cases of excessive risk-taking.

In *Wai Yu-Tsang*, the case was effectively about risk-taking, since no loss was proved. Lord Goff went much further in his dictum by referring to:

> a state of affairs which they realise will *or may* deceive the victim into so acting, or failing to act, that he will suffer economic loss or his economic interests will be put at risk.[258]

The use of 'or may' triggered the question of recklessness which Lord Goff, as stated in the judgment, wanted to avoid. Extending conspiracy to defraud to recklessness would extend the meaning of this offence far beyond the scope of statutory conspiracy.[259] However, as one author argues, it is not necessary to involve the question of recklessness, since the conspirators intended that a certain state of affairs arise, so the proposed reformulation of Lord Goff's dictum would be:

> the conspirators have dishonestly agreed to bring about a state of affairs [so] that he [the victim] will suffer economic loss or his economic interests will be put at risk.[260]

Nevertheless, the definition formulated by Lord Goff seems to have gained acceptance.[261] In any case, both understandings do not require that the perpetrators intend to cause loss, but the intention to cause a state of affairs in which the economic interests of the victim are put at risk is satisfactory for the commission of conspiracy to defraud.

No case similar to *Allsop* and *Wai Yu-Tsang* has reached higher jurisdiction since the adoption of the Fraud Act 2006. The offence of conspiracy to defraud has been widely criticised. While it is still in use, even after the introduction of

[255] *Allsop* (n 27) 32.
[256] Ibid 29.
[257] Farrell et al, *Blackstone's Guide to the Fraud Act 2006* (n 38) 211.
[258] *Wai Yu-Tsang* (n 2) 280, emphasis added.
[259] See, eg Farrell et al, *Blackstone's Guide to the Fraud Act 2006* (n 38) 211.
[260] Montgomery and Ormerod, *Montgomery and Ormerod on Fraud* (n 25) D-7018.
[261] It was cited eg in *R. v Goldshield Group Plc and others* [2009] 1 Cr App R 33.

the Fraud Act,[262] it is difficult to predict its future. Nonetheless, as it stands, if the prosecution has good reasons to use the common law conspiracy to defraud, it allows charging for excessive risk-taking, if the conditions described above are fulfilled. Moreover, it is possible that both decisions influence the understanding of *mens rea* under this Act.

5. Cooperation in the Commission of the Offence

The scope of criminal liability of managers exposing their companies to excessive risk can extend further according to the rules of secondary participation. Also, those who participate in different ways in the offences committed by the managers can be held liable according to these rules.

According to the English criminal law, a person may commit an offence as principal or as a secondary participant.[263] If two (or more) managers participate in taking a decision which is considered to be an abuse of position, or two (or more) persons participate in false representation incriminated under section 2 of the Fraud Act 2006 to the same extent, they will most probably be charged as principals. However, the rules on complicity broaden the scope of liability and may apply to persons whose participation in the commission of the offence would not amount to the level of principal offender. If the conditions are fulfilled, the secondary participant may also be charged for the main offence.[264]

Contrary to the inchoate offences, liability in case of secondary participation is dependent on the commission of the main offence,[265] and the law providing it does not create separate offences.[266] The activity of the secondary participant must take place before the offence is completed.[267] For criminal liability for secondary participation, it is necessary that the action of an accomplice be connected with the commission of the offence. Hence, a person will not be criminally liable if the aid was without influence on the commission or the encouragement was forgotten or never reached the principal.[268] Furthermore, it is possible to avoid criminal liability in case of withdrawal, under certain conditions, mainly consisting in actively counteracting the effects of the accomplice's previous contribution with the aim of preventing the commission of the offence.[269]

[262] For example, the LIBOR scandal is under investigation as conspiracy to defraud. See SFO Press Release (28 October 2014), available at https://www.sfo.gov.uk/2014/10/28/libor-investigation-further-charge/.

[263] Since complicity is understood as the commission of the main offence, it is subject to the same punishment as the latter.

[264] Simester et al, *Simester and Sullivan's Criminal Law* (n 4) 204.

[265] Ibid 204.

[266] Ibid 257.

[267] Ibid 203.

[268] Ibid 213 et seq.

[269] Ibid 259–61.

According to section 8 of the Accessories and Abettors Act 1861, as amended by the Criminal Law Act 1977,[270] complicity is composed of the following elements: the conduct element (aiding, abetting, counselling or procuring), the connection with the commission of the offence by the principal, and the *mens rea*.

The conduct element can take four different forms: aiding, abetting, counselling or procuring. Each of these forms has its own meaning, although in practice they will overlap on various occasions. For example, abetting can easily also constitute aiding or counselling.[271] Moreover, it is not necessary to specify to which of the forms the charge refers, which might prove very helpful for prosecutors in formulating charges in such cases.[272]

Mens rea in case of complicity is composed of two elements: the accomplice must have the intention in respect of his own contributions (aiding, abetting, counselling or procuring) and he must either know or at least foresee the 'essential matters'[273] which constitute the offence of the principal.[274] Furthermore, procurement, as implied by its nature, requires the intention on the side of the accomplice that the principal commit the offence.[275] The accomplice need not know all the details of the foreseen offence (time, place, object, unless relevant for the definition of the offence).[276]

With respect to the second element, there is doubt whether the perpetrator must know the essential matters which constitute that offence[277] or whether also wilful blindness could result in criminal liability in case of secondary participation. It appears in view of the recent jurisprudence that it is enough that the accomplice considers that it is probable that the essential elements of the principal's offence exist.[278]

It is possible that aiding or abetting will be committed by omission. Such a modality is not excluded, but presents certain difficulties as to the conditions of abetting when the person is charged with encouraging the commission of an offence by not preventing it. In such cases, it is required in particular that the person has a legal duty to prevent an offence or by his inaction encourages the perpetrator and intends to encourage him.[279] This could be the case of a senior

[270] 'Whosoever shall aid, abet, counsel, or procure the commission of any indictable offence, whether the same by an offence at common law or by virtue of any Act passed or to be passed, shall be liable to be tried, indicted, and punished as a principal offender.'

[271] Simester et al, *Simester and Sullivan's Criminal Law* (n 4) 210.

[272] Ibid 208.

[273] *Johnson v Youden* [1950] 1 KB 544, 546. It is considered that the accomplice 'must appreciate that [the principal] intends or contemplates doing actions which constitute the actus reus of an offence, although [the accomplice] need not recognise that those actions in fact constitute an offence': Simester et al, *Simester and Sullivan's Criminal Law* (n 4) 229.

[274] Ibid 218.

[275] Ibid 219.

[276] Ibid 229 et seq.

[277] *Johnson v Youden* [1950] 1 KB 544, 546.

[278] Simester et al, *Simester and Sullivan's Criminal Law* (n 4) 226.

[279] Ibid 217.

manager (a director) who tacitly encourages a manager to take an excessively risky decision by not doing anything while being informed about it. A similar situation might occur in case of two senior managers. Such non-intervention might amount to the commission of fraud by abuse of position by omission (Fraud Act 2006, section 4(2)). But if it does not, the manager may be held liable if his inaction encouraged the other to proceed and it was the intention of the former to encourage the latter.[280]

In a reverse case, lower-level management will less likely be held liable for abetting the director by failing to react to his risky policy. To their defence will come, for example, the decision in *Clarkson*, in which the Court of Appeal quashed the convictions of two soldiers who entered a room in which a rape was taking place and observed the occurrence without preventing it but also without encouraging its commission.[281]

It is possible to foresee criminal liability in a case in which a manager or another person embarks on the commission of an offence together with another manager and the latter commits fraud in a way which exposes the company to excessive risk, which was not part of the agreement, but had nonetheless been envisaged as a possibility by the first person.[282]

6. Reasons for Excluding Criminal Liability

6.1. Consent of the Victim

The consent of the victim can, under certain conditions, exclude criminal liability in English law, either because it will render lawful the action of the defendant or because it will exclude one of the elements of *actus reus* or *mens rea*.[283] In case of fraud, consent will arguably be evaluated within the assessment of dishonesty. Moreover, it is difficult to imagine the commission of fraud by false representation or fraud by failing to disclose information with the consent of the victim, unless the victim was somehow tricked into giving it. As to fraud by abuse of position, consent of the victim will not only exclude dishonesty, but also abuse.[284] The defendant is not abusing his position, if he is allowed to act the way he acts. Such consent could be valid only if the victim had the necessary information to properly assess the situation. If the defendant knew that the consent was given by the victim

[280] Ibid 217.

[281] *R v Clarkson* (1971) 55 Cr App R 445.

[282] Such liability would be based on the complicated and controversial concept of joint enterprise. For more details on this concept see Simester et al, *Simester and Sullivan's Criminal Law* (n 4) 232 et seq and Ashworth, *Principles of Criminal Law* (n 56) 420 et seq.

[283] Simester et al, *Simester and Sullivan's Criminal Law* (n 4) 765. For general rules on consent in English criminal law, see ibid 763 et seq.

[284] Parry et al, *Arlidge and Parry on Fraud* (n 41) 167.

who did not have a full understanding of the issue at stake, he acts dishonestly and he commits an abuse. Moreover, if it is the defendant who misinformed the victim, he could be held liable also for fraud by false representation.[285]

The question which will have the crucial impact on the scope of fraud by abuse of position is: who is the victim, ie who is entitled to give consent? The most straightforward answer is that it is the same person whose financial interests the defendant has the duty to safeguard or not to act against. Hence, it will be the company, and in order to be valid, the consent should be given in accordance with the rules of civil and company law. This means that even if consent is given, there might remain persons who did not agree and whose interests were exposed to a risk of loss, which would qualify for criminal liability provided the consent was not given (eg minority shareholders, clients). In such cases, if the prosecutor finds that the wrongdoing justifies prosecution, he might still charge for the conspiracy to defraud, since this offence does not precisely define its victim, but only requires the defrauding of another person.[286]

Another question relates to the problem of belief that the consent was given or the belief that the consent would be given. As to the first, it will be rather difficult to claim that the defendant was dishonest, if he was acting in an honest belief that the victim consented to what he is doing. As to the second possibility, the question is more difficult.

The idea of exonerating the defendant in such scenario is not unknown, which can be demonstrated by section 2 of the Theft Act 1968 which excludes dishonesty of the defendant 'if he appropriates the property in the belief that he would have the other's consent if the other knew of the appropriation and the circumstances of it'.[287] This provision applies, however, to the understanding of dishonesty for the offence of theft and it could only be applied to fraud by analogy. Irrespective of the question if that is probable, it seems justified to claim that juries may in some cases find that the defendant did not act dishonestly, if he honestly believed that such consent would have been given.[288] This would probably be the case if the defendant had to take rapid decisions without having the possibility to ask for permission, while being honestly convinced that consent would be granted, on condition that the victim was in possession of the entire information about the situation.[289]

[285] Ibid 168.

[286] The case of *Wai Yu-Tsang* might be an example: the defendant was charged 'with conspiring … to defraud the bank and its existing and potential shareholders, creditors and depositors', *Wai Yu-Tsang* (n 2) 269.

[287] Theft Act 1968, s 2(1)(b).

[288] Law Com No 276 (n 1) marginal no 7.72; Ormerod and Williams, *Smith's Law of Theft* (n 8) 133.

[289] Parry et al, *Arlidge and Parry on Fraud* (n 41) 31; Montgomery and Ormerod, *Montgomery and Ormerod on Fraud* (n 25) D-1017.

6.2. Orders of Superiors

Superior orders do not provide a justification for criminal conduct under English law.[290] However, an order of a superior may result in acquittal of the defendant because of lack of *mens rea*, in particular and yet again depending on the question of dishonesty. Under the test of *Ghosh*, one could claim that the fact that the order came from a superior might make a manager believe that ordinary and honest people would not consider such act as dishonest. However, if a senior manager is convinced that the orders of a director require him to perform an abuse of position, he cannot escape liability merely because the orders came from a superior.[291]

6.3. Expert Opinions

The question whether the conduct of a manager can be justified by the fact that he based his act on an opinion of an expert can also be solved by reference to the concept of dishonesty. If the manager believed in the correctness of an expert opinion, it will be hard to claim that he committed the act dishonestly. However, if he had doubts about the correctness of the opinion, or, in a worse scenario, he knew it was incorrect but used it to cover his actions, it is likely that honest and reasonable people would consider his act to be dishonest.

7. Offence of Reckless Misconduct in the Management of a Financial Institution

In order to complete the analysis of the English law in relation to criminalisation of managers for excessive risk-taking, it is necessary to mention the new criminal offence of reckless misconduct in the management of a financial institution introduced by the Financial Services (Banking Reform) Act 2013. The interest of this provision results from the fact that, although for criminal liability the provision requires the failure of a financial institution, this result may be brought about recklessly, in particular by excessively risky management. Certain scepticism as to the practical implications of the provision may be justified, as its design (as will be demonstrated below) renders it very difficult to prove.[292] These difficulties were already known at the time of adoption of the offence, but it was considered that it would still positively influence the decision-making processes of senior bank

[290] Simester et al, *Simester and Sullivan's Criminal Law* (n 4) 755.
[291] Ibid 755 et seq.
[292] Christopher Coltart, 'Banking Act is a Paper Tiger', *Law Society Gazette*, 3 February 2014.

management.[293] Its real impact remains to be seen, as the provisions entered into force only on 7 March 2016.[294]

The introduction of the offence was recommended by the Parliamentary Commission on Banking Standards, which was created in the aftermath of the financial crisis:

> to consider and report on professional standards and culture of the UK banking sector … lessons to be learned about corporate governance, transparency and conflicts of interest, and their implications for regulation and for Government policy and to make recommendations for legislative and other action.[295]

The Commission found that, despite the existence of various criminal offences, such as theft and fraud, these 'do not cover the apparent mismanagement and failure of control by senior bankers which has been at the heart of the recent concerns about standards and culture in banking'.[296] In view of this, the Commission recommended creating a new offence of reckless misconduct in the management of a bank.[297]

The offence is defined in Financial Services (Banking Reform) Act 2013, section 36 (1), with various explanations provided in this and the following section.[298] Its application is limited to senior managers of financial institutions concerned. The senior manager is a person who performs a senior management function under an arrangement with the institution.[299] The Act does not define what are the senior management functions, but provides that it will be decided by the Financial Conduct Authority and the Prudential Regulation Authority.[300] In any event, it will be a person belonging to the top management of the bank, since such person must be able to influence the decision-making process as to the way in which the business of the institution is to be carried on. The institutions concerned

[293] Parliamentary Commission on Banking Standards, *Changing Banking for Good, Report of the Parliamentary Commission on Banking Standards*, vol II, June 2013, HL Paper 27-II HC 175-II, recital 1182.

[294] Financial Services (Banking Reform) Act 2013 (Commencement No 9) Order 2015 (SI 2015/490, 4 March 2015).

[295] Parliamentary Commission on Banking Standards, *Changing Banking for Good* (n 293) vol I, 2.

[296] Ibid vol II, recital 1174.

[297] Ibid vol II, recital 1182.

[298] Financial Services (Banking Reform) Act 2013, s 36(1): 'A person ("S") commits an offence if – (a) at a time when S is a senior manager in relation to a financial institution ("F"), S – (i) takes, or agrees to the taking of, a decision by or on behalf of F as to the way in which the business of a group institution is to be carried on, or (ii) fails to take steps that S could take to prevent such a decision being taken; (b) at the time of the decision, S is aware of a risk that the implementation of the decision may cause the failure of the group institution; (c) in all the circumstances, S's conduct in relation to the taking of the decision falls far below what could reasonably be expected of a person in S's position; and (d) the implementation of the decision causes the failure of the group institution'. The punishment is: on summary conviction imprisonment for a term not exceeding 12 months or a fine or both; on conviction on indictment, to imprisonment for a term not exceeding seven years or a fine, or both.

[299] Financial Services (Banking Reform) Act 2013, s 37(7).

[300] Ibid s 37(8).

by the offence are mainly UK incorporated banks, but also under certain conditions building societies or UK investment firms.[301]

Contrary to the offence of fraud, the offence under section 36 contains various requirements of *actus reus* and only one requirement of *mens rea*. Therefore, it will be the former that will mostly shape the scope of application of the offence. In order to be criminally liable it is necessary that:

(i) the defendant either took or agreed to the taking of a decision on how the business of the bank should be carried on or failed to take steps that could prevent such a decision;
(ii) the conduct of the perpetrator in relation to the taking of the decision fell far below what could reasonably be expected of a person in his position; and
(iii) the implementation of the decision caused the failure of the institution.[302]

Hence, criminal liability will only be triggered when the bank effectively fails and the link of causality must be established between the decision, in the taking of which the senior manager participated in the way described above, and the failure of the bank. This requirement may be the biggest hurdle to overcome by the prosecution.

As to the *mens rea* requirement, the offence under section 36 punishes reckless misconduct in the management of a financial institution.[303] Therefore, it is not necessary that the perpetrator intends the failure of the bank or agrees to its occurrence. It is sufficient that he is aware of a risk that the implementation of the decision may cause the failure of the bank. Contrary to the offences described above, section 36 does not contain the requirement of dishonesty.

If it enters into force, the provision might punish a manager who took a decision or participated in taking a decision that the business of the institution should be carried on in an excessively risky way, provided that the manager's conduct in relation to taking this decision falls far below the standard expected from him and he is aware of the risk of failure of the institution that the implementation of this decision may cause. However, the manager can only be found liable once the institution collapses and on the condition of establishing the causal link between the decision and the institution's failure. Since the offence has not yet entered into force, it is very difficult to predict whether any conviction will ever occur, how the courts will interpret the offence, or what its influence on the management culture in the institutions covered by section 36 will be. In any event, in view of the requirement of the effective failure of the institution, this offence can only be used in order to punish an already occurred calamity.

[301] Financial Services (Banking Reform) Act 2013, Explanatory Notes, recital 218.

[302] For the explanation of what amounts to the failure of the institution, see Financial Services (Banking Reform) Act 2013, s 37(9), (10).

[303] For the analysis of the most suitable form of *mens rea* for this offence, see Parliamentary Commission on Banking Standards, *Changing Banking for Good* (n 293) vol II, recital 1176 et seq.

8. Solutions to the Five Cases

As to the first two cases (out of the five described in Chapter 1[304]), both managers occupy a position in which they are expected to safeguard, or not to act against, the financial interests of the bank. The use of the position is improper, since they are supposed to act within the allowed limits of risk, thus their courses of conduct constitute an abuse. It is clear in the second case that the manager intends to make a gain for himself. The first manager might be acting with the same intention (eg intent not to lose work and salary), but even if he does not have such motivation, the extended definition of intention allows us to consider that since he is aware that it will be virtually certain that his decision exposes the bank to a risk of loss, this limb will also be fulfilled. Both managers might possibly be found to have been dishonest, since they are breaching rules governing the way they should execute their duties. The probability of conviction is smaller in the first case, as the perpetrator does not have any personal intention, while in the second case the manager expects a bonus. The fact that they both hope that, at the end of the day, everything works out fine does not preclude proving their *mens rea*, as shown in the case of *Wai Yu-Tsang*.

As to the third case, the director fulfils the limb of the required position. The question whether he committed an abuse of position will be intertwined with the question of dishonesty. If the test proves that the manager acted dishonestly, his conduct will be also abusive. To answer this question, it will be important whether the manager knowingly acted outside the scope of his duties. Hence, the crucial question will be whether the manager was allowed to invest on the stock exchange and whether or not it was outside of the scope of the business of the company, as prescribed by articles of association or other acts. If it can be proved that such investments were not permitted, it is likely that the manager would be considered dishonest. In this case, a conviction for theft would also be possible, since if he was not allowed to invest the money in this way, he usurped the right of the owner. Also, the *mens rea* requirement of intention to permanently deprive would be fulfilled, according to the broad understanding held in *Fernandes*, extending this concept to situations where the perpetrator deals with the property in a way that 'he knows he is risking its loss'.[305] However, if such investing on the stock exchange was indeed permitted, the likelihood of the manager being found dishonest, even if his investment strategy was too risky, is less significant. In such case, he could still be held liable for theft if he retains the gains from the investment.[306]

The manager in case 4 could potentially be held liable for fraud by failing to disclose information (Fraud Act 2006, section 3) and fraud by abuse of position

[304] For the hypotheses of the cases and explanations, see Chapter 1, section 4.
[305] *Fernandes* (n 174).
[306] Theft Act 1968, s 5(3); See also Montgomery and Ormerod, *Montgomery and Ormerod on Fraud* (n 25) D-3011–3014/D. 3.38–3.106.

(section 4). The liability for the first offence will depend on whether the manager had the duty to disclose information about the problems of the new model (which he most probably had). Conviction for the second offence would require demonstrating that by concealing the information and presenting the model as fit for production, the manager abused his position (which is also likely since breaching professional duties can be considered to constitute an abuse). But most of all, the outcome of this case will depend on the evaluation of the dishonesty of the director. As the case stands, the likelihood of conviction is limited, unless it is possible to demonstrate that the manager had a direct interest (eg in the form of commission) to conceal the problems, or that he acted with a particular lack of professional integrity, eg he purposefully shredded documentation concerning the problem. Without such element, the case may rather be considered as misjudgement, but not fraud. It is, however, highly likely that the jury will conclude that a reasonable and honest director would not conceal information on a problem that could hamper the success of a new car model.

The course of conduct of the manager in case 5 will in the first place be evaluated in view of the offence of bribery, and since there is no limitation on prosecution applicable to this offence, so there is no incentive to incriminate this conduct under other offences, as will be seen eg in the analysis of the French legal system.[307] Moreover, the offence does not require proof of dishonesty. The question relevant for this book is whether the manager could be punished also for exposing the company to excessive risk of loss. Without entering into details of corporate criminal liability, it is conceivable that the company would be subject to liability, for example under Bribery Act 2010, section 7. However, even if this is not the case, the company might suffer loss for several other reasons, for example, losing the chance to obtain the contract in question or because of damage to its reputation. The manager's intention is for the company to profit and not to be exposed to risk. However, using the company's money for bribing public officials is not a proper use of these funds, thus all the elements of fraud by abuse of position are fulfilled. A conviction will be much less likely, if the manager used his own funds for the bribery. The likelihood that the jury would find the manager dishonest is diminished by the fact that he acted mainly (or only) for the benefit of the company. Moreover, the risk of loss is not directly linked to his act but remote, and might not materialise. Hence, it is rather unlikely that he would also be prosecuted for fraud. However, he might obviously be prosecuted for bribery, as well as for theft of the company's funds that he used to bribe the public official.

Other offences described in this chapter might also be of application in the cases analysed above. If the perpetrator in the course of his actions made a false representation, he might be liable for fraud as described in Fraud Act 2006, section 2. In particular, this could occur in the last case, which could also result in liability for fraud as described in section 3. If other persons were involved in these

[307] Bribery Act 2010, s 1.

cases, they could be held liable either for conspiracy to defraud or for the statutory offence of conspiracy, or for the main offence through the rules of complicity. In such cases, the inchoate offence of encouraging or assisting could also be applied. The most important threshold in the analysis of all these cases will always be linked to the question of dishonesty. Once this requirement is fulfilled, the English law offers vast possibilities to criminalise managers acting as described in the first four cases.

However, as regards the version of the cases showing negligence only, the English legal system does not provide a possibility to convict the managers.

9. Conclusions

The English legal system offers a plethora of offences which may be applied to managers who expose their companies to excessive risk. They will in the first place fall into the scope of application of the offence of fraud, in particular the modality described in section 4 of the Fraud Act 2006, described as fraud by abuse of position. The manager commits it if he dishonestly abuses the position in which he is expected to safeguard, or not to act against, the financial interests of another person, ie the company (and indirectly of the shareholders). Under this provision, two questions will be pertinent in deciding whether what the manager did could be considered abuse of company assets: whether the excessive risk-taking was an abuse and whether it was dishonest.

Moreover, managers could potentially also be liable for the common law offence of conspiracy to defraud or the offence of theft. Depending on the particularities of concrete cases, other modalities of fraud could also potentially be applied. The English legal system extends also the scope of criminalisation by providing for liability for possession etc of articles for use in fraud; making or supplying articles for use in fraud; encouraging and assisting an offence; attempt; and statutory conspiracy. At the same time, the statutes prescribe the quite severe penalty of a maximum of 10 years' imprisonment for almost all these offences.

However, the application of these offences to excessive risk-taking by managers will be greatly limited and depend on the limb of dishonesty and its particularities. The law does not provide a definition of this notion, but only a formal test, the most recent version of which was established in *Ivey*, which only provides for the standard according to which the limb must be assessed (dishonest according to honest and reasonable people). The question whether a manager was dishonest will be answered by the tribunal of fact, which will be the jury in cases where the latter is involved. The jury is composed of 12 laymen and may not include anybody with any experience in business. Moreover, the jury does not give reasons for their assessments. The difficulty to foresee the outcome of concrete cases leads to very limited use of these offences in cases of excessive risk-taking, which do not provide such obvious wrongdoing as cases of loss.

The Law Commission suggested that fraud is not meant to be a 'general dishonesty offence'.[308] The Commission's intention was that '[d]ishonesty should only function as a negative element to rebut the *prima facie* criminality of the defendant's conduct'.[309] In contrast to this statement, as was shown above in different sections of the analysis, it is dishonesty that makes a criminal offence out of a sometimes very innocent course of conduct. For example, the path from use to abuse in Fraud Act 2006, section 4 will lead through the question of dishonesty. A very broad definition of intent and position contribute to the conclusion that the question of dishonesty will be decisive for the defendant's criminal liability.

The English legal system also provides for an offence of reckless misconduct in the management of a financial institution (Financial Services (Banking Reform) Act 2013, section 36) which does not require proof of dishonesty. The offence may be used to punish senior managers of financial institutions who take excessively risky decisions. However, the requirement that the institution effectively collapsed as a result of the implementation of such decisions, together with other *actus reus* requirements, allow us to doubt whether the offence can ever effectively be used.

[308] Law Com No 276 (n 1) marginal no 5.57.
[309] Ibid.

3

France

1. Introduction and History

Before the enactment of the offence of abuse of company assets (*abus de biens sociaux*) an act of misuse of these assets could be punished only by virtue of the offence of breach of trust (*abus de confiance*), which criminalised fraudulent misappropriation of entrusted property (article 408 of the old, Napoleonic, Penal Code of 1810). This offence, the equivalent of the English embezzlement, was not well suited for this task, since it was designed to punish misappropriation, so it forced the courts to extensively interpret the requirements of this offence.[1] Moreover, the old formulation of the breach of trust contained an enumerative list of contracts on the basis of which the right to use another person's property was transferred to the defendant. The list did not contain the contract creating a company (*contrat de société*), compelling the jurisprudence to develop a theory on the basis of which it was assumed that this contract implies the conclusion of another contract, the one by which the power of attorney was granted (*contrat de mandat*), which *was* on the list.[2]

The broad interpretation of the provision led to criticism for infringement of the principle of legality.[3] Moreover, the creativity of judges did not help to fill all the gaps. For instance, if a director signed in the name of the company a guarantee for his personal debts, it was not possible to consider it as misappropriation (*détournement*), since no use of assets had yet been made.[4] The provision also excluded from its scope situations in which the object of misappropriation was real property.[5]

The shortcomings of the provision, the political and financial scandals of the Third French Republic, in particular the *Stavisky* affair,[6] as well as the need to

[1] For details see 3.2 below, and in particular 3.2.2.

[2] Wilfrid Jeandidier, *Abus de confiance* (JurisClasseur Pénal, Date du fascicule 1 February 2015, Date de la dernière mise à jour 1 Septembre 2017) para 41.

[3] Henri Donnedieu de Vabres, 'IV. Crimes et délits contre les biens' (1938) *Revue de Science Criminelle et Droit Pénal Comparé* 716, 719; Wilfrid Jeandidier, *Abus des biens, du crédit, des pouvoirs ou des voix* (JurisClasseur Sociétés Traité, Date du fascicule 7 February 2017, Date de la dernière mise à jour 7 February 2017) para 2.

[4] Jeandidier, *Abus des biens* (n 3) para 2.

[5] Frédéric Stasiak, *Droit pénal des affaires*, 2nd edn (Paris: LGDJ, 2009) 236.

[6] Ibid 236.

reinforce the confidence of investors during the recovery period from the financial crisis, led in 1935 to the enactment of a new offence, namely the abuse of company assets (*abus de biens sociaux*).[7] The offence was provided by a statutory order (décret-loi) for public limited companies (*société anonyme*)[8] and in the same year its application was extended to limited liability companies (*société à responsabilité limitée*).[9] The scope of this offence was, however, limited, both as to the types of company to which it applied and as to the circle of potential perpetrators. Thus, the offence of breach of trust retained its validity for all those cases to which the offence of abuse of company assets was inapplicable.

The legal basis changed in 1966 but the new law kept the provision almost intact.[10] Finally, the law was incorporated into the Commercial Code, where it remains until today, in article L241-3 4° and 5° for limited liability companies and in article L242-6 3° and 4° for public limited companies.[11] Since its enactment until now, the law has remained almost identical with the original text of 1935.[12] Moreover, the offence was unaffected by different initiatives to decriminalise business activities.[13] In particular, the *Coulon* report recommended retaining the offence.[14]

The legislative technique adopted for the offence of abuse of company assets is fairly complex. The offence is constructed according to four modalities of the commission of this offence. The modalities are grouped respectively in

[7] Jeandidier, *Abus des biens* (n 3) para 3; Annie Médina, *Abus de biens sociaux: Prévention – Détection – Poursuite* (Paris: Dalloz, 2001) 3.

[8] Décret-loi of 8 August 1935.

[9] Décret-loi of 30 October 1935.

[10] Loi of 24 July 1966.

[11] L'ordonnance no 2000-912 of 18 September 2000.

[12] Didier Rebut, *Abus de biens sociaux* (Répertoire de droit pénal et de procédure pénale, Dalloz, January 2010, dernière mise à jour June 2011) para 9. Recent changes concerned the applicable penalities. Loi no 2008-776 of 4 August 2008 de modernisation de l'économie, art 71, provided for disqualifications applicable to the perpetrators of the abuse of company assets provided by the Commercial Code. Most recently, a new aggravating circumstance (Loi no 2013-1117 of 6 December 2013 relative à la lutte contre la fraude fiscale et la grande délinquance économique et financière, art 30), as well as a possibility to apply the forfeiture of civic, civil and family rights (Loi no 2013-907 of 11 October 2013 relative à la transparence de la vie publique, art 27) have also been added.

[13] In the past decades, several initiatives turned into laws, which aimed at limiting the enormous number of criminal provisions concerning business activities (as to company law, Loi no 2001-420 of 15 May 2001 can be cited as the main example). Despite the enactment of these decriminalising statutes, several authors pointed out that no real decriminalisation has taken place. The statutes have mainly abolished provisions that were rarely used in practice anyway and left the core of white-collar offences intact. Moreover, some of the abolished offences reappeared in a different form enforced by means of administrative law, eg as to competition offences (see Rebut, *Abus de biens sociaux* (n 12) para 6 et seq; Stasiak, *Droit pénal des affaires* (n 5) 9; Michel Véron, *Droit pénal des affaires*, 9th edn (Dalloz, 2011) 16 et seq; Agathe Lepage, Patrick Maistre du Chambon and Renaud Salomon, *Droit pénal des affaires*, 4th edn (Paris: LexiNexis Litec, 2015) 3 et seq.

[14] Groupe de travail présidé par Jean-Marie Coulon, *La dépénalisation de la vie des affaires*, Rapport au garde des Sceaux (Ministre de la Justice, January 2008) 22, 33–34. The only exception concerned the suggestion to delete the abuse of votes (although only as regards limited liability company, SARL), which has fallen out of use (33).

two different paragraphs: the abuse of company assets and the abuse of company credit (L241-3 4° and L242-6 3°) and the abuse of powers and the abuse of votes (L241-3 5° and L242-6 4°). However, the jurisprudence is not very strict in differentiating between these modalities, and judgments evoking more than one of these modalities are not unusual. The modalities are not considered to be separate offences, which is proved by the fact that the issue of the relationship between convictions for more than one of the modalities does not appear in this context. It is also a general practice, which this chapter will also respect, to use the name of the first modality – 'abuse of company assets' – while referring to all the modalities, unless it is made clear that only the first modality is meant.[15]

Secondly, one of the particularities of the French approach is that there is no general offence of abuse of company assets, applicable to all types of companies, but instead the French law criminalises the abuse separately for different types of commercial entities. Moreover, the offence has not been provided for all types of business entities. In particular, two groups of companies are not included. The first one is related to the function of the offence, which should help to counterbalance the limited liability of companies. Therefore, entities in which the liability of members is unlimited have been excluded from the scope of the offence, eg general partnerships (*sociétés en nom collectif*), limited partnerships like partnerships limited by shares (*sociétés en commandite simple*) or undisclosed partnerships (*sociétés en participation*), de facto partnerships (*sociétés créées de fait*), economic interest groupings (*groupements d'intérêt économique*) and associations (*associations*).[16] In the case of these companies, the misuse of their assets is only criminalised by use of the breach of trust offence.[17] It is a similar situation as regards the second exclusion, which concerns foreign companies.[18] However, the courts do not treat the requirement that the company must be French very strictly, considering also as French companies those entities which, although formally foreign, function as de facto French companies,[19] in particular if they have their effective headquarters in France.[20] Because an analysis of the plethora of acts criminalising abuse of company assets for different types of entities[21] would be long and necessarily

[15] Rebut, *Abus de biens sociaux* (n 12) para 10.

[16] Lepage et al, *Droit pénal des affaires* (n 13) 319.

[17] Ibid 319.

[18] Cass crim, 3 June 2004, Bull crim, no 152, 567. For an analysis of this problem see the comment of Delphine Caramalli regarding this decision published in (2004) 44 *Receuil Dalloz* 3213.

[19] Jeandidier, *Abus des biens* (n 3) para 5.

[20] Stasiak, *Droit pénal des affaires* (n 5) 238; Cass crim, 31 January 2007, Bull crim, no 28, 102.

[21] The offence of abuse of company assets has been provided not only for entities regulated by the Commercial Code but also for other types of companies provided in other statutes, for instance: *sociétés coopératives, sociétés mutuelles d'assurance, sociétés immobilières de construction, sociétés civiles de placement immobilier, sociétés par actions simplifiées, sociétés en commandite par actions, sociétés civiles faisant publiquement appel à l'épargne, sociétés d'exercice libéral* and *sociétés d'économie mixte*. These provisions are very similar to those provided for the SARL and the SA, although some differences exist. For more details see Eva Joly and Caroline Joly-Baumgartner, *L'abus de biens sociaux: Á l'épreuve de la pratique* (Paris: Economica, 2002) 16; Médina, *Abus de biens sociaux* (n 7) 15 et seq; Lepage et al, *Droit pénal des affaires* (n 13) 319.

encyclopaedic, and in view of the minimal differences between these provisions, this chapter will concentrate on the offence of abuse of company assets provided by the Commercial Code, and in particular with respect to the two major types of limited companies: the limited liability company (*société à responsabilité limitée*, SARL) and the public limited company (*société anonyme*, SA), upon which the law has focused since the enactment of the offence in 1935.[22]

Finally, the scope of application of the offence of the abuse of company assets is limited to persons occupying, de jure or de facto, certain positions in the company.[23] This rule provides for another gap in liability for the abuse, which can be remedied, yet again, only by use of the breach of trust offence.[24] This latter offence, newly formulated for the Penal Code of 1994 (CP), is phrased in more abstract terms, in particular without a limited list of contracts on the basis of which the assets were entrusted. Furthermore, it is not excluded that acts which constitute an abuse of company assets may also fulfil the requirements to constitute a breach of trust. According to the French rules on such conflicts, the perpetrator has to be charged for the former offence as it is *lex specialis* and since it foresees a more severe punishment.[25]

2. Protected Legal Interests

In part of the literature, the abuse is counted amongst offences against property or, in other terms, against another person's assets (*délit d'atteinte aux biens*).[26]

[22] The punishment for all the modalities is of five years' imprisonment and a fine of 375,000 euros (art L241-3, art L242-6). The only exception concerns the liquidator, for whom the fine is of 9,000 euros (L247-8). As to the abuse of company assets provided in different laws, in some of these provisions the punishment is of the same level, eg Code monétaire et financier, art L231-11, whereas in some others it varies, eg Code de la construction et de l'habitation, art L313-32: five years' imprisonment and a fine of 150,000 euros. Article L249-1 adds to this list a possibility to prohibit the perpetrators of abuse of company assets provided by the Commercial Code from exercising certain functions or activities. It is also possible to apply to them the forfeiture of civic, civil and family rights provided for in Penal Code (CP), art 131-26. For more details on additional punishments, see Jeandidier, *Abus des biens* (n 3) para 93 et seq. Furthermore, as to the abuse of company assets enshrined in the Commercial Code, a recent law provided for an additional aggravating circumstance elevating the punishment to seven years' imprisonment and a fine of 500,000 euros. It was introduced by Loi no 2013-1117 of 6 December 2013 relative à la lutte contre la fraude fiscale et la grande délinquance économique et financière, art 30, and may be applied if the offence was conducted or facilitated using either accounts or contracts opened or subscribed with entities established abroad or by interposition of natural or legal persons or any organization, trust or comparable institution established abroad (Commercial Code, arts L241-3 and L242-6).

[23] The scope of application is enlarged by the rules on complicity, see 5 below.

[24] Breach of trust is punished by three years' imprisonment and a fine of 375,000 euros (CP, art 314-1). Additional circumstances may increase the level of punishment to seven years' imprisonment and to a fine of 750,000 euros (CP, art 314-2) or to 10 years' imprisonment and a fine of 1,500,000 euros (CP, art 314-3). In the latter cases, liability for participation in a criminal association for the purpose of committing the breach of trust could be also envisaged.

[25] Frédéric Desportes and Francis Le Gunehec, *Droit Pénal Général*, 14th edn (Paris: Economica, 2007) 246; Jeandidier, *Abus des biens* (n. 3) para 6.

[26] Médina, *Abus de biens sociaux* (n 7) 7.

While that is certainly true, it does not reveal the full nature of the offence.[27] The titles of the respective chapters, in which the abuse of company assets is placed, already provide some limited guidance as to the protected legal interest, since they use the expression 'Offences involving' followed by the type of the company, to which the offences refer, eg 'Offences involving limited liability companies'. These titles suggest that the company is at the centre of attention of the offences, in contrast to those crimes that have been placed under the heading 'Felonies and misdemeanours against property', which is the case of the offence of breach of trust.

Contrary to the latter offence, the abuse of company assets does not require a result in the form of negative financial consequences for the victim (ie the owner of the assets).[28] As will be further explained below, merely exposing the company to abnormal risk is sufficient for criminal liability. The fact that the risk did not materialise in a loss, but the company eventually profited from the act, does not exclude liability.[29] Moreover, the risk need not relate to a financial loss: it may also consist in exposure of the company to fiscal or criminal sanctions (although they will admittedly have financial consequences).[30] These factors have led some authors to consider that the offence punishes abuses of management (*abus de gestion*).[31] In this sense, the offence punishes the managers for making their own interests prevail over the interests of the company, thus punishing disloyalty, which is linked also with the origins of the offence, introduced in 1935 in order to protect the confidence of investors at a time when the French economy was making an effort to recover from the financial crisis.[32]

The above interpretation of the protective scope of the offence of abuse of company assets is similar to the conception focusing on company property insofar as both refer to the interests of the company. The term 'company interests' is also used to define the requirements of the offence. Therefore, the understanding of this is crucial for delineating the protective scope of the abuse of company assets offence.[33] The jurisprudence generally rejects the interpretation associating the interests of the company only with the interests of its shareholders, and opts for an understanding which emphasises the company's own interest. This interpretation is strengthened especially by the refusal to consider the shareholders' consent as exculpatory, as well as by convictions of managers of companies of which they are sole shareholders.[34]

[27] Rebut, *Abus de biens sociaux* (n 12) paras 15–17.

[28] Marie-Paule Lucas de Leyssac and Alexis Mihman, *Droit pénal des affaires, Manuel théorique et pratique* (Paris: Economica, 2009) 187.

[29] Yvonne Muller, 'Le droit pénal des conflits d'intérêts', *Droit pénal* (January 2012), no 1 étude 1, point 13.

[30] Yvonne Muller, 'L'abus réprimé: la correction par le juge', 353 *Gazette du Palais*, 19 December 2009, 30, 31.

[31] Rebut, *Abus de biens sociaux* (n 12) para 10; Muller, 'L'abus réprimé (n 30) 30.

[32] Médina, *Abus de biens sociaux* (n 7) 3.

[33] For more details, see 3.1.3(ii) below.

[34] Alain Dekeuwer, 'Les intérêts protégées en cas d'abus de biens sociaux', 43 *La Semaine Juridique Entreprise et Affaires*, 26 October 1995, 500, para 17.

By adopting such an approach, and as has been recognised in some judgments of the Court of Cassation, the abuse of company assets offence in fact protects the interests of the stakeholders such as employees, creditors or suppliers.[35] However, this is done indirectly as the courts consequently refuse to allow third persons to join the procedure as civil parties by reason of the damage sustained by them.

The focus on company interests does not mean that the interests of the shareholders are neglected. Indeed, as mentioned above, the interests of the latter were one of the original reasons for the enactment of the offence. However, it is considered that shareholders' interests are sufficiently protected if the company interests are protected, since the former benefit from the well-being of the company.[36] Nor are shareholders admitted as civil parties, which may be more surprising than in the case of the stakeholders. Only the company is recognised as the victim of the offence.[37] However, the shareholders are admitted to act in criminal procedure in the name of the company, which is justified by the fact that the management of the company, normally entitled to so to act, might be composed of the alleged perpetrators.[38]

The extension of the application of the offence to cases in which corruption was involved[39] might suggest that the protection offered by this offence extends also to different kinds of legal interest of a public nature.[40] This interpretation, however, is far-fetched. The possibility to punish a manager for abuse of company assets in such a case is provided due to the fact that, because of the act of bribery, the company assets are at risk, not in order to punish the act of corruption itself, which is criminalised by a different offence. Moreover, abuse of company assets is used for a practical reason: its longer limitation period, due to the rules postponing its starting point.[41]

As to breach of trust, despite the fact that the name of the offence could suggest that it aims at protecting the relation between the owner and the person to whom the property is entrusted, its goal is to protect another person's property.[42] This interpretation finds its confirmation in two aspects of the offence. First, those

[35] Joly and Joly-Baumgartner, *L'abus de biens sociaux* (n 21) 93.

[36] Dekeuwer, 'Les intérêts protégées en cas d'abus de biens sociaux' (n 34) para 15.

[37] Rebut, *Abus de biens sociaux* (n 12) para 257 et seq. Interestingly, the jurisprudence went back and forth on this point, as first denying the shareholder the right to participate in the procedure as civil parties, then allowing them to join the procedure in this capacity from the 1970s (Cass crim, 6 January 1970, Bull crim, no 11, 22), only to deny it again in the years following 2000 (Cass crim, 13 December 2000, Bull crim no 373, 1135). See also Lucas de Leyssac and Mihman, *Droit pénal des affaires* (n 28) 220; Rebut, *Abus de biens sociaux* (n 12) paras 262–63.

[38] Lucas de Leyssac and Mihman, *Droit pénal des affaires* (n. 28) 218–19; Rebut, *Abus de biens sociaux* (n 12) para 254 et seq.

[39] For more details, see 3.1.3(ii) below.

[40] Médina, *Abus de biens sociaux* (n 7) 8.

[41] Rebut, *Abus de biens sociaux* (n 12) paras 73, 76.

[42] Corinne Mascala, *Abus de confiance* (Répertoire de droit pénal et de procédure pénale, Dalloz, October 2003) para 2.

breaches of contract which normally fall into the scope of the offence are not punishable if the perpetrator becomes the owner of the item in question before the act, but after the handover of the item.[43] Secondly, the consent of the owner excludes the commission of the offence.[44]

3. Main Offences

3.1. Abuse of Company Assets (*abus de biens sociaux*)

The provisions for the two types of limited company, public limited companies (SA)[45] and limited liability companies (SARL),[46] are analogous and differ only as to the description of the perpetrator according to the functions foreseen for each type of company.[47] All other elements of the offence are identical. The descriptions of the offence of abuse of company assets or credit (Commercial Code, arts L241-3 4° and L242-6 3°) and of the abuse of powers and votes (arts L241-3 5° and L242-6 4°) have exactly the same elements with the only exception being the object of the offence. Therefore, the analysis of these elements will proceed in the following order. The first section will present different categories of functions which fall into the scope of the offence, delimiting the circle of potential perpetrators (3.1.1 below). The second section will analyse the four objects of the abuse and the relationship between them (3.1.2 below). It will be followed by an examination of the description of the course of conduct (3.1.3 below) and of the two different requirements of *mens rea* (3.1.4 below).

[43] Jean Larguier and Philippe Conte, *Droit pénal des affaires*, 11th edn (Armand Colin, 2004) 170 et seq.

[44] Jeandidier, *Abus de confiance* (n 2) para 67.

[45] Commercial Code, art L242-6: 'The following shall be punished by a prison sentence of 5 years and a fine of 375,000 euros: … 3° If the chairman, directors or managing directors of a public limited company use the company assets or credit, in bad faith, in a way which they know to be contrary to the interests of the company, for personal purposes or in order to benefit another company or undertaking in which they are directly or indirectly involved; 4° If the chairman, directors or managing directors of a public limited company use the powers which they possess or the votes which they have in this capacity, in bad faith, in a way which they know to be contrary to the interests of the company, for personal purposes or in order to benefit another company or undertaking in which they are directly or indirectly involved.'

[46] Commercial Code, art L241-3: 'The following shall be punished by a prison sentence of 5 years and a fine of 375,000 euros: … 4° If managers use the company assets or credit, in bad faith, in a way which they know to be contrary to the interests of the company, for personal purposes or in order to benefit another company or undertaking in which they are directly or indirectly involved; 5° If managers use the powers which they possess or the votes which they have in this capacity, in bad faith, in a way which they know to be contrary to the interests of the company, for personal purposes or to encourage another'.

[47] All the translations of legal acts in this chapter use the translation published on the official website run by the French government, http://legifrance.gouv.fr/, which makes available French legal acts as well as provides translations of some of them. However, in case of the Commercial Code, the translation

3.1.1. Manager as Perpetrator

The range of possible perpetrators of the abuse of company assets is relatively restricted and comprises only persons enumerated in the provisions providing for this liability. Instead of an abstract definition, the French model opted for a precise definition of the circle of possible perpetrators, extended, however, by the inclusion of persons who exercise the functions de facto.[48] This latter category will add an element of imprecision to an otherwise very strictly designed law, since it will be subject to case by case evaluation in order to verify whether the defendant fulfilled the criteria to qualify as a de facto manager.[49]

In all companies, only the top management can be held liable as principal offender and within some companies even supervisory bodies are excluded from the scope of the offence. No other senior or junior manager can be held liable, unless it can be proved that he de facto exercised one of the functions enumerated below. However, this circle may be extended by means of the rules on complicity, since for this form of liability French criminal law does not require the fulfilment of the requirement describing the perpetrator's position.[50] Senior and junior managers may thus be punished as secondary participants in the abuse of company assets, provided that the conditions of liability for complicity are fulfilled.[51]

Within the SARL, the liability is limited to managers (*gérants*) (article L241-3 4° and 5°). The SA can be managed according to two models: the traditional French single-board model and the dual-board model. If the company is managed according to the classic system, criminal liability for abuse of company assets is provided for the chairman (*le président*), the directors (*les administrateurs*) and the managing directors (*les directeurs généraux*) (article L242-6 3° and 4°), together

has been corrected where it seemed necessary. The French original of the law is also taken from that website.

[48] Rebut, *Abus de biens sociaux* (n 12) para 200.

[49] For the SARL, Commercial Code, art L241-9 extends criminal liability for abuse of company assets to 'any person who, either directly or indirectly, has in reality managed a limited liability company on behalf of, or in the place of, its legal manager'. An analogous provision extends criminal liability within the SA, SCA and European company. By virtue of art L246-2, provisions on the criminal liability of the chairman, the directors or the managing directors of public limited companies or European companies and the managers of partnerships limited by shares are also applicable to 'any person who, directly or through an intermediary, has effectively managed, administered or run such a company through or on behalf of its legal representatives'. Article L242-30 extends the scope of this extension to those who would de facto exercise the functions of a member of the executive board or of the supervisory board in a company managed according to the dual-board system. The same rule applies to a de facto chairman or director of a SAS (art L244-4). In sum, by force of all these provisions, criminal liability is extended to persons exercising de facto all the functions described in the previous sections. For an analysis of criteria according to which a person is considered a de facto manager, see Joly and Joly-Baumgartner, *L'abus de biens sociaux* (n 21) 230; Médina, *Abus de biens sociaux* (n 7) 197 et seq. See also Lepage et al, *Droit pénal des affaires* (n 13) 333 et seq.

[50] Mirelle Delmas-Marty and Geneviève Giudicelli-Delage (eds), *Droit pénal des affaires*, 4th edn (Paris: Pr Université de France, 2000) 341; Rebut, *Abus de biens sociaux* (n 12) para 216 et seq.

[51] See section 5 below.

with their deputies (article L248-1). In a company structured according to the dual-board system, members of the executive board (*directoire*) and members of the supervisory board (*conseil de surveillance*) may incur criminal liability (article L242-30).

As to other types of companies, in a partnership limited by shares (*société en commandite par actions*) criminal liability for abuse of company assets is limited to the managers (*gérants*) (article L243-1), and in a simplified joint-stock company (*société par actions simplifiée*) to the chairmen (*president*) and directors (*dirigeants*) (article L244-1). In a European Company (*société européenne*), the scope of liability is the same as in the SA and concerns the chairman, directors, managing directors and their deputies, members of the executive board or members of the supervisory board (article L244-5).

Liability for the abuse of company assets is also provided for the liquidators (*liquidateurs*) by an analogous version of the offence foreseen by article L247-8, although limited to the abuse of assets or credit. Interestingly, this offence is applicable to entities whose managers are not subject to criminal liability for that offence, ie general partnerships (*sociétés en nom collectif*) and partnerships limited by shares (*sociétés en commandite simple*), which is supposedly explained by the fact that, in contrast with the latter, the liquidator does not bear unlimited liability for the losses of these companies.[52]

Since the other elements of the offence apply in the same way to all potential perpetrators, in order to avoid cumbersome enumerations, in the sections that will follow this subchapter, the word 'manager' will be used while referring to all persons who can be held liable for the offence of abuse of company assets, unless it is specified that it refers specifically to the function of a *gérant*.

3.1.2. Object of the Abuse

According to the definitions provided by article L241-3 4° and 5° and its equivalents, the abuse may have one of four objects, which are divided into two groups, resulting in four possible modalities of its commission. The first group (L241-3 4°) consists of abuse of company assets or credit, while the second group (L241-3 5°) consists of the abuse of the manager's powers and voting rights. These terms overlap to a considerable extent, and the interpretation given to them by the French jurisprudence does not attempt to delimit the scope of each category.[53]

The expression *bien social* or *biens sociaux* (company asset(s)) is understood as broadly as possible.[54] It comprises any kind of property, financial assets, chattels or real estate.[55] It includes also intellectual property (eg rights of authorship, patents,

[52] Stasiak, *Droit pénal des affaires* (n 5) 239; Rebut, *Abus de biens sociaux* (n 12) para 213.

[53] Médina, *Abus de biens sociaux* (n 7) 52.

[54] Jeandidier, *Abus des biens* (n 3) para 11.

[55] Stasiak, *Droit pénal des affaires* (n 5) p. 241. The extensiveness of this list makes the scope of the offence of abuse of company assets much broader than the range of property offences such as theft (*vol*),

trademarks, etc).[56] It is considered that into this category also fall different rights (*droits*),[57] claims (*créances*),[58] orders (*commandes*)[59] or lists of clients (*clientèle*).[60] However, it has not yet been clarified whether assets resulting from a criminal offence would always be considered a possible object of abuse, but at least one judgment goes in this direction.[61]

The notion of credit (*crédit*) refers to the good reputation of the company as a viable business partner, which normally translates into its ability to get loans or to become guarantor of others' debts. Therefore it can include the moral reputation of the company as well as its financial standing.[62] The classic example given to explain this kind of abuse is when the company becomes a guarantor of the director's personal debt, thus diminishing its capacity to take more loans[63] and running unnecessary risk that it will have to pay the director's debt, if he is not able to do that.[64] This modality also includes situations in which the defendant issues documents in the name of the company which oblige the company to pay at a later date, eg by signing a bill of exchange.[65]

The abuse of company credit is limited to its financial consequences. This offence does not punish cases where damage done to the company concerns only its reputation, if this does not in any way affect the assets of the company.[66] Therefore, a comfort letter (*lettre de confort*) issued by the company (and signed by the defendant in the name of the company) in favour of another person, for instance the defendant in his private capacity, and providing assurances as to that person's credibility, would not constitute the offence of abuse of company credit, since it does not create legal obligations for the company. In such cases, however, the commission of abuse of powers might be considered.[67]

The term 'powers' in the context of the offence of abuse of powers by managers can be understood in two different ways. The first theory considers that it refers to the powers of a shareholder, in case the manager is himself a shareholder of the company. This interpretation would be explained mainly by the legislative technique differentiating between the first pair of modalities, abuse of company assets and credit, which can be committed by managers in the execution of their

fraud (*escroquerie*) or breach of trust, which are excluded for instance with respect to real property. See also Delmas-Marty and Giudicelli-Delage, *Droit pénal des affaires* (n 50) 342.

[56] Jeandidier, *Abus des biens* (n 3) para 12, Cass crim, 14 November 1973, Bull crim, no 415, 102.

[57] Rebut, *Abus de biens sociaux* (n 12) para 115.

[58] Joly abd Joly-Baumgartner, *L'abus de biens sociaux* (n 21) 68; Cass crim, 15 March 1972, Bull crim, no 107, 260.

[59] Joly and Joly-Baumgartner, *L'abus de biens sociaux* (n 21) 68.

[60] Jeandidier, *Abus des biens* (n 3) para 12; Cass crim, 6 May 2009, No de pourvoi: 08-86378.

[61] Jeandidier, *Abus des biens* (n 3) para 12; Cass crim, 3 October 2007, No de pourvoi: 07-81603.

[62] Rebut, *Abus de biens sociaux* (n 12) para 117.

[63] Joly and Joly-Baumgartner, *L'abus de biens sociaux* (n 21) 72.

[64] Rebut, *Abus de biens sociaux* (n 12) para 117.

[65] Cass crim, 10 November 1964, Bull crim, no 291.

[66] Médina, *Abus de biens sociaux* (n 7) 45 et seq.

[67] Ibid 47.

functions, and the second pair, abuse of powers and votes, which the managers can commit, if they influence the general meeting to take a decision, which is against the interests of the company.[68] According to this theory, the offence of abuse of powers, together with the abuse of votes, incriminates managers' behaviour during assemblies or shareholders' meetings, if it is contrary to company interests.[69] This theory and thus also such a strict differentiation between the two pairs of modalities have been generally rejected by both literature and jurisprudence.[70]

The second theory, which won prevalence among both the doctrine and the jurisprudence, understands under the term 'powers' all of the rights to act that the law or the articles of association confer on the manager.[71] This already large interpretation tends to be extended furthermore by the jurisprudence, including also the rights effectively exercised by managers and not only granted by the two mentioned sources.[72] This does not mean nevertheless that the offence may extend without limit. For instance, one court acquitted a manager who, in his personal capacity, asked certain shareholders to manifest their confidence in him, by giving him the right to vote in their place as proxy, while at the same time informing them about their freedom to turn down his request.[73] However, the court decided differently in a case where it found that the powers were correlated with the authority linked to the function of the manager, the authority and influence linked with it that the manager abused.[74] In this case, the court sentenced the defendant for having organised a disadvantageous acquisition of his company by another one, although it was outside the scope of his competences to decide upon it and the decision was taken by the competent body.[75]

The last of the objects of the abuse is denominated in the French original as '*voix*', which can mean vote or votes. This term refers to the shareholders' right to vote, and thus in turn to situations in which shareholders have transferred their right to vote to the managers who become their proxies and cast the vote on their behalf, in particular if it is a blank proxy. The managers may be held liable for this type of offence, if they use this right to vote in a way which is detrimental to the company.[76] The practical application of this modality is currently very

[68] Joly and Joly-Baumgartner, *L'abus de biens sociaux* (n 21) 76.

[69] Iouda Tchernoff, *Traité de droit pénal financier* (Dalloz, 1937) no 68, cited after Jeandidier, *Abus des biens* (n 3) para 14.

[70] Jeandidier, *Abus des biens* (n 3) para 14; Rebut, *Abus de biens sociaux* (n 12) para 121; Joly and Joly-Baumgartner, *L'abus de biens sociaux* (n 21) 77.

[71] Lepage et al, *Droit pénal des affaires* (n 13) 325; Jeandidier, *Abus des biens* (n 3) para 15; Rebut, *Abus de biens sociaux* (n 12) para 121.

[72] Joly and Joly-Baumgartner, *L'abus de biens sociaux* (n 21) 76 et seq.

[73] Delmas-Marty and Giudicelli-Delage, *Droit pénal des affaires* (n 50) 352; Cass crim, 27 February 1978, Bull crim, no 76, 192.

[74] Rebut, *Abus de biens sociaux* (n 12) para 20; Lucas de Leyssac and Mihman, *Droit pénal des affaires* (n 28) 197.

[75] Cass crim, 10 July 1995, Bull crim, no 253, 703.

[76] Rebut, *Abus de biens sociaux* (n 12) para 126.

limited due to the fact that, since the enactment of this offence, various limitations to the possibility of giving a blank proxy have been introduced.[77] Therefore this variation remains unused in practice and will not be analysed hereinafter. In any case, it can be argued that any abuse of vote, whether exercised in the defendant's own capacity or as a proxy of a shareholder, could be considered as an abuse of power.[78]

3.1.3. *Abuse*

In order to describe the course of conduct of the abuse of company assets, it is necessary to analyse its two aspects: a use of one of the four objects described above, which is contrary to the company's interests.

(i) Use

As far as the quantity of cases is concerned, the first variation of the offence, which consists in abusing the assets of the company, outnumbers the other three modalities. Moreover, not only is there no consistency in the delimitation between the modalities, as was mentioned above, but the courts sometimes combine them in one judgment, without necessarily explaining the reasons for doing so. Since the abuse of company assets (*sensu stricto*) and the abuse of company credit are in the same section of their respective articles (L241-3 4° and L242-6 3°), some judgments refer to both of them.[79] The problem does not concern the second pair, the abuse of powers and the abuse of votes (L241-3 5° and L242-6 4°), because its second element has in practice fallen into disuse. In view of the same rules of procedure and of the same punishment foreseen for all the variations, together with a commonly understood wrongdoing behind criminalisation, the perils of infringement of the defendant's rights are rather limited.[80] Taking into account the design of the offence, the focal points deciding upon the manager's liability are the requirement that his act be contrary to the company's interests and that the manager acted in his personal interest.

Although the verb used in the definition of the offence, 'usage', suggests that only active behaviour of the defendant can fulfil this limb,[81] the French jurisprudence admitted the possibility of commission of the offence also by omission.[82]

[77] Joly and Joly-Baumgartner, *L'abus de biens sociaux* (n 21) 87.

[78] Jeandidier, *Abus des biens* (n 3) para 22; Lepage et al, *Droit pénal des affaires* (n 13) 326; Joly and Joly-Baumgartner, *L'abus de biens sociaux* (n 21) 87.

[79] Joly and Joly-Baumgartner, *L'abus de biens sociaux* (n 21) 66 et seq.

[80] Ibid 65.

[81] Stasiak, *Droit pénal des affaires* (n 5) 240 et seq.

[82] Cass crim, 28 January 2004, No de pourvoi: 02-88094; Cass crim, 23 March 2005, No de pourvoi: 04-84756.

An example of such a situation would be where the defendant failed to terminate a contract, which is contrary to the interests of the company (causing losses to the company or exposing it to the risk of loss).[83] In another case, the court convicted a manager of a SARL for not having reduced his remuneration, while the company was generating losses.[84] It is considered to be a case of use of powers not to pursue a claim for a debt which another person owes to the company, which would translate into an abuse of power if the *mens rea* requirements were also fulfilled.[85] The number of cases in which the manager's wrongdoing consisted merely in an omission is very limited.[86]

The literature tends to be critical on extending the understanding of the word 'usage' to inaction.[87] However, authors are inclined to accept the application of the abuse of company assets to cases of omission, taking into account two considerations. First, if the manager is accused of abuse of powers, one can claim that by not using his powers (eg to claim a debt in the name of the company) he in fact wrongly uses these powers. Secondly, by deliberately not terminating a situation which is detrimental for the company, the perpetrator's conduct in fact amounts to what the French literature calls 'omission in acting' (*omission dans l'action*) and accepts as use.[88] A manager who does not prevent another manager from committing the abuse of company assets might also be punished as an accomplice, if the conditions of this modality are fulfilled.[89]

It is a general rule that the offence is considered to be committed at the moment of use.[90] It is also from that point, the moment of use, which will be decisive for evaluating whether the act was contrary to the company's interests. The approach differs in cases where the use (and abuse) starts at a certain point of time (in the moment of the decision or later) and then lasts in time. The jurisprudence, for instance, considers not pursuing a claim for a debt to be a continuous offence.[91] This issue becomes pertinent in view of three different problems: complicity, handling stolen goods (*recel*), and rules on time limitation of prosecution (*prescription*).[92]

The offence of abuse of company assets does not require proof of a certain result, but is focused on the perpetrator's conduct. This conduct is defined by its

[83] Cass crim, 31 October 2000, No de pourvoi: 00-80.824 (assets).

[84] Cour d'Appel Angers, 17 January 1991, Dr pénal 1991, Comm 241, cited by Rebut, *Abus de biens sociaux* (n 12) 69.

[85] Cass crim, 15 March 1972, Bull crim, no 107, 260.

[86] Wilfrid Jeandidier, 'L'Elément matériel des infractions d'affaires où la prédilection pour l'inconsistance' in *Mélange offerts à Raymond Gassin* (Aix-Marseille: Presses Universitaires d'Aix-Marseille, 2007) 245–63, 253.

[87] Jeandidier, *Abus des biens* (n 3) para 25.

[88] Lucas de Leyssac and Mihman, *Droit pénal des affaires* (n 28) 194–95.

[89] See 5 below.

[90] Joly and Joly-Baumgartner, *L'abus de biens sociaux* (n 21) 61.

[91] Cass crim, 15 March 1972, Bull crim, no 107, 260.

[92] Joly and Joly-Baumgartner, *L'abus de biens sociaux* (n 21) 61 et seq. It is in particular the problem of time limitation of prosecution that has resulted in intensive debate.

possible consequences, which are contrary to the interests of the company, and not by the real consequences of the act. Therefore, as far as the liability of the principal is concerned, the offence is already committed at the moment of the abuse, and later occurrences remain without influence.[93] In particular, it has been confirmed by jurisprudence on numerous occasions that restitution or compensation has no impact on the assessment of whether the offence was committed or not.[94]

To use (*faire un usage*) the company's assets means to perform any act affecting these assets.[95] This term certainly comprises the acts of misappropriation, which are of less relevance here. What is more important, it comprises also other acts of management (*actes de gestion*), which can be divided into two categories. The first contains acts, called *actes de disposition*, which affect the assets by a legal act (eg a contract), ie burden them with an obligation (*engager*) or transform them (*transformer*), for example through sale, donation, bequest and constitution of a guarantee. The second group of acts, named *actes d'administration*, comprise any other acts of assets management, eg physically using, maintaining, storing, etc.[96]

The use of credit is generally performed by a legal act, in particular by signing in the name of the company a contract, which affects the company's financial credibility. This will be the case, for example, when the manager signs in the name of the company a contract granting a loan, under conditions which are unfavourable for the company. Such a loan could be granted to the company director or to another person mentioned as potential perpetrator, or also to any other person not targeted by the offence, to whom one of the persons targeted by the offence decides to grant such a loan.[97] The president of the board of directors of an SA was convicted in such a case for having granted in the name of the company a loan to another company in which he was the major shareholder. This loan was approved despite the fact that the company granting it was in financial difficulties and the president was aware of that.[98]

Among the available modalities of the offence, the abuse of powers is the one that causes the most conceptual problems. The difficulties with the understanding of the term 'powers', described in the previous section, extend also to the interpretation of the use of powers. The case law concerning this modality is limited and rather dated.[99] It is, however, possible to point out certain types of acts which the jurisprudence considered to be (ab)use of powers.

[93] Joly and Joly-Baumgartner, *L'abus de biens sociaux* (n 21) 64 et seq.

[94] See, eg Cass crim,16 December 1975, Bull crim, no 279, 735. For further examples, see Joly and Joly-Baumgartner, *L'abus de biens sociaux* (n 21) 64 et seq.

[95] Lepage et al, *Droit pénal des affaires* (n 13) 320.

[96] Joly and Joly-Baumgartner, *L'abus de biens sociaux* (n 21) 57; Jacques-Henri Robert and Haritini Matsopoulou, *Traité de droit pénal des affaires* (Presses Universitaires de France, 2004) 474.

[97] Médina, *Abus de biens sociaux* (n 7) 53.

[98] Ibid 53.

[99] Joly and Joly-Baumgartner, *L'abus de biens sociaux* (n 21) 76 et seq.

The first group of cases comprises situations in which managers signed contracts or took decisions, which were disadvantageous for the company.[100] The fact that this contract is disadvantageous may be related not only to an actual loss that the company will suffer, but also with unnecessarily high exposure to a risk of loss.[101] Some of these cases resemble the abuse of assets (*sensu stricto*), in others the use of assets will be less evident. For instance, a manager was convicted for abuse of powers for having terminated an employee's employment contract in such a way that it exposed the company to judicial procedures.[102]

Another category comprises cases in which the manager omitted to claim repayment of debt, which another person, company or entity owed to the company.[103] Yet again, it could be debated whether this would not also constitute an abuse of assets. In any case, it is less likely that the problem of exposure to excessive risk will occur in this scenario.[104] Another type of situation in which the court convicted for abuse of powers was a take-over of the company organised by its manager, where since the company disappeared it was impossible to claim that it suffered any loss.[105]

A further category of abuse of powers, the common denominator of which could be described as disloyal conduct of managers,[106] is exemplified by a case in which the manager convinced some clients of his bank to withdraw their money from the bank and entrust it to him for further investment. It this case, the court based its judgment (unfortunately without giving further details) on the existence of the risk, which consisted in the fact that were these investments to end in failure, the bank could be held financially liable for the failure vis-à-vis the clients and could also incur sanctions from the banking supervisory authorities.[107] That it is possible to consider this case as an example of abuse of company credit is yet another illustration of the overlap between the available modalities.[108] Similar remarks apply to another judgment in which the court convicted a manager for having transferred to the company an obligation to guarantee debts.[109]

In view of these overlaps and the lack of a precise definition of the abuse of powers, the doctrine encounters difficulties in authoritatively establishing the

[100] Cass crim, 8 January 1990, No de pourvoi: 88-84.675; Cass crim, 15 January 1990, No de pourvoi: 89-80.345; Joly and Joly-Baumgartner, *L'abus de biens sociaux* (n 21) 77.

[101] Cass crim,16 January 1989, Bull crim, no 17, 45.

[102] Cass crim, 30 January 2001, No de pourvoi: 00-84.414.

[103] Joly and Joly-Baumgartner, *L'abus de biens sociaux* (n 21) 81 et seq, eg Cass crim, 15 March 1972, Bull crim, no. 107, 260; Cass crim, 5 January 1989, No de pourvoi: 88-81.217.

[104] See, eg Jeandidier, *Abus des biens* (n 3) para 19; Joly and Joly-Baumgartner, *L'abus de biens sociaux* (n 21) 81.

[105] Robert and Matsopoulou, *Traité de droit pénal des affaires* (n 96) 474; Cass crim, 10 July 1995, Bull crim, no 253, 703.

[106] Joly and Joly-Baumgartner, *L'abus de biens sociaux* (n. 21) 79.

[107] Cass crim, 19 November 1979, Bull crim, no 325, 887.

[108] Joly and Joly-Baumgartner, *L'abus de biens sociaux* (n 21) 80.

[109] Cour d'Appel Grenoble, 25 February 1998, Gaz Pal 17–19 October 1999, Somm 46, cited by Joly and Joly-Baumgartner, *L'abus de biens sociaux* (n 21) 83.

relationship between this and other modalities. In order to solve this problem, different proposals have been formulated. According to the first one, abuse of powers would constitute the broadest modality comprising any kind of decision, while the abuse of assets and credit would constitute special cases of abuse of powers. Another solution would see in the abuse of powers a preliminary step to commit a further offence of abuse of assets or credit, since while committing the abuse of powers or votes, the manager is using the powers conferred on him.[110] The shortcoming of these solutions is that they would render the existence of some modalities obsolete.[111] One of the proposals formulated in the literature has suggested granting abuse of powers an autonomous function among the modalities, which would be applicable in the three following types of situation:

- when the impact on the assets of the company is indirect and thus difficult to quantify (eg organisation of disadvantageous acquisition of the company);
- when the manager infringes the internal rules of the company (eg by granting a loan against such rules);
- when the manager's conduct consisted in omission (eg not claiming debt owed by another person to the company[112]).[113]

An issue, which is usually linked with the course of conduct and its termination, is how to determine the beginning of the limitation period for prosecution. In the context of the abuse of company assets, the jurisprudence regarding this problem inspired an intensive debate in the French doctrine, although it has been tackled rather pragmatically than dogmatically. This period is of three years[114] and it might prove to be too short in various cases, if the abuse does not come to light.[115] The reason for the importance of this problem in the context of the offence of abuse of company assets is that, in many cases, the manager – the perpetrator of the offence – is in a stronger position than the shareholders. He is, for instance, in a position to influence the flow of information within the company and hide the details of the abuse.[116] Moreover, if the company prospers, the shareholders may have a tendency not to monitor the management very meticulously, while managers may not allow information on misconduct to leave their circle. It is therefore much more likely that the abuse of company assets will come to

[110] Jeandidier, *Abus des biens* (n 3) para 21.

[111] Joly and Joly-Baumgartner, *L'abus de biens sociaux* (n 21) 84 et seq.

[112] However, the Court of Cassation sentenced the perpetrator for abuse of company assets and not abuse of powers in the following case: Cass crim, 18 December 1997, No de pourvoi: 96-85657.

[113] Joly and Joly-Baumgartner, *L'abus de biens sociaux* (n 21) 85.

[114] Code of Criminal Procedure, art 8 para 1.

[115] Michel Dobkine, 'Réflexions itératives à propos de l'abus de biens sociaux' (1997) 37 *Recueil Dalloz* 323, 324 et seq.

[116] Jean-François Renucci and Houria Mehdi, 'L'Actualité de l'abus de biens sociaux' (2002) 1 *Revue Pénitentiaire et de Droit Pénal* (April) 27, 28.

light in the case of internal conflicts within the management or involving employees having relevant information, or if the company begins to have financial difficulties. All these situations may occur well after the facts in question.[117] Consideration of this problem resulted in the application of the rules, which were developed by the jurisprudence on breach of trust,[118] postponing the initial moment from which the beginning of the limitation period starts running until the moment when the abuse is discovered.[119] The application of this principle is limited by the rule that, if there was no concealment or covering up of the act (*dissimulation*), the limitation period starts running from the moment of the presentation of the yearly financial statement (*comptes annuels*), which concerns the assets in question.[120] In case of concealment, which could occur if the manager provides no or insufficient information or if the information is wrong or misleading, the limitation period starts running when the abuse is discovered by the prosecutors or by the shareholders.[121] Its discovery by other persons alone is not enough to start the period running.[122] These rules have been subject to criticism for extending the limitation period so much that, as highlighted by one author, it is doubtful whether the abuse of company assets is subject to the limitation of prosecution at all.[123]

(ii) Contrary to the Interests of the Company

In order for the use of assets, credit, powers or votes by the manager to become an abuse, it must be qualified as contrary to the interests of the company (*contraire à l'intérêt de la société*). The provisions criminalising the abuse provide for this requirement with a formulation suggesting that it is a *mens rea* requirement ('in a way which they know to be contrary to the interests of the company'). However, it is considered that the use must be contrary to such interests not only in the perception of the manager, but also must actually be so in fact.

The analysis of this limb will proceed in two steps: first, by examining what is understood by the expression 'the interests of the company', and secondly, by analysing when the use is considered to be contrary to such interests.

Three competing theories explain the expression 'interests of the company' in the French literature. The first, called contractual theory (*théorie*

[117] Lucas de Leyssac and Mihman, *Droit pénal des affaires* (n 28) 115.

[118] Philippe Conte, Chantal Giraud-van Gaver, Jacques-Henri Robert and Jean-Christophe Saint-Pau, *Le risque pénal dans l'entreprise* (Paris: Litec, 2003) 4.

[119] Rebut, *Abus de biens sociaux* (n 12) para 230 et seq.

[120] Cass crim, 27 June 2001, Bull crim no 164, 541.

[121] Rebut, *Abus de biens sociaux* (n 12) para 238 et seq.

[122] Ibid para 236.

[123] Claude Cohen, 'L'abus de biens sociaux, délit imprescriptible?' (2002) *Gazette du Palais* (September/October) 1300. A suggestion, so far not accepted, was formulated to provide for a final limit at which the prosecution of the offence would be barred in any kind of circumstances: Groupe de travail présidé par Jean-Marie Coulon, *La dépénalisation de la vie des affaires*, (n 14) 97 et seq. See also Jean-François Renucci, 'Infractions d'affaires et prescription de l'action publique' (1997) *Recueil Dalloz* 23 et seq.

contractuelle), considers that the only reason for the existence of a company is the satisfaction of the interests and goals of its shareholders, thus the interests of the company are assimilated with the interests of the shareholders.[124] Following this theory, it would be in the interests of the shareholders, at least in the short term, to use the company funds to cause the price of the stock to rise, although it may not necessarily be in the best interests of the company as such.[125]

A rival theory, called institutional theory (*théorie institutionnelle*), perceives the company as:

> an autonomic economic agent, pursuing its own goals, which are distinct from those of its shareholders, employees, creditors, tax authorities, suppliers or clients, but which correspond to the general interest of all those actors, which is to assure the well-being and continuous functioning of the company.[126]

An intermediate third theory takes into account the interests of the shareholders, in particular their interest in making profit from their investment, while at the same time stressing the own interests of the company, especially its long-term survival and well-being.[127]

The French jurisprudence on abuse of company assets demonstrates a clear inclination towards the second and the third interpretations. In one of its judgments, the Court of Cassation rejected the first interpretation, saying: 'The abuses of company assets prejudice not only the interests of shareholders, but also those of the third parties who contract with it'.[128] It is claimed that this interpretation can be justified, inter alia, by the choice of the legislator not to use the expression 'interest of shareholder' or 'company's stated business objectives' (*objet social*).[129] The consequence of adopting this line of interpretation can be seen in the application of the offence of abuse of company property to companies owned by one person, who fulfils the function of its manager, to companies run as family businesses or in cases in which consent to the abuse committed by the manager was granted by the shareholders (see also 6.1 below).[130] An inclination towards the

[124] Joly and Joly-Baumgartner, *L'abus de biens sociaux* (n 21) 90.

[125] Larguier and Conte, *Droit pénal des affaires* (n 43) 342.

[126] Conseil National du Patronat Français (CNPF) and Association Française des Entreprises Privées (AFEP), *Le conseil d'administration des sociétés cotées* (July 1995) 8 (Rapport Viénot), available at www.ecgi.org/codes/documents/vienot1_fr.pdf.

[127] Gilles Mathieu, 'L'acte contraire à l'intérêt social en matière d'abus de biens sociaux' (2002) *Gazette du Palais* (July/August) 1045, 1046.

[128] 'Les abus de biens sociaux portent atteinte non seulement aux intérêts des associes, mais aussi à ceux des tiers qui contractent avec elle': Cass crim, 26 May 1994, Bull crim, no 206, 482. For an extensive list of judgments in this line, see Joly and Joly-Baumgartner, *L'abus de biens sociaux* (n 21) 93.

[129] Rebut, *Abus de biens sociaux* (n 12) para 33, in this respect see also Médina, *Abus de biens sociaux* (n 7) 81 et seq.

[130] Joly and Joly-Baumgartner, *L'abus de biens sociaux* (n 21) 93 et seq.

third theory, rather than the second, could be deduced from the courts' reluctance to grant the right to bring civil actions for damages within the criminal procedure to the shareholders, employees or other parties.[131]

The use is contrary to the interests of the company if it is done without adequate compensation, ie if it will generate loss, or expose the company to an abnormal risk, that is to a risk to which the company should not be exposed.[132] Hence, what is crucial for the cases examined in this book, a manager can be held criminally liable even if the company does not suffer a loss, but is exposed to an abnormal risk.[133]

Although the above definition suggests that it is the result of the act that determines its qualification as contrary to the company's interests (ie a loss or a situation of being exposed to excessive risk), this offence does not require proof of result.[134] The fact that the result already occurred might make proof of this limb easier. However, the judge should not focus on the consequences, but he will have to make an abstract evaluation of the act determining whether at the moment of its commission (eg at the moment the decision was taken or the contract concluded), it was contrary to the company's interests.[135] This rule has important consequences determining the scope of liability for this offence. First, the fact that the act turned out eventually to be profitable for the company does not preclude liability, if it can be established that at the moment when it was committed, it exposed the company to an abnormal risk of loss.[136] Secondly, the fact that the act turned out to be less advantageous than could have been expected at the moment when it was undertaken, and in fact exposed the company to an abnormal risk or even eventually caused loss, does not in and of itself render the act contrary to the company's interests in terms of this offence.[137] This rule corresponds with the philosophy of this offence, which excludes the possibility that it is used to judge the ability of the management to take good decisions and to make the company prosper, but should be applied to punish managers who knowingly take decisions against the company's interests.[138]

As to the abuse of powers, it is important to stress that a breach of duty is not necessary to qualify the use as contrary to the company's interests. It is possible that the manager breaches some of his duties, eg granting a loan against the

[131] Stasiak, *Droit pénal des affaires* (n 5) 243, eg Cass crim, 28 January 2004, No de pourvoi: 03-81345; Cass crim, 9 March 2005, No de pourvoi: 04-85.825; Cass crim, 23 February 2005, No de pourvoi: 04-83.768; Cass crim, 23 February 2005, Node pourvoi: 04-83.792.

[132] Rebut, *Abus de biens sociaux* (n 12) para 38. See also the classification proposed in Lucas de Leyssac and Mihman, *Droit pénal des affaires* (n 28) 199–209.

[133] Joly and Joly-Baumgartner, *L'abus de biens sociaux* (n 21) 86.

[134] Cass crim, 8 December 1971, Bull crim no 346, 869.

[135] Cass crim, 2 December 1991, No de pourvoi: 90-87563.

[136] Rebut, *Abus de biens sociaux* (n 12) para 64; Cass crim, 16 January 1989, Bull crim, no 17, 45.

[137] Joly and Joly-Baumgartner, *L'abus de biens sociaux* (n 21) 101.

[138] Robert and Matsopoulou, *Traité de droit pénal des affaires* (n 96) 477; Stasiak, *Droit pénal des affaires* (n 5) 242; Cass crim, 27 October 1997, Bull crim, no 352, 1169 (so-called *Carignon* affaire).

rules of the bank,[139] but liability under this provision can also result from a use which remains within the boundaries of the manager's powers, eg by signing a contract, which the manager was allowed to sign, but the conditions of which were against the interests of the company.[140] Instead of analysing the breach of rules, the court will have to analyse, as in the context of other modalities, whether the use of powers was of such a nature as to expose the company to an abnormal risk of loss or whether such loss was certain.[141] Consequently, if in spite of a breach of the rules (statutory or internal) the company was not exposed to risk of loss, criminal liability for the abuse would be excluded. This problem has arisen, inter alia, in cases concerning managers' remuneration. It has been argued that the judges ought not to base their judgment on procedural shortcomings related to granting the remuneration, but that the emphasis should be placed on the question of the company's expectation to be compensated sufficiently by the manager's work.[142] Moreover, the judges need not evaluate the exact adequacy of remuneration to the work of a manager, which would constitute an excessive intrusion into the life of corporations, but should limit their intervention to the most serious cases of abuse, such as in the judgment concerning a former manager who was receiving remuneration without performing any service at all for the company.[143]

Whilst use may be considered contrary to the company's interests due to the certitude that it will lead to a loss, what is important for the liability analysed in this book is that the mere risk of such loss is enough. In order to qualify the act as detrimental, the French jurisprudence and doctrine consider that the company should be exposed to an abnormal risk (*risque anormal*), in other words to a risk to which it should not be exposed (*risque auquel il ne devrait pas être exposé*).[144] This expression, which is left for the consideration of the judges in concrete cases, should exclude from the scope of the offence those situations in which the company is exposed to the risk, which are inherent to the market or type of transaction in question.[145] The expression has not been defined by the

[139] Cass crim, 3 May 1967, Bull crim, no 148.

[140] Cass crim, 8 January 1990, No de pourvoi: 88-84675; Cass crim, 15 January 1990, No de pourvoi: 89-80345. In the latter case, the manager did not submit the contract to the executive board, however the abuse of powers resulted from detrimental conditions of the contract, under the terms of which the company was obliged to remunerate an employee for eight years even if the company decided to dispense with the services of this employee.

[141] Joly and Joly-Baumgartner, *L'abus de biens sociaux* (n 21) 86.

[142] Rebut, *Abus de biens sociaux* (n 12) para 50.

[143] Ibid para 49; Cass crim, 28 March 1996, Bull crim, no 142, 407.

[144] Cass crim, 16 January 1964, Bull crim 1964 no 16, 27 (abuse of company assets); Cass crim, 10 November 1964, Crim, no 291 (abuse of credit); Cass crim, 3 May 1967, Bull crim no 148, 350 (abuse of assets, credit and powers); Cass crim, 7 March 1968, Bull crim no 80, 189 (abuse of powers and abuse of assets in case of a cooperative); Cass crim, 24 March 1969, Bull crim no 130, 319 (abuse of assets); Cass crim, 16 March 1970, Bull crim no 107, 245 (abuse of credit); Cass crim, 16 December 1975, Bull crim no 279, 735 (abuse of company assets); Cass crim, 19 November 1979, Bull crim no 325, 887 (abuse of powers); Cass crim, 16 January 1989, Bull crim no 17, 45 (abuse of powers); Joly and Joly-Baumgartner, *L'abus de biens sociaux* (n 21) 98.

[145] Cass crim, 16 January 1989, Bull crim no 17, 45.

jurisprudence. According to one author, the risk can be classified as abnormal when it is 'obviously disproportionate or unnecessary' in relation to the expected advantage.[146]

In this context, the modality of the abuse of company assets (*sensu stricto*) or of the abuse of powers occurs when the act of the manager concerning these assets exposes them to an abnormal risk.[147] This would take place where a manager used the company assets in some way for which the compensation is linked with exposure to abnormal risk. This would be the case if a manager borrows money from the company, or even keeps borrowing on a regular basis, which may lead to confusion between the company assets and those of the manager. Such a practice, even if the manager is the main or only shareholder, is considered to be contrary to the interests of the company if the company does not receive adequate compensation. This applies in particular to cases where no interest is paid on the loaned funds or the situation lasts a relatively long time, since it exposes the company to the abnormal risk that the manager will not pay back the debt.[148] Another case falling into this category is a situation in which the company paid the sum required by the court for the manager's bail or other form of guarantee of this kind, which might translate into a loss should the manager fail to meet its conditions.[149]

The risk need not directly concern financial aspects of the company, but can also consist, for instance, of exposing the company to the risk of legal sanctions, although such sanctions would most probably imply also a financial loss.[150] Such a case might, for example, involve a manager who bribes a tax officer by giving him 15,000 euros, while expecting a reduction of taxes of 250,000 euros. Although the company is intended to receive compensation for the money it spent and would make an important saving, this use of company assets carries a risk that, if discovered, not only will the saving not materialise (so the 15,000 euros would be spent without compensation), but also the company could be sanctioned.[151]

The above examples are linked with an important rule established in the French jurisprudence, which provides that if the act in question is unlawful (which is limited in this context to acts which may be punished with criminal or tax sanctions), it is always considered to be contrary to the interests of the company.[152] Despite a certain reluctance to take this approach at first, it was confirmed by the judgment in *Carignon*, in which the court held:

> whatever short-term benefit it can bring, the use of company funds for the sole purpose of committing a crime such as corruption is contrary to the interest of the company in

[146] Rebut, *Abus de biens sociaux* (n 12) para 61.

[147] Joly and Joly-Baumgartner, *L'abus de biens sociaux* (n. 21) 99; Cass crim, 16 January 1989, Bull crim no 17, 45; Cass crim, 19 November 1979, Bull crim no 325, 887.

[148] Rebut, *Abus de biens sociaux* (n 12) para 45; Cass crim 9 May 1988, No de pourvoi: 87-90069.

[149] Tribunal correctionnel Nantes 2 May1985, RTD com 1985, 830, cited by Joly and Joly-Baumgartner, *L'abus de biens sociaux* (n 21) 171. See also Cass crim, 16 January 1964, Bull crim 1964, no 16, 27.

[150] Rebut, *Abus de biens sociaux* (n 12) para 62.

[151] Example from Joly and Joly-Baumgartner, *L'abus de biens sociaux* (n 21) 98.

[152] Stasiak, *Droit pénal des affaires* (n 5) 243; Cass crim, 22 April 1992, Bull crim 1992 no 169, 441.

> the way that it exposes the legal person to an abnormal risk of being sanctioned with criminal or tax penalties incurred against it and its managers and because it undermines its creditworthiness (or credit according to the terminology of the offence) and reputation.[153]

Following this judgment, it has been considered that not only in relation to corruption, but also in cases of other unlawful (in the above sense) acts, the act is considered contrary to the interests of the company, because it always exposes the company to a risk of a legal sanction.[154] Opposition to this solution diminished following the introduction into the French criminal law of corporate criminal liability in March 1994, which in 2004 was extended to all offences.[155] Explaining this interpretation, one author considered that the reputation of the company is part of its assets and thus exposing that reputation to risk is also contrary to the company's interests.[156] It is important to mention that the factor which contributed to the use of the offence of abuse of company assets in order to punish corruption is that the limitation period for prosecuting the abuse may be longer than in the case of bribery, due to the rules on postponing the moment from which statutory limitation starts to run.[157]

As to the offence of abuse of company credit, it is typically committed by the use of such credit in a way which exposes the company to a risk to which it should not be exposed. A standard example of such use is a situation in which the company guarantees a personal loan taken out by the manager. The exposure to an abnormal risk results from the fact that, should the manager fail to repay the loan, the company might have to pay in his place, whereas there is no compensation for the company in return for this favour.[158]

There exist at least two rebuttable presumptions as to when the act is or is not considered to be contrary to the interests of the company. According to the first, if the act does not enter into the framework of the company's stated business objectives, it is presumed to be contrary to its interests. In such cases, it is the task of the

[153] 'Quel que soit l'avantage à court terme qu'elle peut procurer, l'utilisation des fonds sociaux ayant pour seul objet de commettre un délit tel que la corruption est contraire à l'intérêt social en ce qu'elle expose la personne morale au risque anormal de sanctions pénales ou fiscales contre elle-même et ses dirigeants et porte atteinte à son crédit et à sa réputation'. Cass crim, 27 October 1997, Bull crim, no 352, 1169 (so-called *Carignon* affaire).

[154] Stasiak, *Droit pénal des affaires* (n 5) 243 et seq. Confirmed eg in the following judgment: Cass crim 14 May 2003, Bull crim, no 97, 372.

[155] Joly and Joly-Baumgartner, *L'abus de biens sociaux* (n 21) 108. The extension was provided for by art 54 of Loi no 2004-204 of 9 March 2004 portant adaptation de la justice aux évolutions de la criminalité which modified art 121-2 of the French Penal Code containing the general rule of corporate criminal liability.

[156] Joly and Joly-Baumgartner, *L'abus de biens sociaux* (n 21) 112.

[157] Rebut, *Abus de biens sociaux* (n 12) paras 73, 76. See also 3.1.3(i) above.

[158] Joly and Joly-Baumgartner, *L'abus de biens sociaux* (n 21) 99; for examples in jurisprudence of this and similar situations: Cass crim, 10 November 1964, Bull crim no 291; Cass crim, 3 May 1967, Bull crim no 148, 350; Cass crim, 16 March 1970, Bull crim 107, 245; Cass crim, 8 December 1971, Bull crim no 346, 869. See also Cass crim, 8 December 1971, Bull crim no 346, 869.

defence to prove that the act was not contrary to these interests.[159] On the other hand, if the act in question was within the company's objectives, it is presumed not to be against its interests.[160]

Finally, special alleviated rules have been developed as to the use of assets within corporate groups. It is not uncommon in such groups for one company to be acting in a way which is detrimental to the company itself, but where the act is beneficial to the whole group. This is in particular the case for flows of goods and capital between companies who are members of a group, which may be done according to conditions which are less advantageous than those applicable on the market.[161]

3.1.4. Mens Rea

The *mens rea* requirement of the offence of abuse of company assets in all its modalities is formulated in the same way and is composed of two elements having different functions in the structure of the offence. The first one, *dol général*, which can be translated as intention, requires that while acting the perpetrator knows that his act is contrary to the interests of the company and hence excludes liability for negligence. This requirement excludes from the scope of the offence situations of inaptitude or incompetence of managers.[162] The second element, special intention (*dol spécial*), requires that the defendant acted (broadly understood) in his own interests. This requirement is crucial in drawing the limit between mismanagement, which ought to remain out of focus of criminal law, and criminally punishable acts where the perpetrator gives priority to his own interests over the interests of the company.

For the assessment of the *mens rea*, the hope of the defendant that the company will eventually either benefit from his act or at least not suffer any loss plays no role, since the offence does not require proof of intention to cause damage to the company.[163] It has to be assessed whether, in the very moment of the commission of the act, the defendant knew the act to be contrary to the interests of the company, meaning that it would cause loss or expose the company to an abnormal risk of loss. For example, if the manager guarantees in the name of the company his personal debt hoping that he will be able to repay it, he nonetheless commits the abuse of company credit, since he is aware that his conduct exposes the company to a risk to which it should not be exposed.[164]

[159] Stasiak, *Droit pénal des affaires* (n 5) 244.
[160] Stasiak, *Droit pénal des affaires* (n 5) 244.
[161] Stasiak, *Droit pénal des affaires* (n 5) 245 et seq. For more details see, eg Joly and Joly-Baumgartner, *L'abus de biens sociaux* (n 21) 114 et seq; Lucas de Leyssac and Mihman, *Droit pénal des affaires* (n 28) 209–15; Cass crim, 20 March 2007, Bull crim no 86, 426.
[162] Médina, *Abus de biens sociaux* (n 7) 208.
[163] Stasiak, *Droit pénal des affaires* (n 5) 246.
[164] Médina, *Abus de biens sociaux* (n 7) 44.

(i) Intention

The first *mens rea* condition, intention (*dol général*), is formulated by the expression: 'in bad faith, in a way which they [the managers] know to be contrary to the interests of the company'. The first problem appearing in its analysis is whether the expression 'in bad faith' would be considered to be pleonastic, since a manager who knowingly acts to the detriment to the company is necessarily acting in bad faith,[165] or does the provision formulate here two different requirements and, if so, what does 'bad faith' mean in this context?

The theory opting for autonomous understandings of these two expressions separates the requirement of knowledge from the requirement of intention, considering that bad faith refers to the intention to act (ie in acting), while knowing that the act is against the company's interests.[166] The abuse of company assets is an intentional offence, so its *mens rea* must, at least in theory, be composed of these two elements.[167] However, judgments considering the two elements separately are rare.[168] It is much more common for judgments to focus on proving knowledge,[169] while the intention to act is simply implied from the fact that the defendant acted while knowing that the act was contrary to the interests of the company.[170] Moreover, the Court of Cassation admitted that the fulfilment of some elements could be brought out in a judgment only implicitly.[171] Such an approach has even a further consequence, since some judgments do not elaborate on the fulfilment of general intention, but concentrate on the proof of the special intention (personal interests, see below). This is mainly the case where the proof of special intention renders evident the knowledge of the defendant that the act was contrary to the company's interests.[172] However, the possibility of addressing only implicitly some elements of the offence does not empty the general intention of its function. The French Court of Cassation did not hesitate to quash judgments where the proof of intention was lacking and the reasoning was limited to a description of actual facts.[173]

In certain configurations of facts, the courts have a tendency to presume the existence of bad faith from the material elements of the offence, which will be even more reinforced where additionally the special intention has been proved.

[165] Jeandidier, *Abus des biens* (n 3) para 70.

[166] Rebut, *Abus de biens sociaux* (n 12) para 137.

[167] Desportes and Le Gunehec, *Droit Pénal Général* (n. 25) 418; Rebut, *Abus de biens sociaux* (n 12) para 134 et seq.

[168] Ibid para 138; eg Cass crim, 16 December 1975, Bull crim no 279, 735.

[169] Rebut, *Abus de biens sociaux* (n 12) para 140; Cass crim, 8 February 1968, Bull crim no 42; Cass crim, 28 March1996, Bull crim no 142, 407.

[170] Rebut, *Abus de biens sociaux* (n 12) para 140; Stasiak, *Droit pénal des affaires* (n 5) 246; eg Cass crim, 3 February 1992, Bull crim no 49, 118.

[171] Rebut, *Abus de biens sociaux* (n 12) para 139; Cass crim, 16 March 1970, Bull crim no 107, 245.

[172] Rebut, *Abus de biens sociaux* (n 12) para 142; Cass crim, 5 November 1976, Bull crim no 315, 803; Cass crim, 19 June 1978, Bull crim no 202, 525.

[173] Rebut, *Abus de biens sociaux* (n 12) para 143; Cass crim, 16 February 1987, Bull crim no 72, 194.

This means that the jurisprudence might presume that the manager acted in bad faith, if other elements of the offence are fulfilled.[174] Moreover, due to the professional aspect of the defendants' activities, the expectation as to their understanding of what is beneficial for the company and what is not is set higher than for a normal citizen.[175] In particular, this will be the case where the manager acted in a clandestine way[176] or where dishonest accountancy practices were applied.[177] This does not mean, of course, that the open and transparent character of the manager's act automatically precludes that he acted in bad faith.[178] Some authors have argued that such an approach creates the risk that the offence of abuse of company assets is reduced to its material element.[179] However, the fact that the court presumes from certain occurrences that the manager was aware of the act being contrary to the company's interests, as exemplified above, does not mean that the judgment may abstain completely from explaining why the judges were convinced that it was so.[180]

The knowledge (and the bad faith) of the manager should be assessed at the moment of the commission of the act.[181] More fully, it is in the moment of his act that the manager must know that it will expose the company to, at least, a risk of loss or other negative consequences, to which it should not be exposed.

It follows from the requirement that the manager must be aware that the act is contrary to the company's interests, and from the fact that no requirement of proof of result is necessary, that he need not precisely foresee its consequences. Therefore, even if the manager was convinced that his act would cause a loss, but in fact it resulted only in a risk of loss, he can still be punished for the abuse of company assets. Furthermore, it is submitted here that even if the manager does not know for sure that the act is contrary to the company's interests, but only has some (sufficiently important) doubts on the matter, he can be held liable, as an additional element of risk is present, which renders the risk abnormal.

It can be added as well that the courts are reluctant to accept the lack of the defendant's awareness when it is due to his own fault. A Court of Appeal rejected such a justification in a case in which a manager evoked in his defence deficiencies in the company's accounting practices.[182] Moreover, it is generally held that a

[174] Médina, *Abus de biens sociaux* (n 7) 212.

[175] Stasiak, *Droit pénal des affaires* (n 5) 247.

[176] Joly and Joly-Baumgartner, *L'abus de biens sociaux* (n 21) 154.

[177] Stasiak, *Droit pénal des affaires* (n 5) 246. For other examples, see Médina, *Abus de biens sociaux* (n 7) 211.

[178] Joly and Joly-Baumgartner, *L'abus de biens sociaux* (n 21) 154.

[179] Véron, *Droit pénal des affaires* (n 13) 217.

[180] Jeandidier, *Abus des biens* (n 3) para 70; Cass crim, 16 February 1987, Bull crim no 72, 194; Cass crim, 22 October 1990, no de pourvoi: 89-85019.

[181] Médina, *Abus de biens sociaux* (n 7) 208; Joly and Joly-Baumgartner, *L'abus de biens sociaux* (n 21) 154.

[182] Cour d'Appel Angers, 22 January 2008 : JurisData no 2008-362347, cited by Jeandidier, *Abus des biens* (n 3) para 70.

manager cannot claim that he was acting in good faith because he acted according to the common practice within his company or did 'as everybody does'.[183] Despite this, there have been cases in which the defendant was acquitted for a course of conduct because it was common practice in his company.[184]

There exists older jurisprudence which extended the application of the offence into grounds which have the characteristics of conscious negligence. In one case, the Court of Cassation quashed the acquittal of a manager, reasoning that the fact that he ignored the fraudulent operations of the main offender (several persons were involved in this case and several offences committed) was insufficient as a defence, since his functions include the duty to supervise the company and prevent wrongdoing, which he failed to fulfil.[185] Not only was the element of intention missing in this case, but also special intention was not proved. This line of interpretation has been since abandoned.[186]

(ii) Special Intention (*Dol spécial*)

The second element of *mens rea*, which will significantly shape the contours of the offence, is the requirement that the defendant acted in his personal interest. It is expressed by demanding that the manager acted 'for personal purposes or in order to benefit another company or undertaking in which they are directly or indirectly involved'.

This expression comprises two, not mutually exclusive, alternatives. The first one requires that the defendant act for his direct interest. This interest can be of a material, financial nature, but could also be only immaterial or moral.[187] Under the second alternative, the defendant, while committing the abuse, is driven by an indirect interest, which he holds in another company or undertaking. The term 'company' must be understood according to French company law. The term 'undertaking', which is the translation of the French '*entreprise*', has not been defined by the law and was meant to comprise a variety of different entities. It is not clear how far the meaning of this term extends, for instance, whether it comprises non-commercial entities, such as associations or trade unions.[188]

Since it is a *mens rea* requirement, there is no need that the interest pursued by the manager actually be realised. Some authors claim that seeking a probable or possible advantage is enough to fulfil this limb.[189] It seems, however, that there is no need even to assess the probability of the realisation of the defendant's

[183] Médina, *Abus de biens sociaux* (n 7) 209; Cass crim, 3 December 1992, Bull crim no 49, 118.
[184] Joly and Joly-Baumgartner, *L'abus de biens sociaux* (n 21) 153.
[185] Cass crim, 19 December 1973, Bull crim no 480, 120.
[186] Jeandidier, *Abus des biens* (n 3) para 73.
[187] Delmas-Marty and Giudicelli-Delage, *Droit pénal des affaires* (n 50) 352.
[188] Médina, *Abus de biens sociaux* (n 7) 216.
[189] Maurice Patin and Marcel Rousselet, 'Délits et sanctions dans les sociétés par actions' (1938) 292 *Sirey* 221, cited by Médina, *Abus de biens sociaux* (n 7) 215.

intention. It is the prosecution's task to prove the existence of this element.[190] However, the Court of Cassation in *Rosemain*[191] stated that in case of clandestine operations concerning company funds, the pursuit of the defendant's personal interest is presumed and it is for him to prove the contrary.[192]

The interest of the manager is direct if he benefits from it personally. This interest is material in nature, if the purpose of the defendant was to enrich himself or to avoid a loss.[193] Such interest can also be of a non-material character. The jurisprudence provides various types of motivation, which it has accepted as fulfilling this limb, such as[194] the protection of family reputation;[195] the hope of obtaining recognition from those who benefitted from the abuse;[196] the preservation of good business relations with another person[197] or influential persons;[198] and attaining prestige or renown.[199] In *Willot*, a lower court found the special interest of the manager in his wish to preserve his position and the remuneration linked to it in a situation of a corporate group, where the perpetrator was heading up a subsidiary and did not want to risk disobeying the parent company's management.[200] In another case, the court found the defendant's interest in a wish to obtain the support of different influential persons.[201] The desire to perform an operation which was expected to advance the manager's career was accepted as sufficient motive by the Court of Appeal of Paris.[202]

As to an indirect interest, it refers to the defendant's intention that another company or undertaking, to which he is somehow linked, benefit from his act. The manager can be linked to the company due to the fact that he is also a manager in that company or because he is its shareholder, creditor, supplier or employee.[203] His interest in the other company may also be more remote, which would be the case, for instance, if he is linked to it by a person close to him, a family member or partner, or through another company in which he also has an interest.[204] The text of the offence does not require, however, that the defendant exercise any function within the company or that he have any defined business relationship with

[190] Joly and Joly-Baumgartner, *L'abus de biens sociaux* (n 21) 145.

[191] Cass crim, 11 January 1996, Bull crim no 21, 51.

[192] Joly and Joly-Baumgartner, *L'abus de biens sociaux* (n 21) 146, where other judgments confirming this line are also cited.

[193] As cited by Rebut, *Abus de biens sociaux* (n 12) para 149.

[194] Cited by Rebut, *Abus de biens sociaux* (n 12) para 150.

[195] Cass crim, 3 May 1967, Bull crim no 148.

[196] Cass crim, 7 March 1968, Bull crim no 80.

[197] Cass crim, 9 May 1973, Bull crim no 216, 511; Cass crim, 19 June 1978, Bull crim no 202, 525; Cass crim, 15 September 1999, No de pourvoi 98-83.237.

[198] Cass crim, 9 February 1987, Bull crim no 61, 155; Cass crim, 14 May 2003, Bull crim no 97, 372.

[199] Cass crim, 20 March 1997, No de pourvoi 96-81.361.

[200] Tribunal correctionel Paris 10 June 1985, cited by Médina, *Abus de biens sociaux* (n 7) 217.

[201] Cass crim, 15 September 1999, No de pourvoi 98-83237.

[202] Cour d'Appel Paris, 6 May 1995, *Le Milon/MP, Dr Sociétés* 1995, no 153, 17, cited by Joly and Joly-Baumgartner, *L'abus de biens sociaux* (n 21) 141.

[203] Delmas-Marty and Giudicelli-Delage, *Droit pénal des affaires* (n 50) 352.

[204] Ibid 352.

it, so long as it is possible to prove that he has some interest in that company.[205] The indirect interest of the manager, similarly to the direct one, can be of a moral nature. It can also relate to a future benefit which the manager expects to obtain.[206]

The introduction of the requirement of special intention was meant to ensure that the offence of abuse of company assets is not used to punish mere mismanagement (such as when the manager exposes the company to excessive risk, but in hope that the risk would not materialise and the company would profit), as opposed to mismanagement intended to further the personal interests of the manager(s) to the detriment of those of the company.[207] However, in a number of cases judges have interpreted this requirement widely, in particular as to the moral interest, as set out above. An even more far-reaching example concerns a case in which a personal interest of transferring money to the tax authorities was found in the manager's intent to bring an end to a cumbersome fiscal inspection.[208] In another case, one could argue that the court confused the interest of the manager with the interest of the company, since it considered that the personal interest was constituted by the satisfaction of the president of a football club in having high-class players. Is such motivation not welcome, or even desirable, in any president of a sport club?[209]

This does not mean, however, that there are no examples of cases in which the court was not satisfied with the fulfilment of this limb. The court has acquitted the defendants in cases where the funds were used in a situation when they were owed to a third party. This was, for instance, the case of a manager of a company in financial difficulties, who decided to repay the debt which was due for payment to an association of which he was the treasurer, despite the fact that it was probably not in the best interests of the company.[210] Similarly, the court did not admit the existence of special intention in a case in which the manager issued cheques in the name of the company in order to repay the expenses of undeclared employees, despite the fact that without doubt such acts create a risk of the company being fined.[211]

The vagueness of this requirement has been criticised on various occasions,[212] and has led some authors to conclude that it has become obsolete.[213]

[205] Rebut, *Abus de biens sociaux* (n 12) para 152.

[206] Ibid para 153, eg Cass crim, 19 October 1978, Bull crim no 282, 724.

[207] Médina, *Abus de biens sociaux* (n 7) 213.

[208] Cour d'Appel Colmar, 30 April 1985, JurisData no 1985-601202; *Rev sociétés* 1985, 833, cited by Jeandidier, *Abus des biens* (n 3) para 78.

[209] Jeandidier, *Abus des biens* (n 3) para 78; Cass crim, 22 October 2008, No de pourvoi: 07-88111.

[210] Rebut, *Abus de biens sociaux* (n 12) para 157; Cass crim, 14 June 1993, Bull crim no 208, 526.

[211] Cour d'Appel Toulouse, 1 April 1999, JurisData no 040713, JCP 23 December 1999, Chronique 2064, cited by Joly and Joly-Baumgartner, *L'abus de biens sociaux* (n 21) 143.

[212] See, eg the materials of the conference 'L'abus de biens sociaux: Le particularisme français à l'épreuve de l'Europe' held at the ESCP-EAP (École supérieure de commerce de Paris) on 2 April 2003, published in (2004) *Gazette du Palais* (November/December) 3516 (eg the speech of A Médina, at 3522, and Jean-René Farthouat, at 3543).

[213] Quentin Urban, 'De la difficulté pour le juge de caractériser l'abus de biens sociaux' 37 *La semaine juridique – édition générale*, 14 September 2005, 1619, 1622.

Some critics expressed the need to interpret this limb more strictly.[214] On the other hand, another author questioned the necessity of keeping this requirement, at least in its current wording, since it can be deduced that any act contrary to the company's interests which the manager performs in the knowledge of these circumstances must to some extent be realised for personal interests.[215] As Jean-Pierre Brouillaud pointed out, it is difficult to find judgments, where this element is lacking:

> most of the time, the personal enrichment of the manager is established, and when it is not, the judge will admit the existence of a moral benefit; if this personal interest is accompanied by the interest of the company, the judge will admit the existence of a partial personal interest, and, finally, when no personal interest can be described with certainty, the judge will presume it.[216]

Moreover, in the judgments in which the limb of personal interests was problematic, the failure of the lower jurisdiction consisted in the lack of analysis of this element and not in its overly extensive interpretation.[217] Despite the fact that none of the convictions which relied extensively on this limb appear to be unsafe, it has been suggested that a legislative intervention should be considered in order either to reinforce this requirement, by limiting it, for instance, to an interest of material character, or to delete it, thus making the abuse of company assets a true mismanagement offence.[218] So far, no changes have been introduced.

Such a broad interpretation would have significant consequences for the cases of excessive risk-taking. It would in practice allow applying the offence in order to punish acts contrary to the company's interests and committed with knowledge of their detrimental character, while the requirement of personal interest would be fulfilled by any kind of motivation, such as pursuit of vanity or prestige. However, this interpretation seems to extend the offence too far.

The idea of including the personal interest of the manager as an element of the offence was to guarantee that mere incompetence or lack of information is not punished under this offence, but rather that it targets managers driven by dishonesty or greed which is reflected in the actual mismanagement, in the way in which the manager used the company for their own selfish purposes, neglecting the interests of the company.[219] 'There can be no abuse of company assets, unless

[214] See, eg the speech of M Franck in the materials of the ESCP-EAP conference (n 212) 3517 et seq.

[215] Jean-Pierre Brouillaud, 'Faut-il supprimer la notion d'intérêt personnel dans la définition de l'abus de biens sociaux?' (2008) 6 *Receuil Dalloz* (7 February) 375.

[216] 'La plupart du temps, l'enrichissement personnel du dirigeant est établie; lorsqu'il ne l'est pas, le juge admettra l'existence d'un intérêt moral; lorsque cet intérêt personnel s'accompagne de l'intérêt social, le juge admettra l'intérêt personnel partiel; lorsque, enfin, aucun intérêt personnel n'est caractérisé avec certitude, le juge le présumera.' Brouillaud, 'Faut-il supprimer la notion' (n 215) 377.

[217] Eg Cass crim, 4 November 2004, No de pourvoi: 03-87.327; Cass crim, 15 October 1990, No de pourvoi: 89-83.146. Haritini Matsopoulou, 'Le retour en grâce de l'intérêt personnel dans l'abus de biens sociaux' (2005) 30 *Recueil Dalloz*, 2075; Brouillaud, 'Faut-il supprimer la notion' (n 215) 378.

[218] Brouillaud, 'Faut-il supprimer la notion' (n 215) 378.

[219] Ibid 375; Urban, 'De la difficulté pour le juge' (n 213) 1622.

the manager wanted to make his personal interest prevail over the interest of the company.'[220]

It seems to be a general tendency to admit the 'diluted' personal interest in cases, in which the act undertaken by the manager is of a particularly serious nature. For instance, in one case the court found personal interest in the manager's intention to keep a privileged relationship with a person he considered influential, while also being driven by the wish to enhance the company's possibilities. The court reiterated that for criminal liability, there is no need that the defendant was motivated solely by his personal interests, and confirmed the manager's sentence because his act constituted bribery.[221]

In another judgment, the personal interests of the manager consisted in consolidating his position within the company by increasing the turnover by all possible means. The act was contrary to the company's interests because the transfer of funds occurred without adequate compensation, ie resulted in a loss, and not only in exposing the company to a risk of loss.[222] The requirement that the act be contrary to the company's interests was also fulfilled by lack of compensation in a case in which the personal interest consisted of the intention to maintain good relations with an influential person.[223] In another case, the managers made available to another person large amounts of money belonging to the company because of their friendship with that person. A loss occurred also in a case in which the defendant was motivated by his wish to maintain good business relations.[224] This could be considered as an example of exposing the company to the risk that the person concerned may not return the money, and in this particular case the money was never returned and thus constituted a loss.[225] The outcome was similar in a case in which the defendants agreed to invest in a golf course for reasons of prestige and renown. In theory, the company was exposed to a risk that the course would be unprofitable, although in the reality of the case it seems that its profitability was not even considered by the managers and that the company suffered an effective loss.[226]

An analogous conclusion can be drawn from the analysis of cases in which the requirement that the act be contrary to the company's interests is less evident, since the act consists in exposing the company to abnormal risk of loss. It is rare to encounter a case in which the requirement of personal interests would not be fulfilled in a more evident manner, in particular by using the company assets for personal purposes.[227] In a case in which the defendant's personal interest was to

[220] 'Il ne peut y avoir abus de biens sociaux que si le dirigeant a voulu faire primer son intérêt personnel sur l'intérêt social', Urban, 'De la difficulté pour le juge' (n 213) 1621.

[221] Rebut, *Abus de biens sociaux* (n 12) para 76; Cass crim, 14 May 2003, Bull crim no 97, 372.

[222] Cass crim, 9 February 1987, Bull crim no 61, 155.

[223] Cass crim, 15 September 1999, No de pourvoi: 98-83237.

[224] Cass crim, 19 June 1978, Bull crim no 202, 525.

[225] Cass crim, 8 December 1971, Bull crim no 346, 869.

[226] Cass crim, 20 March 1997, No de pourvoi: 96-81361.

[227] Cass crim, 16 January 1964, Bull crim no 16, 27 (abuse of company assets); Cass crim, 10 November 1964, Bull crim no 291 (abuse of credit); Cass crim, 24 March 1969, Bull crim no 130, 319 (abuse of assets); Cass crim, 16 March 1970, Bull crim no 107, 245 (abuse of credit).

win other persons' gratitude, the court evoked exposure to a risk of loss, but in fact the loss occurred.[228]

However, in another case the court sentenced the defendant for exposing his company to excessive risk by granting a loan to his brother, and the court considered that the personal interest was constituted by his intention to safeguard the reputation of the manager and his family. It appears from the judgment that eventually the bank suffered no loss.[229]

Based on the analysis of the judgments of the Court of Cassation, it is submitted here that in cases in which the fulfilment of the requirement that the act be contrary to the company's interests is limited to the exposure to excessive risk, the courts will likely be reluctant to consider as satisfied the requirement of personal interests, if this does not appear clearly evident, but is limited only to what was called above 'diluted' personal interest. It is certainly true that, as one author pointed out, it is the task of the judge to interpret this requirement in concrete cases and the result will depend on the way the judge perceives the manager's behaviour, while having considerable judicial discretion.[230] It cannot be excluded that a court would accept a 'diluted' personal interest in the case of mere exposure to a risk of loss, but from the above analysis it appears that the likeliness of such a result is limited.

3.2. Breach of Trust (*abus de confiance*)

The offence of breach of trust (*abus de confiance*), provided for in article 314-1 of the French Penal Code, the scope of which, unlike the abuse of company assets, is not limited to the corporate environment, could be assimilated with the offence of embezzlement in the common law system.[231] Before the enactment of the abuse of company assets, it constituted the only possibility to punish managers for the abuse of company assets. Since the entry into force of the latter offence, breach of trust remains applicable to all cases to which the offence of abuse of company assets cannot be applied, because the defendant does not fall into one of the categories of suitable perpetrators. However, the scope of criminalisation of the breach of trust is narrower since it requires that the defendant should have misappropriated the assets in question and also a proof of result.[232]

[228] Cass crim, 7 March 1968, Bull crim no 80, 189.

[229] Cass crim, 3 May 1967, Bull crim no 148, 350.

[230] Urban, 'De la difficulté pour le juge' (n 213) 1623.

[231] CP, art 314-1: 'Breach of trust is committed when a person, to the prejudice of other persons, misappropriates funds, valuables or any property that were handed over to him and that he accepted subject to the condition of returning, redelivering or using them in a specified way'.

[232] In cases in which both offences could apply, eg if a manager included as a potential perpetrator of the abuse of company assets misappropriated the company property, it is for the latter offence that he will be sentenced, since it provides for a more severe punishment. See Robert and Matsopoulou, *Traité de droit pénal des affaires* (n 96) 102, note 8.

In comparison with the abuse of company assets, this offence is composed of more extensive *actus reus* and less exigent *mens rea* requirements. As to the *actus reus*, it is necessary to prove that the defendant committed a misappropriation. This misappropriation should concern, according to the provision, funds, valuables or any property, which expression, although it appears prima facie to comprise literally any kind of property, including intangible property,[233] according to the commonly accepted interpretation in fact excludes real estate.[234] Since the French original uses the same term as in the case of abuse of company assets (*bien*) with regard to breach of trust, this section will also use the term 'assets' when referring to the object of the latter offence. These assets should be handed over to the defendant before the commission of the offence upon the condition of returning them or using them in a specified way. The misappropriation should cause damage to the owner of the entrusted assets. The *mens rea* element is limited to a general intention to commit what the *actus reus* describes, namely misappropriation and the resulting prejudice, while being aware of the circumstances, ie that the assets have been handed over subject to the condition of returning them or using them in a specified way.

The offence of breach of trust is mainly designed to punish cases of effective misappropriation of entrusted assets. However, in view of the broad interpretation of some of the limbs of this offence, namely misappropriation and prejudice, certain cases in which the entrusted assets were exposed to excessive risk may potentially fall into the scope of the offence.

3.2.1. Precondition: Conditional Handover of the Assets

The assets must be handed over to the perpetrator before the misappropriation and it is necessary that he accept the hand-over. The hand-over may result from a contract, a judicial decision or a statute.[235] The fact that this contract was void or declared null does not preclude criminal liability for breach of trust.[236] The acceptance may also be implied from the perpetrator's conduct.[237] The hand-over must be conditional: the perpetrator must use them in a certain way or for a certain purpose, which is the reason for the assets to be handed over, and/or he must return them at a certain point, in particular at the end of his mission. Liability for this offence is excluded therefore, if there has been a transfer of ownership of the assets to the perpetrator.[238]

The assets of the company being handed over to the manager, whether he is a person described in the offence of abuse of company assets or a lower

[233] Véron, *Droit pénal des affaires* (n 13) 55 et seq.
[234] Jeandidier, *Abus de confiance …* (n 2) para 15 et seq; Stasiak, *Droit pénal des affaires* (n 5) 43.
[235] Ibid 43.
[236] Ibid 41.
[237] Jeandidier, *Abus de confiance* (n 2) para 30.
[238] Mascala, *Abus de confiance* (n 42) para 38.

level manager, who cannot be liable for that offence, without doubt fulfils this precondition.[239] The assets belong to the company and the manager receives them only for a certain purpose, which is to use them for the benefit of the company. Moreover, he is obliged to return them after his mandate comes to an end. It is irrelevant whether he receives the assets by virtue of the contract, which created the company (*contrat de société*), under the contract giving the manager the power of attorney (*mandat*), or any other form of contractual relation, including his work contract.[240]

3.2.2. *Misappropriation*

The course of conduct criminalised by the offence of breach of trust, is described in article 314-1 of the French Penal Code by the verb '*détourner*', which can be translated as to embezzle or to misappropriate, but also as to divert, to redirect or to turn away. This translation shows the connotation of the verb, which in the context of the offence should mainly mean use of the assets in a way which is different from the one envisaged in the moment of handing them over.[241] Another way of explaining the understanding of misappropriation would be: to behave, at least for a while, as the owner of the assets.[242]

The most evident case of misappropriation would be constituted by physical destruction of the assets or its loss, eg by a legal transaction (eg donation).[243] Moreover, misappropriation can also be committed where the perpetrator uses the assets in a different way than that originally envisaged, or if he refuses to return them when he is supposed to do so.[244] For the fulfilment of this limb, it is not necessary that the perpetrator have appropriated the object or that he have profited from it in any way.[245] However, not every kind of misuse and not every situation of refusal to return the object will lead to criminal liability.

As to the refusal to return the object, or in case the perpetrator is late in doing so, the French jurisprudence has elaborated criteria in order to distinguish what should remain a civil law dispute in this regard and what constitutes the offence of breach of trust. These situations are of lesser interest here.[246] Exposing the assets to excessive risk would only possibly fall into the scope of the offence if it can be qualified as misappropriation of these assets.

[239] Rebut, *Abus de biens sociaux* (n 12) para 33 et seq, also in the case of de facto manager: Cass crim, 31 January 2007, Bull crim no 26, 98.

[240] Jeandidier, *Abus de confiance* (n 2) paras 39, 41. See also Cass crim, 19 June 2013, Bull crim no 145, in which the court considered that working hours could be subject to breach of trust, if the employee uses his work time for personal purposes.

[241] Stasiak, *Droit pénal des affaires* (n 5) 44; Cass crim, 8 December 1971, Bull crim no 341, 856.

[242] Cass crim, 13 February 1984, Bull crim no 49.

[243] Stasiak, *Droit pénal des affaires* (n 5) 44.

[244] Robert and Matsopoulou, *Traité de droit pénal des affaires* (n 96) 101, 103.

[245] Jeandidier, *Abus de confiance* (n 2) para 60.

[246] In this regard, see, eg Mascala, *Abus de confiance* (n 42) para 66 et seq; Véron, *Droit pénal des affaires* (n 13) 59 et seq.

In order to be considered misappropriation, the misuse must imply that, at least for a moment, the perpetrator wants to behave like an owner of the asset.[247] It is through this intention, but deduced from the way in which the perpetrator acted, that the perpetrator's acts should be evaluated. Hence, the same act can be considered innocent or criminal depending on whether the judges consider that the act disclosed the perpetrator's intention to embezzle it.[248] This intention can be deduced by the judge from the fact that the perpetrator acted for his own benefit, by using the object in question for his own endeavour or personal purpose.[249] According to this interpretation the following situations would fall into the scope of the provision: a banker uses for his personal purpose the funds entrusted by the clients;[250] a driver receives a credit card in order to buy petrol for the car and uses it to cover his personal expenses;[251] an employee uses the employer's computer to visit pornographic websites.[252] This interpretation would assimilate the offence of breach of trust to the abuse of company assets, with its requirement that the perpetrator is acting in his personal interest, however limited to its strict interpretation. Moreover, it is the misuse of assets and not exposure to risk that is targeted by this offence. Cases in which the assets of the company are exposed to a risk of loss, which do not entail that the perpetrator use the assets for his personal purpose, remain outside the scope of this offence.

These limits of the offence could be questioned in view of at least one judgment from the Court of Cassation, in which the court upheld the conviction of a manager of a travel agency. The manager was entitled to issue tickets in the name of Air France and issued these tickets to a company which was subject to procedures related to its insolvency and which had also lost its licence issued by the International Air Transport Association (IATA). The court considered that the defendant, in her capacity as representative of Air France, was obliged to verify these aspects of the partner company's credibility before issuing the tickets. By not doing so, the defendant took the risk of not being able to transfer to Air France the money due for the tickets which she should have obtained from the company to which the tickets were sold. Therefore, the court considered, the defendant behaved as if the tickets were her own property.[253] It is important to take into consideration that Air France suffered an effective loss in this case.

[247] Jeandidier, *Abus de confiance* (n 2) para 52; Cass crim, 13 February 1984, Bull crim no 49; Cass crim, 16 June 2011, No de pourvoi: 10-83.758.

[248] Véron, *Droit pénal des affaires* (n 13) 59, for an example where the court did not find such intention, see, eg Cass crim, 11 January 1968, Bull crim no 10.

[249] Robert and Matsopoulou, *Traité de droit pénal des affaires* (n 96) 101; Mascala, *Abus de confiance* (n 42) paras 62–65; Jeandidier, *Abus de confiance* (n 2) para 52 et seq.

[250] Cass crim, 1 April 1968, Bull crim no 115.

[251] Cass crim, 19 May 2004, Bull crim no 125, 477.

[252] Cass crim, 19 May 2004, Bull crim no 126, 480.

[253] Cass crim, 3 July 1997, Bull crim no 265, 905.

3.2.3. Prejudice

Although the provision requires proof of prejudice to another person, extensive interpretation of this requirement has resulted in its limited influence in shaping the contours of the offence. This interpretation makes it possible to consider that this limb is fulfilled if the prejudice is only a potential one.[254] Moreover, the prejudice need not be of material character, since a moral prejudice is also accepted, in the form, for instance, of risk of damage to the victim's reputation.[255]

3.2.4. Mens Rea

The *mens rea* of the offence consists, on the one hand, of knowing that the assets were handed over only conditionally, and on the other hand, of the intention to embezzle them and cause the resulting prejudice, ie intention either to appropriate, to retain fraudulently or to misuse.[256]

This requirement does not create important problems. However, in the case cited above concerning the sale of Air France tickets, it can be questioned, whether the court did not in fact convict the defendant for negligence, since her wrongdoing consisted in not having foreseen that the company to which she sold the tickets might have been in financial difficulties. The Court of Cassation rejected this criticism formulated by the defence, however without elaborating on the issue.[257] At least two authors questioned this judgment as excessive in this respect,[258] and it seems that this line of jurisprudence has not been confirmed by further judgments.

4. Inchoate Offences

4.1. Preparatory Acts and Attempt

The preparatory acts to committing abuse of company assets or to committing breach of trust are not criminalised as there is no offence or rule that would so provide. As to attempt, it is criminalised only if the offence is felony (*crime*) or in cases provided by the statute (CP, article 121-4). Since there is no such provision

[254] Cass crim, 3 December 2003, Bull crim no 232, 935; Mascala, *Abus de confiance* (n 42) para 86.

[255] Mascala, *Abus de confiance* (n 42) para 87; Robert and Matsopoulou, *Traité de droit pénal des affaires* (n 96) 108; Cass crim, 6 April 1882, Bull crim 1882, no 92, cited by Jeandidier, *Abus de confiance* (n 2) para 65.

[256] Robert and Matsopoulou, *Traité de droit pénal des affaires* (n 96) 109.

[257] Cass crim, 3 July 1997, Bull crim no 265, 905.

[258] Robert and Matsopoulou, *Traité de droit pénal des affaires* (n 96) 108; Lepage et al, *Droit pénal des affaires* (n 13) 85.

for the abuse of company assets or for the breach of trust and neither are felonies, attempting to commit one of these offences is not criminalised.[259]

Due to this rule, an act executed in view of committing abuse of company assets will not be punishable, in particular, if the assets were not yet exposed to a risk of loss.[260] It is possible, however, to consider that the offences of abuse of credit and the abuse of powers in fact criminalise an attempt to commit the abuse of assets (*sensu stricto*).[261] Although, as demonstrated above, the delimitation of these modalities is in practice not very precise, it could be considered that, especially the offence of abuse of powers in cases where it is not accompanied by an abuse of assets, would punish an attempt to commit such abuse. However, it has been suggested that, since the law specifically excluded criminalisation of attempt for this offence, it ought not to be reintroduced through the back door.[262] Moreover, the fact that the abuse of company assets may be committed by an act contrary to the company's interests consisting in exposing the company to a risk of loss, and not causing an immediate loss, is considered to give enough width to the offence, so that the lack of criminalisation of attempt does not constitute an unjustified lacuna.[263]

As to the breach of trust, the literature points out that in view of the extensive concept of misappropriation in the current doctrine, criminalisation of attempts not only appears unnecessary, but it would also be difficult to establish the starting point of an attempt and when the effective commission of the offence begins.[264]

4.2. Conspiracy

The French criminal law provides for criminalisation of criminal association if at least one of the offences involved is punished by at least five years' imprisonment.[265] Since the imprisonment foreseen for the abuse of company assets is indeed of five years, it is possible to convict a person who participates in a group preparing to commit this offence under the condition that these preparations have passed the stage of mere exchange of opinions and at least one preparatory act has been executed.[266] However, known cases concern most often multiple

[259] Mascala, *Abus de confiance* (n 42) para 102; Rebut, *Abus de biens sociaux* (n 12) para 269. See also Cass crim, 7 April 1998, No de pourvoi: 97-83801.

[260] Rebut, *Abus de biens sociaux* (n 12) para 269.

[261] Stasiak, *Droit pénal des affaires* (n 5) 240.

[262] Joly and Joly-Baumgartner, *L'abus de biens sociaux* (n 21) 85.

[263] Larguier and Conte, *Droit pénal des affaires* (n 43) 343.

[264] Lucas de Leyssac and Mihman, *Droit pénal des affaires* (n 28) 120.

[265] CP, art 450-1: 'A criminal association consists of any group formed or any conspiracy established with a view to the preparation, marked by one or more material actions, of one or more felonies, or of one or more misdemeanours punished by at least 5 years' imprisonment'.

[266] André Vitu and Didier Beauvais, Fasc. 20: Participation à une association de malfaiteurs, mise à jour 20 December 2016, JurisClasseur Code Pénal, para 26. Participation in a criminal association with the purpose of committing the abuse of company assets is punished by five years' imprisonment and

offences, where abuse of company assets is only one of the planned or committed offences.[267]

5. Cooperation in the Commission of the Offence

The rules on complicity allow the inclusion into the scope of criminalisation of the offence of abuse of company assets persons who do not exercise within the company the functions required for liability as principal offender.[268] The French criminal law, which follows the theory of unity of the offence (*théorie de l'unité de l'infraction*), requires for liability for complicity that the commission of the main offence, ie abuse of company assets, effectively occurred.[269]

'The accomplice to the offence, in the meaning of article 121-7, is punishable as a perpetrator' (CP, article 121-6).[270] According to CP, article 121-7, there exist two forms of complicity: by helping or assisting the main offender or by instigation.[271] To attract liability for complicity in the form of helping or assisting, the aid must be effectively provided, since an attempt to be an accomplice is not punishable.[272] Moreover this act must be prior or simultaneous to the commission of the main offence; however, subsequent aid is punishable if it was promised before the act, since it is the moment of the agreement that would be decisive.[273] This modality comprises any act helping the main perpetrator. The French jurisprudence has never given precise criteria to differentiate between the two expressions describing the conduct of the aider, helping (*aide*) and assisting (*assistance*), but in practice the first one tends to be used in situations where the accomplice provides the main perpetrator with the necessary tools, and the second for other types of help, in particular physical help in the commission of the offence.[274] The aid or assistance provided by the accomplice need not effectively help the main perpetrators directly. It can also be indirect.[275]

a fine of 75,000 euros, unless this association foresaw committing also other, more serious offences, in which case it could be of 10 years' imprisonment and a fine of 150,000 euros. The same punishment would also apply to breach of trust, in the case described by CP, art 314-3.

[267] See, eg Cass crim, 15 January 2014, Bull crim no 11; Cass crim, 12 October 2011, Bull crim, no 205.

[268] Rebut, *Abus de biens sociaux* (n 12) para 218.

[269] Desportes and Le Gunehec, *Droit Pénal Général* (n 25) 504. As regards offences of which attempts are also punishable, it is sufficient for the accomplice's liability that the main perpetrator attempts to commit the main offence.

[270] Following this approach, the punishment provided for the main offence also applies to the accomplice. Desportes and Le Gunehec, *Droit Pénal Général* (n 25) 510.

[271] Catherine Elliott, *French Criminal Law* (Willan Publishing, 2001) 88.

[272] Desportes and Le Gunehec, *Droit Pénal Général* (n 25) 497.

[273] Ibid 498.

[274] Ibid 497.

[275] Ibid 497.

As to instigation, CP, article 121-7 provides for two modalities of this category of complicity.[276] The first one consists in provoking a person to commit an offence. The criminalisation of provocation is limited to situations in which the accomplice uses one of the means enumerated in the article: a gift, promise, threat, order or an abuse of authority or powers. This limitation does not apply to the second modality, which consists in giving instructions to the main perpetrator. The instructions given by the accomplice do not need to prove essential to the commission of the offence.[277] Similar to the first modality, the instigation must be addressed to a concrete person, be prior or simultaneous to the commission of the main offence, and needs to be effectively committed, since its attempt is not punishable. It can however be indirect.[278]

The *mens rea* requirement of all the modalities of complicity is knowledge concerning the foreseen main offence and the intention to participate in its commission as accomplice. It is important to stress that the accomplice does not need to fulfil the *mens rea* requirement foreseen for the main offence, which will be particularly important in view of the special intention required for the abuse of company assets. In the case of this offence, the accomplice need not act in his personal interests. It is enough (but necessary) that he knows that the main perpetrator is animated by such reasons.[279]

The above rules also apply in the same way to breach of trust. However, it is in the case of the abuse of company assets that the rules on complicity will significantly broaden the boundaries of the offence. All these persons that do not fulfil the requirement as to the function within the company may fall into the scope of this provision, provided that they help the main perpetrator, furnish him with instructions or provoke him in accordance with the requirements of the rules of complicity. The criminalisation would thus include other categories of managers (senior or junior), assistants, internal accountants, other employees and also persons from outside the company, such as auditors or chartered public accountants.[280] For criminal liability, it is necessary that these persons have knowledge of the planned offence, in particular of the main perpetrator's special intention, and that the abuse is effectively committed. It is not necessary, however, that the main perpetrator be convicted for it.[281]

In addition, complicity plays an important role as regards punishing for omission. The general rule requires that the act of an accomplice is not limited to his mere passiveness. However, the French jurisprudence overcomes this rule on

[276] CP, art 121-7: 'Any person who, by means of a gift, promise, threat, order, or an abuse of authority or powers, provokes the commission of an offence or gives instructions to commit it, is also an accomplice'.

[277] Desportes and Le Gunehec, *Droit Pénal Général* (n 25) 502.

[278] Ibid 500.

[279] Ibid 502.

[280] See, eg Cass crim, 6 September 2000, No de pourvoi: 00-80989, in which the court considered criminal liability of a public accountant, but decided to quash the sentence for lack of proof of his actual help prior or simultaneous to the commission of the main offence.

[281] Desportes and Le Gunehec, *Droit Pénal Général* (n 25) 508.

various occasions, notably in the context of abuse of company assets.[282] A manager may become an accomplice by not preventing another manager from committing an abuse, if it was within his competence or if it was his duty to prevent it, provided he was aware of this abuse.[283] Furthermore, there is no need to prove the special intention of the accomplice. If that intention was present, liability for abuse of powers could be envisaged.

6. Reasons for Excluding Criminal Liability

6.1. Consent of the Victim

Since the assets in question belong to the company, consent to the manager's act would need to be given by a supervisory body or by the shareholders. It is generally accepted that such consent, regardless whether it is prior or subsequent to the manager's act, has no relevance to his criminal liability.[284] The courts' reluctance to accept consent as a defence is linked to the above-mentioned understanding of company interests as independent of the interests of the shareholders, on the one hand, and of consideration given to the interests of third parties, on the other.[285] Further reasons given for this approach are that it is a general rule in French criminal law that the consent of the victim does not have an exonerating effect, and that the bodies giving consent could be manipulated by the manager(s) or even taken over completely, if the managers are majority shareholders.[286] The solution is similar as regards the offence of breach of trust.[287]

6.2. Orders of Superiors

The problem of the exonerating effect of orders of superiors has not been extensively treated in the French doctrine, but it is submitted here that the solution to it can be deduced, in particular from the rules of consent. Denying exonerating effect to the consent of shareholders or supervisory bodies demonstrates the philosophy behind this offence, which is the responsibility of managers for the well-being of the company.

[282] Ibid 498.
[283] Cass crim, 20 March 1997, No de pourvoi: 96-81361; Cass crim, 7 September 2005, No de pourvoi: 05-80163; Joly and Joly-Baumgartner, *L'abus de biens sociaux* (n 21) 60, 242–43; Jeandidier, *Abus des biens* (n 3) para 25.
[284] Cass crim, 8 March 1967, Bull crim no 94; Rebut, *Abus de biens sociaux* (n 12) para 35 et seq; Jeandidier, *Abus des biens* (n 3) para 37; Larguier and Conte, *Droit pénal des affaires* (n 43) 342 et seq.
[285] Médina, *Abus de biens sociaux* (n 7) 208.
[286] Joly and Joly-Baumgartner, *L'abus de biens sociaux* (n 21) 95.
[287] Jeandidier, *Abus de confiance* (n 2) para 67.

As to the abuse of company assets, the configurations that can be envisaged are limited, since the persons considered apt to become perpetrators of this offence are already at the top of the company hierarchy. In the limited cases where managers are ordered to perform certain acts by the shareholders or by other bodies (eg the supervisory board in case of the SA under the dual-board regime), such orders cannot release them from considering whether what they are ordered to do is contrary to the company's interests. If the manager considers that it is contrary to such interests, he should abstain from performing the act and he is subject to criminal liability if he does not do so.

As regards breach of trust, the orders of superiors may be treated in the same way as for consent, except if they amount to a situation where the scope of the permitted use is validly enlarged.

6.3. Expert Opinions

In theory, it would be difficult to claim that a manager was aware that his act was contrary to the interests of the company, if he was convinced of its correctness in view of an expert opinion, where there was no reason to doubt its accuracy.[288] If the manager's act is based on an opinion of the expert, according to which it would not be contrary to the company's interests, the defence could try to claim that the *mens rea* requirement of knowledge is missing and thus criminal liability for abuse of company assets is excluded. However, the courts have a tendency not to give easy admission to a defence based on that requirement, and often presume knowledge on the grounds that a high level manager 'couldn't not know'.[289]

As regards breach of trust, the existence of an expert opinion cannot be considered an exonerating circumstance as such, since this offence does not contain the requirement that what the perpetrator did was contrary to the owner's interests, but it focuses on whether the perpetrator acted as if he was the owner. An expert opinion could be proof that the manager acted diligently, as expected from him according to the contract, by virtue of which he received the assets in question, and thus that he did not embezzle those assets. However, it is also possible that the expert opinion demonstrates his intention to go beyond the scope of tasks he was supposed to perform with the assets, and that he therefore did misappropriate them.

7. Solutions to the Five Cases

Despite the fact that excessive risk-taking was subject to some discussion in the doctrine and notwithstanding existing jurisprudence, it is impossible to answer

[288] Joly and Joly-Baumgartner, *L'abus de biens sociaux* (n 21) 152.
[289] Muller, 'Le droit pénal des conflits d'intérêts' (n 29) point 13.

with certainty whether the judges would convict managers in the cases described in the introductory chapter.[290]

In order to envisage liability for the abuse of company assets, it is first necessary that perpetrators in these cases fulfil the requirement concerning their function within the company. If this is not the case, two other possibilities exist for managers to become liable for this offence: either it is possible to consider that a person exercises one of these functions de facto and in this way falls into the scope of the offence, or a person becomes liable as an accomplice, provided that the main perpetrator committed the abuse of company assets. If this is not the case, only liability for breach of trust can be taken into account (see below).

As to case 1, it concerns without doubt a positive act of using the company assets. This act is contrary to the company's interests: since the risk associated with the credit is greater than should be taken and the company is not adequately compensated for the risk it takes in granting the loan, in other words, the risk the bank takes is abnormal, so it can be considered that this limb is also fulfilled. The *mens rea* requirement of intention does not seem to be a problem, since the manager is aware of the abnormal risk the transaction is running. The question which is much more difficult to answer is whether the manager fulfils the requirement of personal interest. As was explained above, the cases in which the courts have sentenced managers for excessive risk-taking concerned, in the main, situations in which the personal interest was evident. It cannot be excluded, however, that the court would admit a 'diluted' personal interest, for example, in the form of the manager's intention to secure a promotion or a bonus or reinforce the position within the company, as the case may be. The probability of conviction would rise to near certainty where the manager grants the credit to a member of his family or to a company in which he had an interest.

As to the second case, the solution would be similar, with the exception of the requirement of personal interest, which is much more evident (financial gratification). Therefore, the probability of conviction is much higher. As to the fact that the manager does not perform the act himself, it can be remedied by the use of abuse of powers or by considering that he was an 'intellectual author' of the offence (*auteur intellectuel*), which is allowed in the French system.[291]

In the third case, the requirement that the act be contrary to the company's interests is clearly met, since aggressively investing the funds necessary to pay the company debts exposes the company to an abnormal risk that these funds would be lost. The issue will again be the manager's personal interest, especially if he wished that only the company should benefit from his act. However, taking into account that the company business is construction and not investing on the stock exchange, and that the manner in which the funds were invested goes far beyond what could be accepted only as a way to secure the funds or to allow them to return

[290] For the hypotheses of the cases and explanations see Chapter 1, section 4.
[291] Desportes and Le Gunehec, *Droit Pénal Général* (n 25) 499.

a reasonable profit, it is possible that the courts would accept even the 'diluted' personal interest. The case would be more evident if the manager was intending to keep at least part of the winnings for himself.

The likelihood of conviction is the lowest in case 4. It is already problematic to consider whether what the perpetrator did amounted to 'use' under the terms of this offence, since it was an omission, which as such rarely leads to a conviction. Moreover, the use did not directly concern the assets of the company. It would be necessary to analyse it as an abuse of credit and to verify whether the risk to the company's reputation would allow the use of this modality. Even if the court would find that these requirements are met, the requirement of personal interest is very difficult to establish, even in its 'diluted' version. If the court were satisfied of this requirement by saying that the manager did not want to fall out of favour among the other senior managers, all the requirements would be fulfilled, but in a fairly weak form, so criminal liability in this case is more likely to be excluded.

The fifth case, in contrast, is the least problematic, since the French jurisprudence has expressly tackled the issue of unlawful acts in relation to the judgment in *Carignon*, considering them to be contrary to the company's interests by exposing it to an abnormal risk of sanctions. Due to the seriousness of the act constituting the abuse, the courts tend to admit a 'diluted' personal interest, so it will be sufficient to prove that the manager sought to strengthen his position within the company or appear as a successful manager. If a bonus was linked to his performance, the case would be even stronger.

The use of the offence of breach of trust could be envisaged if the manager in question does not perform any of the functions making him a potential perpetrator of the abuse of company assets. Because of the requirement of misappropriation, it will find only very limited application for excessive risk-taking.

In order to envisage criminal liability for breach of trust, it is necessary to verify whether the defendant received an object which may be subject to embezzlement by virtue of CP, article 314-1. With the exception of real property, any assets could fall into this category. In all five cases, assets of the company were entrusted to the managers. Moreover, these assets were entrusted to them in order to be used for the benefit of the company and must be returned to the company at the end of the manager's mission. Only if the act in question concerned exclusively real property would the fulfilment of this limb be problematic.

If the interpretation given to this term in the judgment concerning the Air France tickets is to be disregarded as too extravagant, it is uncertain whether the conduct of the manager in cases 1 and 2 would be considered as misappropriation. It is true that the perpetrator in these cases uses the assets of the bank in a way which is not in accordance with the conditions of this use and breaches the regulations of the bank. However, the manager does not use the assets for his personal interests (or such interest is remote), so it remains a case of mismanagement, which as such is not targeted by the offence. If some kind of personal interest of the manager were deemed to be present, as in case 2, the chances of conviction would be much higher, as it would be possible to claim that the manager used the bank's funds as if they were his own. The case would probably be even more straightforward if the loans were granted, for example, to the manager's brother.

As to case 3, it is the most likely to result in conviction, although it is not possible to foresee this with certainty. The assets of the company, which are intended to be used to pay its debts, ought not to be used for risky investment. There remains some doubt, however, as to whether the court would take into account in the manager's defence that he wished the company to profit from the funds, which would otherwise remain profitless in the company account. The fact that he was aware of the excessive risk of his investment would be an argument in support of admitting fraudulent misuse. However, it seems rather unlikely that the court would convict the manager, if no loss occurred. The probability of conviction would be much higher were the manager to plan on keeping the profit from the investment for himself.

Case 4, which consists of an omission to inform, would most probably fall outside the scope of the offence of breach of trust, since there is no direct link to entrusted assets which could have been misappropriated or even misused.

As to Case 5, in spite of the liability for corruption, it is difficult to expect a conviction for a breach of trust, if the assets were entrusted to the perpetrator for the purpose of committing bribery. However, if the perpetrator used the funds of the company in order to commit an act of corruption, even for the benefit of the company, it can be argued that he misused the assets by using them in a different way than agreed, and that he put at risk the company's reputation. Although the absence of a personal interest might help the defendant's defence, in view of the gravity of the act the court will more likely admit a misuse.

To conclude, the probability of conviction for breach of trust is high only in cases 3 and 5. Furthermore, an element of personal interest would probably be necessary in the former. This result would probably be different were the case of the Air France tickets to be considered as authoritative, since it would probably allow for the admission of liability in cases 1 and 2. In these cases, the manager knowingly disobeyed the rules, while also being aware of the risk of loss for the bank. However, he did not intend to misappropriate the funds and he wanted the company to profit. Although he intentionally exposed the company to a risk of loss, he did not want to cause prejudice to the company. Moreover, in the Air France tickets case, the loss eventually occurred, whereas the hypothesis of cases 1 and 2 is that there is no proof of such a result. In order to convict a manager for a breach of trust in these cases, it is necessary to interpret extensively practically all of the elements of the offence and move away from the wrongdoing punished by this offence, and as such conviction remains highly unlikely.

As regards the negligent version of the cases, there exists no possibility to convict managers for these acts.

8. Conclusions

The French legal system offers two offences which may be applied to managers who misuse the assets of their companies: the abuse of company assets and abuse of trust. Of the two, mainly the first one can be applied to punish for excessive risk-taking. The offence of abuse of company assets criminalises acts by senior managers which are against the company's interests, when committed intentionally and for personal interest. An act is against the company's interests if it leads (in normal circumstances) to a loss, or exposes the company to abnormal risk of loss. The main objective of the offence is the protection of the financial interests of the company and indirectly of the shareholders and the stakeholders. In this sense, the offence also penalises disloyalty of the managers towards the company. Furthermore, the French law emphasises that the interests of the stakeholders as managers cannot escape criminal liability by evoking consent given by shareholders or other bodies of the company to acts against the interests of the company.

The analysis in this chapter has demonstrated that two elements of the offence will limit its applicability to a great extent. First, it is the requirement that the perpetrator acted in his personal interest. This requirement excludes cases in which the only interest that animated the manager was the well-being of the company. Moreover, it is generally admitted that the offence should not punish acts of mere mismanagement. However, the court has extended the understanding of this requirement to include 'diluted' personal interests. While so far most cases using such an interpretation have concerned an effective loss, it cannot be excluded that also in cases of excessive risk-taking, the court would consider that the defendant acted in his personal interest, if he was motivated only by his intention to maintain an important relationship or simply acted in pursuit of vanity.[292] These observations lead to the conclusion that the cases of interest in this book fall into a grey zone of liability for abuse of company assets, and the answer to the question whether the defendant will finally be convicted or acquitted will depend on the particularities of the case.

Secondly, the scope of the offence is further limited as to the circle of potential perpetrators. It applies only to senior managers, although the circle can be extended to persons acting de facto as senior managers and by the rules on complicity. In respect of all categories of managers to whom the offence of abuse of company assets cannot be applied, the offence of breach of trust remains to be considered. Its applicability to the cases which are relevant for this book will be even more limited because of the requirement of misappropriation, which, although interpreted broadly, might be difficult to apply to cases of excessive risk-taking, unless it is accompanied by certain additional elements. If the perpetrator acted in his personal interest, it is more likely that the court would consider that

[292] '*Fumées de la vanité*', Conte et al, *Le risque pénal dans l'entreprise* (n 118) 2.

he demonstrated by his act a will to behave like an owner, which would fulfil the definition of misappropriation. This makes an interesting parallel between the two offences, suggesting that, in relation to both of them, the decisive element concerning criminal liability will be the proof of personal interest. Taking into account the fact that managers committing economic crimes are often driven by greed and ambition, this requirement cannot be considered an insurmountable hindrance to establishing criminal liability in cases of excessive risk-taking.

4

Germany

1. Introduction and History

In the German legal system, the offence criminalising improper use of entrusted assets is described in section 266 of the German Penal Code (Strafgesetzbuch, StGB)[1] as *Untreue*, which could be translated as breach of trust, but the same word may also mean infidelity or disloyalty. This offence consists in breaching one's duty to safeguard another person's financial interests, thereby causing financial damage to this person.[2]

According to this definition, the offence of *Untreue* is composed of two alternative modalities, namely the *Missbrauchstatbestand* (the abuse of power

[1] '266 – (1) Whosoever abuses the power accorded him by statute, by commission of a public authority or legal transaction to dispose of assets of another or to make binding agreements for another, or violates his duty to safeguard the financial interests of another incumbent upon him by reason of statute, commission of a public authority, legal transaction or fiduciary relationship, and thereby causes damage to the person, whose financial interests he was responsible for, shall be liable to imprisonment not exceeding 5 years or a fine. (2) Section 243(2), section 247, section 248a and section 263(3) shall apply mutatis mutandis.' The English version of the German laws used in this section is cited according to the (unofficial) translation published on the webpage of the Federal Ministry of Justice and Consumer Protection (www.gesetze-im-internet.de/); the translation of the German Criminal Code (StGB) has been provided by Prof Dr Michael Bohlander.

[2] Pursuant to StGB, s 266, *Untreue* is punishable by imprisonment not exceeding five years or a fine. The minimum length of imprisonment is one month (StGB, s 38(2)). The fines provided by the StGB are daily unit fines (s 40(1)), which are calculated according to the personal and financial circumstances of the offender and should typically reflect his current average one-day net income or the average income he could achieve in one day (s 40(2)). The minimum fine provided for *Untreue* consists of 5 units and the maximum of 360. Section 266(2) provides for a more severe penalty (imprisonment from six months to 10 years) if one or more aggravating circumstances provided in s 263(3) occur. Within the corporate context, the most pertinent aggravating circumstance is described under point 2 of this section: the offender 'causes a major financial loss or acts with the intent of placing a large number of persons in danger of financial loss by the continued commission of offences of fraud'. The provision makes reference to the offence of fraud, as it is part of its description, and applies *mutatis mutandis* to the offence of *Untreue*. It is the first part of the sentence – causing a loss of great value – that may in particular occur in the corporate context. It remains unclear what the minimum value at which this rule finds application is. The threshold of €50,000 is often cited in this context, see Edward Schramm, 'Untreue, § 266 StGB' in Carsten Momsen and Thomas Grützner, *Wirtschaftsstrafrecht. Handbuch für die Unternehmens- und Anwaltspraxis* (Munich: CH Beck, 2013) marginal no 161. The fact that the average loss in *Untreue* cases is €75,000 may render this exceptional aggravation of punishment part of the normal practice, increasing the level of punishment, see Jürgen Seier, 'Untreue' in Hans Achenbach and Andreas Ransiek (eds), *Handbuch Wirtschaftsstrafrecht*, 3rd edn (Heidelberg /Munich /Landsberg /Frechen /Hamburg: C.F Müller, 2012) marginal no 35. See also 3.5.2 below in the context of risk-damage.

alternative) and the *Treubruchstatbestand* (the breach of trust alternative).[3] The *Missbrauch* alternative consists in abusing the right or power granted to the perpetrator to make binding agreements in the name of another person, while the *Treubruch* alternative punishes for breaching the duty to safeguard another person's financial interests.[4] The offence requires the same result for both alternatives: damage (*Nachteil*). The relevance of this offence to the topic of this book comes in particular from interpretations which accept, under certain conditions, that exposure to the risk of damage may satisfy the requirement for damage in section 266.

The history of this offence goes back to the Constitutio Criminalis Carolina from 1532.[5] The offence of *Untreue* was enacted in the original German Penal Code in 1871, which also drew inspiration from criminal codes of former German States.[6] This version of the offence was highly casuistic, enumerating different categories of persons who could be liable for it.[7] The cumbersome formulation also prompted a debate between scholars who wanted to limit its scope to the course of conduct described as *Missbrauch* and those who opted for a broader criminalisation as described by the *Treubruch* alternative (the details of these two variants will be explained below).[8] Over decades none of the schools gained prevalence and eventually the reform of the law, which was adopted on 26 May 1933,[9] incorporated both of them in the alternative form.[10] The circle of possible perpetrators of the offence of *Untreue* remained limited, but, unlike in the pre-1933 version, the new version used a general clause. The definition of the offence in the version from 1933 remains practically intact until today. Smaller modifications concerned the legislative technique and the punishment provided.[11] Despite the lack of significant changes as to the language of the provision, the interpretation evolved considerably through jurisprudential input.[12]

[3] Because of the fact that the translation into English of these three terms (*Untreue*, *Missbrauch* and *Treubruch*) would give very similar results, and would thus not evoke the differences between them, these terms will be used in the German original.

[4] Seier, 'Untreue' (n 2) marginal no 38.

[5] Alfred Dierlamm, '§ 266 Untreue' in Roland Hefendehl and Olaf Hohmann (eds), *Münchener Kommentar zum Strafgesetzbuch*, vol 5, §§ 263–358 StGB, 2nd edn (Munich: C.H Beck, 2014) marginal no 18.

[6] Urs Kindhäuser, '§ 266 Untreue', in Urs Kindhäuser, Ulfrid Neumann and Hans-Ullrich Paeffgen (eds), *Strafgesetzbuch*, 4th edn (Baden-Baden: Nomos, 2013) marginal nos 5–6.

[7] Schramm, 'Untreue, § 266 StGB' (n 2) marginal no 25.

[8] Seier, 'Untreue' (n 2) marginal no 15. For the analysis of both modalities, see 3 below.

[9] Gesetz zur Abänderung strafrechtlicher Vorschriften, entered into force on 1 June 1933; Bernd Schünemann, '§ 266 Untreue' in Heinrich Wilhelm Laufhütte, Ruth Rissing-van Saan and Klaus Tiedemann (eds), *Strafgesetzbuch. Leipziger Kommentar*, vol 9/1, §§ 263–266b, 12th edn (Berlin: de Gruyter, 2012) before marginal no 1 (at 664).

[10] Seier, 'Untreue' (n 2) marginal no 16.

[11] Kindhäuser, '§ 266 Untreue' (n 6) marginal no 10; Schünemann, '§ 266 Untreue' (n 9) before marginal no 1 (at 664–67).

[12] Moreover, the scope of the offence was influenced by abolishing certain other provisions, such as special *Untreue* in certain types of companies (former Public Limited Companies Act (Aktiengesetz,

The reform of 1933 was adopted under the Nazi regime and reflected the criminal policy of that time.[13] Its goal was to fight 'profiteering and corruption' ('*Schiebertum und Korruption*') and 'to catch all cases deserving punishment without a gap'.[14] However, the notions used in the definition of the offence did not belong to the Nazi legal terminology.[15] The concept of legal interests protected by this offence was also dissociated from its Nazi historical context by post-war interpretation. Nevertheless, the broad and abstract definition of the offence survived and troubled further generations of German lawyers.[16] In particular, the problems concerned the scope of criminalisation of this offence and whether it meets the requirement of certainty enshrined in article 103(2) of the German Basic Law of 1949. A popular quote from the German penalist Hellmuth Mayer from 1954 expressed this issue in the following way: 'Unless there is a classic old case of *Untreue*, no court and no prosecution office may know, whether s 266 StGB is applicable or not'.[17] The offence was critically assessed on so many occasions[18] that *Perron* ironically called *Untreue* 'a goose that brings golden eggs to the doctrine and to the defence lawyers'.[19] The task of rendering the understanding of the general concept of the offence and of its different elements more precise was left to the jurisprudence and to the doctrine.[20] The Federal Constitutional Court of Germany (Bundesverfassungsgericht, BVerfG) expressed itself as satisfied with these efforts in two judgments verifying the conformity of *Untreue* with the German Constitution, in particular article 103(2) thereof, which provides for

AktG), s 294 and Limited Liability Companies Act (Gesetz betreffend die Gesellschaften mit beschränkter Haftung, GmbHG), s 81a) or by introducing new ones, as was the case for StGB, s 266b ('Misuse of cheques and credit cards'). See Schramm, 'Untreue, § 266 StGB' (n 2) marginal no 26; Martin Paul Waßmer, '§ 266 Untreue' in Jürgen Peter Graf, Markus Jäger and Petra Wittig (eds), *Wirtschafts- und Steuerstrafrecht* (Munich: CH Beck, 2011) marginal no 8.

[13] Seier, 'Untreue' (n 2) marginal no 14.

[14] Schramm, 'Untreue, § 266 StGB' (n 2) marginal no 25; Ernst Schäfer, 'Gesetz zur Abänderung strafrechtlicher Vorschriften vom 26. Mai', *Deutsche Juristenzeitung* (*DJZ*) 1933, 788 et seq (cited after Schramm, 'Untreue, § 266 StGB' (n 2) marginal no 25).

[15] Schramm, 'Untreue, § 266 StGB' (n 2) marginal no 27.

[16] Schramm, 'Untreue, § 266 StGB' (n 2) marginal no 27. On the influence of the laws adopted under the Nazi regime on today's German criminal law, see Joachim Vogel, *Einflüsse des Nationalsozialismus auf das Strafrecht* (Berlin: Berliner Wissenschafts-Verlag, 2004); Richard F. Wetzell, 'Introduction: Crime and Criminal Justice in Modern Germany' in Richard F. Wetzell (ed), *Crime and Criminal Justice in Modern Germany* (New York/Oxford: Berghahn Books, 2014) 1–30, 14–17. It is interesting to note that the criminal law under the Nazi regime attached criminal liability much more in view of the subjective elements of the offence, in particular the perpetrator's attitude (so called *Gesinnungsstrafrecht*); see in particular Vogel, cited above, in particular at 16–17 and 81–87.

[17] 'Sofern nicht einer der klassischen alten Fälle der Untreue vorliegt, weiss kein Gericht und keine Anklagebehörde, ob §266 StGB vorliegt oder nicht.' Hellmuth Mayer, 'Die Untreue' in *Materialien zur Strafrechtsreform*, vol 1, *Gutachten der Strafrechtslehrer* (Bonn, 1954) 333–56, 337, cited by Schramm, 'Untreue, § 266 StGB' (n 2) marginal no 14 and Daniel Schilling, *Fragmentarisch oder umfassend?* (Frankfurt: Peter Lang, 2009) 12; Seier, 'Untreue' (n 2) marginal no 18.

[18] Schünemann, '§ 266 Untreue' (n 9) marginal no 3 with further references.

[19] Walter Perron, 'Probleme und Perspectiven des Untreuetatbestandes', *Goltdammer's Archiv für Strafrecht* (2009) 219–34, 220.

[20] Seier, 'Untreue' (n 2) marginal no 17.

the legality principle;[21] the Court did, however, require a strict interpretation, in particular as regards the limb of result.[22] Nonetheless, some authors in the doctrine still express concerns as to the precise delimitation of the boundaries of *Untreue* and call for a legislative reform of the offence.[23]

The application of *Untreue* to cases wherein a manager exposes a company's assets to a risk of loss by taking excessively risky business decisions is not new: examples of it can be found throughout the history of the offence.[24] For instance, in 1927, the Imperial Court of Justice (Reichsgericht) sentenced a bank director for granting overly-risky credit in order to help the financial recovery of an enterprise in economic difficulties.[25] Other cases concern under-secured loans[26] or speculation with securities.[27] Another relevant notion within the interpretation of this offence is the concept of risk-damage, according to which, in certain circumstances, exposure to risk amounts to actual damage. This concept also goes back to the early time of section 266 of the (then Imperial) Penal Code 150 years ago. It was developed under the offence of fraud from which *Untreue* borrowed its conceptual framework of damage and under *Untreue* itself.[28] However, the judgments which have shaped the current interpretation of the offence in this context were issued in the last 10 years.

The offence of *Untreue* belongs to the core of white-collar offences within the German system,[29] a key crime in the context of the separation of management and ownership of limited companies.[30] It was applied to different types of relationship, including business relationships, but in particular in recent years the jurisprudence has focused on abuses committed in the corporate environment, ie by organs of the companies or their employees.[31] The debate on the interpretation of this offence has generated an enormous amount of literature and abundant jurisprudence. Practically every possible aspect of *Untreue* has been debated. It is impossible to present here all of these problems and all of the formulated theories. Therefore, this chapter will focus only on issues relevant for excessive risk-taking and will be limited to the details which are necessary and useful for the

[21] For more detail on this principle, see Chapter 6, 2.4.2.

[22] BVerfG (10 March 2009) NJW 2009, 2370; BVerfG (23 June 2010) NJW 2010, 3209.

[23] See, eg Seier, 'Untreue' (n 2) marginal no 22; Schramm, 'Untreue, § 266 StGB' (n 2) marginal no 27 with further references.

[24] Martin Paul Waßmer, *Untreue bei Risikogeschäften* (Heidelberg: CF Müller, 1997) 13.

[25] So called *Sanierungskredit, Entscheidungen des Reichsgerichtes in Strafsachen* (*RGSt*) 65, 211; cited by Waßmer, *Untreue bei Risikogeschäften* (n 24) 13.

[26] Reichsgericht, *Juristische Wochenschrift* 1934, 2923 No 29; Reichsgericht, *Juristische Wochenschrift* 1936, 934, cited by Waßmer, *Untreue bei Risikogeschäften* (n 24) 10.

[27] *RGSt* 53, 194, cited by Waßmer, *Untreue bei Risikogeschäften* (n 24) 10.

[28] Schünemann, '§ 266 Untreue' (n 9) marginal nos 177–78. Fundamental judgments: Beschluss der Vereinigten Strafsenate des Reichsgerichtes, 20 April 1887, *RGSt*16, 1, 11 (as regards fraud, StGB, s 263); *RGSt* 16, 77, 81 (as regards *Untreue*). Both judgments cited by Schünemann, '§ 266 Untreue' (n 9) marginal no 178.

[29] Seier, 'Untreue' (n 2) marginal no 1.

[30] Schünemann, '§ 266 Untreue' (n 9) marginal no 2.

[31] Ibid marginal no 3.

comparison with the other two legislative orders. The reader must also be warned that the analysis provided here is based on jurisprudence that is contradictory on various occasions and may be subject to further changes or adjustments.[32] Further difficulty results from the fact that many judgments were issued with regard to specific, concrete types of activities and it thus remains unclear whether their findings can be extrapolated to the understanding of *Untreue* in general. The analysis will focus mainly on the two major types of limited companies: the limited liability company (*Gesellschaft mit beschränkter Haftung*, GmbH) and the public limited company (*Aktiengesellschaft*, AG).

Lastly, in view of the difficulties encountered in practice in using *Untreue* to punish misconduct in connection with the most recent financial crisis, in 2013 the German legislator introduced specific criminal provisions in relation to the banking and insurance sector, namely section 54a of the Banking Act and section 142 of the Insurance Supervision Act. These two sections provide very similar offences, which penalise violation of risk management rules by senior managers, which result in the concrete endangerment of the existence of the undertakings under their direction. While the violation must be committed intentionally, criminal liability is also foreseen if the result was brought about with negligence. So far, the German legal system has tackled excessive risk-taking through the offence of *Untreue*, and at the time of writing, there has been no jurisprudence concerning this new offence and the relevant literature is very limited. The offence is a clear post-crisis attempt to address excessive risk-taking in crucial financial institutions, thus a presentation of the German system without a brief analysis of this new law would be incomplete.

2. Protected Legal Interests

According to the dominant view, the only legal interests protected by the offence of Untreue are property or assets (*Vermögen*).[33] The fact that the required course of conduct consists of breaching the trust of the victim only describes the way

[32] Seier, 'Untreue' (n 2) marginal no 18.

[33] Walter Perron, '§ 266 Untreue', in Adolf Schönke, Horst Schröder, Albin Eser et al (eds), *Strafgesetzbuch Kommentar*, 29th edn (Munich: CH Beck, 2014) marginal no 1; Dierlamm, '§ 266 Untreue' (n 5) marginal no 1; Kindhäuser, '§ 266 Untreue' (n 6) marginal no 1; Schramm, 'Untreue, § 266 StGB' (n 2) marginal no 2; Seier, 'Untreue' (n 2) marginal no 10; BGH (20 July 1999) NJW 2000, 154, 155; BVerfG (23 June 2010) NJW 2010, 3209, 3212. On the difficulties of translating '*Vermögen*' into English, see 3.5 below. German jurisprudence and doctrine explains the justification for criminalisation by reference to a highly debated term '*Rechtsgut*', which can be translated into English as: protected goods or goods-in-law. Further on that debate see: Claus Roxin, *Strafrecht. Allgemeiner Teil*, vol 1, 4th edn (Munich: C.Beck, 2006) 14 et seq; Roland Hefendehl, Andrew von Hirsch and Wolfgang Wohlers, *Die Rechtsgutstheorie. Legitimationsbasis des Strafrechts oder dogmatisches Glasperlenspiel?* (Baden Baden: Nomos, 2003); Claus Roxin, 'The Legislation Critical Concept of Goods-in-law under Scrutiny' (2013) 3(1) *European Criminal Law Review* 3. From a theoretical point of view, this concept will be also analysed in Chapter 6.

in which the assets are targeted, in the same way as deception describes the way the perpetrator targets property while committing the offence of fraud (*Betrug*, StGB, s 263).[34] It is the fact that the owner of the assets entrusts them to another person and thus loses control of them that requires a counterbalance in the form of criminal protection.[35] Thus, *Untreue* is applicable when the person to whom the assets were entrusted misuses the power to decide upon another person's property.[36]

The literature enumerates several other possible protected interests, which, however, have not gained acceptance. Under the Nazi regime, the interpretation of the offence put the emphasis on the aspect of betrayal (*Verrat*), which has now been abandoned.[37] The offence does not protect the freedom to make use of one's own assets,[38] although one of the judgments of the Federal Court of Justice (Bundesgerichtshof, BGH) seems to admit such an interpretation.[39] The confidence in the integrity of the person to whom the assets are entrusted (*Vertrauen in die Integrität des Treunehmers*) or confidence in the integrity of the legal and business environment (*Vertrauen in die Redlichkeit des Rechts- und Wirtschaftsverkehrs*) are also excluded.[40] The main reasons given for this approach are the following. First, *Untreue* is systematically connected to the offence of fraud (*Betrug*) as they are in the same chapter of the StGB and the former borrows some of its conceptual framework from the latter (in particular concerning the result). There is an agreement in the German doctrine that fraud is focused only on protecting property (it is referred to as a genuine property offence, *reines Vermögensdelikt*) and *Untreue* should be interpreted in the same way.[41] Secondly, if the resulting damage is of minor value, *Untreue* is prosecuted only upon the request of the victim, which

[34] Seier, 'Untreue' (n 2) marginal no 10; Dierlamm, '§ 266 Untreue' (n 5) marginal no 1. Contrary Meyer, according to whom the trust between the principal and the agent is also protected by the offence: Dieter Meyer, 'Nochmals: Ist die Begebung ungedeckter Schecks mittels Scheckkarte durch ihren berechtigten Inhaber strafbar?' (1971) 11 *Monatschrift für Deutsches Recht (MDR)* 893, 894.

[35] Dierlamm, '§ 266 Untreue' (n 5) marginal no 2.

[36] Kindhäuser, '§ 266 Untreue' (n 6) marginal no 3.

[37] Dierlamm, '§ 266 Untreue' (n. 5) marginal no 1; Kindhäuser, '§ 266 Untreue' (n 6) marginal no 1. For the exposition of the interpretation based on betrayal, see Georg Dahm, 'Untreue' in Franz Gürtner, *Das kommende deutsche Strafrecht, Besonderer Teil*, 2nd edn (Berlin: Verlag Franz Vahlen, 1936) 448 et seq.

[38] Dierlamm, '§ 266 Untreue' (n 5) marginal no 1; for critical analysis see Frank Saliger, 'Wider die Ausweitung des Untreuetatbestandes' (2000) 3(112) *Zeitschrift für die gesamte Strafrechtswissenschaft (ZStW)* 563, 589 et seq.

[39] BGH (29 August 2008) NStZ 2009, 95, 99.

[40] Seier, 'Untreue' (n 2) marginal no 11; Schramm, 'Untreue, § 266 StGB' (n 2) marginal no 2. Contrary view: Wolfgang Schmid, '§ 31 Treupflichtverletzungen' in Christian Müller-Gugenberger and Klaus Bieneck, *Wirtschaftsstrafrecht. Handbuch des Wirtschaftsstraf- und – ordnungswidrigkeitenrechts*, 5th edn (Köln: Dr Otto Schmidt, 2011) marginal no 3, who considers that *Untreue* also protects confidence in the integrity of the legal and business environment. See also in this line: Wolfgang Dunkel, 'Nochmals: Der Scheckkartenmißbrauch in strafrechtlicher Sicht' (1977) *Goltdammer's Archiv für Strafrecht* 329.

[41] Waßmer, '§ 266 Untreue' (n 12) marginal no 9; Schünemann, '§ 266 Untreue' (n 9) marginal no 23.

should demonstrate the focus on property as opposed to the relationship between the principal and the agent.[42]

Considering property or assets to be the only protected interests of Untreue has several substantive law and procedural consequences. First, the owner of the assets and the person who suffered damage from the breach of duty (*Geschädigter*) must be identical. However, it is possible that the person who entrusts the property and the owner are not identical, if the assets are already being managed by a third person.[43] Secondly, since property is an individual protected interest, the consent of the owner, including presumed consent, may under certain conditions exclude criminal liability.[44] However, as regards limited companies, the shareholders' ability to consent is restricted, for example, by the requirement that the act would not endanger the existence of the company.[45] Such a limitation demonstrates that although the offence focuses on the owner's (ie the company's and the shareholders') assets, it takes into account some interests of other stakeholders.[46] Thirdly, the interests of third persons such as creditors or employees are not protected by this offence.[47] Only the person who suffered damage from the offence can become an aggrieved party (*Verletzter*) within the criminal procedure (for example, as described in section 403 et seq of the Code of Criminal Procedure (Strafprozessordnung, StPO)). This category includes shareholders in the cases of the GmbH and AG.[48]

3. Offence of *Untreue*

The two modalities of the offence under StGB, section 266, *Missbrauchstatbestand* (the abuse of power alternative, consisting in abusing the right of the perpetrator to make binding agreements in the name of the victim) and *Treubruchstatbestand* (the breach of trust alternative, consisting in breaching the duty to safeguard another person's financial interests) have identical requirements of result and *mens rea* but differ as to the description of the potential perpetrator and the criminal conduct. It is because of this differentiation that the relation between the two modalities has been the subject of intensive debate within the German doctrine, resulting in two competing theories.[49]

Whereas one theory considers that the two modalities constitute two different offences (dualistic theory), the opposite theory claims that *Untreue* is one offence,

[42] Seier, 'Untreue' (n 2) marginal no 11; Waßmer, '§ 266 Untreue' (n 12) marginal no 9.
[43] Seier, 'Untreue' (n 2) marginal no 12.
[44] Ibid marginal no 12; for details see 6.1 below.
[45] For further details see 6.1 below.
[46] See also Kristina Nattkemper, *Die Untreuestrafbarkeit des Vorstands einer Aktiengesellschaft* (Berlin: Duncker & Humblot, 2013) 75–76.
[47] Schramm, 'Untreue, § 266 StGB' (n 2) marginal no 2.
[48] Kindhäuser, '§ 266 Untreue' (n 6) marginal no 129; Seier, 'Untreue' (n 2) marginal no 13.
[49] Dierlamm, '§ 266 Untreue' (n 5) marginal no 24.

with the *Treubruch* modality encompassing all its possible occurrences and *Missbrauch* representing a particular form of its commission (monistic theory).[50] The core of this debate concerns the question whether it is necessary to prove in the case of the *Missbrauch* modality a *Vermögensbetreuungspflicht* (the duty to safeguard the financial interests of another person), which is necessary for the *Treubruch*. In other words, the question is whether the criteria for defining this duty elaborated for the *Treubruch* modality apply also for the *Missbrauch* alternative or whether it is enough that the perpetrator has the right to make binding agreements in the name of or for another.[51] Those claiming that proof of the duty is necessary consider it a common platform for the offence – *Vermögensbetreuungspflicht* defines here the perpetrator and his conduct is the breach of this duty – and thus consider *Untreue* to be one offence, where a *Missbrauch* is just a special case of *Treubruch* (monistic theory). If such necessity is denied, then the two modalities can be considered two different offences (dualistic theory).[52]

Currently, the monistic approach has gained prevalence in the jurisprudence[53] and among the German doctrine, so the duty to safeguard the financial interests of another person has to be established for both modalities.[54] Two consequences result from the preference for the monistic theory. First, on a procedural level, if *Untreue* is considered to be one offence with two modalities, it would theoretically be unnecessary to warn the defendant that he may be convicted of the offence as defined in the other modality, rather than the one of which he was originally accused. In the case of two different offences, such a change would

[50] Seier, 'Untreue' (n 2) marginal nos 10–11; Kindhäuser, '§ 266 Untreue' (n 6) marginal no 11. In view of limited practical impact of this debate on the topic of excessive risk-taking, a detailed account has not been given. For more detailed information see, eg Kindhäuser, '§ 266 Untreue' (n 6) marginal nos 12–26; Dierlamm, '§ 266 Untreue' (n 5) marginal nos 24–31; Schünemann, '§ 266 Untreue' (n 9) marginal no 6 et seq.

[51] Kindhäuser, '§ 266 Untreue' (n 6) marginal no 20; Schünemann, '§ 266 Untreue' (n 9) marginal no 18 et seq.

[52] Seier, 'Untreue' (n 2) marginal nos 9–10.

[53] Seier, 'Untreue' (n 2) marginal no 52; BGH (26 July 1972) NJW 1972, 1904; BGH (5 July 1984) NJW 1984, 2539, 2540; BGH (13 June 1985) NJW 1985, 2280, 2282; BGH (6 December 2001) NJW 2002, 1585 et seq; BGH (21 December 2005) NJW 2006, 522, 525.

[54] Seier, 'Untreue' (n 2) marginal no 52. The monistic theory is sustained eg by Dierlamm, '§ 266 Untreue' (n 5) marginal no 31; Kindhäuser, '§ 266 Untreue' (n 6) marginal no 26; Johannes Wessels and Thomas Hillenkamp, *Strafrecht. Besonderer Teil 2, Straftaten gegen Vermögenswerte*, 36th edn (Heidelberg: CF Müller, 2013) marginal nos 749–50. The opposite view is represented eg by Schramm, 'Untreue, § 266 StGB' (n 2) marginal no 13 and to some extent by Schünemann in '§ 266 Untreue' (n 9) marginal nos 13–17. Martin Heger, '§ 266 StGB Untreue' in Kristian Kühl and Martin Heger, *Strafgezetzbuch Kommentar* (Lackner/Kühl), 28th edn (Munich: CH Beck, 2014) marginal nos 4, 21; Thomas Fischer, *Strafgesetzbuch*, 61st edn (Munich: CH Beck, 2014) ch 'Untreue § 266', marginal no 6. The main argument in favour of choosing that option refers to the wording of the provision and considers that the expression '*dem, dessen Vermögensinteressen er zu betreuen hat*' (to the person, whose financial interests he was responsible for) refers to both modalities. Moreover, the reaction of the legislator (Law Reform 2. WiKG, 15 May 1986) to one of the judgments of the BGH (BGH (26 July 1972) NJW 1972, 1904) demonstrates his preference toward the monistic theory (Dierlamm, '§ 266 Untreue' (n 5) marginal nos 26, 31, and Schünemann, '§ 266 Untreue' (n 9) before marginal no 1 (at 665)).

require prior warning, as provided for[55] in StPO, section 265(1).[56] However, even though the jurisprudence has accepted the monistic theory, it still considers that such a warning is necessary.[57] Secondly, should the criteria defining the *Vermögensbetreuungspflicht* be applied also to the *Missbrauch* modality, then the perpetrator of *Missbrauch* must have some room for manoeuvre and not only have the right to make a binding agreement for the principal according to detailed and precise instruction leaving him no space for decision-making.[58]

3.1. Duty to Safeguard the Financial Interests of Another Person (*Vermögensbetreuungspflicht*)

The expression 'duty to safeguard the financial interests of another' is as such very wide and only through restrictive interpretation by the jurisprudence and the doctrine have its boundaries been shaped toward compliance with the principle of legality.[59] Not every duty which a person may have not to act in a way which would infringe the financial interests of another will turn the person having such a duty into a potential perpetrator of *Untreue*.[60] The German doctrine and jurisprudence have developed three criteria which qualify a relationship as a 'duty' in the sense of section 266.

First, the perpetrator must be acting in the interests of another person. This criterion requires that the relationship between the perpetrator and the principal is of such a nature that the perpetrator is expected to take care of the principal's interests.[61]

Secondly, safeguarding someone else's interests should be at the core of his relationship with the principal and the perpetrator and does not constitute mere accessory obligations.[62] This requirement is meant to guarantee that *Untreue* does not become a tool to punish every failure to honour contractual obligations.[63]

[55] StPO, s 265(1) 'The defendant may not be sentenced on the basis of a penal norm other than the one referred to in the charges admitted by the court without first having his attention specifically drawn to the change in the legal reference and without having been afforded an opportunity to defend himself'.

[56] Schramm, 'Untreue, § 266 StGB' (n 2) marginal no 12.

[57] Seier, 'Untreue' (n 2) marginal no 60; BGH (15 July 1954) NJW 1954, 1616; BGH (5 July 1984) NJW 1984, 2539, 2540.

[58] Schramm, 'Untreue, § 266 StGB' (n 2) marginal no 12.

[59] Petra Wittig, *Wirtschafsstrafrecht* (Munich: CH Beck, 2010) marginal no 94.

[60] Ibid marginal no 95.

[61] Kindhäuser, '§ 266 Untreue' (n 6) marginal no 43; Wittig, *Wirtschafsstrafrecht* (n 59) marginal no 97. In other words, it must serve the interests of another person (*Fremdnützigkeit*), BGH (15 June 1976); *Goltdammer's Archiv für Strafrecht* 1977, 18–19. This requirement excludes from the scope of the offence situations in which there exist contractual obligations, but the parties act mainly in their own interests (for instance, contracts of sale or loan).

[62] Perron, '§ 266 Untreue' (n 33) marginal nos 23–28; BGHSt (30 October 1985) NStZ 1986, 361; BGH (4 November 1988) NStZ 1989, 72–73; BGHSt (22 May 1991) NJW 1991, 2574.

[63] Wittig, *Wirtschafsstrafrecht* (n 59) marginal no 104; BGH (3 May 1978) NJW 1978, 2105, 2106 et seq.

This issue is quite clear as to bilateral contracts (*Synallagmatischer Verträge*), eg the contract of sale, where both parties have certain obligations that have an impact on each other's financial interests, but they are acting for their own good, without taking responsibility for another's financial interests.[64] Therefore, a contract for work and labour (*Werkvertrag*), an employment contract (*Arbeitsvertrag*), and a loan (*Darlehen*) are in principle excluded.[65] The opposite is true, however, if the contract is designed in a way that gives the perpetrator power of attorney (eg an employment contract containing such a clause, or a contract of sale in the form of commission sale).[66]

Thirdly, while executing it, he would be granted at least a certain degree of independence in taking the decisions (*Selbstständigkeit*).[67] This requirement is essential in determining the position of the perpetrator in the sense that it eliminates from the scope of the offence those types of relationship where the person is only 'the extended arm of the principal',[68] while the latter is not losing control of his affairs and thus is not in need of criminal law protection.[69]

3.2. *Missbrauch* Alternative (Abuse of Power)

However, it is currently not uncommon for judgments not to establish whether the conditions of the *Missbrauch* have been fulfilled, and to limit their analysis to the establishment of the existence of the duty to safeguard another person's financial interests (and breach thereof),[70] a practice criticised by the German doctrine, in view of the duty to precisely ascertain the offence of which one is accused or in respect of which one is sentenced.[71]

Besides the above described duty to safeguard the financial interests of another, the perpetrator of the *Missbrauch* alternative must have been granted the power to administer the property of another (*Verfügungsbefugnis*[72]) or to make binding agreements for another (*Verpflichtungsbefugnis*). The first of these powers, *Verfügungsbefugnis*, enables a person to modify, transfer or dispose of someone

[64] The obligation to act in good faith (BGB, s 242) or duties to avoid damage to another party are not enough to constitute the duty required for the offence. Dierlamm, '§ 266 Untreue' (n 5) marginal no 65; Kindhäuser, '§ 266 Untreue' (n 6) marginal no 45.

[65] Kindhäuser, '§ 266 Untreue' (n 6) marginal no 45.

[66] Ibid marginal no 46.

[67] 'so dass der Verpflichtete … einen gewissen Spielraum, eine gewisse Bewegungsfreiheit oder Selbstständigkeit hat' BVerfG (23 June 2010). See also NJW 2010, 3209, para [108]; BGH (11 December 1957) NJW 1960, 53; BGH (3 August 2005) NStZ 2006, 38, 39; BGH 22 May 1991, NJW 1991, 2574; Schünemann, '§ 266 Untreue' (n 9) marginal no 82–85.

[68] 'der verlängerte Arm des Vermögensinhabers' (Kindhäuser, '§ 266 Untreue' (n 6) marginal no 47).

[69] Kindhäuser, '§ 266 Untreue' (n 6) marginal no 47.

[70] Seier, 'Untreue' (n 2) marginal no 39, eg BGH (27 February 1975) NJW 1975, 1234; BGH (21 December 2005) NJW 2006, 522; BGH (22 November 2005) NJW 2006, 453.

[71] Seier, 'Untreue' (n 2) marginal no 40.

[72] It can be also translated as the power to dispose of assets of another.

else's property, whilst the second one, *Verpflichtungsbefugnis*, empowers him to legally bind the principal by an agreement made on his behalf.[73] The perpetrator may be entitled to act in his own name on someone else's behalf or as an agent.[74]

The power may come from a statute, a commission of a public authority or a legal transaction. A factual possibility to influence one's property situation is not enough. The power must be given to the perpetrator through a valid act. If it occurs that the act was invalid, the perpetrator cannot be liable for the *Missbrauch* alternative, however his liability might still be possible under the *Treubruch* modality.[75] On the other hand, if the power was legally granted to the perpetrator but in the meantime it was withdrawn or expired, but it continues to be valid in relation to third persons (eg on the basis of German Civil Code (Burgerliches Gesetzbuch, BGB), section 170 et seq), the perpetrator may be held liable for *Untreue* in the *Missbrauch* alternative.[76]

The fact that the perpetrator co-owns the assets in question does not exclude his liability, thus a partner in a partnership (*Personengesellschaft*) may also commit *Untreue* with assets of the partnership.[77] The qualification of property as belonging to someone else must be assessed according to civil law criteria and not with regard to whom the assets belong in the economic sense.[78] It results that if the company is the owner of the assets, the ultimate owner of the shares can be liable for *Untreue* concerning the assets of this company, which is in particular relevant in cases of limited companies owned by one person.[79] In the same sense, if the owner loses control over his property (eg in the course of an insolvency procedure), he remains its owner and therefore cannot commit *Untreue* in relation to these assets.[80]

Situations to which this modality applies consist of making use of the power to conclude a valid transaction or to make a legally binding statement, which goes beyond the scope of authorisation granted internally to the perpetrator.[81] A necessary condition is a discrepancy between the power vested in the perpetrator as regards binding the company towards third parties, and the internal agreement on the use of this power (the agreement between the owner and the agent).[82]

[73] Seier, 'Untreue' (n 2) marginal no 100.

[74] Dierlamm, '§ 266 Untreue' (n 5) marginal no 34.

[75] Wittig, *Wirtschafsstrafrecht* (n 59) ch '§ 20 Untreue', marginal no 27.

[76] Eg on the basis of BGB, s 170 et seq. For instance, BGB, s 170 provides that: 'If authority is granted by declaration to a third party, it remains in force in relation to this third party until he is notified by the principal of the expiry thereof'. See Kindhäuser, '§ 266 Untreue' (n 6) marginal no 89; Dierlamm, '§ 266 Untreue' (n 5) marginal no 34.

[77] Kindhäuser, '§ 266 Untreue' (n 6) marginal no 30.

[78] Perron, '§ 266 Untreue' (n 33) marginal no 6.

[79] Schünemann, '§ 266 Untreue' (n 9) marginal no 72; Perron, '§ 266 Untreue' (n 33) marginal no 6.

[80] Kindhäuser, '§ 266 Untreue' (n 6) marginal no 30.

[81] Wittig, *Wirtschafsstrafrecht* (n 59) marginal no 33.

[82] A classic example of such a situation is the German procuration (*Prokura*). Although the procuration might be limited by agreement or law (eg in accordance with Commercial Code (Handelsgesetzbuch,

The internal limits of the authorisation for the perpetrator are generally provided by the relationship between him and the owner, in other words by his duty to safeguard the financial interests of another.[83] In the case of foreign companies, the scope of authorisation might need to be sought in the law of the jurisdiction which applies to the company.[84]

It is possible to commit the *Missbrauch* alternative by omission.[85] However, this possibility is necessarily limited to situations where omission is equal to a statement with legal consequences, ie leads to a conclusion of a transaction or to a renunciation of a right.[86]

3.3. *Treubruch* Alternative (Breach of Trust)

The perpetrator of the general *Treubruch* alternative need not have the powers described in the previous section. It is sufficient that he has the duty to safeguard the financial interests of another. The duty may be enshrined in a statute, a commission of a public authority, or a legal transaction, similarily to the *Missbrauch*, as well as in an additional source, a fiduciary relationship. This source extends the application of the offence in particular to the following categories of situations.[87]

The first group includes situations, in which the source of power turned out to be invalid.[88] This might be the case if the management of a company has been nominated by an invalid decision, for example in case of an AG in which the management board (*Vorstand*) has been nominated by an irregularly appointed supervisory board, and despite that fact (or possibly not being aware of that) the

HGB) s 49(2)), this limitation has no effect on third parties (HGB, s 50). Similar discrepancies may occur as to the external power and internal authorisation of: a commission agent (*Kommissionär*) (HGB, ss 383, 385); a managing partner of a general partnership (*offene Handelsgesellschaft*) (HGB, s 126(1), (2)); manager of a GmbH (GmbHG, s 37) and the management board of an AG (AktG, s 82); Kindhäuser, '§ 266 Untreue' (n 6) marginal no 86; Petra Wittig, '§ 266 Untreue' in Bernd von Heintschel-Heinegg (ed), *Beck'scher Online-Kommentar StGB*, 38th edn (Munich: CH Beck, 2018), marginal no 13, available at www.beck-online.beck.de.

[83] Kindhäuser, '§ 266 Untreue' (n 6) marginal no 92.

[84] Wittig, '§ 266 Untreue' (n 82) marginal no 18a.2.

[85] Wittig, *Wirtschafsstrafrecht* (n 59) marginal no 34.

[86] Perron, '§ 266 Untreue' (n 33) marginal no 16.

[87] The third category of situations falling under this category, although not without controversy, concerns situations where the assets have been entrusted for a purpose which is *contra bonos mores* or against the law (*gesetzes- oder sittenwidrige Rechtsgeschäfte*), BGH (17 November 1955) NJW 1956, 151; BGH (19 January 1965) NJW 1965, 770; BGH (6 December 1983) NJW 1984, 800. The mere fact that the perpetrator did not perform the act (eg in order to bribe a public official or to speculate in a way which is against the market regulations), for which purpose the assets were entrusted, cannot in and of itself make him responsible for *Untreue*. This problem concerns the situation where the perpetrator misuses the assets entrusted with such a purpose. For details of this debate, see Dierlamm, '§ 266 Untreue' (n 5) marginal nos 166–68; Kindhäuser, '§ 266 Untreue' (n 6) marginal nos 41–42; Schünemann, '§ 266 Untreue' (n 9) marginal no 64.

[88] Schünemann, '§ 266 Untreue' (n 9) marginal no 63.

management exercises its functions normally.[89] The second category comprises situations where the perpetrator's legal relationship has terminated, but he continues to exercise it assuming that this is the will of the principal.[90] The duty will only be admitted when the perpetrator continues to execute his function as such and not in cases where only some particular duties remain after the cessation of the function related to the termination of the contract.[91] Eventually, the inclusion of fiduciary relationships extends the application of *Untreue* to de facto management.

A person fulfilling the requirements described above commits *Untreue* in the form of the *Treubruch* alternative by breaching the duty to safeguard the financial interests of another (*Verletzung der Vermögensbetreuungspflicht*) in any other way than by committing *Missbrauch*. An important issue, which will determine whether what the perpetrator did can be considered a breach of this duty, concerns the standards applicable to determine the fulfilment of the duty. These standards are provided for by the same sources establishing the relationship at the basis of the duty: a statute,[92] a commission of a public authority or a contract. If none of these sources provide for more precise instructions, they should be sought in rules setting the general standards for certain types of relationship, such as 'reasonable care' (*übliche Sorgfalt*);[93] 'care of a prudent mercantile trader' (*Sorgfalt eines ordentlichen Kaufmanns*);[94] 'care of a prudent businessman' (*Sorgfalt eines ordentlichen Geschäftsmanns*);[95] or 'care of a prudent and conscientious manager'[96] (*die Sorgfalt eines ordentlichen und gewissenhaften Geschäftsleiters*).[97]

Only breach of the duty that constitutes the special position of the perpetrator towards the owner's property can be the basis for responsibility for *Untreue* (*Sachlich-Inhaltlich Zusammenhang*).[98] Furthermore, not every rule that the perpetrator breaches may lead to criminal liability, but only of those rules which aim at protecting property.[99] Moreover, the breach must concern the scope of competences of the perpetrator. Therefore, for example, if an angry manager throws his mobile phone on the floor and destroys it, he is not liable for *Untreue*.[100]

[89] Seier, 'Untreue' (n 2) marginal no 137; Dierlamm, '§ 266 Untreue' (n 5) marginal no 163; BGH (22 September 1982) NJW 1983, 240.

[90] Seier, 'Untreue' (n 2) marginal no 138; see also BGH (14 July 1955) NJW 1955, 1643.

[91] Dierlamm, '§ 266 Untreue' (n 5) marginal no 164.

[92] Eg BGB, ss 1639 et seq, 1664, 1802 et seq, 2216 et seq; see Kindhäuser, '§ 266 Untreue' (n 6) marginal no 63.

[93] Kindhäuser, '§ 266 Untreue' (n 6) marginal no 63, citing the following provisions: BGB, ss 276, 665, 677, 27 Abs 3, 86, 713.

[94] HGB, s 347.

[95] GmbHG, s 43 Abs 1.

[96] AktG, s 93 Abs 1.

[97] The list in this paragraph after Kindhäuser, '§ 266 Untreue' (n 6) marginal no 63.

[98] Dierlamm, '§ 266 Untreue' (n 5) marginal no 185; BGHSt (30 October 1985) NStZ 1986, 361, 362; OLG Hamm (20 January 2000) NStZ-RR 2000, 236, 237.

[99] Wittig, '§ 266 Untreue' (n 82) marginal no 35b; Kindhäuser, '§ 266 Untreue' (n 6) marginal no 63.

[100] Urs Kindhäuser, *Strafrecht. Besonderer Teil II*, 4th edn (Baden Baden: Nomos, 2005) 41.

In the case of *Treubruch*, the duty can be breached not only through an act which has legal consequences and which is an expression of will, but also through material acts that are not legal acts. The following behaviour can be cited as examples: taking money from the cash till;[101] or the combination or intermixture of movable things that will lower their value.[102] However, not every breach of duty will constitute *Treubruch*; it must be related to the scope of functions (*Aufgabenkreis*) of the perpetrator.[103]

In cases of granting credits and sponsoring, the First Senate of the Federal Court of Justice required that the breach be 'severe' (*gravierend*).[104] The reasoning behind this decision was to differentiate between a breach of a duty, which constitutes a mere violation of civil law or company law rules, and a violation which would lead to criminal liability.[105] This approach would guarantee asymmetrical 'accessoriness' of criminal provisions to civil or company law provisions since not every breach of duty will constitute a *Treubruch* in the sense of StGB, section 266, whereas every *Treubruch* will necessarily entail a violation of civil or company law duties.[106]

This solution resulted in controversy. The Third Senate of the BGH considered that the First Senate had added a requirement to the definition of the offence which had not been provided by the legislator, and denied the necessity that the breach of duty be severe.[107] However, this criticism was rejected by the BVerfG in a recent judgment which re-confirmed the requirement.[108]

It remains unclear whether this requirement will remain within the structure of the offence, in particular as to cases other than granting credits and sponsoring. It has been pointed out that, while in these two domains its use may be justified to curb excessive criminalisation in view of a particularly broad discretion of the managers, the use of it in other areas may be unnecessary and doubtful in the absence of legislative expression of such a requirement.[109] Moreover, the use of this clause may also have limited impact, since it is as such rather vague.[110] However,

[101] BGH (17 November 1955) NJW 1956, 151, 151 et seq; BGH (11 December 1957) NJW 1960, 53.

[102] Kindhäuser, '§ 266 Untreue' (n 6) marginal no 64.

[103] Ibid marginal no 62.

[104] Schramm, 'Untreue, § 266 StGB' (n 2) marginal no 53; BGH (15 November 2001) NJW 2002, 1211–16, 1214; BGH (6 December 2001) NJW 2002, 1585,1587; also in LG Düsseldorf (22 July 2004) NJW 2004, 3275, 3280. See also BGH (13 April 2011) NJW 2011, 1747, 1749, para [30].

[105] Kindhäuser, '§ 266 Untreue' (n 6) marginal no 75a.

[106] Dierlamm, '§ 266 Untreue' (n 5) marginal no 174; Klaus Lüderssen, 'Gesellschaftsrechtliche Grenzen der strafrechtlichen Haftung des Aufsichtsrats' in Dieter Dölling, *Jus Humanum. Grundlagen des Rechts und Strafrechts, Festschrift für Ernst-Joachim Lampe* (Berling: Duncker & Humblot, 2003) 727–42, at 729; Wolfgang Wohlers, 'Die strafrechtliche Bewältigung der Finanzkrise am Beispiel der Strafbarkeit wegen Untreue' (2011) 123 *ZStW* 791, 801.

[107] Kindhäuser, '§ 266 Untreue' (n 6) marginal no 75b; Schramm, 'Untreue, § 266 StGB' (n 2) marginal no 54; BGH (21 December 2005) NJW 2006, 522, 526 et seq.

[108] BVerfG (23 June 2010) NJW 2010, 3209, 3215, para [112].

[109] Schramm, 'Untreue, § 266 StGB' (n 2) marginal no 55.

[110] Ibid marginal no 55; Kindhäuser, '§ 266 Untreue' (n 6) marginal no 75b.

the recent judgment regarding the management board of the HSH Nordbank AG seems to confirm the requirement of severe breach.[111]

Treubruch, similarily to *Missbrauch*, can be committed by omission.[112] Seier gives the following examples of such cases: failure to prevent existing danger; neglect of control duties; omission to insure entrusted property; allowing valuable products or real estate to decay; lack of proper book-keeping; failure to declare a claim into the insolvency estate; missing an opportunity to increase the assets.[113] Silence which leads to the prolongation of a contract is to be regarded as *Missbrauch*; failing to terminate a(n) (unfavourable) contract should be analysed as *Treubruch*.[114] In view of these rules, a manager who is helping another to commit *Untreue* by turning a blind eye to the latter's actions and against his duty could also be criminally liable.

3.4. Managers of Companies and Excessive Risk-Taking

3.4.1. Senior Management in GmbH

The manager(s) (*Geschäftsführer*) of a limited liability company (*Gesellschaft mit beschränkter Haftung*, GmbH) have the duty to safeguard their company's financial interests and they can be liable for *Untreue*, if they breach this duty and cause damage or risk-damage to the company.[115] The managers manage the company and represent it in transactions with third parties.[116] Therefore, they can be liable for both modalities of *Untreue*. The duty of the managers is, in particular, enshrined in GmbHG, sections 35 and 43.[117] Section 43 sets the standard,

[111] BGH (12 October 2016) 5 StR 134/15.

[112] According to the dominant view, the punishment for *Untreue* committed by omission benefits from legal reduction in view of StGB, s 13. See Seier, 'Untreue' (n 2) marginal nos 72–79; Waßmer, '§ 266 Untreue' (n 12) marginal no 11; Schünemann, '§ 266 Untreue' (n 9) marginal no 202. See also Michael Bohlander, *Principles of German Criminal Law* (Oxford/Portland, OR: Hart Publishing, 2009) 40 and Wolfgang Wohlers and Karsten Gaede, '§ 13 Begehen durch Unterlassen' in Urs Kindhäuser, Ulfrid Neumann and Hans-Ullrich Paeffgen (eds), *Strafgesetzbuch*, 4th edn (Baden-Baden: Nomos, 2013), marginal nos 65–66.

[113] Seier, 'Untreue' (n 2) marginal no 75.

[114] Perron, '§ 266 Untreue' (n 33) marginal no 35a.

[115] Seier, 'Untreue' (n 2) marginal no 311; BGH (27 August 2010) NJW 2010, 3458. Besides managers of GmbH and AG, the following types of persons could be liable for *Untreue* (this list is after Seier, 'Untreue' (n 2) marginal no 109): persons specifically authorised to make agreements in the name of the company, *Prokuristen* (HGB, s 48 et seq); *Handlungsbevollmächtigte* (HGB, s 54 et seq); managing associates/partners of different partnerships, *Die Geschäftsführende Gesellschafter einer BGB-Gesellschaft* (BGB, s 714); *einer oHG* (HGB, ss 125, 126); *einer KG* (HGB, ss 161, Abs 2, 170, 125); *einer KG auf Aktien* (AktG, s 282); *einer GmbH & Co KG* (HGB, ss 161 Abs 2, 125; GmbHG, s 35), as well as liquidators appointed contractually (*Vertraglich eingesetzte Liquidatoren*).

[116] Mads Andenas and Frank Wooldridge, *European Comparative Company Law* (Cambridge University Press, 2009) 301.

[117] Dierlamm, '§ 266 Untreue' (n 5) marginal no 92.

according to which they should 'manage the company with the degree of care and skill of a prudent businessman'.[118] Further duties may be stipulated either in the law, in the service agreements, or in resolutions of general meetings.[119] While representing the company, the managers are obliged to observe the restrictions provided in the articles of the company or by resolutions of shareholders (GmbHG, section 37(1)). However, these limitations are not binding in relation to the third parties, unless the third party was aware of these restrictions (GmbHG, section 37(2)).[120] This discrepancy may result in liability for *Missbrauch*, if the managers conclude an agreement in disregard of these limitations.[121]

According to GmbHG, section 44, the above-described rules concerning the managers apply also to their deputies (*stellvertretende Geschäftsführer*).[122]

In a GmbH, a supervisory board may also be established and in certain cases its establishment is obligatory.[123] In many aspects, the rules concerning this board follow the analogous provisions which apply to the AG, where the supervisory board is always obligatory. In particular concerning the standard of care in the execution of the board members' duties, the law refers to the statute on the AG (GmbHG, section 52(1)), which will be described below.

Shareholders (*Gesellschafter*) of a GmbH are not bound by the duty to safeguard the company's interests in the sense of StGB, section 266, regardless of the proportion of shares a shareholder owns. Nonetheless, a shareholder might become liable for *Untreue* for his acts performed as a de facto manager, but the scope of his duties will be defined according to the rules for this category of executives (see below).[124]

Particular problems occur in cases concerning one-man GmbHs, in which the sole shareholder is also the manager of the company. The majority view is that such companies should be treated in the same way as any other GmbH.[125] Although earlier jurisprudence considered that the position of such a sole shareholder and manager is no different to that of any other GmbH manager,[126] it has been suggested that the doctrine on consent ought to be taken into account.[127] Accordingly, the criminal liability for *Untreue* would be limited only to acts which affect the nominal capital of the company (*Stammkapital*), its liquidity

[118] Andenas and Wooldridge, *European Comparative Company Law* (n 116) 301; GmbHG, s 43 (1): 'Die Geschäftsführer haben in den Angelegenheiten der Gesellschaft die Sorgfalt eines ordentlichen Geschäftsmannes anzuwenden'.

[119] Andenas and Wooldridge, *European Comparative Company Law* (n 116) 301.

[120] Ibid 301.

[121] Kindhäuser, '§ 266 Untreue' (n 6) marginal no 86; Wittig, *Wirtschafsstrafrecht* (n 59) marginal no 33.

[122] Dierlamm, '§ 266 Untreue' (n 5) marginal no 92.

[123] Andenas and Wooldridge, *European Comparative Company Law* (n 116) 304.

[124] Dierlamm, '§ 266 Untreue' (n 5) marginal no 97.

[125] Seier, 'Untreue' (n 2) marginal no 324.

[126] BGH (29 May 1987) NJW 1988, 1397, 1398 et seq.

[127] Seier, 'Untreue' (n 2) marginal no 324, see also BGH (20 December 1994) NStZ 1995, 185.

or survival.[128] However, this solution has been also criticised as too formalistic, since it does not reflect the reality of company life, where shareholders are allowed to decide on the life and death of the company, while criminalising company-life-threatening acts performed by sole managers.[129]

De facto managers (*faktische Geschäftsführer*) are also among potential perpetrators, regardless of whether their status is due to the fact that their nomination was void or in cases where the person intentionally does not want to officially undertake the managerial function, however he assumes control of the company.[130] His liability for *Untreue* will necessarily be limited to the *Treubruch* modality.[131] In order to assess if a person can be considered a de facto manager, the intensity with which he executes the management function, the timespan, as well as whether he is in practice considered a manager in relation to third parties should be taken into account.[132] The so-called 'strawperson' (*Strohmann*) who is only formally the manager, but does not execute this function in practice, will not be held criminally liable unless he effectively uses the powers formally granted to him.[133]

3.4.2. Senior Management in AG

In a public limited company (*Aktiengesellschaft*, AG), members of the management board (*Vorstand*) have the duty to safeguard the financial interests of the AG. Since they have the right to take binding decisions in its name, they can be liable for both *Missbrauch* and *Treubruch* modalities.[134] Their internal duties are shaped in particular by AktG, sections 76 and 93. In particular, section 93(1) sets the standard for assessment of management duties by providing that the board members must apply in their management activities the diligence of a prudent (*ordentlich*) and conscientious (*gewissenhaft*) manager.[135] This standard should be applied to all managerial responsibilities and is generally considered to be objective in the sense that it does not take into account individual abilities and shortcomings.[136] It is not an ordinary businessman who is the model person here, but 'a person in a

[128] BGH (20 December 1994) NStZ 1995, 185; BGH (24 August 1988) NJW 1989, 112. See also the analysis of the problem of consent at 6.1 below.

[129] Seier, 'Untreue' (n 2) marginal no 325.

[130] Ibid marginal no 299; BGH (24 June 1952), BeckRS 1952, 31196211.

[131] Schmid, '§31 Treupflichtverletzungen' (n 40) marginal no 100.

[132] Dierlamm, '§ 266 Untreue' (n 5) marginal no 94; see also Alfred Dierlamm, 'Der faktische Geschäftsführer im Strafrecht – ein Phantom?' NStZ 1996, 153.

[133] Schünemann, '§ 266 Untreue' (n 9) marginal no 246; Seier, 'Untreue' (n 2) marginal no 305.

[134] Seier, 'Untreue' (n 2) marginal no 226, eg BGH (6 December 2001) NJW 2002, 1585; BGH (27 February 1975) NJW 1975, 1234; BGH (27 August 2010) NJW 2010, 3458.

[135] Alternative formulation: 'Care of a careful and conscientious businessman', Andenas and Wooldridge, *European Comparative Company Law* (n 116) 310; AktG, s 93 Abs 1 Satz 1: 'Die Vorstandsmitglieder haben bei ihrer Geschäftsführung die Sorgfalt eines ordentlichen und gewissenhaften Geschäftsleiters anzuwenden'.

[136] Andenas and Wooldridge, *European Comparative Company Law* (n 116) 310.

leading and responsible position in a specific enterprise'.[137] Section 93(1) clarifies, however, that a board member does not breach his duty of care if, while taking the managerial decision, he could reasonably consider that he is acting on the basis of adequate information and for the benefit of the company.[138] According to AktG, section 78(1), the management board represents the company in relations with third parties. The members of the board might be bound towards the company by limitations of this power of representation (AktG, section 82(1)). In the same way as in the case of the empowerment of managers of a GmbH, these limitations may create discrepancies between what the management can do and what the management is allowed to do, and thus the members of this board are potential perpetrators of the *Missbrauch* alternative.[139]

Similarly, as regards de facto managers of a GmbH, criminal liability for *Untreue* is also possible for de facto members of the management board.[140]

Members of the supervisory board (*Aufsichtrat*) of an AG can be also liable for *Untreue*, however only for its *Treubruch* modality, since the board does not make binding agreements.[141] A supervisory board member can be liable for *Untreue* only in respect of his main function, which is the monitoring of the management board's decisions (AktG, section 111(1)). Hence, members of the board who breach other duties, as for example confidentiality duties or by accepting forbidden premiums, will not be liable for *Untreue*.[142] Although according to AktG, section 116, the standard of care provided for the management board should be used accordingly for the members of the supervisory board, it is in practice less demanding and adapted to the functioning of this board, which is due to the different scope of duties of this body and to the fact that these activities are generally performed as an auxiliary occupation.[143] For this reason, members of the board are allowed in principle to trust the documents provided by the managerial board and are not obliged to perform their own inquiries.[144] They could be liable for *Untreue*, for example, if they fail to reverse or they expressly accept a decision of the management board, which is damaging for the company.[145] However, they do not breach their duty if they fail to report to the police an offence they deem to have been committed by one or more members of the management board.[146]

[137] Ibid 310.

[138] See also BGH (12 October 16) 5 StR 134/15.

[139] Kindhäuser, '§ 266 Untreue' (n 6) marginal no 86.

[140] Waßmer, '§ 266 Untreue' (n 12) marginal no 49. On the problem of de facto managers of limited companies, see also Bernd Groß, *Die strafrechtliche Verantwortlichkeit faktischer Vertretungsorgane bei Kapitalgesellschaften* (Berlin: Duncker & Humblot, 2007).

[141] Schramm, 'Untreue, § 266 StGB' (n 2) marginal no 114.

[142] Seier, 'Untreue' (n 2) marginal no 236.

[143] Ibid marginal no 235.

[144] Dierlamm, '§ 266 Untreue' (n 5) marginal no 79; Lüderssen, 'Gesellschaftsrechtliche Grenzen' (n 106) 730–31.

[145] Seier, 'Untreue' (n 2) marginal no 236.

[146] Dierlamm, '§ 266 Untreue' (n 5) marginal no 79.

Only exceptionally does the supervisory board perform tasks of a managerial nature. In particular, this is the case for the appointment and dismissal of members of the management board and for setting their remuneration (AktG, section 87), as well as approving certain transactions as provided by AktG, section 111(4) sentence 2. These decisions are to be assessed according to the standard of duty described above (diligence of a prudent and conscientious manager) and, for instance, the board members could be liable for *Untreue* if they fail to approve a decision which is profitable for the company.[147] The most extensive debate has concerned the board's task to set the management's remuneration. In the *Mannesmann/Vodafone* case, the court had to assess criminal liability of the supervisory board for *Untreue* for granting very large bonuses, ie remuneration granted after the performance of the management's activity. The Regional Court of Düsseldorf considered that although the members of the supervisory board breached their duty, that breach was not severe (*gravierend*).[148] This judgment would have altered the structure of the offence by adding this latter criterion to the assessment of the breach of duty. However, the BGH subsequently rejected this solution in its review of the judgment and considered that the additional requirement of 'severity' need not be proven.[149] These judgments prompted not only an abundant reaction from the doctrine, but also a legislative change of AktG, section 87, which provides more detailed rules according to which the supervisory board has to set the management's remuneration, which may result in less difficulty in assessing whether the supervisory board breached their duty during this assessment.[150]

The shareholders of the AG, as persons who can in any case terminate the life of the company, are considered not to have the duty to safeguard the company's financial interests in the sense of StGB, section 266, regardless whether they are minority or majority shareholders, provided that they do not hold office within the company with which such a duty is associated (eg as members of the management board or de facto managers).[151]

According to AktG, section 94, the rules concerning the members of the management board apply also to their deputies (*Stellvertreter von Vorstandsmitgliedern*).[152]

The German jurisprudence and doctrine were also confronted with the problem of how to define the scope of duty, and its breach, in the case of foreign companies such as the English Private Company limited by shares (Ltd), whose

[147] Seier, 'Untreue' (n 2) marginal no 236.

[148] LG Düsseldorf (22 July 2004) NJW 2004, 3275, 3280 et seq.

[149] BGH (21 December 2005) NJW 2006, 522, 526 et seq. But the following judgment seemed to confirm it: BGH (12 October 16) 5 StR 134/15.

[150] Seier, 'Untreue' (n 2) marginal no 239; Andreas Ransiek, 'Anerkennungsprämien und Untreue – Das "Mannesmann"-Urteil des BGH', NJW 2006, 814. See also Dierlamm, '§ 266 Untreue' (n 5) marginal nos 267–71 and references cited there.

[151] Wittig, *Wirtschafsstrafrecht* (n 59) marginal no 124; Schramm, 'Untreue, § 266 StGB' (n 2) marginal no 114; Seier, 'Untreue' (n 2) marginal no 243.

[152] Dierlamm, '§ 266 Untreue' (n 5) marginal no 95.

managers act within the scope of jurisdiction of the German criminal courts. It is considered that the rules provided by the law according to which the company was established define this duty, regardless of whether Germany company law contains equivalent rules or not.[153]

3.4.3. Other Managers in GmbH and AG

In order to assess if other managers, who do not fulfil the above functions, have the duty to safeguard their company's financial interests and thus can be held liable for *Untreue*, it is necessary to verify in each case whether the conditions describing this duty are fulfilled. It must be verified that the perpetrator was in a relationship with the company requiring that he act in the interest of the company, that safeguarding this company's financial interests was the core of this relationship, and that in performing this role he enjoyed a certain degree of independence. The work contract alone does not imply the existence of a duty to safeguard the financial interests of the employer.[154] Although the position of each manager must be considered individually in concrete cases in view of the rules describing his position (whether based in the law or according to the terms of his contract), it can be assumed that the managers will in most cases fulfil these criteria. That is, the position of manager implies that the main task of the person is to act for the benefit of the company while managing its affairs. The main criterion which will decide whether a specific manager can be held liable for *Untreue* is whether he was granted the required independence while executing this function.

For example, the jurisprudence has repeatedly held that an employee of a bank who has some management function has the duty to safeguard the bank's financial interests.[155] Similarly, commercial representatives or sales agents (*Handelsvertreter*) have also been considered to have such a duty.[156]

3.4.4. Excessive Risk-Taking as Breach of Duty

The situations in which managers expose their companies to excessive risk can fall into several categories of cases treated by the German jurisprudence and analysed by the doctrine. Many of these cases would fall into the category of so-called *Risikogeschäfte* (*Risikogeschäft* in singular), which can be translated, albeit imprecisely, as 'risky business' or 'speculative transaction'. *Risikogeschäfte*

[153] Perron, '§ 266 Untreue' (n 33) marginal no 21e; Schramm, 'Untreue, § 266 StGB' (n 2) marginal no 116; BGH (13 April 2010) NStZ 2010, 632, 634.

[154] Schmid, '§31 Treupflichtverletzungen' (n 40) marginal no 117a.

[155] Dierlamm, '§ 266 Untreue' (n 5) marginal no 82. For instance: BGH (11 January 1955) NJW 1955, 508; BGH (23 March 1993) wistra 1993, 222.

[156] Dierlamm, '§ 266 Untreue' (n 5) marginal no 98; OLG Koblenz (13 February 1968) MDR 1968, 779–80; OLG Hamm (12 March 1957), NJW 1957, 1041; OLG Köln (20 June 1967) NJW 1967, 1923.

are 'business decisions in which it is uncertain whether they lead to a loss or to a gain',[157] or decisions which may prove to be a failure.[158] If defined as such, the *Risikogeschäfte* are a rather normal element of business life and as such are not criminalised.[159]

Such a situation becomes relevant for criminal liability if the manager, who has the duty to safeguard his company's financial interests, breaches this duty by undertaking risky business or concluding a speculative transaction and as a result the company suffers harm in the form of damage or risk-damage. The question of result in this context will be dealt with in the next section. The problem discussed here concerns the issue of when the perpetrator, in taking a risk-bearing decision, breaches his duty to safeguard the company's financial interests.

The following transactions can be cited as examples of typical *Risikogeschäfte*: transactions in which one party executes its obligation immediately while the other's contribution is stretched over time:[160] speculation (for example with financial instruments),[161] or investments in particular in longer-term projects such as research or advertising campaigns.

In order to answer the question, whether the perpetrator breaches his duty in venturing a risky transaction, it is necessary to establish how much risk the person in question is allowed to take. This will result in the first place from the rules governing the internal relations between the manager and the company enshrined in the applicable law, the provisions of his contract, rules governing the execution of his duties and applicable standards of care.[162] Furthermore, it will depend on the agreement between the manager and the principal. Hence, if the principal agreed that the manager would be permitted to pursue very daring business, there is no breach of duty, even if such acts would be considered not to fulfil the normal standards of care in the given circumstances.[163] However, the agreement must comply with the rules on valid consent. Moreover, the scope of possible consent may be limited, as is the case for both GmbH and AG.[164] At the same time, the principal may narrow the scope of risk which the manager is allowed to take in comparison to the standards of the business in question. In such a case, the

[157] Wittig, *Wirtschafsstrafrecht* (n 59) marginal no 42: 'unternehmerische Entscheidung, bei der ungewiss ist, ob sie zu einer Vermögensminderung oder -mehrung führt'.

[158] Thomas Hillenkamp, 'Risikogeschäft und Untreue' NStZ 1981, 161, 165; Kindhäuser, '§ 266 Untreue' (n 6) marginal no 73; Waßmer, *Untreue bei Risikogeschäften* (n 24), 10.

[159] Kindhäuser, '§ 266 Untreue' (n 6) marginal no 73; BGH (22 November 2005) NJW 2006, 453, 455.

[160] Uwe Hellmann, 'Risikogeschäfte und Untreuestrafbarkeit' (2007) 11 *Zeitschrift für Internationale Strafrechtsdogmatik* (*ZIS*) 433.

[161] Hellmann, 'Risikogeschäfte und Untreuestrafbarkeit' (n 160) 433.

[162] Perron, '§ 266 Untreue' (n 33) marginal no 20; BGH (27 February 1975) NJW 1975, 1234, 1234 et seq; BGH (21 March 1985) wistra 1985, 190; Fischer, *Strafgesetzbuch* (n 54) marginal no 63; Kindhäuser, '§ 266 Untreue' (n 6) marginal no 73 et seq.

[163] Seier, 'Untreue' (n 2) marginal no 382.

[164] Ibid marginal no 382; BGH (20 December 1994) NStZ 1995, 185; BGH (24 August 1988) NJW 1989, 112. For more detail, see 6.1 below.

manager would not be able to successfully claim that he fulfilled this standard and would be liable for *Untreue*.[165]

If the above sources do not provide for precise direction as to the level of risk allowed to be taken and the principal did not give any particular instructions, it is assumed that the level of allowed risk should be assessed according to the purpose of the business and standards of care typical for this type of business activity.[166] Hence, in certain situations speculation will be completely forbidden. This is the case, for instance, for the managers of foundations or cooperatives as far as the preservation of their assets is concerned.[167] Speculation with the money of a savings bank (*Sparkassen*) is also considered to be forbidden.[168] Nonetheless, within the market of financial instruments, for example in undertakings dedicated to investment in commodity futures, the permitted level of risk is much higher.[169]

It is impossible to define such rules in an abstract manner, since the standard of care varies according to the type of business activity.[170] In particular, it should not be implied from the mere fact that the act exposed the company to risk or that the risk materialised in damage that the perpetrator's decision was necessarily contrary to his duty.[171] The breach of duty can occur in two situations: the perpetrator omits to perform a necessary risk analysis and takes his decision intuitively, or he performs such analysis but despite its suggestions ventures into risky business 'like a gambler'.[172] The BGH considered in the *Bundesligaskandal* case that the transaction is forbidden if 'the risk of loss is more probable than the prospect of gain'.[173] However this approach, although possibly correct in most situations, appears to be too restrictive, as there may be situations in which pursuing a more daring business can be allowed, as for example granting credit to enterprises in difficulty (so called *Sanierungskredite*) or to victims of a flood disaster.[174] A definition which would also encompass such situations would therefore consider it a breach of duty where the transaction, all circumstances taken into account, cannot be economically justified.[175]

[165] Hillenkamp, 'Risikogeschäft und Untreue' (n 158) 166.

[166] Perron, '§ 266 Untreue' (n 33) marginal no 20; BGH (4 February 2004), StV 2004, 424.

[167] Wittig, *Wirtschafsstrafrecht* (n 59) marginal no 43; Seier, 'Untreue' (n 2) marginal no 381; see, eg BGH (11 October 2000) NStZ 2001, 155.

[168] Wittig, *Wirtschafsstrafrecht* (n 59) marginal no 43. See, eg BayObLG (20 July 1965) BayOblGSt 1965, 88.

[169] BGH (6 December 1983) NJW 1984, 800, 801.

[170] Waßmer, *Untreue bei Risikogeschäften* (n 24) 28.

[171] Wittig, *Wirtschafsstrafrecht* (n 59) marginal no 44; BGH (21 March 1985) wistra 1985, 190.

[172] Seier, 'Untreue' (n 2) marginal no 385.

[173] BGH (27 February 1975) NJW 1975, 1234, 1236: 'die Gefahr eines Verlustgeschäftes wahrscheinlicher ist als die Aussicht auf Gewinnzuwachs'.

[174] Seier, 'Untreue' (n 2) marginal no 385.

[175] Perron, '§ 266 Untreue' (n 33) marginal no 20; Waßmer, *Untreue bei Risikogeschäften* (n 24) 73 et seq; Seier, 'Untreue' (n 2) marginal no 385. See also critically: Schünemann, '§ 266 Untreue' (n 9) marginal no 116.

A particular area where *Risikogeschäfte* take place is the banking industry, with granting credit as a particular example of such a transaction.[176] As far as the breach of duty is concerned, the following situations are typically considered to breach this duty in the terms required by StGB, section 266: breaching the legal or internal rules on credit limitations;[177] transactions accomplished without the necessary procedural steps (eg without necessary agreement of another person); breaches of instructions received from senior management; and granting credits for which the client's credibility was insufficiently verified.[178]

In order to establish whether the representative of the bank can be liable for *Untreue* in the case of erroneously granted credits, it is necessary to verify whether he breached his duty to safeguard the financial interests of the bank. This can definitely not be inferred from the success or the failure of the transaction as such, but rather from the assessment concerning the fulfilment of different obligations imposed by the legal framework and internal rules of the bank, in particular the Banking Act (Gesetz über das Kreditwesen, KWG).[179] Not only the rules as such should be taken into account but also their application, which means that if the banker is allowed in exceptional cases to disregard these norms, it ought to be considered within the assessment of his criminal liability as well.[180]

In general the representative of the bank who decides upon granting the credit has to be sufficiently informed in order to correctly assess the risk of loss and the chances of profit.[181] Since the banking law contains specific rules on how to make such assessments, the question has arisen of the impact of the breach of one of such rules for the general assessment of the breach of duty. This issue was subject to several judgments of the BGH, in particular in the context of KWG, section 18, which sets a higher standard for the gathering of information about the client by the bank in the context of large loans.[182] The BGH considered that although a breach of KWG, section 18 rules can signify a breach of duty in the sense of StGB, section 266, the banker has the duty to perform an overall assessment of the client's credibility. This means that even while fulfilling KWG, section 18 requirements, he might breach his duty to safeguard the bank's financial interest, but also that even if he breaches this provision, he might not be criminally liable if the assessment had been correctly performed in a different way.[183] In a subsequent

[176] Potential perpetrators could be eg branch managers (*Filialleiter*); independently acting credit men or credit analysts (*eigenverantwortlich handelnde Kreditsachbearbeiter*); senior executives (*leitende Angestellte*), as well as control personnel such as internal auditors or agents or members of supervision bodies, Seier, 'Untreue' (n 2) marginal no 272.

[177] BGH (21 March 1985) wistra 1985, 190, 191.

[178] After Seier, 'Untreue' (n 2) marginal no 271; Hillenkamp, 'Risikogeschäft und Untreue' (n 158) 166. In the context of banking, see Susanne Martin, *Bankuntreue* (Berlin: Duncker & Humblot, 2000) 87–97 with abundant jurisprudence cited there.

[179] Perron, '§ 266 Untreue' (n 33) marginal no 20a; Seier, 'Untreue' (n 2) marginal no 273.

[180] Seier, 'Untreue' (n 2) marginal no 273.

[181] Schramm, 'Untreue, § 266 StGB' (n 2) marginal no 69.

[182] Ibid marginal no 70.

[183] BGH (6 April 2000) NJW 2000, 2364, 2365.

judgment, the BGH continued this line by confirming that if certain information, which was supposed to be obtained, is missing, there is no breach of duty if it was substituted by different yet equivalent information.[184] The court considered that if the obligation to gather information, such as the one established in KWG, section 18, is breached in a particularly serious way (*gravierend*), it constitutes in any case a breach of duty in terms of StGB, section 266.[185]

Credits granted to enterprises in difficulties (so called *Sanierungskredite*) can imply a much higher level of risk than loans granted in normal circumstances. It is, however, allowed to take that risk if the credit is granted in the framework of a plan to allow the enterprise to regain stability, and if the existence of the bank would not be threatened. The purpose of such a loan is so that older claims on that enterprise, which it is temporarily unable to repay, may also be recovered in future.[186] Such credit may be considered in such circumstances 'the least evil' and thus a higher level of risk is allowed.[187]

If it is established according to these rules that the person responsible for granting the loan breaches his duty, and provided that it resulted in damage (in the form of risk-damage or actual harm), then he may be liable for *Untreue*. If the credit transaction is valid externally, but the breach of duty concerns only the internal limitations, the perpetrator will be liable for the *Missbrauch* alternative. If it is not valid, then only the *Treubruch* modality can be considered.[188]

Active corruption committed by managers, for instance in order for their company to obtain a lucrative contract, has not been qualified as *Untreue* as such at the current time.[189] The reluctance of the courts might be explained by two problems. First, while paying bribes without the consent of the owner of the assets would normally be considered *Untreue*,[190] it is not uncommon that the perpetrator acts with such a consent, whether expressed, tacit or hypothetical.[191] The second problem concerns difficulties in establishing the damage and, relatedly, intent to cause such damage.[192] The lack of instructive jurisprudence helping to clarify this problem is due to the fact that the major cases, in particular the *Siemens/ENEL*

[184] BGH (15 November 2001) NJW 2002, 1211, 1214.

[185] BGH (15 November 2001) NJW 2002, 1211, 1214; Kindhäuser, '§ 266 Untreue' (n 6) marginal no 77.

[186] Dierlamm, '§ 266 Untreue' (n 5) marginal no 239; BGH (15 November 2001) NJW 2002, 1211, 1215.

[187] Dierlamm, '§ 266 Untreue' (n 5) marginal no 241.

[188] Schramm, 'Untreue, § 266 StGB' (n 2) marginal no 68. In the context of banking mismanagement and the financial crisis, see also Christian Schröder, 'Die strafrechtliche Bewältigung der Finanzkrise am Beispiel der Untreue' (2011) 123 *ZStW* 771; Wolfgang Wohlers, 'Die strafrechtliche Bewältigung der Finanzkrise am Beispiel der Strafbarkeit wegen Untreue' (2011) 123 *ZStW* 791; Thomas Fischer, 'Die strafrechtliche Bewältigung der Finanzkrise am Beispiel der Untreue – Finanzkrise und Strafrecht' (2011) 123 *ZStW* 816.

[189] Kindhäuser, '§ 266 Untreue' (n 6) marginal no 113.

[190] Ibid.

[191] Seier, 'Untreue' (n 2) marginal no 401.

[192] Ibid, see also OLG Frankfurt (26 February 2004) NStZ-RR 2004, 244.

case, were treated as problems of creating so-called slush funds or hidden funds (*schwarze Kassen*).

While the slush fund or other hidden money might serve the purpose of corruption, this need not always be the case. The breach of duty is said to consist in the fact that a certain amount of money is set apart and hidden, which might result in different types of problems.[193] This issue came to light, first, in the public sphere, namely in the context of political parties or the use of resources of public institutions, where the lack of financial transparency exposed the party to a risk of having to repay received public subventions.[194] Only with the judgment in the *Siemens/ENEL* case has this issue been extended to the private sector, in which the secret fund was created for the purposes of corruption in order to obtain attractive contracts for Siemens.[195] In this case, the BGH found that the breach of duty consisted in hiding the funds and also in making it impossible to correctly enter them into the company's books,[196] while the damage consisted in that the company could no longer use the funds.[197] It was, however, pointed out in the literature that it is difficult to conceive of a sense in which the company loses the possibility to use the assets moved to the hidden fund, if these persons are in control of it.[198] Although the valid consent of the management board could have kept the perpetrator's act within the scope of what he was permitted to do, there was no consent of the supervisory board or of the shareholders and in any case it would have been excluded because of the breach of compliance rules.[199]

Whether the establishing of the hidden fund constitutes *Untreue* in the form of *Missbrauch* or of *Treubruch* depends upon the classification of the transfer of money as a valid transaction (eg on the basis of BGB, section 138).[200] In the same way as above, a person who does not establish the hidden fund himself, but takes over its administration from another person, can also be convicted of *Untreue* for not having entered the funds into the company's books and for not having returned the funds to the company, which resulted in the impossibility to use the funds, provided that this person has the required duties towards the company.[201]

3.5. Result

A breach of duty to safeguard the financial interests of another person becomes criminally relevant, save for the *mens rea*, if it causes damage (*Nachteil*) to the

[193] Schramm, 'Untreue, § 266 StGB' (n 2) marginal nos 58–63, 142–46.
[194] Seier, 'Untreue' (n 2) marginal no 197.
[195] BGH (29 August 2008) NStZ 2009, 95, 96 et seq.
[196] Ibid 97, para [37].
[197] Ibid 98, para [43].
[198] Seier, 'Untreue' (n 2) marginal no 407 et seq.
[199] Dierlamm, '§ 266 Untreue' (n 5) marginal no 244.
[200] Schramm, 'Untreue, § 266 StGB' (n 2) marginal no 63.
[201] Ibid marginal no 145.

entrusted assets. Already from the text of the provision it becomes clear that the damage must affect the assets of the person, to which the duties refer.[202]

3.5.1. Determination of Damage

The method used in order to verify whether damage occurred is called *Gesamtsaldierung*, which can be translated as 'comprehensive balancing'.[203] This method consists in comparing the sum of the assets before and after the conduct (the breach of duty) and establishing whether a loss occurred.[204] This means that there is no damage if directly through the conduct (even constituting a breach of duty) the loss is compensated by a gain in the assets which is equal to or higher than the loss,[205] for instance by liberation from a debt.[206] Damage must be understood here only in an economic sense.[207] Hence, loss in creditworthiness or reputation can be considered only if it is financially quantifiable.[208]

Typical examples of damage would be situations where goods are given away or sold below the market price or damaged, when goods are acquired above the market price, or if private use is made of them, contrary to their original purpose.[209]

The compensation must result directly from the conduct and not from a subsequent action, since a subsequent compensation is irrelevant for criminal liability.[210] However, there is a standing line of jurisprudence considering that, if at the moment of the commission of the breach of duty the perpetrator is able to compensate the loss with his liquid means and is willing to do so (*ersatzwillig und -fähig*), it is considered that there is no damage.[211] Although this rule has

[202] Wittig, *Wirtschafsstrafrecht* (n 59) marginal no 135; BGH (11 November 1982) NJW 1983, 461, 462; BGH (25 April 2006) NStZ 2006, 401, 402, para [7].

[203] Schramm, 'Untreue, § 266 StGB' (n 2) marginal no 125.

[204] Perron, '§ 266 Untreue' (n 33) marginal no 40; BGH (17 August 2006) NStZ-RR 2006, 378: 'Ob ein Vermögensnachteil eingetreten ist, muss grundsätzlich durch einen ex-ante vorzunehmenden Vergleich des gesamten Vermögens vor und nach der beanstandeten Verfügung unter wirtschaftlichen Gesichtspunkten geprüft werden. An einem Nachteil fehlt es regelmäßig, wenn wertmindernde und werterhöhende Faktoren, zu denen auch Gewinnerwartungen zählen können, sich gegenseitig aufheben'. BGH (9 February 2006) NStZ-RR 2006, 175; BGH (27 February 1975) NJW 1975, 1234. Also BVerfG (23June 2010) NJW 2010, 3209, 3216, para [119]: 'Grundsätzlich soll der Vermögensnachteil als Taterfolg der Untreue nach heutiger Rechtsprechung und herrschender Lehre durch einen Vergleich des gesamten Vermögens vor und nach der beanstandeten Verfügung unter wirtschaftlichen Gesichtspunkten geprüft werden'.

[205] Wittig, *Wirtschafsstrafrecht* (n 59) marginal no 138; BGH (27 August 2003) NStZ 2004, 205, 206: 'Ein Nachteil liegt deshalb nicht vor, wenn durch die Tathandlung selbst zugleich ein den Verlust aufwiegender Vermögenszuwachs begründet wird'; BGH (15 March 1979) MDR 1979, 636(b).

[206] Schramm, 'Untreue, § 266 StGB' (n 2) marginal no 125.

[207] See, eg BGH (2 July 1997) NStZ 1997, 543.

[208] Seier, 'Untreue' (n 2) marginal no 167.

[209] Ibid marginal no 168.

[210] BGH (6 May 1986) NStZ 1986, 455.

[211] Kindhäuser, *Strafrecht. Besonderer Teil II* (n 100) 44; BVerfG (23 June 2010) NJW 2010, 3209, 3217, para [126]; BGH (16 December 1960) NJW 1961, 685; BGH (6 April 1982) NStZ 1982, 331; BGH (30 October 2003) NStZ-RR 2004, 54.

been considered to be breaking the logic excluding the influence of subsequent compensation, it remains in keeping with the logic of the offence of *Untreue*. Since its objective is the protection of assets, a perpetrator keeping liquid means ready to compensate any damage to such assets at the moment of the act does not in fact create even an endangerment of these assets.[212]

In general, different acts should be analysed separately according to the method of *Gesamtsaldierung*. However, if several acts are economically closely linked, then the assessment would have to address them as a whole.[213] This rule is relevant in particular to publicity campaigns, the introduction of new production methods, or efforts intended for saving a company in crisis.[214]

It is generally admitted that damage in terms of StGB, section 266 can be incurred also by omitting to make a gain by a regularly conducted business, although this rule also meets strong opposition among the doctrine.[215] In this regard, uncertain expectations or unfounded hopes are not sufficient for establishing criminal liability.[216] The jurisprudence requires that the profit or the saving can be expected 'with certainty' (*mit Sicherheit*) had the perpetrator used the given opportunity.[217] For example, damage occurs in this sense if the perpetrator acquires land or signs a contract in the name of the owner of the assets for a less advantageous price than one which was available.[218]

The method of *Gesamtsaldierung* is complemented by the rules on the individual impact of damage (*individuellen Schadenseinschlag*) in order to take into account particularities which result from the fact that the same goods might not have the same value for different persons,[219] and that an analysis in terms of exchange might not make sense in order to assess the correctness of the act.[220] This 'individualised' approach allows the costs of an exuberant birthday party of the CEO to be considered as damage. The service received for the funds spent

[212] Seier, 'Untreue' (n 2) marginal no 177 et seq.

[213] Kindhäuser, '§ 266 Untreue' (n 6) marginal no 112; BGH (23 May 2002) NStZ 2002, 648, 650.

[214] Seier, 'Untreue' (n 2) marginal no 173.

[215] Kindhäuser, *Strafrecht. Besonderer Teil II* (n 100) 43; Seier, 'Untreue' (n 2) marginal no 169; Schramm, 'Untreue, § 266 StGB' (n 2) marginal no 126. Vehement criticism has been formulated by Schünemann, '§ 266 Untreue' (n 9) marginal no 173. One of the focal points of this discussion concerned so-called 'kick-back' payments (*Kick-Back Zahlungen*), which consist in contracting a supplier for an increased price and the management receiving a benefit from the amount by which the price was increased. The main problem is whether the contract could have been concluded for the lower (not increased) price. For more information see eg Schramm, 'Untreue, § 266 StGB' (n 2) marginal no 147 et seq; Seier, 'Untreue' (n 2) marginal no 392 et seq; Nickel Szebrowski, *Kick-Back* (Köln/Berlin/Munich: Heymanns, 2005).

[216] BGH (28 January 1983) NJW 1983, 1807, 1808; OLG Stuttgart (18 September 1998) NJW 1999, 1564, 1566.

[217] BGH (28 January 1983) NJW 1983, 1807, 1809.

[218] BGH (9 March 1989) wistra 1989, 224. For more examples, see Dierlamm, '§ 266 Untreue' (n 5) marginal no 210.

[219] BGH (16 August 1961) NJW 1962, 309.

[220] Kindhäuser, '§ 266 Untreue' (n 6) marginal no 108.

on the party might have been equal in economic terms, but the company had no interest in spending its funds in this way.[221] In the same line is the so-called 'theory of missed objective' (*Zweckverfehlunglehre*), which is used instead of the *Gesamtsaldierung* in order to assess the damage in cases where funds are spent for purposes which do not bring an equivalent benefit for the giver (eg sponsoring).[222] According to this method, damage occurs if funds were assigned to be given for a concrete objective and they were not used for it.[223] For example, if a manager is supposed to spend funds in order to finance a campaign aiming to help victims of an earthquake, and he instead spends them on a homelessness charity or buys paintings for the company's headquarters, damage in terms of *Untreue* occurs.[224]

Concerning slush funds, as examined in the above-mentioned case of *Siemens/ENEL*, the court found that the damage lay in the fact that the hidden funds were unavailable to the company, and the fact that the perpetrator intended to use the money for the benefit of the company was considered irrelevant.[225] According to the dominant legal-economic concept of assets, the benefit obtained through illegal activities (corruption) cannot be taken into account.[226] This approach provoked an intensive critical reaction from the doctrine, which accused the court of changing the nature of the offence.[227] In particular, the judges were reproached for allegedly transforming *Untreue* into an offence which protects the freedom of using one's assets[228] or criminalises preparation to commit corruption or accounting offences.[229] Despite the criticism, this line of jurisprudence appears to have solidified. The Federal Constitutional Court considered that it does not raise constitutional concerns,[230] and the BGH followed it in its judgment in the *Trienekens* case.[231]

[221] Schramm, 'Untreue, § 266 StGB' (n 2) marginal no 133. See also OLG Hamm (21 June 1985) NStZ 1986, 119.

[222] Schramm, 'Untreue, § 266 StGB' (n 2) marginal no 134; Stephan Beukelmann, '§ 263 Betrug' in Bernd von Heintschel-Heinegg (ed), *Beck'scher Online-Kommentar StGB*, 27th edn (Munich: CH Beck, 2015) marginal no 60, available at www.beck-online.beck.de; as to breach of duty in cases of sponsoring, see Kindhäuser, '§ 266 Untreue' (n 6) marginal no 79 et seq.

[223] Seier, 'Untreue' (n 2) marginal no 183.

[224] Kindhäuser, '§ 266 Untreue' (n 6) marginal no 105; Schramm, 'Untreue, § 266 StGB' (n 2) marginal no 134.

[225] BGH (29 August 2008) NStZ 2009, 95, 98 et seq. The extent of this case (*Siemens*) renders impossible the discussion of its details here. This summary is based on the résumé of Seier, 'Untreue' (n 2) marginal no 404 et seq.

[226] Schramm, 'Untreue, § 266 StGB' (n 2) marginal no 143.

[227] Seier, 'Untreue' (n 2) marginal no 405.

[228] Dierlamm, '§ 266 Untreue' (n 5) marginal no 248; Matthias Jahn, 'Untreue durch die Führung "schwarzer Kassen" – Fall Siemens/ENEL' (2009) *Juristische Schulung* (*JuS*) 173, 175.

[229] Frank Saliger, '§ 266 Untreue' in Helmut Satzger, Wilhelm Schluckebier and Gunter Widmaier (eds), *StGB Strafgesetzbuch Kommentar*, 2nd edn (Carl Heymanns Verlag, 2014) marginal no 77.

[230] BVerfG (23 June 2010) NJW 2010, 3209, 3217.

[231] BGH (27 August 2010) NJW 2010, 3458, 3462.

3.5.2. *Risk-Damage* (Schadensgleiche Vermögensgefährdung)

What is crucial for criminal liability for excessive risk-taking is that not only an effective loss, but also a situation in which there exists a risk that the assets will be damaged, fulfils the requirement of damage.[232] The German doctrine and jurisprudence use mainly two expressions to describe this type of damage: *schadensgleiche Vermögensgefährdung*, which means 'endangerment equal to damage', and *Gefährdungsschaden*, which could be translated as 'risk-damage'.[233]

The concept of risk-damage has been developed within the doctrine and jurisprudence concerning the offence of fraud and has been incorporated into the analysis of *Untreue* similarly to other concepts related to the notion of result.[234] The translation of this concept was not frictionless, as important differences resulted in the risk that the offence would through this notion expand far beyond the boundaries given in the law. The first major difference concerns the rules of attempt of both offences. While an attempted fraud is punishable, an attempt to commit *Untreue* is not.[235] On one hand, it may prompt the judges to use the concept of risk-damage, especially in particularly striking cases, and thus overcome the lack of actual damage.[236] On the other hand, since the law excludes the criminalisation of attempt it ought not to be introduced through the back door.[237] The second difference is in the *mens rea* requirement, which for fraud requires that the perpetrator acts with the intent of obtaining for himself or a third person an unlawful material benefit.[238] By contrast, *Untreue* can be committed without such intent and it is punishable even if the perpetrator hoped for a final positive outcome of his actions for the principal (although he considered possible and accepted causing economic harm).[239] In the case of *mens rea* in the form of conditional intent, this allows punishment of the perpetrator who does not want to cause loss, but is aware that his act may result in the risk-damage situation and proceeds with his plan accepting such a possibility.[240] The problems of interpreting *mens rea* will be further developed in the next section.

Not all types of endangerment of the assets may be considered risk-damage; this is only possible where the situation of risk economically analysed results in an actual decrease of the value of the victim's assets.[241] The assets must be

[232] Wittig, *Wirtschafsstrafrecht* (n 59) marginal no 149.
[233] Schramm, 'Untreue, § 266 StGB' (n 2) marginal no 136.
[234] Seier, 'Untreue' (n 2) marginal nos 166, 179.
[235] Schramm, 'Untreue, § 266 StGB' (n 2) marginal no 137; see also section 4 below.
[236] Schramm, 'Untreue, § 266 StGB' (n 2) marginal no 137.
[237] Wittig, *Wirtschafsstrafrecht* (n 59) marginal no 150.
[238] StGB Betrug, s 263.
[239] Perron, '§ 266 Untreue' (n 33) marginal no 49.
[240] For further analysis of the *mens rea* in case of risk-damage see 3.6 below.
[241] BGH (17 February 1999) NJW 1999, 1489, 1491. Kindhäuser, '§ 266 Untreue' (n 6) marginal no 110: 'Im Grundsatz wird ein Schaden dieser Art unter der Voraussetzung angenommen, dass

endangered in a concrete and not merely abstract way.[242] In other words, the existing risk must result in the assets being worth less than if the risk situation had not occurred.[243] For instance, if a bank decides to alienate a claim for repayment of a credit, it is worth less, if it was given with insufficient guarantees. However, it is not excluded that the debtor might repay it entirely without problem. Hence, the risk-damage is different to the actual damage in that the eventual loss might still not occur.

One of the arguments evoked in order to explain this interpretation is of an economic character. Through the notion of risk-damage, the jurisprudence and the doctrine take into account that 'the prices in a market-driven economic system are formed according to the laws of demand and supply' and within this process the expectations as to possible prices define the value of assets as well.[244] The concept of risk-damage takes into consideration the accounting rules based on the above consideration, which require the inclusion of foreseeable risk and costs related to the depreciation of the value of the endangered assets.[245]

In the case of 'risky business' or 'speculative transactions' (*Risikogeschäfte*) the earlier jurisprudence considered that if the perpetrator fulfilled the criteria which allowed the court to consider that he took excessive risk in comparison to that which he was authorised to take, and thus breached his duty to safeguard the financial interests of the owner of the assets, in such situations the result in the form of risk-damage can be admitted.[246] The court used normative formulae in order to define the result, such as:

> a financial loss exists if the offender behaving just like a gambler deliberately and against the rules of professional diligence accepts a highly increased risk of loss only in hope of a highly dubious gain.[247]

Risk-damage can be admitted where the principal ought to have seriously considered that the loss would occur, or that its occurrence was obvious.[248] Further jurisprudence introduced the concept to different areas of application of *Untreue*, such as improper book-keeping, granting credits or creating slush funds.[249]

bereits die Gefährdungslage bei wirtschaftlicher Betrachtung zu einer gegenwärtigen Minderung des Vermögensgesamtwertes führt.' Dierlamm, '§ 266 Untreue' (note 5) marginal number 211: 'Eine konkrete Vermögensgefährdung soll dem effektiven, real eingetretenen Vermögensnachteil gleichstehen, wenn sie bei wirtschaftlicher Betrachtung bereits zu einer Minderbewertung der gegenwärtigen Vermögenslage führt.'

[242] Dierlamm, '§ 266 Untreue' (n 5) marginal no 212.

[243] BVerfG (23 June 2010) NJW 2010, 3209, 3218, para [137].

[244] Ibid para [140].

[245] See, eg HGB, s 253(I), (IV); BVerfG (23 June 2010) NJW 2010, 3209, 3219, para [141].

[246] Seier, 'Untreue' (n 2) marginal no 386; Hillenkamp, 'Risikogeschäft und Untreue' (n 158) 166; Andreas Ransiek, 'Risiko als Problem des Untreuetatbestandes' (2004) 116(3) *ZStW* 634, 658–59.

[247] BGH (27 February 1975) NJW 1975, 1234, 1236.

[248] BGH (9 July 1987) NJW 1987, 3144, 3145.

[249] For extensive analysis of the jurisprudence, see eg, Dierlamm, '§ 266 Untreue' (n 5) marginal no 212 et seq.

The concept was met with criticism in the doctrine for extending the scope of the offence beyond the will of the legislator, in particular by introducing criminalisation of attempt, which was not provided for this offence.[250]

The Federal Constitutional Court of Germany analysed the concept of risk-damage from the point of view of its conformity with the German Basic Law, in particular with the imperative of certainty, in its judgment in 2010.[251] The Court held that the use of this concept does not infringe the German Basic Law. However, it insisted on a restrictive interpretation of the concept and provided essential rules on its use.[252]

First, it must be possible to quantify the loss due to the risk-damage situation.[253] These kinds of assessments are daily practice in business or commercial activities.[254] The BVerfG considered the use of the concept of risk-damage without such quantification, but based only on above-mentioned normative criteria, to be constitutionally questionable. The use of these criteria might be tempting in order to circumvent the limitative function of the limb of result.[255] However, such practice blurs the difference between the element of conduct (breach of duty) and its result (damage), which have separate functions within the structure of the offence and in setting boundaries of criminalisation.[256] In this way, the interpretation would go against the wishes of the law-makers, who expressly excluded the possibility of punishment for attempted *Untreue* since they wanted to criminalise the damaging of entrusted assets, and not their mere endangerment.[257] Therefore, the court requires that in each case damage caused by the exposure to risk must be quantified according to recognised (eg accounting) methods, and if necessary expert witnesses should be called.[258] If it is impossible to assess it precisely, then the minimum level would be taken into account,[259] and if the quantification is doubtful, the defendant must be acquitted.[260]

The jurisprudence has used the concept of risk-damage in the context of several types of breaches of duty to safeguard another person's financial interests causing the exposure of the assets of the victim to a risk of loss.

For example, the repayment claim that the bank has towards its debtor can be sold and its price is determined by the assessment of the probability that the debt will be repaid. If the credibility of the debtor was incorrectly assessed or insufficient guarantees were taken, the value of such a claim may be lower than the

[250] Waßmer, '§ 266 Untreue' (n 12) marginal no 184; Seier, 'Untreue' (n 2) marginal no 186.
[251] BVerfG (23 June 2010) NJW 2010, 3209, 3218 et seq.
[252] Schramm, 'Untreue, § 266 StGB' (n 2) marginal no 138.
[253] BVerfG (23 June 2010) NJW 2010, 3209, 3220, para [151].
[254] Ibid 3219 et seq, para [146].
[255] Ibid 3220, para [149].
[256] Ibid.
[257] Ibid 3220, para [150].
[258] Ibid 3220, para [151].
[259] Schramm, 'Untreue, § 266 StGB' (n 2) marginal no 139.
[260] BVerfG (23 June 2010) NJW 2010, 3209, 3220, para [151].

one initially assumed.[261] This consideration led the First Criminal Panel of the BGH to consider in one case that the concept of risk-damage is unnecessary and that it is in fact a case of actual damage.[262] However, the judgment of the Federal Constitutional Court suggests that this kind of result will remain the domain of risk-damage.[263] That being so, the BVerfG pointed out that through the use of this concept, the offence does not punish the mere endangerment of the assets, but the actual decrease in their value. The value of risk-damage is not equal to the possible damage if the risk materialises, but to the amount by which the value of the assets has been diminished because of the risk.[264]

In order to establish whether, in the context of granting credit, the bank suffered harm in the form of risk-damage, it is necessary to assess the impact of this result using economic tools, since the normative criteria have been rejected, as described above.[265] Such analysis must take into account the whole economic context of the credit (and not only, for example, its initial value), expected interests and other revenues, and the analysis of the financial standing of the debtor, and must be expressed in concrete money value and not only by means of assertions or suppositions.[266]

Another example can be improper accountancy. It can fulfil the criteria of risk-damage, if the fact that the book-keeping is not done diligently creates a concrete risk that valid claims are not enforced and debts not recovered in time.[267] Yet another example consists of situations where the act creates the risk that the victim may be called to pay compensation or damages because of the perpetrator's conduct.[268] The risk-damage result has also been accepted in situations where the perpetrator's act created the risk that the owner of the assets will be damaged by losing subventions, contracts or having to pay fines.[269]

The notion of risk-damage also gave rise to debates as regards two issues related to punishing for the offence of *Untreue*. First, causing 'a major financial loss' constitutes an aggravating circumstance, which elevates the possible punishment. It is so far unclear whether the result in the form of risk-damage can have the same effect, and if so, at what level it becomes 'major'.[270] The second problem

[261] BGH NJW 2002, 1211, 1216.

[262] BGH (20 March 2008) NJW 2008, 2451, 2452.

[263] Schramm, 'Untreue, § 266 StGB' (n 2) marginal no 138 et seq.

[264] BVerfG (23 June 2010) NJW 2010, 3209, 3219, para [142]; BGH (24 August 1999) wistra 2000, 60, 61.

[265] Dierlamm, '§ 266 Untreue' (n 5) marginal no 240.

[266] Dierlamm, '§ 266 Untreue' (n 5) marginal no 240. Compare also BGH (15 November 2001) NJW 2002, 1211, 1216; BGH (20 March 2008) NJW 2008, 2451, 2452; BGH (20 October 2009) NStZ 2010, 329.

[267] Schramm, 'Untreue, § 266 StGB' (n 2) marginal no 140; Seier, 'Untreue' (n 2) marginal no 196.

[268] Schramm, 'Untreue, § 266 StGB' (n 2) marginal no 140.

[269] BGH (18 October 2006) NJW 2007, 1760, 1765.

[270] See, eg against: Seier, 'Untreue' (n 2) marginal no 35; in favour: Schramm, 'Untreue, § 266 StGB' (n 2) marginal no 161. While the BGH considered that only a real loss can be deemed as a loss in the

is linked with the limitation period for prosecution. This period for *Untreue* is five years (AktG, section 78(3) point 4), and starts running from the moment when the damage occurs.[271] If the damage is aggravated in time by subsequent occurrences, the limitation period begins at the moment of the last occurrence.[272] In the case of risk-damage, although in the moment when it occurs the offence is committed (*vollendet*), it is considered completed (*beendet*) only in the moment when the actual damage occurs or it becomes clear that the risk will not materialise.[273] Reconciling this rule with the understanding of risk-damage as actual damage, however, is problematic. It appears as if at the moment of the occurrence of risk-damage, a quantifiable loss emerges with which the offence is both committed and completed and the limitation period starts running.[274] If this risk-damage cannot be quantified, then there is no risk-damage at all.[275]

Although the recent understanding of risk-damage narrowed this concept, since it now requires that it constitute a quantifiable loss for the assets of the company, it is still subject to critical remarks from the German doctrine, mainly for extending the scope of criminalisation (this despite the lack of criminalisation of attempt) and the still imprecise terms used to define the offence.[276] Further attempts to curb the scope of application of the concept of risk-damage concern the *mens rea* requirements and will be analysed in the section devoted to this limb of *Untreue*.

3.5.3. Attribution of Damage/Causality

As for any offence requiring a result, the offence of *Untreue* requires linking the result with the conduct of the offence and it naturally concerns both actual damage and risk-damage.[277] The German criminal law requires that the link between the

context of StGB, s 263(3), it allowed this provision to be applied to risk-damage, if the value exceeded €100,000, BGH (2 December 2008) NJW 2009, 528, 532. In another judgment, however, the BGH considered that the risk-damage could be deemed as a loss in terms of s 263(3), since in view of the approach requiring that the endangerment have real influence on the value of the assets, there exists a decrease of value and thus a loss, NStZ (18 February 2009) 2009, 330, 331.

[271] Schramm, 'Untreue, § 266 StGB' (n 2) marginal no 168. For rules on the interruption of the limitation period see StGB, s 78c.

[272] Perron, '§ 266 Untreue' (n 33) marginal no 58, BGH (11 July 2001) NStZ 2001, 650.

[273] BGH (11 July 2001) NStZ 2001, 650; Schramm, 'Untreue, § 266 StGB' (n 2) marginal no 149; critically: Schünemann, '§ 266 Untreue' (n 9) marginal no 207, pointing out the conflict with art 103(2) of the German Constitution (Basic Law).

[274] Dierlamm, '§ 266 Untreue' (n 5) marginal no 284.

[275] Andreas Ransiek, '"Verstecktes" Parteivermögen und Untreue' NJW 2007, 1727, 1730.

[276] Seier, 'Untreue' (n 2) marginal no 186.

[277] Hans-Heinrich Jescheck and Thomas Weigend, *Lehrbuch des Strafrechts* (Berlin: Duncker & Humblot, 1996) 277; Schmid, '§31 Treupflichtverletzungen' (n 40) marginal no 175; BGH (6 April 2000) NJW 2000, 2364, 2365. Furthermore, the requirement of causality is already expressed in StGB, s 266, which requires that the perpetrator 'abuses the power … or violates his duty … and *thereby* causes damage' (emphasis added, in German original: *dadurch*); Saliger, '§ 266 Untreue' (n 229) marginal no 79.

perpetrator's act and the result be established according to an evaluation consisting of two steps: establishment of causality (*Kausalität*) and objective ascription (*objektive Zurechnung*).[278]

In the first step, it is necessary to establish whether the conduct (the breach of duty in case of *Untreue*) was a '*conditio sine qua non*' of the damage. This is done through an intellectual operation consisting of imagining the course of action without the conduct in question. If in such a situation the damage as it *in concreto* occurred would be impossible, then the causal link must be denied and hence so too criminal liability.[279] However, it is not necessary that the perpetrator's conduct be the only cause of the damage.[280] The condition would not be fulfilled only if the result was caused solely by other events.[281]

In the second step, it must be established whether it is possible to objectively ascribe the causation of the damage to the perpetrator.[282] It is generally accepted that there is a need to establish the connection with the breach of duty (*Pflichtwidrigkeitszusammenhang*) and the connection with the legal interests protected by the offence (*Schutzzweckzusammenhang*).

The criterion of the connection with the breach of duty is not fulfilled if the damage would also have occurred had the perpetrator acted according to his duty.[283] For illustrating this requirement the literature gave the following examples. If the breach of duty consisted in not observing a rule requiring another manager to approve the decision of the perpetrator, but this manager would have agreed to it anyway, the criterion of connection is not fulfilled, and criminal liability is excluded.[284] Another example would be constituted by a case in which a bank employee responsible for granting loans did not assess credit suitability according to the rules and subsequently the borrower was unable to repay the loan; liability for *Untreue* is excluded if the creditworthiness of the borrower was in any case unquestionable at the moment of granting the loan.[285] One can argue whether even causation exists in these cases, while it is not the lack of another manager's

[278] Jescheck and Weigend, *Lehrbuch des Strafrechts* (n 277) 277. The notion of objective ascription is subject to debates within the German doctrine. For more information on causality and objective ascription see Jescheck and Weigend, *Lehrbuch des Strafrechts* (n 277) p277 et seq; Roxin, *Strafrecht. Allgemeiner Teil* (note 33) 343 et seq. or Uwe Murmann, *Grundkurs Strafrecht* (Munich: CH Beck, 2015) 152–202; in English: Bohlander, *Principles of German Criminal Law* (n 112) 45 et seq, including literature cited in these publications. In the context of *Untreue* see Frank H Gerkau, *Untreue und objektive Zurechnung* (Hamburg: Kovač, 2008).

[279] Jescheck and Weigend, *Lehrbuch des Strafrechts* (n 277) 277 et seq; Saliger, '§ 266 Untreue' (n 229) marginal no 78.

[280] Saliger, '§ 266 Untreue' (n 229) marginal no 78.

[281] Seier, 'Untreue' (n 2) marginal no 203.

[282] The discussion on the scope of applicability of the theory of objective ascription is still ongoing in the German doctrine. See Saliger, '§ 266 Untreue' (n 229) marginal no 79; Martin, *Bankuntreue* (n 178) 134 et seq; Bernd Schünemann, 'Die "gravierende Pflichtverletzung" bei der Untreue: dogmatischer Zauberhut oder taube Nuss?' NStZ 2005, 473, 475 et seq.

[283] Saliger, '§ 266 Untreue' (n 229) marginal no 81.

[284] Example given by Seier, 'Untreue' (n 2) marginal no 204.

[285] BGH (6 April 2000) NJW 2000, 2364, 2365.

approval or lack of observing the rules while assessing the credit suitability that increased the risk of damaging the company's financial interest. The requirement of connection with the breach of duty would be lacking in a case where the assessment of creditworthiness, even if carried out correctly, would lead to granting the credit and was based on falsified data provided by the borrower and the bank employee was unaware of the falsification.[286]

The question is how probable this putative scenario must be in order to exclude liability for *Untreue*. The view represented in the jurisprudence and by one group of scholars requires that, in order for the harm to be ascribed to the perpetrator, it must be certain that the harm would not have occurred, had the perpetrator acted according to the rules.[287] However, another group of scholars considers that it is sufficient for criminal liability that the perpetrator increased the risk that the forbidden result would occur.[288]

According to the criterion of connection with the legal interests protected by the offence, only harm which the norm forming the duty and breached by the perpetrator aimed at preventing must be objectively ascribed to the offender.[289] In other words, the perpetrator should have breached a norm the purpose of which was to prevent the harm caused by the perpetrator, ie financial damage.[290] For example, the perpetrator who caused financial damage to the budget of a political party by infringing rules prescribed by the statute on political parties would not be liable for *Untreue*, since the function of this statute is to ensure the transparency of political party funding, and not preventing them from financial damage.[291] The outcome would be similar for the granting of credits. Criminal liability would depend on whether the perpetrator breached one of the duties which regulate the policy of the bank in general and are not aimed at protecting its financial interests, or that regulate the granting of concrete credits. Only in the latter case could the damage be ascribed to the perpetrator.[292]

At least two problems are associated with this criterion. The first, of a more dogmatic nature, concerns the allocation of this issue within the structure of the offence. While some authors consider it a problem of duty and its breach,[293] other authors analyse it within the problem of causality and objective ascription of

[286] Saliger, '§ 266 Untreue' (n 229) marginal no 81.

[287] The classic jurisprudence is BGH (25 September 1957) NJW 1958, 149. For abundant literature references see Roxin, *Strafrecht. Allgemeiner Teil* (n 33) 392.

[288] Roxin, *Strafrecht. Allgemeiner Teil* (n 33) 392 et seq; Jescheck and Weigend, *Lehrbuch des Strafrechts* (n 277) 584–86. For criticism of this theory see Günther Jakobs, *Strafrecht. Allgemeiner Teil*, 2nd edn (Berlin/New York: Walter de Gruyter, 1993) 235 et seq.

[289] Saliger, '§ 266 Untreue' (n 229) marginal no 82.

[290] Seier, 'Untreue' (n 2) marginal no 207.

[291] Hans-Ludwig Günther, 'Die Untreue im Wirtschaftsrecht' in Bernd Heinrich et al (eds), *Festschrift für Ulrich Weber* (Bielefeld: Verlag Ernst und Werner Gieseking, 2004) 311–17, at 316.

[292] Martin, *Bankuntreue* (n 178) 140.

[293] See, eg Perron, '§ 266 Untreue' (n 33) marginal no 19a; Dierlamm, '§ 266 Untreue' (n 5) marginal no 47.

result,[294] as is also the case in this chapter.[295] Nonetheless, the decision on where to place this issue does not change the scope of criminal liability for *Untreue*. The latter will be influenced by the solution to the second major problem, namely the extent to which the breached norm focuses on protecting the assets of the victim. While the doctrine formulated requirements that the norm should be originally designed in order to prevent damage,[296] or serve specifically and directly this purpose,[297] according to some recent jurisprudence it is enough if the norm serves also and even indirectly the purpose of damage prevention.[298] According to the Federal Constitutional Court of Germany, there must be a specific connection to prevention of damage to the assets.[299] Despite these discrepancies it is admitted by the majority that the fulfilment of this requirement is necessary for criminal liability and that the lack of a breach of a norm which has no connection with the protection of the victim's assets should exclude criminal liability for *Untreue*.[300]

3.6. *Mens Rea*

Untreue can only be committed intentionally.[301] The offence does not require any kind of special intent. In particular, there is no need for the perpetrator to act for his personal interest or with intent to make a gain for himself or another person.[302] The fact that the perpetrator perceived that in general he acted for the benefit of the victim does not exclude criminal liability.[303]

German criminal law distinguishes three grades of intent: direct intent in the first degree (*Absicht*); direct intent in the second degree (*Direkter Vorsatz* or *dolus directus*); and conditional intent (*Bedingter Vorsatz* or *dolus eventualis*).[304] The perpetrator acting with *Absicht* wants to perform the act described by its elements and at least hopes that the result may occur. In the case of *dolus directus*, the perpetrator's ultimate goal might be different than described by the offence, but the perpetrator knows that while realising this goal it is certain or highly probable

[294] Saliger, '§ 266 Untreue' (n 229) marginal no 82 et seq; Seier, 'Untreue' (n 2) marginal no 207 et seq.

[295] Jescheck and Weigend, *Lehrbuch des Strafrechts* (n 277) 287 et seq.

[296] 'genuine zum Zwecke der Schadensverhinedung aufgestellt', Seier, 'Untreue' (n 2) marginal no 207.

[297] 'spezifisch und unmittelbar dem Vermögensschutz dienen', Dierlamm, '§ 266 Untreue' (n 5) marginal no 47.

[298] 'wenigstens auch, und sei es mittelbar', BGH (13 September 2010) NJW 2011, 88, 91. See also BVerfG (23 June 2010) NJW 2010, 3209, 3218 et seq.

[299] 'der spezifische Vermögensbezug' BVerfG (23 June 2010) NJW 2010, 3209, 3218, para [133].

[300] Seier, 'Untreue' (n 2) marginal no 208. Against: Saliger, '§ 266 Untreue' (n 229) marginal no 83.

[301] Wittig, *Wirtschafsstrafrecht* (n 59) marginal no 163; Schünemann, '§ 266 Untreue' (n 9) marginal no 189.

[302] Schünemann, '§ 266 Untreue' (n 9) marginal no 189; Perron, '§ 266 Untreue' (n 33) marginal no 49.

[303] BGH (6 May 1986) NStZ 1986, 455; Perron, '§ 266 Untreue' (n 33) marginal no 49.

[304] Terminology used in this section according to Bohlander, *Principles of German Criminal Law* (n 112) 63.

that he will perform the act described by the *actus reus*. If the perpetrator acts with *dolus eventualis*, the realisation of the *actus reus* is not the perpetrator's goal, but he considers it as possible and accepts this possibility.[305]

It is admitted that *Untreue* can be committed with any of the three grades of intention, including *dolus eventualis*.[306] This means that for criminal liability it is necessary that the perpetrator wanted (*Absicht*) or knew with certainty, regarded as highly probable (*dolus directus*) or considered possible and accepted (*dolus eventualis*) that, while being aware of his duty to safeguard the financial interests of another person, he either abused the rights given to him (*Missbrauch*) or breached the duty to safeguard these interests (*Treubruch*) and thereby caused the damage (or risk-damage).[307]

As to *dolus eventualis*, this is the grade of intention which is the closest to negligence. Hence, the jurisprudence requires a strict approach to its requirements, in particular in cases where the perpetrator did not act for his own benefit.[308] As the BGH explained in one of its judgments, the perpetrator acting with advertent negligence (*bewußte Fahrlässigkeit*),[309] although aware of the risk of result (damage or risk-damage), hopes that this risk does not materialise, whereas the perpetrator acting with *dolus eventualis* accepts the possibility that the risk may materialise if he cannot realise his objective otherwise, although he does not want this to happen.[310] However, this requirement has been criticised in the doctrine as an attempt to curb the extent of criminalisation of *Untreue*, which according to these authors should be done by a restrictive interpretation of the *actus reus* instead.[311]

It is the general rule that intention in all its three forms should concern all of the elements of the *actus reus*.[312] As to the result element in the form of risk equal to damage (*schadensgleiche Vermögensgefährdung*), the *mens rea* requirement is certainly fulfilled in the case of the first two grades of intention, ie if the perpetrator is willing while acting to expose the owner of the assets to the risk as described in the previous section or is certain or holds it to be highly probable

[305] Jescheck and Weigend, *Lehrbuch des Strafrechts* (n 277) 297. See also Bohlander, *Principles of German Criminal Law* (n 112) 63 et seq.

[306] Seier, 'Untreue' (n 2) marginal no 82; BGH (6 April 2000) NJW 2000, 2364, 2365.

[307] Schramm, 'Untreue, § 266 StGB' (n 2) marginal no 152, whose terminology differentiates, however, between *dolus directus* in the first degree in case of certainty, and *dolus directus* in the second degree if the perpetrator contemplates (*beabsichtigen*) the possibility that he commits the act described in the *actus reus. Dolus eventualis* is defined in the same way as above.

[308] BGH (27 February 1975) NJW 1975, 1234, 1236; BGH (23 May 2002) NStZ 2002, 648, 650.

[309] This term after Bohlander, *Principles of German Criminal Law* (n 112) 63; as he points out, no German concept of *mens rea* fully corresponds with the English concept of recklessness, therefore English criminal law terminology is avoided and the terms used in this section should be understood only as translations of German terms without the English law connotations.

[310] BGH (27 February 1975) NJW 1975, 1234, 1236. See also Schünemann, '§ 266 Untreue' (n 9) marginal no 191.

[311] Perron, '§ 266 Untreue' (n 33) marginal no 50; Schünemann, '§ 266 Untreue' (n 9) marginal no 190.

[312] Jescheck and Weigend, *Lehrbuch des Strafrechts* (n 277) 295.

that such risk will be the result of his act. There has, however, been a controversy concerning the volitional element of *mens rea* in case of *dolus eventualis*.[313] The classic solution required that the perpetrator considered it possible that his act causes a risk to the assets he had the duty to safeguard and accepts this possibility, although it is not his will that such risk is created.[314] However, the Second Criminal Panel of the BGH in the *Kanther/Weyrauch* case required that the perpetrator in such case not only accepts the possibility of creating the risk, but must also accept the prospect of the occurrence of the actual damage.[315] The case concerned the creation of hidden funds by certain members of the Hessen branch of the Christian Democratic Union (CDU). Since the introduction of the rules on transparency of political parties' finances, the maintaining of such accounts infringed these rules and created a risk that the CDU would lose the state subsidy to which political parties were entitled depending on the electoral support they received.[316]

The solution given by the court was mainly motivated by concerns about the scope of the offence, which the court attempted to curb by means of a restrictive interpretation of *mens rea*.[317] The court was in particular concerned that conviction for *Untreue* with a result limited only to risk-damage and with *mens rea* in the form of *dolus eventualis* would in fact mean introducing punishment for attempted *Untreue*, which had been excluded by the StGB.[318] However, this solution created incongruence between the *actus reus* and *mens rea* requirements, as the *mens rea* would go further by referring to (conditional intention of) actual damage, while for the *actus reus* the risk-damage would suffice.[319] Although some authors welcomed the court's attempts at limiting the scope of the offence, the method used by the court evoked criticism.[320] The doctrine's disapproval stemmed not only from the above-mentioned incongruence, but also from the classification of the perpetrator's intention as *dolus eventualis*. It has been established that the perpetrator knew (and accepted) the risk which was created by his act, which means that while acting, his intention took the form of *dolus eventualis* as to damage. However, if as regards the *actus reus*, it is risk-damage (*Gefährdungschaden*) which is assumed, then the perpetrator acted with direct intention (*dolus directus*), since he knew with certainty that his act would create the risk of damage.[321]

[313] Kindhäuser, '§ 266 Untreue' (n 6) marginal no 123; Seier, 'Untreue' (n 2) marginal no 187 et seq.

[314] BGH (6 April 2000) NJW 2000, 2364, 2366; BGH (15 November 2001) NJW 2002, 1211, 1216.

[315] BGH (18 October 2006) NJW 2007, 1760, 1766.

[316] Ibid 1761.

[317] Seier, 'Untreue' (n 2) marginal nos 186–88.

[318] BGH (18 October 2006) NJW 2007, 1760, 1766. On attempted *Untreue*, see section 4 below.

[319] In fact this problem was already addressed in the judgment where the court, curiously, justified it by comparison with attempt, where the intention of the perpetrator goes further than his *actus reus*. BGH (18 October 2006) NJW 2007, 1760, 1767; Seier, 'Untreue' (n 2) marginal no 188.

[320] Schünemann, '§ 266 Untreue' (n 9) marginal no 196; Andreas Ransiek, '"Verstecktes" Parteivermögen und *Untreue*' NJW 2007, 1727; Bernd Schünemann, 'Zur Quadratur des Kreises in der Dogmatik des Gefährdungsschadens' NStZ 2008, 430. Also Perron, '§ 266 Untreue' (n 33) marginal no 50.

[321] Ransiek, '"Verstecktes' Parteivermögen" (n 320) 1729.

The solution set out in the above judgments was confirmed in two subsequent judgments issued by the Second Criminal Panel[322] and by the Fifth Criminal Panel of the BGH.[323] However, the First Criminal Panel of the BGH rejected outright the solution given in these judgments.[324] The Court solved the problem in a different way, namely by considering that in cases of capital investment or credit transactions, exposure to risk can already be considered as actual damage, as was discussed in the previous section, and the perpetrator does not act with *dolus eventualis* but with direct intention, since he intended to expose the company to this risk.[325]

This judgment draws attention to the following problem relating to admitting discrepancies between the description of the *actus reus* and the *mens rea* of the offence of *Untreue*. If the theory requiring the perpetrator to accept the actual damage gains acceptance within the doctrine, then a perpetrator who accepted the damage, but whose act was limited to creating a risk-damage situation, would be punished for *Untreue*. At the same time, a perpetrator who only accepted the possibility that he may create a risk-damage situation and did not accept the actual damage, but in fact caused it, would have to be acquitted. Such a solution elevates *mens rea* to a decisive factor for criminal liability and gives it prevalence over the *actus reus*. This interpretation is doubtful since a person who accepts that he will create a risk of damage, in particular a risk of the type that it fulfils the criteria of risk-damage as described above, might find it difficult to claim that he only agreed to create a risk, but did not want to create the damage as such. The acceptance of risk of damage implies the possibility that the harm occurs.

In a judgment issued after the above-mentioned judgments of the BGH, the Federal Constitutional Court of Germany did not repeat the requirements formulated by the Second and repeated by the Fifth Criminal Panel, stating only that intention in form of *dolus eventualis* should be sufficient for criminal liability for *Untreue*.[326] This may suggest, together with elaborate analysis of the *actus reus*, in particular in the context of risk-damage, that the court did not approve of the attempts to limit these concepts through *mens rea* requirements, but considered, as did several authors in the doctrine, that the solution ought to be sought rather in a strict interpretation of the limbs of the *actus reus*.[327]

The fulfilment of the *mens rea* requirement of intention may be excluded because the perpetrator erroneously perceived a fact which constitutes one of the elements of the offence.[328] In relation to the offence of *Untreue*, this can be

[322] BGH (25 May 2007) NStZ 2007, 704.

[323] BGH (2 April 2008) NJW 2008, 1827, 1830.

[324] BGH (20 March 2008) NJW 2008, 2451, 2452.

[325] Ibid 2451 et seq.

[326] BVerfG (23 June 2010) NJW 2010, 3209, 3214, para [105].

[327] Ibid 3218, para [137]; Schramm, 'Untreue, § 266 StGB' (n 2) marginal no 141; Kindhäuser, '§ 266 Untreue' (n 6) marginal no 123.

[328] StGB, s 16(I): 'Whosoever at the time of the commission of the offence is unaware of a fact which is a statutory element of the offence shall be deemed to lack intention'. For more information on the mistake of facts (*Tatbestandsirrtum*) see Jescheck and Weigend, *Lehrbuch des Strafrechts* (n 277) 306 et seq.

considered in particular in two situations. First, there exists common agreement that criminal liability is excluded if the perpetrator erroneously thought that he acted in accordance with the owner's will.[329] Criminal liability is not excluded, however, if the perpetrator acted hoping that the owner would subsequently approve of his act.[330]

Secondly, a mistake as to whether the perpetrator had the duty to safeguard the victim's financial interests or about its breach may also exclude criminal liability. The scope of this error is subject to debate, in which three positions have been formulated and reflected also in the jurisprudence.[331] The core of the issue is whether the error as to the duty ought to be considered a mistake of fact (*Tatbestandsirrtum*) or analysed as a problem of mistake of law (*Verbotsirrtum*). The classification of the perpetrator's mistake as one of these categories may have a significant impact on the final outcome as to his criminal liability, since a mistake of fact excludes the perpetrator's intent and thus the commission of the offence per se, while a mistake of law excludes criminal liability (because of lack of guilt) only if it was unavoidable (StGB, section 17, first sentence). If the perpetrator's mistake was avoidable, it can still have influence on the final sentence, but only by mitigating the penalty (StGB, section 17, second sentence).

The first theory considers that any mistake which concerns the duty to safeguard the victim's financial interests, including mistakes concerning the legal background of this duty, should be considered to be a mistake on the facts, thus excluding that the perpetrator acted intentionally.[332] The contrary view considers that only mistakes as to the factual aspects of the background of the duty can be considered mistakes of fact, while a mistake as to the assessment of legal aspects of the duty ought to be viewed as a mistake of law.[333] A compromise view requires that in order for the perpetrator to act intentionally, it is necessary that he have a 'layman's insight into the normative evaluation of the underlying facts'[334] (*Parallelwertung in der Laiensphäre*).[335]

There exists so far no agreement as to the solution of this problem and different approaches can also be found in the jurisprudence.[336] One author suggests that a pragmatic and plausible approach, which the BGH seem to apply as well,[337]

[329] Schramm, 'Untreue, § 266 StGB' (n 2) marginal no 153; Kindhäuser, '§ 266 Untreue' (n 6) marginal no 122; Dierlamm, '§ 266 Untreue' (n 5) marginal no 282; BGH (17 June 1952) BeckRS 1952 30397513.

[330] Seier, 'Untreue' (n 2) marginal no 83.

[331] Ibid marginal no 84.

[332] Dierlamm, '§ 266 Untreue' (n 5) marginal no 282.

[333] Kindhäuser, '§ 266 Untreue' (n 6) marginal no 122. See also Schünemann, '§ 266 Untreue' (n 9) marginal nos 192–97.

[334] This English explanation of the German expression *Parallelwertung in der Laiensphäre* used in the context of mistake of law is taken from Bohlander, *Principles of German Criminal Law* (n 112) 120.

[335] Perron, '§ 266 Untreue' (n 33) marginal no 49; Schmid, '§ 31 Treupflichtverletzungen' (n 40) marginal no 199. See also Günther Jakobs, 'LG Düsseldorf: *Untreue*-Vorwurf wegen Verletzung gesellschaftsrechtlicher Sonderpflichten – Mannesmann/Vodafone' NStZ 2005, 276, 277 et seq.

[336] For examples for the first theory: BGH (17 June 1952) BeckRS 1952 30397513; BGH (6 May 1986) NStZ 1986, 455; second theory: BGH (17 September 2009) NStZ 2009, 694, 696; Saliger, '§ 266 Untreue' (n 229) marginal no 105. See also BGH (21 December 2005) NJW 2006, 522, 527 et seq.

[337] BGH (18 October 2006) NJW 2007, 1760, 1766. See also BGH (21 December 2005) NJW 2006, 522, 531.

would favour the application of a mistake of fact where the legal background of the breached duty reaches a certain degree of complexity. If the legal background is evident, however, it should be the mistake of law that comes into play.[338]

4. Inchoate Offences

Neither preparatory acts, nor attempt[339] nor conspiracy[340] to commit *Untreue* is criminalised in German criminal law.[341]

5. Cooperation in the Commission of the Offence

According to German law, criminal liability can be incurred by different types of participation in the offence (*Beteiligung*), which can be divided into two groups: liability as a principal (*Täterschaft*) and liability as a secondary participant (*Teilnahme*).[342] The latter category will be explained in more detail below. As to the principals, leaving aside the cases of sole perpetrator, this form of liability can also occur in two forms: joint principals (*Mittäterschaft*) and principals by proxy (*Mittelbare Täterschaft*).

5.1. Principals

The notion of joint principals addresses the situations in which several persons act according to a common plan, which entails commission of an offence, and the tasks within this plan are distributed in a way that they do not all fulfil the required elements of the offence. If this is the case, these persons are liable as principals regardless of the nature of their contribution(s).[343] This form of liability would

[338] Saliger, '§ 266 Untreue' (n 229) marginal no 105.

[339] According to StGB, s 23(1), attempts to commit a felony entail criminal liability, whereas attempted misdemeanours are punishable only if expressly provided so by law. *Untreue* belongs to the category of misdemeanours (in view of the level of punishment) and the law does not foresee such a provision.

[340] The German criminal law provides in StGB, s 30(2) for liability for conspiring to commit an offence. However, the application of this provision is limited to felonies. See Bohlander, *Principles of German Criminal Law* (n 112) 175.

[341] The debates over the boundaries of criminalisation through the offence of *Untreue* pointed out that extensive interpretation of certain elements, in particular the notion of risk-damage, result in practice in introducing the criminalisation of attempted *Untreue* through the back door (Alfred Dierlamm, 'Untreue – ein Auffangtatbestand?' NStZ 1997, 534, 535). It seems, however, that the recent constitutional jurisprudence largely addressed this criticism.

[342] Bohlander, *Principles of German Criminal Law* (n 112) 154. This section is mainly based on ibid 153 et seq, including the English terminology he uses.

[343] Jescheck and Weigend, *Lehrbuch des Strafrechts* (n 277) 674; Bohlander, *Principles of German Criminal Law* (n 112) 161 et seq; Urs Kindhäuser, *Strafrecht. Allgemeiner Teil*, 4th edn (Baden Baden: Nomos, 2009) 342.

find its application in cases where only the cooperation of two or more managers constitutes a breach of duty, or where it is only due to their parallel breach of duty that the required harm occurred (eg if a collegiate decision needs to be taken).[344]

The category of principals by proxy[345] encompasses persons who do not commit the offence themselves, but use another person (an agent) as an instrument (*als 'Werkzeug'*)[346] for this purpose, controlling the situation due to superior knowledge or superior powers over the agent.[347] It is the element of control of the act (*Tatherrschaft*), which is crucial for the differentiation between this form of committing the offence and secondary participation in its commission.[348]

This form of liability may be applied if managers (duty holders) use other persons to perform acts which are contrary to the duty of those managers and result in harm, as required by StGB, s 266. However, it is possible that the order given by the duty holder to perform such an act may constitute a breach of duty in itself, thus the person would be liable as sole perpetrator, without invoking liability as principal by proxy.

Only a person who has the duty to safeguard the financial interests of another person can commit *Untreue* as a principal.[349] Persons who do not have such a duty can fall into the scope of criminal liability for this offence only as secondary participants, ie instigators or aiders.[350] The majority of scholars follow the so-called *Einheitstäterbegriff*.[351] According to this theory, if a person has the duty to safeguard another person's financial interests and breaches this duty, causing the required result, he commits *Untreue* as a principal even if what he did would amount to secondary participation (aiding or instigating).[352] For instance, if a manager provides assistance to another person in the commission of *Untreue* or induces this person to commit this offence, the manager breaches his duty and fulfils the definition of the offence, thus he will be liable as a principal and not as a secondary participant (provided that the requirements of secondary participation are fulfilled; see below).[353] Similarly, in the case of two

344 BGH (21 December 2005) NJW 2006, 522, 527; see also Gerhard Seher, 'Grundfälle zur Mittäterschaft' (2009) *Juristische Schulung (JuS)* 304, 307 et seq. In view of the explained theories, one can argue that in the context of liability as joint principal, the relevant contribution must in fact be necessary to the commission of *Untreue*.

345 Under StGB, s 25(1): '[a]ny person who commits the offence himself or through another shall be liable as a principal'. It is the latter part of the sentence that designates the commission by proxy.

346 Jescheck and Weigend, *Lehrbuch des Strafrechts* (n 277) 664.

347 Bohlander, *Principles of German Criminal Law* (n 112) 156.

348 Jescheck and Weigend, *Lehrbuch des Strafrechts* (n 277) 664.

349 Seier, 'Untreue' (n 2) marginal no 61; Schramm, 'Untreue, § 266 StGB' (n 2) marginal no 156; Kindhäuser, '§ 266 Untreue' (n 6) marginal no 127; BGH (10 November 1959) NJW 1960, 158.

350 Seier, 'Untreue' (n 2) marginal no 62; Kindhäuser, '§ 266 Untreue' (n 6) marginal no 127; Perron, '§ 266 Untreue' (n 33) marginal no 52; BGH (21 October 1983) wistra 1984, 22, 23; BGH (21 December 2005) NJW 2006, 522, 530.

351 This term could arguably best be explained as 'lack of distinction between principals and participants'.

352 Schramm, 'Untreue, § 266 StGB' (n 2) marginal no 156.

353 Seier, 'Untreue' (n 2) marginal no 64. Against this theory and in favour of application of rules of control (*Tatherschaft*): Reihart Maurach, Friedrich-Christian Schroeder and Manfred Maiwald,

managers (both duty holders) where one successfully instigates the other to commit *Untreue*, both could be considered principals. However, liability as principal is limited to breaches of the given person's duties. As a result, where a person is a duty holder towards the victim but the latter is damaged because of the breach of another duty (a duty that this person does not have), such act does not classify this person as a principal.[354] For example, in the *Mannesmann/Vodafone* case, the liability of the members of the management board was considered as aiding to commit *Untreue* by their involvement in granting excessive remuneration, but not as principals, since the duty as regards this competence was vested only in the members of the supervisory board.[355]

5.2. Secondary Participants

There are two forms of secondary participation: instigation (*Anstiftung*) and aiding (*Beihilfe*).[356] Besides an intentional act of instigating or aiding, in order for the secondary participant to be criminally liable, it is necessary that the principal intentionally commit an unlawful act, *Untreue*, ie that he is a duty holder. It is, however, not necessary that he is held criminally liable for it.[357] In view of the *Einheitstäterbegriff*, the secondary participant cannot be a duty holder.

Instigation consists in causing another person to commit an unlawful and intentional act.[358] Instigation does not need to be the only cause of the main perpetrator's act; it is sufficient if it is one of the prompting factors.[359] The instigator is liable only if the main perpetrator actually committed *Untreue*.[360] If, at the moment of instigation, the future main perpetrator had already decided to commit the offence, the

Strafrecht Besonderer Teil, vol 1, *Straftate gegen Persönlichkeits- und Vermögenswerte*, 9th edn (Heidelberg: CF Müller Verlag, 2003) § 45 Untreue, marginal no 21.

354 Wittig, *Wirtschafsstrafrecht* (n 59) marginal no 7.

355 LG Düsseldorf (22 July 2004) NJW 2004, 3275, 3283; BGH (21 December 2005) NJW 2006, 522, 528.

356 The punishment for the secondary participant is the same as for the principal, although it should be mitigated according to the rules provided for in StGB, s 49(1) (StGB, ss 27 and 28). This mitigation can even be applied twice in certain cases of aiding. The dominant view, represented also in the jurisprudence, considers that if a person qualifies for the category of aider only by lacking the quality of duty holder, then the punishment may be mitigated only once (pursuant to StGB, s 28(1)). If, however, the person acts in a way which would fulfil the definition of aider in general terms, he should benefit from double mitigation of punishment. BGH (8 January 1975) NJW 1975, 837, 838; Schramm, 'Untreue, § 266 StGB' (n 2) marginal no 157; Dierlamm, '§ 266 Untreue' (n 5) marginal no 286. The question is, however, subject to debate, see also Perron, '§ 266 Untreue' (n 33) marginal no 52; Seier, 'Untreue' (n 2) marginal no 63.

357 The main perpetrator's liability might be excluded eg because of insanity. This approach is known as limited dependence of aiding and instigating on the main offence (*limitierte Akzessorietät*). See Jescheck and Weigend, *Lehrbuch des Strafrechts* (n 277) 685 et seq; Bohlander, *Principles of German Criminal Law* (n 112) 167–68.

358 StGB, s 26. See also Jescheck and Weigend, *Lehrbuch des Strafrechts* (n 277) 686.

359 Kindhäuser, *Strafrecht. Allgemeiner Teil* (n 343) 348.

360 As a general rule, the main perpetrator must at least enter the phase of a criminal attempt to commit the offence, but since attempted *Untreue* is not criminal, for the liability of instigators the commission of the main offence is necessary, Jescheck and Weigend, *Lehrbuch des Strafrechts* (n 277) 689.

instigator's liability is excluded.[361] The law does not specify in what way the secondary participant has to instigate the main perpetrator; this can be done by any means, for instance, gifts, promises, use of influence or reputation, or even threats.[362]

Instigation must be committed intentionally, which requires a so-called double intention (*doppelter Anstiftervorsatz*): the intention that the concrete intentional offence is committed and the intention to induce its commission.[363] Intention in the form of *dolus eventualis* is enough.[364] The intention to instigate must be directed at a concrete person or circle of persons.[365] Public incitement to commit an offence directed at an unspecified group of persons may, however, be punished pursuant to StGB, section 111. The instigator does not need to know all the details of the main offence, only its essential elements.[366]

An aider is a person who intentionally assists another in the intentional commission of an unlawful act.[367] This help may consist in acts of a different nature, such as providing instruments or tools, helping to execute the act, by providing information or advice, as well as by giving psychological support – although this last category is subject to controversy.[368] The majority view accepts aiding by providing psychological support if the secondary participant helps the main perpetrator, who has already decided to commit the offence, to overcome fear as to its execution,[369] or by strengthening the main perpetrator's will to execute the act (also by promising help, which the main perpetrator does not use in the end).[370] In instances other than providing psychological support, the main perpetrator does not need to be aware of the fact that aid is being provided.[371] Aid can be provided at any point of time until the main offence is completed (*beendet*).[372] According to the dominant view, the aid must be one of the elements that influenced the main act which facilitated, intensified or ensured its commission, although it does not need to be the only or main factor.[373]

[361] In cases where at the moment of instigation the main perpetrator had already decided to commit the offence, only liability for attempted instigation is possible (pursuant to StGB, s 30(1), see Bohlander, *Principles of German Criminal Law* (n 112) 168). However, in order for such a liability to be possible, it is necessary that the attempts to commit the main offence are criminalised. As this is not the case for *Untreue*, also attempted instigation is not punishable.

[362] Jescheck and Weigend, *Lehrbuch des Strafrechts* (n 277) 687.

[363] Kindhäuser, *Strafrecht. Allgemeiner Teil* (n 343) 351.

[364] Jescheck and Weigend, *Lehrbuch des Strafrechts* (n 277) 687.

[365] Günter Heine and Bettina Weißer, '§ 26 Anstiftung' in Adolf Schönke, Horst Schröder, Albin Eser et al (eds), *Strafgesetzbuch Kommentar*, 29th edn (Munich: CH Beck, 2014) marginal no 19; Jescheck and Weigend, *Lehrbuch des Strafrechts* (n 277) 688.

[366] Bohlander, *Principles of German Criminal Law* (n 112) 169.

[367] StGB, s 27(1). See also Jescheck and Weigend, *Lehrbuch des Strafrechts* (n 277) 691.

[368] Kindhäuser, *Strafrecht. Allgemeiner Teil* (n 343) 355.

[369] Ibid 355.

[370] Jescheck and Weigend, *Lehrbuch des Strafrechts* (n 277) 692.

[371] Günter Heine and Bettina Weißer, '§ 27 Beihilfe' in Adolf Schönke, Horst Schröder, Albin Eser et al (eds), *Strafgesetzbuch Kommentar*, 29th edn (Munich: CH Beck, 2014) marginal no 18.

[372] Jescheck and Weigend, *Lehrbuch des Strafrechts* (n 277) 692; Schünemann, '§ 266 Untreue' (n 9) marginal no 207.

[373] Wolfgang Joecks, '§ 27 Beihilfe' in Bernd von Heintschel-Heinegg (ed), *Münchener Kommentar zum Strafgesetzbuch, Band 1: §§ 1-37 StGB*, 2nd edn (Munich: CH Beck, 2011) marignal no 23 et seq; Heine and Weißer, '§ 27 Beihilfe' (n 371) marginal no 4.

The *mens rea* requirement is similar to the one as regards the instigator (double intention).[374] The aider must want the unlawful act to be effectively committed, however he does not need to know all the details concerning the act. The jurisprudence tends to require even less knowledge as to these details than in cases of instigation.[375]

Aid can be provided in any form, be it by preparing documents, gathering information, advising on the decision-making process or psychologically supporting the act.[376] Help can also be provided by accountants or auditors advising the main perpetrator or attesting (contrary to the facts) to the correctness of the company's accounts, unless they have the duty themselves.[377] In the *Mannesmann/Vodafone* case, the aid for the accused (member of the management board and head of department) consisted in preparing decisions of the supervisory board, the members of which breached their duty by adopting these decisions, and assisting in their enforcement.[378]

Assistants and other personnel collaborating with the managers may perform all of these activities and remain innocent. The crucial factor, which might turn them into secondary participants, is *mens rea*. According to the rule of double intention, the secondary participant must know that the person to whom he is providing help is a duty holder and, more pertinently, must want him to breach his duty or know that the act furthered by his aid may constitute a breach of duty and accept this possibility. Moreover, the secondary participant must want to assist in the commission of this breach, or at least know that it is possible that his help will facilitate the main act and accept this possibility. Finally, secondary participants must intend the company to suffer damage or risk-damage or consider it probable that this result will take place and accept this.

6. Reasons for Excluding Criminal Liability

6.1. Consent of the Victim

The valid consent (*Einverständnis*) of the victim, ie the owner of the assets,[379] to the act of the perpetrator excludes criminal liability for *Untreue*.[380] According to

[374] Jescheck and Weigend, *Lehrbuch des Strafrechts* (n 277) 695.

[375] Kindhäuser, *Strafrecht. Allgemeiner Teil* (n 343) 362; Bohlander, *Principles of German Criminal Law* (n 112) 173.

[376] See, eg BGH (15 November 2001) NJW 2002, 1211, 1213.

[377] BGH (18 October 2006) NJW 2007, 1760.

[378] BGH (21 December 2005) NJW 2006, 522, 522 et seq, 528.

[379] See 2 above.

[380] Kindhäuser, '§ 266 Untreue' (n 6) marginal no 66; Seier, 'Untreue' (n 2) marginal no 89; BGH (20 July 1999) NJW 2000, 154, 155; BGH (18 June 2003) NJW 2003, 2996, 2998–3000; BGH (21 December 2005) NJW 2006, 522, 525 et seq; Wittig, '§ 266 Untreue' (n 82) marginal no 20.

the majority opinion, consent in cases of Untreue is not a ground of justification (such as self-defence), but broadens the scope of what the perpetrator is allowed to do within these boundaries of his duty.[381]

In order to exclude criminal liability, consent must be valid and this validity is defined by several rules. First of all, consent must be given before the act. If it is given afterwards it cannot exclude criminal liability.[382] Secondly, the person giving consent must be entitled to decide upon the assets, which is particularly important in the context of legal persons (see below).[383] Thirdly, the person must have the legal capacity to consent, and the consent was not obtained by means of deception (*Täuschung*) or constraint (*Zwang*).[384] Moreover, the person must have enough insight into the situation.[385] Although lack of experience does not exclude the validity of consent *a priori*, consent could be invalid, for example, in a situation in which an inexperienced person gives consent to a transaction bearing an uncommonly high risk.[386] Some authors also think that consent is invalid when it authorises an illegal act (eg corruption) or is given in violation of legal provisions (eg consent given by an organ with respect to an act which, according to the by-laws, is beyond the scope of its remit).[387]

Shareholders of a GmbH are entitled to give valid consent to an act which may be damaging for the company, however the limits of this consent are subject to debate.[388] The dominant view considers such consent valid as long as it does not authorise an act which endangers the existence of the company (in economic terms), for example, if it risks illiquidity of the company or affects its nominal capital (*Stammkapital*).[389] The opposing view claims that such an interpretation aims at protecting mainly the creditors of the company, which is not the function of *Untreue* and that it should not limit the freedom of shareholders (owners) to decide upon their assets, and thus considers their right to give consent as unlimited.[390]

[381] Schramm, 'Untreue, § 266 StGB' (n 2) marginal no 74; Dierlamm, '§ 266 Untreue' (n 5) marginal no 143; BGH (27 August 2010) NJW 2010, 3458, 3461. On the problem of consent and the offence of *Untreue*, see the monograph of Edward Schramm, *Untreue und Konsens* (Berlin: Duncker & Humblot, 2005).

[382] Seier, 'Untreue' (n 2) marginal no 92; Schramm, 'Untreue, § 266 StGB' (n 2) marginal no 76. However, the latter discussed situations in which such consent could be valid, if given during the commission of the offence, see Schramm, 'Untreue, § 266 StGB' (n 2) marginal no 77 and Schramm, *Untreue und Konsens* (n 380) 186–87; Wittig, '§ 266 Untreue' (n 82) marginal no 21; BGH (21 December 2005) NJW 2006, 522, 526.

[383] Schramm, 'Untreue, § 266 StGB' (n 2) marginal no 78.

[384] Seier, 'Untreue' (n 2) marginal no 90.

[385] BGH (7 November 1996) NStZ 1997, 124, 125.

[386] Kindhäuser, '§ 266 Untreue' (n 6) marginal no 67; Waßmer, *Untreue bei Risikogeschäften* (n 24) 44.

[387] Schramm, 'Untreue, § 266 StGB' (n 2) marginal no 80. Contrary: Seier, 'Untreue' (n 2) marginal no 90, who considers that such view is not in agreement with the protected legal interest of the offence of *Untreue*.

[388] Schramm, 'Untreue, § 266 StGB' (n 2) marginal no 85.

[389] Kindhäuser, '§ 266 Untreue' (n 6) marginal no 71; Schramm, 'Untreue, § 266 StGB' (n 2) marginal no 85.

[390] Perron, '§ 266 Untreue' (n 33) marginal no 21b. See also Dierlamm, '§ 266 Untreue' (n 5) marginal no 143 et seq.

Similar rules apply to consent given by the shareholders of an AG. Here too, as in the context of the GmbH, part of the doctrine opposes limiting consent.[391] It must be granted by all shareholders or a valid shareholders' meeting.[392]

As the shareholders are not considered duty holders, they cannot be liable for *Untreue* for consent given against the interests of the company.

Presumed consent (*mutmaßliches Einverständnis*) can also in certain circumstances exclude criminal liability for *Untreue*. It may be considered only in situations where obtaining a valid consent from the entitled person was impossible, at least in the necessary timeframe.[393] Presumed consent is a justification developed mainly in the domain of criminal law in medicine, but its general rules apply here as well.[394] It excludes criminal liability if 'an evaluation of all circumstances, conducted with due diligence at the time of the act by D[efendant], leads to the conclusion that, if asked, V[ictim] would consent'.[395] The fact that the victim subsequently denies that he would have given consent does not exclude the validity of this justification, if its conditions were fulfilled.[396]

6.2. Orders of Superiors

If a lower-tier manager performs at the request of a senior manager an act which he knows to be in breach of his duty and may result in a loss to the company, there is nothing to suggest that the request excludes his criminal liability. However, the senior manager's order may influence the *mens rea* of the lower-level manager, if the senior manager assures him that the decision is correct. Moreover, a question of consent may also arise, however in very exceptional cases, where the senior manager would be entitled to give valid consent in the name of the company.

6.3. Expert Opinions

The existence of expert opinion may influence the *mens rea* of the perpetrator if it indicates that the decision in question will not expose the company to unacceptable risk, unless the perpetrator has reason to doubt the accuracy of that opinion.

In the case of collective decisions, each member of the decisive body is obliged to fulfil his duty and do all that he can reasonably do to stop a decision which

[391] Dierlamm, '§ 266 Untreue' (n 5) marginal no 159.

[392] BGH (21 December 2005) NJW 2006, 522, 522 et seq, 525.

[393] Dierlamm, '§ 266 Untreue' (n 5) marginal no 145.

[394] Schramm, 'Untreue, § 266 StGB' (n 2) marginal no 81 et seq; Dierlamm, '§ 266 Untreue' (n 5) marginal no 145.

[395] Bohlander, *Principles of German Criminal Law* (n 112) 88.

[396] Ibid 88 et seq.

might be detrimental to the company.[397] It has also been considered in the context of granting credit that members of the decisive body may rely on the opinion of the manager in charge, or of an expert called for this purpose, unless particular circumstances exist, such as doubts or diversity of expert opinions or particularly high risk.[398]

7. Special Provisions for Banking and Insurance Executives

The so-called Ring-fencing Act (Trennbankengesetz),[399] which concerns banking and insurance undertakings and was enacted in reaction to the most recent financial crisis, introduced two special criminal provisions concerning senior banking and insurance managers, which penalise violations of a listed number of risk-management rules, resulting in a situation of concrete endangerment to the existence of a financial or insurance institution.[400] The reason for introducing these provisions was the German legislature's consideration that the instances in which senior managers of banking, financial and insurance undertakings could be held criminally liable for failures in risk management were insufficient.[401] These new offences should contribute to the prevention of a new financial crisis and, were one to occur nonetheless, ought to permit a criminal law response to wrongdoing.[402] The provisions entered into force on 2 January 2014.[403] Since the law has been in force for a relatively short period of time, the literature concerning it is so far rather limited and there is no jurisprudence.

The Ring-fencing Act introduced the offence concerning banking executives by creating a new section 54a of the Banking Act (Gesetz über das Kreditwesen,

[397] Seier, 'Untreue' (n 2) marginal no 80.

[398] Ibid marginal no 280; Kindhäuser, '§ 266 Untreue' (n 6) marginal no 78; BGH (6 April 2000) NJW 2000, 2364, 2366; BGH (15 November 2001) NJW 2002, 1211, 1216.

[399] Gesetz zur Abschirmung von Risiken und zur Planung der Sanierung und Abwicklung von Kreditinstituten und Finanzgruppen (Act on Ringfencing of Risks and on Recovery and Resolution Planning for Credit Institutions and Financial Groups), adopted on 7 August 2013 (Bundesgesetzblatt Jahrgang 2013 Teil I No 47, 3090 et seq), entered into force on 13 August 2013, available at http://dipbt.bundestag.de/extrakt/ba/WP17/508/50871.html. The author is very grateful to HammPartner and in particular to Thomas Richter for providing the English translation of the provisions of KWG and VAG used in this section. The author remains responsible for alterations made to this translation.

[400] The punishment provided for the offences of KWG, s 54a and VAG, s 142 is five years' imprisonment and a fine, or two years and a fine if the result was caused negligently. The limitation period is of five years regardless of the form of *mens rea*, and it starts running from the moment of the occurrence of the foreseen result. See Peter Häberle, 'KWG 54a Strafvorschriften' in Georg Erbs, Max Kohlhaas and Friedrich Ambs (eds), *Strafrechtliche Nebengesetze, Loseblattausgabe*, 199th edn (MüMunich: CH Beck, 2014) marginal nos 1, 6, 9.

[401] Deutscher Bundestag, Drucksache 17/12601 (4 March 2013) 2.

[402] Alexander Schork and Tilman Reichling, 'Der strafrechtliche Schutz des Risikomanagements durch das sog. Trennbankengesetz' (2013) *Corporate Compliance Zeitschrift* (*CCZ*) 269.

[403] Häberle, 'KWG 54a Strafvorschriften' (n 400) marginal no 1.

KWG), and a similar provision concerning insurance undertakings: section 142 of the Insurance Supervision Act (Gesetz über die Beaufsichtigung der Versicherungsunternehmen, VAG).

7.1. Protected Legal Interests

The question of what legal interests are protected by the offence of VAG, sections 54a and 142 is subject to debate. Indisputably, the overall aim of the offence is to ensure the stability of the financial system as a whole, but the question is whether other legal interests are also protected by the offence.[404] The document explaining the reasons for introducing the provisions of the Ring-fencing Act mentions also '[aiming at] securing the entrusted assets and [ensuring] proper conduct of banking and insurance and financial services'.[405] However, the unclear wording of the text and the possible overlap in this respect with the offence of *Untreue*, which also protects entrusted assets, does not facilitate giving a clear answer to this problem.[406] The fact that KWG, section 54a and VAG, section 142 punish only those infringements of risk-management rules that impact on the functioning of the whole institution and not only on interests of particular clients suggests that systemic interests prevail over individual ones in the context of this offence.[407]

7.2. Perpetrator

Criminal liability for the offence under KWG, section 54a, as well as for the one provided for in VAG, section 142, is applicable only to a limited circle of persons called *Geschäftsleiter* (senior managers). According to the definition in KWG, section 1(2), senior managers are those who by virtue of the law or the articles of association manage the business affairs of the undertaking and represent it. Generally, this circle will be limited to the most senior managers, for example, members of management boards in public limited companies (AG).[408] VAG, section 7a(1), provides a similar definition as regards senior insurance managers.

[404] Deutscher Bundestag, Drucksache 17/12601, 2, Häberle, 'KWG 54a Strafvorschriften' (n 400) marginal no 1.

[405] Deutscher Bundestag, Drucksache 17/12601, 28.

[406] Häberle, 'KWG 54a Strafvorschriften' (n 400) marginal no 1. To the contrary, Cichy, Cziupka and Wiersch consider that both legal goods are protected by the offence as well as 'avoiding harm to economy in general'; See Patrick Cichy, Johannes Cziupka and Rachid René Wiersch, 'Voraussetzungen der Strafbarkeit der Geschäftsleiter von Kreditinstituten nach § 54 a KWG n. F.' (2013) *Neue Zeitschrift für Gesellschaftsrecht* (*NZG*) 846, 847.

[407] Häberle, 'KWG 54a Strafvorschriften' (n 400) marginal no 1.

[408] Thomas Richter, 'The New German Ringfencing Act Establishing Criminal Liability of Banking and Insurance Executives for Failures in Risk Management' (2013) 6(4) *Journal of Risk Management in Financial Institutions* 433, 440.

Persons who do not fulfil these criteria may be liable for the offence according to the general rules on aiding and instigating (see 5.2 above). Such persons can be members of the supervisory board (*Aufsichtsrat*), lower level managers or even third persons.[409] The requirement of a previous order from the BaFin (see below) applies also to the liability of these persons.[410]

7.3. Conduct, Result and Condition for Prosecution

The legislative technique, as well as the wording of the provision as regards the description of the conduct and its result, is not reader-friendly and does not translate easily into English. Section 54a describes the criminal conduct as:

> [failing] to ensure, contrary to Section 25c subsection (4a) or Section 25c subsection (4b) sentence 2, that an institution or a group set out therein has in place a strategy set out therein, a process set out therein, a procedure set out therein, a function set out therein or a concept set out therein and hereby causes a threat to the existence of the institution, the subordinated enterprise or an institution belonging to the group.

The elements of this description will be explained in turn.

The application of this provision is limited to certain types of institutions. According to KWG, section 1(1b), these are credit institutions (*Kreditinstitute*) or financial services institutions (*Finanzdienstleistungsinstitute*) as defined by KWG, sections 1 and 1a or groups mentioned in section 25a(3). The offence in VAG, section 142 is applicable to insurance undertakings (*Versicherungsunternehmen*) as defined by VAG, section 1(1). These institutions must be under the supervision of the Federal Financial Supervisory Authority (Bundesanstalt für Finanzdienstleistungsaufsicht, BaFin). Currently, BaFin supervises in Germany around 1,850 banks and 700 financial services institutions, as well as around 600 insurance undertakings.[411]

Criminal conduct consists in failing to ensure that the credit and financial institution or the insurance undertaking has in place the risk management measures set out in the respective catalogues to which KWG, section 54a and VAG, section 142 make reference. Risk-management measures as regards credit and financial institutions are foreseen in the KWG, in particular in section 25c. The implementation of these measures is the responsibility of senior managers. Section 25c(4a) and (4b) sentence 2 provide catalogues of risk-management measures. These are measures that section 54a refers to as: strategy (*Strategie*); process (*Prozess*); procedure (*Verfahren*); function (*Funktion*); or concept (*Konzept*).[412] Similar duties,

[409] Häberle, 'KWG 54a Strafvorschriften' (n 400) marginal no 2.

[410] Richter, 'The New German Ringfencing Act' (n 408) 440.

[411] See www.bafin.de.

[412] The following quotes from KWG, s 25c give examples of these measures: '1. a business strategy aimed at the sustainable development of the institution and a consistent risk strategy as well as processes for the planning, implementation, review and adjustment of the strategies … as a minimum

adapted to the type of activities in question, have been formulated for the senior managers of insurance institutions in VAG, section 64a(7).

Despite the extensive catalogue of measures, it had been raised during the legislative process that it could still be unclear for the addressees of these provisions when the implementation of these measures could be considered insufficient, and thus that this law might infringe the constitutional principle of legal certainty.[413] The legislator addressed this problem by introducing a requirement that, for criminal liability, it is necessary that BaFin first ordered the responsible person to remedy the violation of risk-management rules, which this person contravened and thereby caused the foreseen result (KWG, section 54a(3) and VAG, section 142(3)).[414]

The last *actus reus* requirement of these offences is that the violation of risk-management rules caused a result, which is described differently for the banking executives and for the insurance executives. The requirement formulated in KWG, section 54a reads as follows: 'and hereby causes a threat to the existence (*Bestandsgefährdung*) of the institution, the subordinated enterprise or an institution belonging to the group'. This situation of concrete endangerment of the institution was defined by the now repealed KWG, section 48b, as 'the risk of a collapse of the credit institution due to insolvency in the absence of corrective actions'.[415] KWG, section 48b described this concept further, in particular by providing for a presumption on the basis of which it can be decided when the situation of the institution can be described as under '*Bestandsgefährdung*'. It is doubtful whether these presumptions, provided for regulatory purposes, could be used in criminal procedure, instead it is necessary to prove that the institution is actually at risk of collapse.[416]

the senior managers must ensure that (a) the overall objective, the objectives of the institution for each material business activity as well as the measures for implementing such objectives are documented at all times; (b) the risk strategy at all times takes into account the objectives or risks management with regard to the material business activities as well as the measures for implementing such objectives; 2. procedures for determining and ensuring the risk-bearing capacity … as a minimum the senior managers must ensure that (a) the material risks of the institution, in particular counterparty, market price, liquidity and operational risks are identified and defined at regular intervals and on an event-driven basis (overall risk profile); (b) as part of the risk inventory, risk concentrations are taken into account and potential material impairments of the asset, revenue or liquidity statutes are examined; 3. internal control procedures with an internal control system and an internal audit … as a minimum the senior managers must ensure that … 4. appropriate staffing levels and technical and organizational resources of the institution … as a minimum the senior managers must ensure that … 5. appropriate contingency plans for emergencies relating to time-critical activities and processes … as a minimum the senior managers must ensure that …'.

413 Häberle, 'KWG 54a Strafvorschriften' (n 400) marginal no 3. In this regard, see also Rainer Hamm and Thomas Richter, 'Symbolisches und hypertrophes Strafrecht im Entwurf eines "Trennbankengesetzes"' (2013) 19(67) *Zeitschrift für Wirtschafts- und Bankrecht* 865.

414 For discussion on the nature of this requirement see Häberle, 'KWG 54a Strafvorschriften' (n 400) marginal no 4.

415 Translation after Richter, 'The New German Ringfencing Act' (n 408) 437.

416 Häberle, 'KWG 54a Strafvorschriften' (n 400) marginal no 3; Richter, 'The New German Ringfencing Act' (n 408) 438.

The offence in VAG, section 142 also has the limb of result, although formulated differently. It requires that by violating the risk-management measures (which BaFin ordered him to remedy) the perpetrator:

> (1.) caused the insolvency or over-indebtedness of the undertaking or (2.) caused that the insolvency or over-indebtedness can only be averted through recourse to state aid within the meaning of Article 107 subsection (1) of the Treaty on the Functioning of the European Union.

Both offences also require proof of causality and objective ascription between the violation of the rules on risk-management and the result, according to the rules provided for this purpose in the German doctrine (see 3.5.3 below on 'Attribution of damage/Causality'). There is no criminal liability for attempt to commit any of these offences (StGB, section 23(1)).[417]

7.4. *Mens Rea*

Both offences have similar *mens rea* requirements. For criminal liability, they must be committed intentionally (at least with *dolus eventualis*) as regards criminal conduct.[418] As to the result, they can be committed either intentionally (KWG, section 54a(1) and VAG, section 142(1)) or negligently (KWG, section 54a(2) and VAG, section 142(2)).[419] This means that it is not necessary for criminal liability that the senior manager even agreed to the occurrence of the result described above.[420] He could still be held liable, under subsection (2), if he foresaw the possibility of the occurrence of the '*Bestandsgefährdung*' although hoped that it would not take place (advertent negligence, *bewusste Fahrlässigkeit*) or did not foresee such a possibility, but was able to foresee it (inadvertent negligence, *unbewusste Fahrlässigkeit*).[421]

8. Solutions to the Five Cases

In view of the broad definition of perpetrator, the managers in all five cases presented in the introductory chapter will fulfil the criteria delimitating the scope of perpetrators of *Untreue*.[422]

As to cases 1 and 2, insufficient guarantees attached to granting of credit constitute typical cases of *Untreue*. In both cases, the manager will be liable as

[417] Häberle, 'KWG 54a Strafvorschriften' (n 400) marginal no 6.
[418] Ibid marginal no 5.
[419] According to StGB, s 11(2), the offences thus formulated are still considered to be intentional.
[420] For details on different types of intention in the German criminal law, see 3.6 above.
[421] Häberle, 'KWG 54a Strafvorschriften' (n 400) marginal no 5.
[422] For the hypotheses of the cases and explanations, see Chapter 1, section 4.

main perpetrator. In the second case, by telling the employees to grant the credit he violates his duty, which is sufficient for the liability as a principal. The breach of duty does not consist in failing to ask for some documents or information, instead the manager grants the credit outright, under conditions which are not acceptable.[423] Therefore, it is probable that the court may consider this breach as 'evident'[424] and consider the requirement of 'severity' of the breach to be fulfilled. As to case 1, provided that the granting of credit is not invalid because of civil law rules, the manager would commit the *Missbrauch* modality, since he was entitled to grant the credit (bind the bank externally), but (internally) should not have allowed it under these conditions.

The main question for deciding upon his liability concerns the result of his act and the *mens rea* requirements. In view of the most recent approach to the concept of risk-damage, it is necessary that the insufficient guarantee of the loan resulted in diminishing the value of the assets of the bank. In both cases, this requirement most probably is fulfilled, since if the bank decides to alienate it the value of the claim would be lower. As to the *mens rea*, in both cases the managers know that they are exposing the company to an excessive risk contrary to their duty. In both cases, they have at least direct intention to cause risk-damage, so there is no need to refer to *dolus eventualis* and the problems associated with it can be avoided.

As to case 2, it may also result in criminal liability under KWG, section 54a, provided that it can be proved that the senior manager violated one of the rules on risk-management and that BaFin ordered this violation to be remedied. Moreover, it is necessary to prove that by violating this rule, the senior manager concretely endangered the existence of the bank.

As to case 3, the breach of duty may also not be difficult to prove, as gambling with the company's money does not meet the standards of diligence as required, for example, by GmbHG, section 43 or AktG, section 93(1). Since the investment will be valid externally, the manager would be liable for the *Missbrauch* modality. Here again, the question of result will be the most problematic, since the approach presented in older jurisprudence, which would allow an admission that the requirement of risk-damage is fulfilled if the manager acts 'like a gambler', is no longer accepted. If it is impossible to quantify the loss of value of the company's assets (invested on the stock exchange) by the mere fact of investing them, then only the final result of this investment will determine whether criminal liability exists. Therefore, a manager might be liable only if his investment has resulted in a loss. As to *mens rea*, it may take the form of *dolus eventualis*, since he was most probably aware of the fact that investment in the stock exchange might bring a loss and accepted this possibility.

In case 4, in order to establish a breach of duty, it is necessary to find the legal basis of the rules and standards governing the way the manager should execute

[423] Compare BGH (15 November 2001) NJW 2002, 1211, 1214.
[424] Schramm, 'Untreue, § 266 StGB' (n 2) marginal no 55.

his function. This case can only be *Treubruch*, since there is no question of binding the company externally. It is probable that by hiding the problem, which may lead to significant extra costs for the company, he breached standards of diligence applicable to him. Moreover, it is also possible to calculate an estimate of the costs incurred by the company were it to sell the cars in question, fulfilling the requirement of risk-damage. On the other hand, one can argue that the risk is fairly uncertain, while the postponing of the presentation and reprogramming of the electronics would generate more immediate costs. As to the *mens rea*, the perpetrator was aware of the risk and of the possible loss and, it would seem, agreed with it. However, if he perceived that the costs would have been higher had the presentation been postponed, then he acted in a way so as to diminish the loss (in his perception), thus the *mens rea* would not be fulfilled.

As to case 5, according to the current jurisprudence, giving bribes as such does not constitute *Untreue*, if it is performed in the interests of the company and upon valid agreement of the owner.[425] However, some authors consider that consent is always invalid if given to an illegal act such as corruption. So far, the German jurisprudence has dealt with cases of corruption by punishing managers for creating slush funds. In order for criminal liability for *Untreue* to be possible, the manager must have used slush funds for the purpose of hiding the money, to be used thereafter for the bribing of public officials. This may constitute a violation of book-keeping rules and in this way the breach of duty would occur. If such a violation might incur negative consequences for the company (eg administrative fines, etc), then it may be considered as risk-damage. The courts have also found damage in the fact that the owner lost the possibility of using the assets hidden in the slush fund. However, in this case scenario, it is unknown whether the manager indeed used a slush fund to bribe the public official. If the use of company funds to corrupt a public official is to be considered a breach of duty, criminal liability would depend on whether the risk-damage could be proved, which requires that the negative consequences if the corruption becomes known offset the gain from the contract.

As to the negligent version of the cases, there is no possibility to convict the managers, since *Untreue* does not provide for liability for negligence.

9. Conclusions

Untreue is one of the most debated offences in the German Criminal Code. Its original sins lay in the compromise between the *Missbrauch* and *Treubruch* theories, which resulted in including both of them in the definition of the offence, and in the broad terminology used in defining the limbs of this crime.

[425] Seier, 'Untreue' (n 2) marginal no 401.

Decades of efforts by the jurisprudence and doctrine have brought much more clarity as to the scope of criminalisation, which was confirmed in the recent judgments of the Federal Constitutional Court of Germany. However, since so many aspects of the offence are debatable and debated, it is impossible to affirm that the understanding of certain limbs will not be broadened or narrowed by further jurisprudence.

From the point of view of the cases under examination in this book, the least problematic requirement is the definition of the perpetrator. In view of the broad general clause used in German law, managers of different levels are included in the scope of this provision, since the crucial element – discretion – will necessarily be fulfilled. This may be the case even if they perform their functions only de facto or if the basis of their relationship entitling them to make decisions concerning another person's assets is void or no longer valid. The provision also allows for the inclusion of members of supervisory bodies. Moreover, persons who do not fulfil the requirements to become perpetrators of *Untreue* may be criminally liable for aiding or instigating the commission of this offence.

The perpetrator's conduct consists in breaching his duty to safeguard the financial interests of the principal, which may take place while managing his assets or when making binding agreements in the name of the principal. In order to verify whether a manager breached his duty, it is necessary to examine the rules and standards which are enshrined in legal sources governing his position (statute, commission of a public authority, legal transaction or fiduciary relationship). These sources may provide concrete requirements or more general standards of conduct. The former may require a certain act of risk-management, while the latter may serve as benchmarks in order to determine whether the risk involved in certain acts is excessive or not. If the appropriate level of risk cannot be determined in this way, it should be done by examining the purpose of the business and standards of care typical for this type of business activities. Furthermore, the duty breached should aim, at least indirectly, at protecting the entrusted assets.

Moreover if, as asserted by recent jurisprudence, there exists a requirement of severity, it will be necessary to establish not only that a duty was breached, but also that this breach was severe. The level of risk that the perpetrator is allowed to take may be heightened by the valid consent of the shareholders, however, this would only be the case under certain conditions, including, according to the dominant opinion, that it would not endanger the existence of the company.

The breach of duty must cause a result, which may constitute an actual damage or risk-damage. In view of the recent jurisprudential development of the interpretation of the concept of risk-damage, the possibilities of its use are more limited, since the risk must be quantifiable and cannot be assessed by means of normative clauses. Therefore, in order to use the concept of risk-damage, the risk to which the company is exposed must result in a concrete decrease in value of the assets of the company.

The result in the form of risk-damage must be causally connected to the breach of duty.[426] The test consists of two elements: causality and objective ascription.[427] The first element verifies whether the breach of duty was effectively part of the causal chain that led to the result, ie that the result would not have happened without this breach. According to the second part of the test, the connection is not established if the result would have occurred even if the perpetrator did not commit the breach of duty. The required probability of this alternative scenario is subject to debate. The dominant view considers it sufficient that it is impossible to exclude it based on significant elements of the case (in other words it must be certain that the harm would not have occurred, had the perpetrator acted according to the rules).[428]

Untreue is an intentional offence, which can be committed with all three forms of intention: direct intent in the first degree, *dolus directus* and *dolus eventualis*. As to the latter form in the context of risk-damage, there is a debate over whether it is necessary that the perpetrator accept not only the possibility of the occurrence of risk-damage, but also of actual damage. The first approach seems to prevail, as the latter results in discrepancies between *actus reus* and *mens rea* and loses its relevance in view of the more restrictive interpretation of the concept of risk-damage.

As can be inferred from the above analysis, the offence of *Untreue* offers broad but not boundless possibilities of prosecution of managers' wrongful behaviour. The judgments issued in recent years, in particular the 2010 sentence of the BVerfG, have curbed an over-extensive interpretation of the offence's definition. In particular, the concept of risk-damage has been restrained by requiring a quantifiable decrease in value. Also, the requirement of 'severity' as to the breach of duty significantly limits the possibility of punishing those who commit minor breaches of such duties. Both restrictions will also influence the requirements of *mens rea*.

On the other hand, the terms used in order to limit the scope of the offence are of a general and imprecise nature, and are open to question from the point of view of legal certainty. This results in continued pleas for the reform of the offence.[429] Moreover, even if the stricter approach does not permit boundless criminalisation of any kind of mismanagement, the use of these broad terms may give the offence a wide scope from the procedural perspective, and allow every dubious business decision or practice to result in the opening of a criminal investigation.[430]

Due to its novelty, it is very difficult to make any sensible conclusions as regards the special offences for senior managers in the banking and insurance industry.

[426] Jescheck and Weigend, *Lehrbuch des Strafrechts* (n 277) 277; Schmid, '§ 31 Treupflichtverletzungen' (n 40) marginal no 175; BGH (6 april 2000) NJW 2000, 2364, 2365.

[427] Jescheck and Weigend, *Lehrbuch des Strafrechts* (n 277) 277 et seq.

[428] Saliger, '§ 266 Untreue' (n 229) marginal nos 78, 81.

[429] Schramm, 'Untreue, § 266 StGB' (n 2) marginal no 27.

[430] Seier, 'Untreue' (n 2) marginal no 21.

These new offences also require a breach of duties, but provide a specific catalogue of them. For criminal liability, the breach of one of these rules does not need to lead to concrete loss, but to concrete endangerment of the existence of the undertaking. As to *mens rea*, the latter result may be caused by the perpetrator even negligently. However, the offence is only punishable if the BaFin has issued a warning as to violations of risk-management rules and ordered their remedy. It remains to be seen whether they will shape the practice of risk-management within the sectors concerned, and what the interplay between the scope of criminalisation of these offences and *Untreue* will be.

5

Comparative Analysis

1. Introduction

Criminalising managerial misbehaviour linked to damaging company assets has a long history in each of the three legal systems. The French and the German offences, the abuse of company assets and *Untreue* respectively, date back to the 1930s. Both offences were introduced in response to the financial crisis of that period, however they remained in constant use after the time of crisis, although they might tend to receive more attention in times of financial difficulties.

None of these offences expressly targeted excessive risk. Nonetheless, excessive risk was introduced through the interpretation of the elements of these offences. One of the modalities of committing the French offence of abuse of company assets consisting in acting against the company interests was exposing it to abnormal risk, an interpretation confirmed by the jurisprudence. The introduction of excessive risk into the definition of the German *Untreue* was also accomplished through jurisprudence, which transplanted the concept of risk-damage, developed for the offence of fraud. While this concept has a long history in German law, dating back to the nineteenth century, its modern understanding in the context of *Untreue* has been developed in the last 15 years. These developments were, inter alia, influenced by criticism formulated over the years in the doctrine and the need to provide boundaries for the allegedly overly vague terms used in the definition of the offence.

Until 2006, English law had no provision targeting excessive risk-taking as such. The traditional common law offence of conspiracy to defraud could have been used for this purpose, but there is very little jurisprudence demonstrating its regular use to combat misdealings in the form of excessively risky management. Nevertheless, three major judgments were in fact issued applying the common law offence to risk-taking (*Sinclair*, *Allsop* and *Wai Yu-Tsang*). Since the introduction of the Fraud Act 2006, the common law offence of conspiracy to defraud is supposed to be used only exceptionally, and the Act, in particular the provisions on fraud by abuse of position provided in section 4, should be the main offence charged in such cases. While no major judgments have been handed down so far, the formulation of section 4 clearly indicates that it may be used to punish managers exposing their companies to excessive risk, together with a handful of other offences, which are set out below.

2. Protected Legal Interests

The studied offences mainly aim at protecting the property of the company or the relationship of confidence between the agent and the principal. This approach grants protection mostly to the shareholders and to some extent to the stakeholders. The attention to the latter group depends largely on the extent to which the consent of shareholders can influence the scope of what is permissible for the managers. None of the analysed offences (with the exception of the special provisions for banking and insurance executives) aim at protecting the economic system or society as a whole. One may say, however, that while the offence grants protection to the assets entrusted by the shareholders to the management, the economic system is protected at large. This claim is based on the following argument. It is in the interest of the economic system, which is based to a large extent on limited companies, where the principle is for division between ownership and management, that such companies function well and that the management make proper use of the entrusted assets. Therefore, by protecting the interests of the shareholders, the offence indirectly protects the economic system. This can be seen, for instance, in the motivation of the French legislators who wanted to win back the confidence of investors in companies in order to foster economic recovery after the financial crisis.

While safeguarding economic interests is not the express purpose of any of the above-mentioned offences, the latter consideration is directly addressed by the new English and German offences targeting excessively risky management of banks (and also the insurance companies as regards Germany).

The English offence of fraud by abuse of position is aimed mainly at defending the property of the company, but also that of the shareholders and the stakeholders.[1] As to the latter category, the offence does not seem to be rigidly defined, as the consent of the shareholders would justify the act. Moreover, it has been pointed out that preserving trust in the relationship between the manager and the person entrusting the assets to him is also a motive for criminalisation, in particular the belief that the manager receiving the assets should use them for the benefit of the owner (the company and the shareholders in this case).[2]

The German offence of *Untreue* is aimed at protecting the legal interest of property (*Vermögen*).[3] Through this, it protects the assets of the company and

[1] Wai Yu-Tsang v R [1992] 1 AC 269, at 269.

[2] Simon Farrell, Nicholas Yeo and Guy Ladenburg, *Blackstone's Guide to the Fraud Act 2006* (Oxford University Press, 2007) 31 et seq.

[3] Alfred Dierlamm, '§ 266 Untreue' in Roland Hefendehl and Olaf Hohmann (eds), *Münchener Kommentar zum Strafgesetzbuch*, vol 5, §§ 263–358 StGB, 2nd edn (Munich: CH Beck, 2014) marginal no 1; Urs Kindhäuser, '§ 266 Untreue' in Urs Kindhäuser, Ulfrid Neumann and Hans-Ullrich Paeffgen (eds), *Strafgesetzbuch*, 4th edn (Baden-Baden: Nomos, 2013) marginal no 1; Walter Perron, '§ 266 Untreue' in Adolf Schönke, Horst Schröder, Albin Eser et al (eds), *Strafgesetzbuch Kommentar*, 29th edn (Munich: CH Beck, 2014) marginal no 1; Edward Schramm, 'Untreue, § 266 StGB' in Carsten Momsen and Thomas Grützner, *Wirtschaftsstrafrecht. Handbuch für die Unternehmens- und Anwaltspraxis*

of the shareholders. Only the shareholders can give consent to acts which would otherwise be considered excessively risky,[4] as well as bring actions as aggrieved party within the criminal procedure.[5] The validity of such consent is, however, limited, according to the dominant view, excluding acts which endanger the existence of the company (in economic terms).[6] In view of this, while the offence mainly protects the interests of the shareholders, the latter rule gives indirect consideration to the interests of other stakeholders.

The French offence of abuse of company assets sanctions those acts of management which are contrary to the interests of the company and done for personal purposes. By punishing such acts, the offence certainly protects the assets of the company. However, several authors have pointed out that the focus is placed on abuses of management and on the duty of loyalty towards the company, since the offence does not require proof of a result (ie a loss).[7] Even a positive outcome of the manager's decision does not exclude criminal liability, if the act exposed the company to excessive risk. The offence protects the company's own interests and only indirectly those of the shareholders. If the interests of the shareholders are in conflict with the company's prosperity, the latter is given priority, which is reflected in criminalisation of abuses committed by managers who are only shareholders of their companies, or in companies run as family businesses, as well as in lack of exculpatory effect of the shareholders' consent. Moreover, by focusing on the interests of the company and understanding them as independent of the interests of the shareholders, the offence takes into account the interest of other stakeholders, which are linked to the general well-being of the company.[8]

In conclusion, the English and the German offences mainly protect the assets of the company. They give most consideration to the interests of the shareholders. Within the German system, the interests of the stakeholders are also taken into account, but only indirectly, through limitation to the validity of consent by which the shareholders may agree to managers' acts exposing the company to a risk which is above the normal level. The French model focuses more on the company as an independent entity, protecting not only the shareholders' interests, but also those of other actors in the economic system, who might be interested in the company's well-functioning. While none of the legal orders concentrates on the protection of the economic system or of society, the existence of these offences,

(Munich: CH Beck, 2013) marginal no 2; Jürgen Seier, 'Untreue' in Hans Achenbach and Andreas Ransiek (eds), *Handbuch Wirtschaftsstrafrecht*, 3rd edn (Heidelberg et al: CF Müller, 2012) marginal no 10; BVerfG (23 June 2010) NJW 2010, 3209, 3212.

[4] Seier, 'Untreue' (n 3) marginal no 12.

[5] Kindhäuser, '§ 266 Untreue' (n 3) marginal no 129; Seier, 'Untreue' (n 3) marginal no 13.

[6] Kindhäuser, '§ 266 Untreue' (n 3) marginal no 71; Schramm, 'Untreue, § 266 StGB' (n 3) marginal no 85.

[7] Didier Rebut, *Abus de biens sociaux, Répertoire de droit pénal et de procédure pénale* (Dalloz, January 2010, dernière mise à jour, June 2011) para 10; Yvonne Muller, 'L'abus réprimé: la correction par le juge', 353 *Gazette du Palais*, 19 December 2009, 30.

[8] Eva Joly and Caroline Joly-Baumgartner, *L'abus de biens sociaux. Á l'épreuve de la pratique* (Paris: Economica, 2002) 93.

which, inter alia, protect limited companies, adds to the security of the system based on the existence of these types of entities.

This problem is interestingly linked with a procedural question of who may be considered as an aggrieved party for the purposes of criminal procedure. The German system considers the aggrieved party to be the company and the shareholders of limited liability companies (GmbH) and public limited companies (AG), which is a consequence of the approach described above.[9] The French system restricts this circle even more and limits it to only the company. The stakeholders, as well as the shareholders as such, are excluded.[10] The shareholder used to be admitted in this role until the Court of Cassation put an end to this practice in 2000.[11] They may, however, be allowed to represent the company in the procedure.[12] The English system does not adopt the institution of aggrieved party in the same sense as, for example, in the French system (*partie civile*).[13] While the victim may commence a private prosecution for the offence, the practical modalities limit the application of this possibility.[14]

3. Managers as Possible Perpetrators

As far as company managers are concerned, who falls within the definition of perpetrators varies as regards the hierarchy, and also over time. As regards the hierarchy, while all the analysed offences include the top management, they vary in criminalisation of acts committed by middle and low-level managers. The legislative technique used to describe the potential perpetrator is also relevant to this problem. The main question is why certain groups would be excluded from criminal liability or subjected to a less strict regime. The reason may be that certain groups of persons, in particular top management, may be considered primarily responsible for the well-being of the company and for the decisions they take. However, lower level managers may also have important influence on the company's actions and the possibility to take excessively risky decisions, which could result in highly detrimental consequences. Including all types of managers would seem to be a more just approach, which allows taking into account the level of guilt of the manager (linked also to his position within the hierarchy), reflected then in the level of concrete punishment.

[9] Kindhäuser, '§ 266 Untreue' (n 3) marginal no 129; Seier, 'Untreue' (n 3) marginal no 13.

[10] Alain Dekeuwer, 'Les intérêts protégées en cas d'abus de biens sociaux', 43 *La Semaine Juridique Entreprise et Affaires*, 26 October 1995), 500, para 15; Rebut, *Abus de biens sociaux* (n 7) para 257 et seq.

[11] Rebut, *Abus de biens sociaux* (n 7) paras 262–63; Cass crim, 13 December 2000, Bull crim, no 373, 1135.

[12] Rebut, *Abus de biens sociaux* (n 7) para 254 et seq.

[13] John Spencer, 'The Victim and the Prosecutor' in Anthony Bottoms and Julian V Roberts (eds), *Hearing the Victim: Adversarial Justice, Crime Victims and the State* (Cullompton: Willan Publishing, 2010) 143.

[14] For a thorough analysis of this right, see ibid 145 et seq.

Within the English system, the most relevant provision, section 4 of the Fraud Act 2006, includes not only persons who are given access to the principal's assets by virtue of a legal relationship, but also those persons whose access is granted by virtue of a legal basis which turned out to be invalid or is no longer valid, provided that it can be proved that they were expected to safeguard, or not to act against, the financial interests of another person.[15] All kind of managers can be included in the scope of this offence, including low-level ones. The other offences available in the English system do not limit the scope of potential perpetrator, with the exception of section 3 on fraud by failing to disclose information, where the duty to make such disclosures must be established. This results in a broadly designated circle of potential perpetrators, including not only all kinds of managers, but also other persons assisting them in these acts (either employees of the company or external to it, eg external advisors).

As far as the German offence of *Untreue* is concerned, it is applicable to persons who have the duty to safeguard the financial interests of another person. The duty is defined by three conjunctive requirements: the perpetrator must be acting, at least partially, in the interests of another person; safeguarding someone else's interests must be the core of his relation with the principal; and while acting, he should be granted some discretion. The duty should be embedded in at least one of the four enumerated sources: a statute, a commission of a public authority, a legal transition or a fiduciary relationship. This definition includes all categories of managers, namely top level management (*Geschäftsführer* in the GmbH and members of the *Vorstand* in the AG as well as their deputies); members of supervisory boards (*Aufsichtrat* in the AG); persons executing these functions de facto, as well as lower level managers, provided that in the act in question it was possible for them to exercise some discretion.[16] Persons who are not managers and do not otherwise have a duty towards the company may be held liable according to the rules on secondary participation, since the commission of these modalities does not require the perpetrator to have such a duty.[17]

Contrary to the English and German provisions, the French provision restricts the application of the offence of abuse of company assets to a limited circle of perpetrators. This limitation comes in two forms. First, the application of the offence is provided only for certain enumerated types of companies, mainly limited liability companies, in particular the limited liability company (*société à responsabilité limitée*, SARL) and the public limited company (*société anonyme*, SA). This limitation follows the logic that criminal liability of managers compensates for

[15] Clare Montgomery and David Ormerod (eds), *Montgomery and Ormerod on Fraud: Criminal Law and Procedure* (Oxford University Press, Release 9, December 2012) D-2108.

[16] BVerfG (23 June 2010) NJW 2010, 3209, para [108]; BGH (11 February 1982) NStZ 1982, 201; BGH (14 January 1986) StV 1986, 203.

[17] Seier, 'Untreue' (n 3) marginal no 62; Kindhäuser, '§ 266 Untreue' (n 3) marginal no 127; Perron, '§ 266 Untreue' (n 3) marginal no 52.

lack of full liability.[18] Secondly, liability is restricted to a circle of enumerated types of functions within the company. These functions can be grouped in two categories: leading company managers (eg *gérants* in the SARL, managing director or members of the executive board in the SA); and members of the supervisory bodies, if such a body has been established (*conseil de surveillance*). This circle is, however, extended by the rules providing that any person who exercises one of these functions de facto without being appointed is subject to the same criminal liability provisions.

Managers left out of the scope of the offence of abuse of company assets may nonetheless be subject to criminal liability for the offence of breach of trust or as accomplices.[19] As to the first possibility, it has limited applicability to cases of excessive risk-taking due to the requirement of misappropriation. The second one will necessarily be restricted by the requirements of criminal liability for complicity, in particular the commission of the offence by one of the top managers.

Another question as regards the scope of application of the offence concerns the temporal aspect of the circle of perpetrators. A manager might still be exercising his duties de facto, while no longer being formally appointed to this function or not having the duty described in the general definition. A similar question is whether a manager can be held liable if the basis of his relationship is formally invalid. Criminal liability in such situations is possible in all analysed systems, either in view of the breadth of the definition or, as for the French offence of abuse of company assets, by means of rules on de facto managers.

The final aspect which can be analysed as regards the scope of possible perpetrators concerns the question whether persons who are not managers could be liable for participating in excessively risky acts of management. All three systems offer the possibility to incur criminal liability by means of rules of complicity. Moreover, in the English and the French systems, these persons could fall within the scope of the offence through the rules on conspiracy or as perpetrators of the English common law offence of conspiracy to defraud. While all these possibilities require the involvement of more than one person, the English regulation extends criminal liability to certain inchoate acts, committed alone.

The three national models differ as regards the legislative technique used to delimit the circle of possible offenders. It is possible to use a general offence, which would in no way restrict its scope of application, therefore allowing all types of managers and persons cooperating with them to be possible perpetrators of the offence. The verification of whether these persons committed the offence would be entirely focused on the conduct (and result) element as well as on *mens rea*. The common law offence of conspiracy to defraud is an example of such an approach.

[18] Agathe Lepage, Patrick Maistre du Chambon and Renaud Salomon, *Droit pénal des affaires*, 2nd edn (Paris: LexiNexis Litec, 2010) 319.

[19] In one case, the court convicted for the breach of trust by excessive risk-taking. However, this case seems to be exceptional. See Cass crim, 3 July 1997, Bull crim no 265, 905.

In all three legal systems, however, it is more common that the offence particularly targets situations where the perpetrator is granted access to another's assets. There can be two principal methods of delimiting the circle of perpetrators: by enumerating concrete functions the perpetrator may be fulfilling (eg member of the board of director); or by an abstract definition.

The first method would have the benefit of providing more legal certainty as it would normally be immediately verifiable whether a particular person could be subject to criminal liability for the offence or not. However, it would bear the natural risk of the casuistic technique, ie of excluding persons potentially deserving to be included into the scope of criminal liability as much as those included. Moreover, persons foreseeing the risk of criminal liability may preclude criminal liability by avoiding the functions enumerated by the criminal provision. The latter problem could be remedied through rules extending the circle (eg the inclusion of those who execute the function de facto). This approach is used in the French offence of abuse of company assets.

The abstract definition method may focus on access to one's assets or on empowerment to make binding decisions (agreements) in another person's name, or on the duty to safeguard the interests of another or not to act against such interests. The definition may also combine all of these aspects. Such definition would normally include all managers (regardless of their level in the management). Most of the analysed offences use this method: the English fraud by abuse of position, the German *Untreue*, and also the French breach of trust.

The technique used is closely linked with the scope of possible perpetrators. While the enumeration of functions will necessarily define a more limited group of persons (otherwise it would become either extremely casuistic or effectively a general definition), the general definition will involve a rather larger circle of possible perpetrators. Hence, the choice of the legislative technique will follow the criminal policy decision on the personal scope of the offence.

The problem of the general definition is that it may become very broad and include types of relationships that may not necessarily deserve criminal law reaction. It will mainly depend on what criteria are chosen for the definition and what sources can be the background of the relationship between the perpetrator and the person whose assets are entrusted to him or whom he represents.

The English definition of the circle of perpetrators of the offence of fraud by abuse of position has been criticised for being too broad and encompassing trivial civil law disputes within the offence.[20] The German definition of *Untreue* is relatively complex, which is also linked to the debates around the relationship between the *Missbrauch* and the *Treubruch* modalities of the offence and the exact understanding of the duty to safeguard the financial interests of another, which the definition accommodates. Regardless of these shortcomings, there is no doubt that both modalities include all levels of managerial hierarchy in limited liability companies.

[20] Montgomery and Ormerod, *Montgomery and Ormerod on Fraud* (n 15) D-2106.

4. Exposing to Excessive Risk as Criminal Conduct

Each of the analysed criminal law systems provides for an offence which incriminates under various conditions excessive risk-taking. However, the English system offers a variety of other offences, which might also be of application to certain acts related to taking excessively risky decisions. The French law, which limits the scope of application of the offence of abuse of company assets, provides for the offence of breach of trust, which punishes acts of managerial misconduct, although according to the current state of the jurisprudence is not applicable to excessive risk-taking. The model of criminalisation offered by these two systems would be incomplete without taking into account these additional offences. However, analysing them together with the offence most adequately targeting excessively risky managerial decisions would blur the image of the system. Therefore, the analysis of the main available offence will be followed by the analysis of these additional offences in a separate section (4.2 Additional offences). In all three systems, persons who do not commit the offence but participate in the act consisting in taking excessively risky business decisions may also potentially be punished for their involvement in this act. The criminalisation of these acts within the three systems will be compared in a further section (4.3 Criminalisation of secondary participation).

4.1. Standard Offence

The English provision describes the conduct as abuse of position, which can be considered dishonest. Abuse is a very broad notion (it can also be committed by omission) and the legislator has not provided any definition of it.[21] The word 'to abuse' comprises also such use that exposes the entrusted assets to excessive risk. While this category would comprise a large variety of acts of mismanagement, the mere improper use of the assets is not enough in view of the second and crucial requirement: dishonesty. The problem of dishonesty, which is partly also an issue of *mens rea*, will also influence the way the conduct is understood and thus pertain also to the analysis of the *actus reus*. As to the latter aspect, the jury needs to consider whether the perpetrator's act was dishonest according to the ordinary standards of reasonable and honest people.[22] Whilst it can be considered that abuse of position may consist in exposing the company to excessive risk, the mere fact of knowingly acting in too risky a fashion will be insufficient for conviction for fraud by abuse of position, since additional elements will most probably be necessary to prove that the manager was dishonest (see below).

[21] Home Office, *Explanatory Notes Fraud Act 2006* (8 November 2006) Recital 21.
[22] *R v Ghosh* [1982] QB 1053.

The criminal conduct targeted by the French offence of abuse of company assets consists of using the company assets, credit or the manager's powers in a way which is contrary to the company's interests. While the delimitation between these three elements is not very strict, the French law does not require that only one, precise modality is chosen.[23] In result, the use of all these three elements allows including a broad scope of acts of use of different possibilities that the function of top managers grants to the potential perpetrator, including omissions (eg non-termination of a detrimental contract when possible). The use will become abuse if it can be proved that it was contrary to the interests of the company, which can be understood, inter alia, as exposing it to abnormal risk, or in other words, to a risk to which it should not be exposed.

The criminal conduct of the German offence of *Untreue* consists of breaching the duty to safeguard another person's financial interests, which results in damage or in a situation of concrete exposure to the risk of such damage (see below). The question of the scope of the duty and of its breach is evaluated according to the standards applicable to this duty, in particular those enshrined in company law.[24] Only those duties that concern the relationship between the manager and the entrusted assets, and the aim of which (at least indirectly[25]) is to protect the entrusted property, are considered.[26] The evaluation of these standards and whether the perpetrator fulfilled them or not should be made according to the interpretation provided within the doctrine and jurisprudence of these provisions. However, the assessment has to be done in an ample and comprehensive way, since a breach of only one concrete rule need not lead to liability for *Untreue*. Furthermore, the Federal Court of Justice (Bundesgerichtshof, BGH) considered in various cases that the breach of duty must be severe, which results in an asymmetrical relation between civil and company law versus criminal law. While this solution caused controversy in the German jurisprudence and doctrine, it was confirmed by the recent fundamental judgment of the Federal Constitutional Court.[27]

All three systems provide criminalisation for all possible types of managerial acts, whether these are binding legal acts or only physical use of the entrusted assets, including omissions. Various similarities and differences will be analysed

[23] Annie Médina, *Abus de biens sociaux. Prévention – Détection – Poursuite* (Paris: Dalloz, 2001) 52.

[24] An example of a concrete duty is the bank's obligation to gather client information for significant loans (Banking Act (Gesetz über das Kreditwesen, KWG), s 18). However, it may refer to more general duties, as the breach of duty may consist in not fulfilling a certain applicable standard of care. In particular, in the case of limited companies, it will be the standard of 'care of a prudent businessman' (*Sorgfalt eines ordentlichen Geschäftsmanns*, § 43 Abs 1 of the Limited Liability Companies Act (Gesetz betreffend die Gesellschaften mit beschränkter Haftung, GmbHG)) or of 'care of a prudent and conscientious manager' (*die Sorgfalt eines ordentlichen und gewissenhaften Geschäftsleiters*, § 93 Abs 1 of the Public Limited Companies Act (Aktiengesetz, AktG)).

[25] 'wenigstens auch, und sei es mittelbar': BGH (13 September 2010) NJW 2011, 88, 91. See also BVerfG (23 June 2010) NJW 2010, 3209, 3218 et seq.

[26] Dierlamm, '§ 266 Untreue' (n 3) marginal no 185; Kindhäuser, '§ 266 Untreue' (n 3) marginal no 63.

[27] BVerfG (23 June 2010) NJW 2010, 3209, 3215, para [112].

in detail in the sections below. The first major difference between the three legal systems consists in the way it is defined, which has important consequences for the scope of application of each of the offences. Two models for defining criminal conduct result from the analysis of the three legal systems. The first one represented by the German offence of *Untreue* criminalises breaches of duty by referring to other branches of law for description of such duties, as well as for criteria as to when the duty is effectively breached.[28] The second model represented by the English and the French offences provides for an autonomous understanding of when the act becomes criminal. Neither model is, however, absolute in its approach.

As to the second model, the French offence considers that it is contrary to the company's interest to expose it to a risk to which it should not be exposed. In order to establish whether the risk was one which the manager was not allowed to take, the judge must evaluate the scope of competencies of the manager and the particularities of the business pursued, possibly by calling on expert evidence. Although the judge will not have to point to a concrete rule, he will have to explain why he considers that the act in question was excessively risky. This will not be the case for the English system, where the jury deciding whether the manager dishonestly abused his position will not have to justify their verdict. However, the prosecution will have to convince the jury that the manager was indeed dishonest, which might be done by showing that he failed to respect some of his duties.[29] It is likely though that the prosecution will not engage in complicated elaborations of details of company law. On the other hand, the requirement to prove a severe breach of duty might grant more autonomy to the German criminal judge, who, having established that the duty was breached according to the non-criminal law standard, may still decide that the breach was not sufficient for the purposes of *Untreue*.

The first model may appear to guarantee more legal certainty than the second. However, the German system has been criticised for not being sufficiently clear as to which conditions establish the duty and which do not, with different approaches present in the doctrine and the jurisprudence. The English system relies on the decision of the jury on dishonesty, which necessarily cannot be considered certain. However, the wish to allow laymen to assess the manager's act according to the standards of normal (reasonable and honest) people, and not fellow managers, prevails in the English system. Among the three systems, the French approach appears to be the least problematic, entrusting the criminal judge with the task of assessing whether an act was contrary to the company's interests.

[28] See also Klaus Lüderssen, 'Primäre oder sekundäre Zuständigkeit des Strafrechts?' in *Menschengerechtes Strafrecht, Festschrift für Albin Eser* (Munich: C.H Beck, 2005) 163–80, at 177 et seq.

[29] Fraud is an offence which is 'triable either way', meaning that it can be tried either in a magistrates' court or in the Crown Court. However, the text will refer to the jury, as their involvement will be much more decisive for the interpretation of the offence (especially the requirement of dishonesty) and the more serious cases are tried in the Crown Court.

4.1.1. Criminalisation of Exposing to Risk Within the Definition of the Offence

None of the provisions focuses on risk in its definition. This is linked to the fact that these provisions aim at protecting the entrusted property against loss, so they tend to focus more on damage. However, all of them include exposing to excessive risk as a form of committing these offences, although they differ in the way this is done.

There are three ways of including exposing the company (or its assets) to excessive risk in the definition of the offence: within the definition of conduct; as a requirement of result; or within the *mens rea*. This section will analyse different modalities of how risk is included in the definitions of conduct of the main offences in the three systems. Only the German provision contains the requirement of result, which will be analysed in the following section. The English system also makes separate reference to exposing to risk as one of the modalities of special intention, which will be addressed in the relevant part of the analysis of *mens rea*.

The English offence of abuse of position may be committed by exposing the company to excessive risk (provided that it was dishonest). The examples of abuse given by the Crown Prosecution Service (CPS) do not concern excessive risk-taking.[30] The Home Office Explanatory Notes, however, provide an example of abuse which consists of investing entrusted money into highly risky business (although not in a corporate context, but when caring for elderly or disabled people and done for private purposes).[31] While a reading of the law and jurisprudence might suggest that in demonstrating that the manager acted too riskily, there should be no problem convincing the jury that he was dishonest,[32] it seems in practice that the jury might not find it sufficient. Dishonesty must be inferred from evidence, so there must be a way to convince the jury that the manager acted without integrity. This might be proved by demonstrating how the manager profited from the transaction. Dishonesty would more likely be established if it can be shown that the only purpose of the perpetrator was to increase his commission. Otherwise, it would also be more convincing if it can be demonstrated that the manager did something wrong in the process of taking the risky decision (eg shredding documents, concealing information). What would make dishonesty more obvious might be, for example, that acts of false accounting were also committed, but in such circumstances the prosecution might opt to use an applicable offence targeting this act rather than fraud (eg Theft Act 1968, section 17). Finally, a complex process of decision-taking may blur the image of who was responsible for what and therefore make it more complicated to convince the jury

[30] Crown Prosecution Service, *The Fraud Act 2006: Legal Guidance*, available at www.cps.gov.uk/legal/d_to_g/fraud_act/.

[31] Home Office, *Explanatory Notes Fraud Act 2006* (8 November 2006) Recital 23.

[32] '[I]t is fraudulent to take a risk to the prejudice of another's rights, which risk is known to be one which there is no right to take': *Sinclair* [1968] 1 WLR 1246, at 1251.

that what the perpetrator did was dishonest. For all the above reasons, the prosecution may abstain from proceeding with a case where certain elements allowing the building of a strong argument for dishonesty are lacking.

The French offence does not mention the problem of risk, but the doctrine understood the formulation 'contrary to the company's interest' as either absence of adequate compensation or exposure to an abnormal risk, or a risk to which it should not be exposed.[33] While this should in theory address excessive risk-taking relatively straight-forwardly without problems, the judges tend to be stricter (and require actual loss) depending on the fulfilment of the *mens rea* requirement of acting for personal interest.

The German jurisprudence and doctrine regarding the offence of *Untreue* specifically addresses the question of criminalisation of excessively risky decisions through the offence of *Untreue* under the topic of so-called *Risikogeschäfte* (risky or speculative transactions). The question of the breach of duty is interlinked with the question of how much risk the person is allowed to take. It will depend in the first place on the instructions given by the shareholders, limited by the rules on consent (ie especially not putting the life of the company in danger). If such instructions have not been given, the level of risk should be established according to the purpose of the business and standards of care typical for this type of business activities.[34] These standards are therefore different, for example, as regards institutions (whether it is a savings bank or an aggressive investment fund) and as to the concrete transactions (eg credit for a well-functioning company or a loan granted in order to help an enterprise in difficulty to recover, which might allow the bank to recover previous credits).

4.1.2. Requirement of Result

There is substantial difference between offences that require proof of result and those which describe the wrongdoing only in the definition of the conduct. The result in question may be a loss, but also, more interestingly, a situation of concrete endangerment to the company assets. By requiring a proof of result, the offence makes it necessary that the prosecution prove that a situation occurred in which the company assets were endangered, as well as connect this situation with the conduct of the perpetrator by means of applicable rules of causality. Since risk is

[33] Cass crim, 16 January 1964, Bull crim 1964 no 16, 27 (abuse of company assets); Cass crim, 10 November 1964, Bull crim no 291 (abuse of credit); Cass crim, 3 May 1967, Bull crim no 148, 350 (abuse of assets, credit and powers); Cass crim, 7 March 1968, Bull crim no 80, 189 (abuse of powers and abuse of assets in case of a cooperative); Cass crim, 24 March 1969, Bull crim no 130, 319 (abuse of assets); Cass crim, 16 March 1970, Bull crim no 107, 245 (abuse of credit); Cass crim, 16 December 1975, Bull crim no 279, 735 (abuse of company assets); Cass crim, 19 November 1979, Bull crim no 325, 887 (abuse of powers); Cass crim, 16 January 1989, Bull crim no 17, 45 (abuse of powers); Joly and Joly-Baumgartner, *L'abus de biens sociaux* (n 8) 98.

[34] Perron, '§ 266 Untreue' (n 3) marginal no 20.

an inherent element of business, such endangerment must necessarily be defined in a way which limits it to situations where the risk is abnormal. This requirement places the focus not only on how the perpetrator acted (addressed by the description of conduct), but also what was the eventual result of this conduct. Therefore, the objective reality created by the perpetrator becomes part of the assessment of his guilt.

The situation is different if the offence does not contain the requirement of result and only concentrates on the conduct. It is focused on the moment the manager took the excessively risky decision, and requires a verification whether in that moment the decision was of such a nature that it exposed the company to abnormal risk, regardless of whether that was really the case (or was avoided due to fortunate events). This is the approach represented by the French system. While the latter does not require proof of any result (not even concrete endangerment of the company), it might be used in order to prove that the use was contrary to the company's interests. However, this aspect of the use must be determined from the point of view of the moment of the perpetrator's act,[35] which demonstrates clearly that the offence aims at punishing managers who (knowingly) take decisions against the company's interests.[36] If a decision which could be considered contrary to the company's interests by chance brings positive results, it can still be charged as an offence,[37] while disastrous results arising from a decision which involved only normal risk would not make it a crime.[38]

The lack of requirement of result may also allow a more flexible approach, as in the English system, where the prosecution can focus on the detrimental results of the manager's act, but also on the fact that his conduct exposed the company to excessive risk, depending on which argument can best be used to convince the jury of the dishonesty of the manager.

The necessity to prove these elements, risk-damage and causality, in particular according to the new approach to risk-damage, results in a major difference in the German offence compared to the English and the French ones, as the former is the only legal system, out of the three analysed, which contains the requirement of result as a separate element of the *actus reus*. The offence of *Untreue* requires proof of result, which may be a loss, but more importantly here, also so-called risk-damage.[39] The latter notion extends the understanding of damage to situations where actual loss has not yet materialised. At first used more broadly, the importance of this notion appears to have shrunk to a certain extent in view of the newest jurisprudential interpretation. According to the latter, the effect of risk

[35] Cass crim, 2 December 1991, No de pourvoi: 90-87563.

[36] Jacques-Henri Robert and Haritini Matsopoulou, *Traité de droit pénal des affaires* (Presses Universitaires de France, 2004) 477; Frédéric Stasiak, *Droit pénal des affaires*, 2nd edn (Paris: LGDJ, 2009) 242; Cass crim, 27 October 1997, Bull crim, no 352, 1169 (so-called Carignon affaire).

[37] Rebut, *Abus de biens sociaux* (n 7) para 64; Cass crim,16 January 1989, Bull crim, no 17, 45.

[38] Joly and Joly-Baumgartner, *L'abus de biens sociaux* (n 8) 101.

[39] For more details on this notion see Chapter 4, 3.5.2; Schramm, 'Untreue, § 266 StGB' (n 3) marginal no 136.

must be quantifiable according to recognised methods, and if necessary by an expert witness. The value of the loss which the company would suffer if the risk materialises does not represent the value of the risk-damage, but it is rather the impact of the risk that must be calculated.

4.1.3. Consent and the Approach to the Company

The approach of the three legal systems to the consent of the shareholders reveals the general understanding of the legislator (at least in the context of the analysed offences) as to whether the company is to be understood as a separate entity with its own interests or only a function of the interests of its economic owners, ie the shareholders. The question here is whether consent granted by the shareholders to a decision of the manager, which in normal circumstances should be considered excessively risky, excludes criminal liability for the offence. If the company is to be understood as a separate entity with its own interests, independent from those of the shareholders, consent to such acts should not have exculpatory effect. This is the case in the French offence of abuse of company assets.[40]

By contrast, in the German system, the scope of duty, in particular the level of risk that may be taken by the manager, may be influenced by the valid consent of the shareholders. For its validity, it is necessary that it is granted before the act and that the shareholders had enough understanding of the situation.[41] Moreover, according to some authors consent is invalid if it authorises the performance of an illegal act (eg corruption).[42] The shareholders must also be entitled to decide upon the matter in question (the matter has not been reserved for another body). According to the dominant view, consent is also invalid if it concerns an act that would put the existence of the company in danger. The approach is similar in the English system, although there is no jurisprudence to corroborate this statement. One can assume, however, that it would be difficult to claim that the manager acted dishonestly or abused his position if he acted with the consent of the shareholders, provided that they had sufficient information to assess the context and the content of their decision.

The question of the validity of consent is also linked to the problem of whose interests are protected by the offence. The exculpatory effect of consent highlights the prevalence of the interests of the shareholders. On the other hand, limits to its validity grant more protection to the stakeholders, who have interests in the correct functioning of the company, and which should be ensured by the managers in spite

[40] Cass crim, 8 March 1967, Bull crim no 94; Rebut, *Abus de biens sociaux* (n 7) para 35 et seq; Wilfrid Jeandidier, *Abus des biens, du crédit, des pouvoirs ou des voix* (JurisClasseur Sociétés Traité, date du fascicule 7 February 2017, date de la dernière mise à jour 7 February 2017) para 37; Jean Larguier and Philippe Conte, *Droit pénal des affaires*, 11th edn (Armand Colin, 2004) 342 et seq.

[41] Presumed consent might also be applicable in certain circumstances, which has a different set of conditions for its exculpatory effect.

[42] Schramm, 'Untreue, § 266 StGB' (n 3) marginal no 80.

of the decisions of the shareholders. In conclusion, the French offence takes into account the interests of the stakeholders, contrary to the English offence of fraud. As to the German offence of *Untreue*, the approach described above favours the shareholders vis-à-vis the stakeholders, although their interests are protected to a certain extent by limiting the validity of consent, in particular as regards any acts which might cause danger to the company's existence or affect its nominal capital.

4.1.4. Superior Orders and Expert Opinions

The analysis of the national chapters also discussed the possibility to acquit managers who took excessive risk in cases where they acted upon the orders of their superiors or were informed by expert opinion. There may be various possibilities as to what would be the place of such a factor within the structure of the offence, if admitted. While the orders of superiors will have only limited influence on the assessment of criminal liability (potentially with the exception of England), the fact that an expert opinion shaped the decision of the manager may be crucial for his innocence.

The possibility that a situation arises where the perpetrator of the French offence of abuse of company assets acted upon superior orders is rather unlikely, as the managers who may be subject to criminal liability for this offence are already at the top of the managerial hierarchy. Such orders will have little influence on the liability of a manager in the German legal system, if he breached his duty and fulfilled the *mens rea* requirement. Its impact would be practically limited only to situation where such an order convinced the lower level manager about the correctness of the decision or about the impossibility of detrimental consequences for the company, thus excluding the *mens rea*. As to England, the question will be part of the assessment of dishonesty, so it will be necessary to evaluate in concrete cases whether the fact that the manager was instructed by the superior may exculpate his act.

Expert opinion may play a role as regards criminal liability in all three countries. In the German legal system, whilst members of the decision-taking bodies must perform their duties according to applicable standards, they may rely on an expert opinion unless there are reasons to doubt such opinion (diversity of views between experts or the decision is particularly high risk). Similarly in England, a manager would arguably not be dishonest if he based his decision on an expert opinion, unless he had strong reasons to doubt the correctness of the advice (a similar remark can be made as regards the orders of superiors). As to France, an expert opinion might exclude the *mens rea* requirement of knowing that the act is contrary to the company's interests, if there were no reasons to doubt that the opinion was accurate. There is, however, no certainty that the court would follow this line of reasoning.[43]

[43] See also Joly and Joly-Baumgartner, *L'abus de biens sociaux* (n 8) 152.

4.1.5. Criminalisation of Attempt

The problem of criminalising attempts to commit offences of excessive risk-taking is strongly linked to the general approach towards attempts in the analysed legal systems. At the same time, the solution may potentially have an important influence on the scope of the offence. The approach chosen by the legislator reflects the choice as to how far protection of property against exposure to risk should be stretched. If the offence focuses only on losses, making attempts to commit it punishable adds criminalisation of excessive risk. If risk is already included in the offence, adding criminalisation of attempts stretches the protection of property truly wide.

In all three systems, excessive risk is already included in the definitions of the analysed offences, but the approach to attempt differs. Neither the French nor the German system provide for criminalisation of attempting to commit the relevant offences. Hence, it is required that the manager effectively perform an act contrary to the company's interests (France) or create a situation of risk-damage (Germany).

By contrast, attempts to commit the offences provided by the English system, in particular fraud by abuse of position, are also criminalised.[44] In view of the generally broad design of these offence, especially the lack of the requirement of result, the role of criminalisation of attempt is limited, as many courses of conduct would already constitute an accomplished offence. It may, however, be applicable, for instance, if the manager prepared a contract which would result in exposing the company to excessive risk, and was about to sign it.

4.2. Additional Offences

The purpose of this section is to analyse the offences that may punish managerial mismanagement, including potentially excessive risk-taking, although their application to cases of excessive risk-taking might not be the first choice of the prosecution. As will be seen below, there is great disparity between the English and the two other legal systems, since most of these additional offences are offered only in the former legal system. Therefore, a symmetrical comparison is impossible.

While Germany offers only one offence, which tackles mismanagement committed by any possible manager, the French legal system allows for punishing all those managers to whom the offence of abuse of company assets is not applicable by using the offence of breach of trust. It has, however, very limited application to cases of excessive risk-taking, as it requires that the perpetrators misappropriated the funds. Only an extensive understanding of misappropriation (which is considered in the French jurisprudence to be equal to behaving, at least

[44] Except for case of omission, see AP Simester, JR Spencer, GR Sullivan and GJ Virgo, *Simester and Sullivan's Criminal Law: Theory and Doctrine*, 5th edn (Oxford/Portland, OR: Hart Publishing, 2013) 344.

momentarily, as the rightful owner of the assets[45]) would include excessive risk-taking within its scope. So far, the jurisprudence does not tend in this direction, with one notable exception.[46] Limited possibilities of using this offence would exist, if it can be proved that the perpetrator intentionally behaves as an owner of the asset.[47] This might be the case if he invests the assets, not in accordance with the company policy, but for a personal endeavour. This offence requires proof of result, but its extensive interpretation includes potential result (ie risk of loss)[48] and also moral prejudice. Hence, if the criteria of misappropriation can be met, this requirement will not limit the application of the offence.

The English system offers an abundance of other offences, which might potentially be applicable to punish managers exposing their company to excessive risk. A manager who asked for approval of his decision by the shareholder and furnished them with inaccurate information might be liable for fraud by false representation (Fraud Act 2006, section 2). If the manager has the duty to disclose information and he fails to do so, he may be liable for fraud by failing to disclose information (Fraud Act 2006, section 3). To this list one can add also the offence of theft (Theft Act 1968, section 1), which provides an additional ground for punishing too risky management of company assets due to its extensive definition. For all of these offences, dishonesty must be proved. It is understood in the same way as for the main offence of fraud by abuse of position as explained above, hence also the same limitation on the use of these offences to cases of excessive risk-taking.

The English Fraud Act 2006 extends criminalisation much further by providing for two inchoate offences criminalising possession of articles for use in frauds[49] and making, adopting, supplying or offering any article.[50] It does not seem that while designing these offences, the legislator wanted to specifically target excessively risky transactions. It is more likely that these offences are supposed to be primarily used to penalise persons preparing or helping in committing the classical fraud by false representation. However, the law might, at least theoretically, be used for punishing managers who were caught in the moment of preparing the excessively risky decision or preparing documents meant to hide shortcomings in the process of preparing such decisions, as well as their helping staff. The relevance of these offences might be enhanced by lack of requirement of dishonesty.

Another extension of the scope of criminalisation comes from two types of conspiracy provided by English law, namely the general statutory conspiracy[51] and the common law offence of conspiracy to defraud.[52] Neither requires that the

[45] Cass crim, 13 February 1984, Bull crim no 49.

[46] Cass crim, 3 July 1997, Bull crim no 265, 905.

[47] Wilfrid Jeandidier, *Abus de confiance* (JurisClasseur Pénal, date du fascicule 1 February 2015, date de la dernière mise à jour 1 September 2017) para 52; Cass crim, 13 February 1984, Bull crim no 49, Cass crim, 16 June 2011, No de pourvoi: 10-83.758.

[48] Cass crim, 3 December 2003, Bull crim no 232, 935.

[49] Fraud Act 2006, s 6.

[50] Ibid s 7.

[51] Criminal Law Act 1977, s 1.

[52] *Scott v Metropolitan Police Commissioner* [1975] AC 819.

effective fraud occurred, although it is necessary that more than one person be involved. The broadening effect comes not only from the fact that it extends criminal liability to those who do not have the required position, but also because they enable punishment for mere agreement to commit fraud, without requiring that the offence be attempted or any preparatory acts committed. The common law conspiracy has a very broad *actus reus* consisting of an agreement to prejudice another person's economic interests, including by exposing them to risk. Its use is limited, however, by the requirement of dishonesty as well as by the need to demonstrate good reasons for not using the statutory version instead.

4.3. Criminalisation of Secondary Participation

Finally, in all three legal systems, persons who did not take the excessively risky decision, but were somehow involved in it, may also be punished. This type of liability may be relevant for all the categories of persons who take part in taking excessively risky decisions, but do not fall into the scope of the offences analysed above. These can be junior managers (where liability is limited to the senior ones) or other persons: assistants, employees or external advisors.[53]

In all three systems, assisting and inciting to commit the offence may lead to criminal liability, however the conditions and the scope of liability differs significantly between the English system and the French and the German ones. The first essential difference between the systems concerns the relationship between the act of assisting or inciting the commission of the main offence and the latter. Whereas in the French and the German systems, the punishment of secondary participants requires that the main perpetrator effectively committed the offence (although he need not be convicted of it), the English law opens up much larger possibilities of criminal liability. Not only does it punish certain preparatory acts (upon similar conditions as in France or Germany), but also assisting and encouraging, without requiring any effect on the main perpetrator or the effective commission of the offence by the latter.[54]

To the contrary, in the French and in the German system, help must be effectively provided (and must also assist in practice in the latter system), although it does not have to be the only factor in the commission of the main offence. It must be delivered before or during its commission. In both systems, the aider might also be held liable for assistance provided after the commission of the offence on the

[53] This section focuses only on the aspects relevant for criminalisation of excessive risk-taking. For comparison of different regimes of complicity in general, see in particular Johannes Keiler, *Actus Reus and Participation in European Criminal Law* (Intersentia, 2013) 153 et seq.

[54] Although it is a *mens rea* issue, it is important to signal here already that criminal liability for encouraging or assisting in the commission of an abuse of position is possible even without requiring that the person who would effectively perform this act would do so dishonestly or with the necessary intention, if these *mens rea* elements can be proved in the person assisting or encouraging.

condition of having promised it before the offence occurred (in Germany, it must be possible to qualify it as psychological aid).[55]

The scope of criminalisation of incitement is similar in the French and the German system. As to the former, the act of incitement must be effectively executed, and in the German system, it must also have at least some influence on the decision of the principal. If the latter had already decided to commit the offence, criminal liability is excluded.[56] In both systems, instigation can be committed only by means of gift, promises, threats, abuse of authority, or also, in the French system, giving instructions. In this sense, the English system is yet again much broader, by extending the scope of punishment also to simple encouragement, and even if it never reached the addressee. The act need only be capable of encouraging.

In addition to the rules pointed out above, the English system offers further possibilities to punish persons collaborating with a (potential) perpetrator of fraud. The two inchoate offences provided by the Fraud Act 2006 criminalising possession of articles for use in frauds and making, adopting, supplying or offering any article would also allow for punishment, without having recourse to the regulation on complicity, for those who help in the process of preparing such a decision, if it takes the form of acts described in the definition of these two offences. In addition, persons who collaborated with the manager in view of an agreement made between them beforehand could potentially be held liable for conspiracy to defraud as well as the statutory conspiracy.

The English and the French systems provide for modalities sanctioning managers who did not take the excessively risky decision themselves, but did not prevent another manager from taking it. The English system requires that such a manager have the duty to prevent such a decision being taken, or by his inaction encourage the perpetrator.[57] The French system also formulates two alternative requirements: preventing the abuse has to be within a manager's competences or be his duty (while being aware of the abuse).[58] Furthermore, the offence of encouraging and assisting crime does not seem to preclude its commission by an omission, for instance, by lack of proper control or help by an expert from outside the company who (knowingly) gives an incorrect assessment of the risk associated with a given transaction. It could also be applied to senior managers whose silence as regards the manager's deeds could be clearly interpreted as encouragement.

[55] The latter can be understood as reinforcing the perpetrator's decision to act, including by promising help; this promise need not materialise eventually; Hans-Heinrich Jescheck and Thomas Weigend, *Lehrbuch des Strafrechts* (Berlin: Duncker & Humblot, 1996) 692.

[56] Michael Bohlander, *Principles of German Criminal Law* (Oxford/Portland, OR: Hart Publishing, 2009) 168.

[57] Simester et al, *Simester and Sullivan's Criminal Law* (n 44) 217. The mere non-prevention of the commission of an offence without encouraging its commission does not constitute secondary participation, as was decided in *R v Clarkson* (1971) 55 Cr App R 445.

[58] Joly and Joly-Baumgartner, *L'abus de biens sociaux* (n 8) 60, 242–43; Jeandidier, *Abus des biens* (n 40) para 25. See also Cass crim, 20 March 1997, No de pourvoi: 96-81361; Cass crim, 7 September 2005, No de pourvoi: 05-80163.

The person who aids a manager to commit *Untreue* by omission is also liable under the condition that it is his duty to prevent the abuse. However, such a person would be considered a main perpetrator in view of the *Einheitstäterbegriff* (lack of distinction between principals and participants). In view of this approach, if an aider or an instigator is subject to a duty to safeguard the company's financial interests, which the main perpetrator breached, he will be liable as principal and not as secondary participant, which has consequences as to the scope of applicable punishment.

5. *Mens Rea*

All the offences described in the previous section require that the conduct was committed intentionally and the scope of protection granted by them depends to a large extent on the details of the *mens rea* requirements. It is composed of cognitive and volitional aspects, as well as of the presence or lack of the requirement of special interest. The requirements of *mens rea* are also shaped by general rules in each of the analysed systems.[59] However, the decisive feature comes from the particular requirements of each offence, such as dishonesty or acting in personal interest. Therefore, the same act could fulfil the *actus reus* of offences provided for in various legal systems, but might not be punishable in one of them in view of the different formulation of the *mens rea*.

5.1. Standard Offence

The offence of fraud by abuse of position, as well as the two other modalities of fraud (fraud by false representation and by failing to disclose information) contains two *mens rea* requirements: knowledge about the abuse and special intention. The *means rea* of the French offence of abuse of company assets (including all its modalities) is composed of two elements. First, the perpetrator, at the moment of the commission of the act, must know and be willing to act against his company's interests (*dol général*). Secondly, he must do so because of personal interest broadly construed, which is understood as personal interest (material or moral), or as interest of a company or undertaking in which he is directly or indirectly involved (*dol spécial*).[60] The German offence of *Untreue* contains a classic requirement of intention composed of the cognitive and volitional aspect and includes the possibility to be committed with *dolus eventualis*.[61]

[59] For comparative analysis of *mens rea* requirements in general, see in particular Jeroen Blomsma, *Mens Rea and Defences in European Criminal Law* (Intersentia, 2012) 39 et seq.

[60] Mirelle Delmas-Marty and Geneviève Giudicelli-Delage (eds), *Droit pénal des affaires*, 4th edn (Paris: Pr Univ de France, 2000) 352.

[61] This terminology according to Blomsma, *Mens Rea and Defences* (n 59) 60.

5.1.1. *Cognitive Aspect*

All three offences require that while committing the act, the perpetrator is aware of certain aspects of what he is doing. These cognitive requirements correspond generally with the requirements of criminal conduct. While in all three systems the manager must be aware that his particular position entails a duty to safeguard the interests of the company, it is the German system that makes this request more specific, although the degree of knowledge required is subject to debate. Similarly, the three systems require that the perpetrator be aware of the negative aspect of his act. However, they differ fundamentally as to the criteria for assessment of this negative feature and its standards.

Until recently, the manager exposing the company to excessive risk in the English legal system had to be aware of the fact that what he was doing could be regarded as dishonest by the standards of reasonable and honest people.[62] However, this requirement has been abolished by the recent judgment in *Ivey*.[63] This limits significantly the requirements of *mens rea*. The English law of fraud is very laconic as regards other elements of the cognitive aspect of intention. However, it seems that it might be presumed that the manager needs to be at least aware that he is abusing his position.[64] While it is unclear whether special proof of that would be required, it can be assumed that the lack thereof would make it difficult to prove that he was dishonest and aware of it.

The French system formulates the requirement much more precisely in the text of the offence: the perpetrator must be aware that what he does is against the company's interests, ie that it exposes the company to an abnormal risk of loss.[65] The lack of knowledge of the manager as to the excessively risky character of the act will not exclude his liability, if it is due to faults for which he is responsible.[66] It has been pointed out in the French doctrine that courts are not always scrupulous in proving all the elements of the *mens rea*, but imply the existence of *dol général* from other elements of the offence. The Court of Cassation confirmed in one judgment that some elements of the offence might be indicated implicitly.[67] Intention could then be deduced from material elements of the offence, in particular, from the lack of transparency in the manager's acts[68] or because of the application of some accountancy tricks.[69] The courts have also sometimes the tendency to infer it from the presence of the requirement of special intention, ie the personal

[62] *R v Ghosh* [1982] QB 1053, at 1064.

[63] *Ivey v Genting Casinos (UK) Ltd t/a Crockfords* [2017] UKSC 67, para [74].

[64] *B v DPP* [2000] 2 AC 428; *R v K (Crown Prosecution Service v K)* [2002] 1 AC 462.

[65] Médina, *Abus de biens sociaux* (n 23) 208.

[66] Cour d'Appel Angers, 22 January 2008, JurisData no 2008-362347, cited by Jeandidier, *Abus des biens* (n 40) para 70.

[67] Rebut, *Abus de biens sociaux* (n 7) para 139; Cass crim, 16 March 1970, Bull crim no 107, 245.

[68] Joly and Joly-Baumgartner, *L'abus de biens sociaux* (n 8) 154.

[69] Stasiak, *Droit pénal des affaires* (n 36) 246. For other examples, see Médina, *Abus de biens sociaux* (n 23) 211.

interest.[70] There is, however, a limit to the use of this technique, as judgments where the reasoning was limited to a presentation of fact did not pass the scrutiny of the Court of Cassation.[71]

The most rigid approach to the cognitive requirements concerns the offence of *Untreue*: the perpetrator needs to be aware of the fact that he has the duty to safeguard the company's financial interests as well as that what he is doing breaches this duty.[72] There is no agreement within the German jurisprudence and doctrine as to the consequences of lack of awareness of the duty. The problem of awareness as regards the duty is composed of two aspects: the factual background of the duty and its legal interpretation. While mistakes as to all these aspects might be considered mistakes on the facts and exclude intention and therefore criminal liability,[73] an adverse theory considers only mistakes as to the factual background to have this consequence and associates legal misinterpretation with mistake of law (excluding criminal liability only if it was unavoidable).[74] A compromise theory proposes that for acting intentionally, the perpetrator should have at least some understanding of the normative consequences of the underlying facts.[75]

The level of perception by the manager of the act's disadvantageousness for the company also varies among the three systems. The French system is the least strict and accepts implying knowledge from other aspects of the offence. Even clear lack of such knowledge cannot excuse the manager, if he was responsible for mistakes that led to his unawareness. The German system, on the contrary, requires proof of the manager's knowledge, although liability for *Untreue* cannot be excluded if the perpetrator was not fully aware of the legal consequences of the duty according to the strictest of competing theories in the German doctrine. While the English approach was the strictest out of the three under the rule in *Ghosh*, which held that the jurors had to be convinced that the manager knew that his act was dishonest, this requirement no longer exists.

Different types of insight in order to assess the said disadvantageousness are also necessary depending on the national system. The French offence of abuse of company assets limits the requirement to the manager's knowledge that the risk he is undertaking is abnormal in the given circumstances. To the contrary, in the German system, the manager must also understand that by taking excessive risk he is breaching a concrete duty. While these two approaches appear different, with

[70] Rebut, *Abus de biens sociaux* (n 7) para 142; Cass crim, 5 November 1976, Bull crim no 315, 803; Cass crim, 19 June 1978, Bull crim no 202, 525.

[71] Rebut, *Abus de biens sociaux* (n 7) para 143; Cass crim, 16 February 1987, Bull crim no 72, 194.

[72] In particular, he will not be liable if he considered (mistakenly) that the shareholders consented to the act. Schramm, 'Untreue, § 266 StGB' (n 3) marginal no 153; Kindhäuser, '§ 266 Untreue' (n 3) marginal no 122; Dierlamm, '§ 266 Untreue' (n 3) marginal no 282.

[73] Dierlamm, '§ 266 Untreue' (n 3) marginal no 282.

[74] Kindhäuser, '§ 266 Untreue' (n 3) marginal no 122. See also Bernd Schünemann, '§ 266 Untreue' in Heinrich Wilhelm Laufhütte, Ruth Rissing-van Saan and Klaus Tiedemann (eds), *Strafgesetzbuch. Leipziger Kommentar*, vol 9/1, §§ 263–266b, 12th edn (Berlin: de Gruyter, 2012) marginal nos 192–97.

[75] Perron, '§ 266 Untreue' (n 3) marginal no 49.

one requiring factual insights and the other more legal ones, the difference between them is not in fact so great. In order to assess that the risk taken is abnormal, the manager in the French system needs to understand not only the economic aspects of his decision, but also the scope of discretion in which he is allowed to exercise his powers. In the German system, whereas one theory requires the acquittal of a manager who did not understand the legal aspects of his duty, the other theory is satisfied to convict where the manager has some understanding of it, as long as he has insight into the factual aspect, which would lead to the breach of duty.

5.1.2. Volitional Aspect

All three legal systems agree that the manager's hope or intention that despite being exposed to excessive risk, the company will eventually profit from his act, are without relevance for criminal liability.[76] Otherwise, the solutions vary to an important extent as regards the volitional requirements of the offence. The English offence of fraud does not formulate it at all and *mens rea* is satisfied with the proof of knowledge and special intention. The French offence of abuse of company assets contains a requirement that the manager act intentionally, while knowing that the act is contrary to the company's interests (ie exposes the company to abnormal risk of loss). This system does not attach great importance to the proof of this requirement. It is implied from the fact that the perpetrator knew that the risk was excessive and he acted anyway. This requirement may also be inferred from the other aspects of the offence, in particular from the special intention.

This volitional aspect is of the greatest importance to the offence of *Untreue*, which contains the requirement of result, hence the perpetrator must have intention to cause this result, in principle at least in the form of *dolus eventualis*. As regards risk-damage, it is, however, unclear whether the latter form suffices or whether the perpetrator needs to at least consider possible and accept the actual loss occuring (although without intending to create it).[77] The latter solution, proposed in some judgments in order to curb over-extensive interpretation of the offence, can lead to paradoxical results and was strongly criticised. So far there is no certainty as to the direction in which further jurisprudence will go, although the recent judgments seem not to follow this line.[78] In any case, while the prosecution in England and France may neglect the volitional aspect of the case, as regards *Untreue*, it must be established that the perpetrator intended to breach his duty and cause the result.

[76] England: Anthony Arlidge et al, *Arlidge and Parry on Fraud*, 3rd edn (London: Sweet & Maxwell, 2007) 13/2-024; France: Stasiak, *Droit pénal des affaires* (n 36) 246; Germany: BGH (6 May 1986) NStZ 1986, 455; Perron, '§ 266 Untreue' (n 3) marginal no 49.

[77] BGH (6 April 2000) NJW 2000, 2364, 2366; BGH (15 November 2001) NJW 2002, 1211, 1216.

[78] Eg the Federal Constitutional Court of Germany accepted the possibility to commit *Untreue* with *dolus eventualis* and did not repeat the requirement of accepting the actual loss, BVerfG (23 June 2010) NJW 2010, 3209, 3214, para [105].

5.1.3. *Special Intention*

The requirement of special intention is the element of the *mens rea* which, contrary to the 'normal' intention, goes beyond willing to perform what is described by the *actus reus*. It may be included in the definition of the offence for reasons of legislative technique, while in reality not adding a requirement which would drastically change the scope of the offence (eg fraud). However, it may also add an element which significantly limits the scope of application of the offence, and possibly also changes the image of the wrongdoing addressed by the offence. This will mainly be the case of the French offence of abuse of company assets, where the requirement of personal interest will be a decisive factor for criminal liability, but also in England, where it will potentially play a crucial role in proving dishonesty.

The requirement of special intention significantly differentiates the three systems. On one side of the spectrum is the German system, which does not contain such a requirement at all. It is without relevance for *Untreue* whether the perpetrator performs his act in view of his personal benefit, a benefit of another person or without any such motivation.[79]

The definition of fraud in the English system contains three possible purposes as to why the perpetrator would dishonestly abuse his position (or commit other modalities of fraud): intention to make a gain for himself or another; or to cause loss to another; or to expose another to a risk of loss. In view of how broadly this requirement is formulated, it will have very little influence on the scope of the offence. On the other hand, proof of personal interest, without formally being part of the definition of the offence, may in practice influence the assessment of the perpetrator's dishonesty. Therefore, it can be considered part of the design of the offence as one of the alternative ways supporting the proof of dishonesty.

At the other end of the spectrum is the French system, where the requirement of broadly-designed personal interest will be crucial to determining the perpetrator's criminal liability. It will eliminate from the scope of the offence all of those situations where the perpetrator exposed the company to excessive risk, but did not seek any personal gain or was not acting in the interest of another person or an undertaking in which he has an interest. In particular, this requirement will eliminate situations where the risk deliberately taken was excessive, but the manager acted solely for the benefit of the company. The interpretation of this requirement given by the French courts extended the definition of this requirement to almost any human motivation, such as seeking renown or advancement of career,[80] or recognition from other persons, as well as honing personal business relationships,[81] or caring for family reputation.[82] Such a reading would render the

[79] Schünemann, '§ 266 Untreue' (n 74) marginal no; 189; Perron, '§ 266 Untreue' (n 3) marginal no 49.

[80] Cass crim, 20 March 1997, No de pourvoi 96-81.361.

[81] Cass crim, 9 May 1973, Bull crim no 216, 511; Cass crim, 19 June 1978, Bull crim no 202, 525; Cass crim, 15 September 1999, No de pourvoi 98-83.237.

[82] Cass crim, 3 May 1967, Bull crim no 148.

difference between the French and the German or English systems almost non-existent, as one can assume that perpetrators in these systems would present similar types of motivations.

However, the 'diluted' personal interest, such as seeking prestige, career advancement or strengthening of position within the company, is rarely sufficient in cases where the aspect of being contrary to the company's interests results from the fact that it exposes the company to excessive risk. Out of the two crucial elements of the offence (acting contrary to the company's interests or personal interests), at least one must be strongly convincing.[83] Therefore, in order to punish the taking of excessive risk, it is necessary that the manager was acting for personal interests amounting to more than merely his own ambition or willingness to please other (more important) persons.[84] It would be necessary to prove that, for example, he intended to directly profit from the act, or provide benefits for his relatives or undertakings. Although it cannot be excluded that the courts would accept the 'diluted' personal interest in cases of mere excessive risk-taking, so far it should be considered that in practice it has not been criminalised.[85]

5.2. Additional Offences

Contrary to the offence of abuse of company assets, the French offence of breach of trust contains no requirement of special intention, but only classic requirements of intention. It is therefore necessary to know that the assets were entrusted conditionally (which is normally the case for managers) and that the perpetrator had the intention of misappropriating them. If the understanding of the *actus reus* requirement of misappropriation is extended to excessive risk-taking, which so far is not the case (with the exception of very limited jurisprudence), the *mens rea* will not add significant limitation to the scope of the offence.

As to the additional offences available in the English legal system, they are all intentional, although they vary as to the details of the *mens rea* requirements. Most of these offences contain also the requirement of dishonesty, including its *mens rea* aspect. This requirement has much less impact on the application of the offence to excessive risk-taking as regards the two alternative modalities of fraud and the

[83] These cases are examples of the broad interpretation of the requirement of personal interest, but in all of them the company suffered a loss: Cass crim, 8 December 1971, Bull crim no 346, 869; Cass crim, 19 June 1978, Bull crim no 202, 525; Cass crim, 20 March 1997, No de pourvoi: 96-81361; Cass crim, 15 September 1999, No de pourvoi 98-83.237.

[84] Cass crim, 16 January 1964, Bull crim 1964 no 16, 27 (abuse of company assets); Cass crim, 10 November 1964, Bull crim no 291 (abuse of credit); Cass crim, 24 March 1969, Bull crim no 130, 319 (abuse of assets); Cass crim, 16 March 1970, Bull crim no 107, 245 (abuse of credit).

[85] Another aspect, which would heighten the probability of the perpetrator's conviction, would be if he performs clandestine operations with company funds. According to the Court of Cassation, in such case the presence of personal interest can be presumed, and the defendant must prove that this was not the case. Cass crim, 11 January 1996, Bull crim no 21, 51. See also Joly and Joly-Baumgartner, *L'abus de biens sociaux* (n 8) 146 (and the judgments cited there, which confirm this line).

common law conspiracy to defraud after the judgment in *Ivey*.[86] As to the latter offence, the other requirement of intention to defraud will not be an obstacle to prosecution as it is fulfilled if the manager intentionally exposes the company to a risk to which it should not have been exposed, even if the overall motive is the company's profit.[87]

As to the other analysed offences in the English legal system – the offence of possession of articles for use in fraud, the offence of making or supplying such articles and the statutory conspiracy to commit fraud – they do not require proof that the perpetrator was dishonest. The *mens rea* is mainly focused on the perpetrator's intention that the article is used to commit fraud (by the perpetrator or another person) as to the first two,[88] or the intention that the intended plan to commit fraud be carried out.[89]

5.3. Criminalisation of Secondary Participation

All three legal systems provide for punishment for complicity in the commission of offences consisting in the exposure of a company to excessive risk. In all three systems, secondary participation requires intention to make one's contribution as an accomplice. They vary, however, as regards the attitude towards the commission of the main offence.

Whereas mere knowledge concerning the foreseen main offence will suffice in England and France, in the German legal system the secondary participant must intend also that the main offence be committed (so-called double intention). In view of that requirement, a person must not only intentionally incite or help, but also know (or at least take it to be possible) that the person is a duty holder and at least be aware that the excessively risky act which he incites or aids to undertake may constitute a breach of duty of the main perpetrator and result in risk-damage (or actual loss) and accept that possibility. There is, however, no need in order for criminal liability to arise that the secondary participant know all of the details of the main offence.[90]

The less rigid approach of the English and French systems eliminates the crucial requirements limiting liability for the main offence: dishonesty and personal interest. Hence, the accomplice to the French offence of abuse of company assets

[86] The other cognitive requirements are: as to fraud by false representation: the person making the representation would need to know that the representation is, or might be, untrue or misleading; as to fraud by failing to disclose information: knowledge about the duty to disclose such information. The latter is contested by the CPS, who consider the offence to be of strict liability in this regard.

[87] *R v Allsop* (1977) 64 Cr App R 29; *Wai Yu-Tsang v R* [1992] 1 AC 269; David Ormerod and David Huw Williams, *Smith's Law of Theft*, 9th edn (Oxford University Press, 2007) 210.

[88] As to the inchoate offence of making or supplying such articles, it would also be sufficient if the perpetrator knew 'that it is designed or adapted for use in the course of or in connection with fraud'.

[89] As to the statutory conspiracy, it must include the conspirer's knowledge or intention that the eventual perpetrator of fraud be dishonest (at the moment of the agreement or the commission of fraud).

[90] Bohlander, *Principles of German Criminal Law* (n 56) 169, 173.

must know that the main perpetrator is acting for personal interest, although he need not himself pursue his own personal goals.[91] Therefore, a lower level manager or an assistant who deliberately helps in an excessively risky transaction, knowing that the principal would get a bonus linked to the company turnover, but who is motivated by personal ambition only (he wants to please the hierarchical superior or improve his position in the company) might be held liable for complicity.

Criminal liability of the accomplice to the English fraud does not depend on proving dishonesty. For liability as an accomplice, the perpetrator must have intention to make his contribution to the commission of the offence (aiding, abetting, counselling or procuring) and be aware or foresee the 'essential matters'[92] of the offence committed by the main perpetrator.[93] Hence, there is no need that the accomplice intend that the principal commit the offence, with the exception of procuring.[94] While complicity requires that the main offence be committed, the English systems offers possibilities to convict other persons for acts of planning, aid or encouragement independently of the commission of the ultimate fraud. However, in general, these offences require a form of intention or belief that this ultimate offence be committed or that the victim be defrauded. This is the case for the inchoate offence of encouraging and assisting crime, statutory conspiracy, as well as the common law conspiracy to defraud. The connection with the ultimate offence is more distant in the definition of the offence of possession, etc of articles for use in frauds, which requires the intention that the article be used in the course of or in connection with fraud, and even less so in the offence of making or supplying articles for use in frauds, which would also be satisfied if the perpetrator knew 'that it is designed or adapted for use in the course of or in connection with fraud'.

Interestingly, the inchoate offence of assisting and encouraging crime offers a possibility to convict a person who aids or abets in the commission of the offence. This would enable the punishment of a person who helps or incites a manager to expose the company to excessive risk, while the manager is unaware of this aspect or does not act dishonestly, provided that the person assisting or encouraging fulfils these *mens rea* requirements.

6. Special Provisions for Banking and Insurance Executives

The English and the German systems contain provisions expressly punishing excessively risky management of banks.[95] The German law also provides an

[91] Frédéric Desportes and Francis Le Gunehec, *Droit Pénal Général*, 14th edn (Paris: Economica, 2007) 502.

[92] *Johnson v Youden* [1950] 1 KB 544, at 546.

[93] Simester et al, *Simester and Sullivan's Criminal Law* (n 44) 218.

[94] Ibid 219.

[95] Financial Services (Banking Reform) Act 2013, s 36 and Banking Act (Gesetz über das Kreditwesen KWG), s 54a.

analogous offence applicable to the insurance industry.[96] Both offences are a reaction to the financial crisis and the deficiencies in risk management which led to it. As the existing offences focused on the relationship between the principal (the company, shareholders) and the agent, they were deemed unsuitable to address the need to protect the economic system from the dangers of excessively risky management of systemically important companies. While protecting the banks (and insurance companies, respectively) from failure, these new offences mainly aim at protecting the economic system and society from its consequences.

The analysis below will briefly point out major similarities and differences between the English and German approaches. However, the reader needs to be aware of several features of these pieces of legislation. They are both very new law, with no jurisprudence at the time of writing. The available doctrine is also limited, in particular as regards the English law. Furthermore, the English provision entered into force only on 7 March 2016, which further postpones the possibility to verify what its practical implications will be.[97] Finally, analysis of the provision leads to the conclusion that the applicability of these offences is likely to be limited in view of their relatively complicated definitions which run the risk of existing more as law in the books than in the courts.

The provisions limit their scope of application to senior managers, which effectively means in both legal orders only top-level management. The German provision is fairly precise in describing what act is forbidden, as the conduct consists in one of the enumerated risk-preventive measures failing to be implemented. Moreover, it requires that the failure be first detected by the national Financial Supervisory Authority (BaFin), which issues an order requiring that the failure be remedied. Only the contravention of this order fulfils the *actus reus* requirement. The English Financial Services (Banking Reform) Act 2013, section 36, is more abstract in its description, requiring that the manager's conduct in relation to the taking of the decision by or on behalf of the financial institution as to the way in which its business is to be carried out, encompassing a failure to take steps to prevent such a decision, fall far below what could reasonably be expected of a person in the manager's position. While the terms are general, the threshold set by this offence seems very high and difficult to argue before a jury.

For criminal liability for both offences, it is necessary that the manager's failures lead to a detrimental result for the financial institution. As regards the German provision, it requires that the institution, as a result of the manager's failure, find itself in a state of concrete danger to its existence. The English law goes even further as to this condition: the implementation of the manager's decision must cause the failure of the group institution.

[96] Insurance Supervision Act (Gesetz über die Beaufsichtigung der Versicherungsunternehmen, VAG), s 142.

[97] Financial Services (Banking Reform) Act 2013 (Commencement No 9) Order 2015 (SI 2015/490, 4 March 2015).

On the *mens rea* side, under the English offence in section 36, the manager must be aware that the implementation of the decision he took or failed to prevent carries a risk of causing the failure of the institution. The German offence does not require that the manager foresee such a consequence of his act, as he may be negligent regarding the result. He must, however, have acted intentionally as regards the violation of the risk-management rule.

Both offences set their requirements in such a way that, arguably, it will be very difficult to secure a conviction, in particular since the defendant will by definition be a high profile manager, likely with a potent defence team. As to the German law, the requirement that the BaFin first give a warning limits the possibility of the commission of the offence itself (although one cannot exclude that the solution might be effective in preventing the financial or insurance institution being brought to the brink of collapse). Furthermore, it may not be so straightforward to prove that the concrete danger to the existence of the institution occurred due to the manager's decision. Regarding the English provision, it is submitted here that the combination of the requirements that it be the manager's decision that caused the failure of the group institution and that his conduct fall far below what could reasonably be expected of a person in his position, together with the *mens rea* requirement, results in very low likelihood of conviction. In view of these reservations, these provisions remain only law on paper until the first successful conviction is secured, and it is difficult to predict whether this will indeed ever come to pass.

7. Comparison of the Results of the Five Cases

All the national systems have been examined in the light of the five sample cases presented in Chapter 1.[98] The first requirement, which needs to be verified, concerns the position of the perpetrator and the problem whether it fulfils the requirement of perpetrator as foreseen by the offence. While this requirement is sufficiently broadly defined by the English offence of fraud by abuse of position and the German *Untreue* to include managers at different levels of corporate hierarchy, the French offence of abuse of company assets limits significantly the scope of potential perpetrators. Therefore, the solutions to the cases given below as regards this offence will be applicable only on the condition that the perpetrator belongs to the top management as required by this offence.

The first two cases present a typical example of transactions which are detrimental to the company, because they bear excessive risk or because the risk taken is not sufficiently compensated. The difference between case 1 and 2 consists in that, whilst in the former the manager is taking the decision himself, in the latter he only directs his subordinates to act in that way.

[98] For the hypotheses of the cases and explanations, see Chapter 1, section 4.

The conviction of a manager in the situation described in case 1 is the most likely within the German system. Granting a loan without sufficient guarantee is a typical example of a breach of duty by the responsible manager and the court is likely to consider the requirement of risk-damage as fulfilled as well, since such a loan has lower value than one granted under normal conditions. The *actus reus* of the French offence of abuse of company assets will also be fulfilled, since granting credit under such detrimental conditions is against the company's interests. However, the manager must also have acted in his personal interest. While a 'diluted' personal interest, such as the hope of being promoted, might not be enough, an expectation of a bonus for the contract already increases the chances of conviction. If the manager granted the credit to a family member under such conditions, the requirement of personal interests will most likely be considered fulfilled. If such strong element of personal interest would be present, it would be also possible to argue that the manager used the funds as if they were his own, and thus committed misappropriation in terms of the offence of breach of trust. That would allow punishing managers who do not fulfil the criteria to become perpetrators of the abuse of company assets.

Liability for the English offence of fraud by abuse of position will depend on whether the act of the manager is considered dishonest by the jury. The sole fact of granting insufficiently secured credit is not likely to convince the jury. It is more likely to be admitted if some other elements could be added, for example, if the manager was clearly acting outside of the scope of his discretion or acting motivated only by his personal interest. Hence, he would be considered dishonest if a breach of the rules for granting credits was evident, or he granted the credit to a member of his family, or did so only in order to obtain the commission directly linked to authorising the loan. The latter aspect, despite not being included in the wording of the offence, renders the solution similar to the French offence.

The manager in case 2 will be convicted for *Untreue* for the same reasons as in case 1, and without having recourse to different rules on participation in the commission of the offence, as by giving the order he has already breached his duty. As to the English system, the solution given above will also be applicable here, since abuse of position can be proved and the element of dishonesty presents the most significant difficulty. As to the French system, the solution is also similar to case 2, but the personal interest is much more evident as the manager expected a bonus, so the probability of conviction would be high.

For senior managers, the special banking provisions could also be considered, provided that the various conditions prescribed by these offences are fulfilled, for which there is no indication in the facts of the case.

The situation presented in case 3 illustrates management of company assets which is certainly very risky, since the manager invests on the stock exchange in an aggressive way. Moreover, he exposes the company to an abnormal risk, because the company's activity is construction. The manager is not acting in his direct interest, as he is intending to keep the eventual profit from the investment for the company.

This case may be considered fraud by abuse of position according to the English law, since all limbs seem to be fulfilled, on the condition that investing the money on the stock exchange was outside of the scope of business of the company (in view of the articles of association or other relevant documents). It is likely that such investment would be considered dishonest, as the manager's act is in clear breach of diligent management. The offence of theft could also be applicable in this case, if he was not permitted to invest the money in this way or if he retained the gains made from the investment.

Conviction will be less likely in the two other legal systems, unless additional circumstances occur. In the German law, if investing on the stock exchange is not part of the company's activities, then by doing that, the perpetrator commits a breach of duty. The difficulty will be in determining the value of risk-damage. It is necessary to verify how the value of assets endangered through investment in risky securities diminished. This might be difficult to establish and in fact depend on the ultimate outcome of the investment. If the investment turns out to be profitable, then there is no *Untreue*.

The issue in the French law would be the requirement of personal interest. The investment as such exposes the company to abnormal risk, so the requirement of acting against the company's interests for the offence of abuse of company assets would be met. It is, however, necessary to demonstrate that the manager had some personal interest in the investment. This would, of course, not be a problem where he wanted to keep the gain for himself, a condition that would also make conviction for breach of trust very likely. However, if the manager acted only in order for the company to profit, only abuse of company assets could come into play, and then only provided that the court would be satisfied with a 'diluted' personal interest. This cannot be excluded, since one can argue that the high risk taken by the manager and potentially very detrimental results make his conduct sufficiently evident to accept even personal interest in such form. If this line of thought was rejected, conviction would to a large extent depend on the final outcome of the investment. If it turns out to bring loss to the company, there is a strong likelihood that personal interest would be admitted even in its weaker form. Also, the offence of breach of trust might be applied in such a case.

Case 4 presents a scenario where a technical internal decision leads to a situation of exposing the company to a risk of loss. The chances of conviction will be limited in all the legal systems. For the German offence of *Untreue*, it will be necessary in the first place to point out a concrete legal basis for a duty that the manager breached by allowing the car to be declared ready or by not disclosing the problems. It is necessary that such a provision aim principally at protecting the assets of the company. If that can be established, the crucial question becomes whether the requirement of risk-damage has been fulfilled and if it can be quantified. On the one hand, it could be estimated, eg by assessing how much the value of the investment is diminished by the risk of repairs necessary. On the other hand, the damage from repairs is less immediate than the costs of postponing the presentation and reprogramming the electronics. The question how the perpetrator perceived his act would be crucial to the question of *mens rea*. On the one hand, he foresaw the costs of repairs and accepted that the company may suffer loss because of them. On the other hand, if he acted so as to diminish the most immediate costs (which would result from postponing the presentation and reprogramming), which he considered more significant, than his intention is excluded.

It will be much more difficult to gain a conviction in the English or the French legal system. The prosecution in the English system will be rather reluctant to proceed with the case under these circumstances, as the probability that the manager would be considered dishonest is low. It might be a misjudgement on the side of the director to clear the car for production or not to inform the other executives, but it will most probably not be considered dishonest. The case would be different if the director did something that would compromise his integrity, such as shredding documents related to the issue, or if he was acting mainly for the commission he was in line to receive for the new model.

The probability of conviction is very low in the French legal system as regards both available offences. Already, the conduct element would be difficult to prove for both offences in question (especially for breach of trust). Even if this element is considered to be fulfilled as regards the abuse of company assets, the problem would be, yet again, with the proof of personal interest. If the case goes to trial after the real loss occurred, it is likely that the judges would admit 'diluted' personal interest, if present. However, before the eventual loss occurs, conviction would be possible only on the condition that there was a concrete personal interest, eg in the form of a commission.

The situation presented in case 5 is in the first place a case of bribery. Regardless of criminal liability for this offence, it may present a situation of exposing the company, for whose benefit the manager acts, to a risk of being sanctioned. Such cases are known to the French legal system and present an evident case of abuse of company assets. The reason for using this offence is the possibility to postpone the starting point of the limitation period, which in result becomes longer than that which applies to corruption. For such cases, the jurisprudence accepts even 'diluted' personal interest. If the manager does not belong to the head management as required by the offence of abuse of company assets, the offence of breach of trust might also be of application, on the condition, however, that the perpetrator himself decided to use the assets of the company for this purpose and not that he received them from his superiors in order to commit corruption.

Within the German system, cases of *Untreue* involving corruption are also known. However, the breach of duty has so far been found not in the act of corruption but in creating slush funds for these purposes. By transferring funds to such a fund, the manager breaches his accounting duties. The jurisprudence found damage in that, because of the transfer, the company lost control over these assets. The manager would also be liable for *Untreue* if he uses the funds for bribery without the owner's consent. Some authors consider that shareholders' consent to illegal acts, including bribery, is always invalid.[99]

[99] Schramm, 'Untreue, § 266 StGB' (n 3) marginal no 80.

The English jurisprudence does not address cases of using fraud or similar types of offences to tackle the problem of managers corrupting public officials in order to obtain contracts for their companies. The limitation period is not a problem, as the English system provides none for the offence of bribery. However, in view of the remoteness of the risk of loss and the fact that the manager acts for the benefit of the company, it is unlikely that he would be found dishonest. This does not exclude the manager's liability for bribery or theft as regards misapplication of company's funds for this purpose.

As regards the negligent version of the cases, none of the analysed legal systems offers a possibility of conviction.

8. Conclusions: Models of Criminalisation of Excessive Risk-Taking

The above comparative analysis examined three models of criminal liability of managers for excessively risky decisions. These models can be summarised as follows.

All three systems contain offences which could be used in order to punish managerial decisions endangering the assets of the company, without requiring that the eventual loss occur.[100] The main focus of these provisions is the relationship between the principal (the company and the shareholders) and the agent (the manager). Thus, the offences protect mainly the company's interests and those of its economic owners. To some extent, the interests of stakeholders, such as creditors or employees, are taken into account by the French offence of abuse of company assets and the German *Untreue* due to the limited influence of shareholders' consent on managers' criminal liability. The analysed offences do not directly protect the economic system. However, Germany and England have introduced offences which incriminate excessively risky management of systemically important banking (and in the case of Germany insurance) institutions.

[100] All three legal systems provide for penalties of imprisonment and fines in relation to the standard offence. While for the French abuse of company assets and the German *Untreue*, maximum terms of imprisonment are limited to five years, the English offence of fraud carries a maximum sentence of 10 years. However, on summary conviction, this penalty is a maximum of 12 months. The German offence of *Untreue* may also be punished with imprisonment of up to 10 years, if it can be classified as causing a major financial loss. It is subject to debate whether risk-damage can fulfil this requirement. If it were included, the value of risk-damage has been suggested as €100,000: BGH (2 December 2008) NJW 2009, 528, 532. The punishment for the French offence of abuse of company assets may also be increased (up to 7 years' imprisonment) if the offence was conducted or facilitated using either accounts or contracts opened or subscribed with entities established abroad or by the interposition of natural or legal persons or any organization, trust or comparable institution established abroad. As regards alternative possibilities of conviction, the English system provides for the same level of punishment as for fraud, with the exception of possession, etc of articles for use in frauds (Fraud Act 2006, s 6), which limits imprisonment to five years. The maximum sentence provided for the French offence of breach of trust is three years.

Besides the common approach as regards protected legal interests, the three models of incrimination present various similarities in the design of the offences. All these offences incriminate misdealing in the management of the company assets. Not only excessively risky management leading to an effective loss, but also merely endangering the assets of the company may lead to criminal liability. In all three legal systems, the act must be committed intentionally (including *dolus eventualis*) and liability for advertent or inadvertent negligence is excluded. In general, it will be sufficient that the intention of the perpetrator be directed at exposing the company to excessive risk. Hence, it will not be indispensable that the perpetrator intended to cause loss or foresaw such a possibility. The three legal systems also concur in including indiscriminately the senior management into their scope.

However, the three models differ as regards key requirements which shape the scope of liability and will be ultimately decisive for the focus of the prosecution. They also reflect the policy choices as well as criminal law traditions of each system.

The distinctive feature of the English model, which is constructed around the offence of fraud by abuse of position and the common law offence of conspiracy to defraud, is its reliance on the concept of dishonesty. It is a notion that has long been present in the English law and been used in definitions of various offences related to the protection of property or white-collar crime (eg theft, conspiracy to defraud, false accounting, and until recently in the cartel offence). Dishonesty will define the conduct from the point of view of *actus reus* and *mens rea*, since it is necessary that the conduct of the manager be considered dishonest (according to the standard of honest and reasonable people) and that he be aware that it is so according to these standards. Therefore, it is not so much a breach of particular rules or the detrimental results of the perpetrator's act, but this negative feature of his deeds will be crucial for criminal liability. Since it will be assessed by a jury of laymen giving no reasons for their decision, it will depend on concrete cases how the prosecution can best convince the jurors that the manager's act was dishonest. The mere fact that the manager handled the entrusted assets in an excessively risky manner will most probably be insufficient for that purpose. The case will certainly be more convincing if the manager gravely breached the standard of conduct or acted in personal interest, which will create a parallel between the English system and the German and the French systems, respectively. However, the presence of these elements is neither an obligatory requirement nor a guarantee of conviction.

The French system, based on the offence of abuse of company assets, is shaped by two requirements that will be decisive for criminal liability and will significantly curb the possibilities to punish managers taking excessively risky decisions. First of all, contrary to the two other systems, the French one restricts liability to head management. Secondly, the manager must act in personal interest. Although this concept is relatively broad, including acting in the interest of a person or persons related to the manager or companies in which he might be interested, it excludes all the acts, even extremely risky, which were performed only in the interests of the company (according to the perception of the manager), or only due to such motivations as a desire for prestige, the will to strengthen his position within the company or to please important persons ('diluted' personal interest). While the latter motivation was admitted as personal interest in terms of the offence of abuse of company assets, this was only so in the context of effective loss to the company. Hence, if the abnormally risky decision results in a loss, the importance of the requirement of personal interest diminishes. Moreover, it cannot be excluded that the courts will decide to apply the concept of 'diluted' personal interest to cases of risk.

The distinctive feature of the German model based on the offence of *Untreue* is that it requires establishing that the manager breached a concrete rule defining his conduct and that this rule was aimed at protecting the financial interests of the company. The question whether the rule was breached needs to be answered according to the standards of the domain to which the rule pertains (eg company law) and there seems to be an agreement in the German law that the breach of this rule must be severe. The consideration of whether the manager breached such a rule would not be surprising in a case against the manager in England or France, it is only in the German system, however, that it is an imperative.

The second element defining the German system is the requirement of a concrete result, which needs to be a situation, separate from the conduct, in which the assets are endangered in a way that lowers their value in a a manner that is possible to quantify. While in many cases it will be possible (eg an improperly secured loan is worth less than a loan subject to adequate guarantees), if the risk cannot be assessed in this way, the judge must acquit the manager.

Whilst the above presentation of the French and the German models is based on dominant jurisprudence, it is also important to note that certain ways of understanding the relevant offences, represented by few judgments and remaining so far at the fringe of dominant interpretation, might change the image of the models, if they gain wider acceptance. In this respect, two aspects in particular deserve attention. First, the French offence of breach of trust, which requires that the person misappropriate the entrusted property, has so far been interpreted in such a way as to preclude the construal of endangerment of those assets as a modality of the commission of the offence (unless the assets are used for personal purposes). However, one judgment has admitted such an interpretation.[101] If such an understanding were to gain acceptance in the jurisprudence, this would extend the application of this offence to other managers who cannot be perpetrators of the offence of abuse of company assets, ie middle- and lower-level management, who expose their companies to excessive risk.

Secondly, as regards the *mens rea* of the German *Untreue*, a minority line of jurisprudence interpreted the requirement of intention in the form of *dolus eventualis* in such a way as to exclude situations wherein the manager was aware that his act was exposing the company to excessive risk (in the form of risk-damage)

[101] Cass crim, 3 July 1997, Bull crim no 265, 905.

and accepted it, but did not accept the eventual damage.[102] If such an interpretation were to be admitted, it would exclude from the scope of the offence situations where the manager was acting whilst convinced that the company would not be damaged by his act, or at least not accepted that it occur, although aware of the excessively risky nature of his decision.

The image of the three models is complemented by the possibility, offered in all three legal systems, to punish persons assisting or encouraging managers to take excessively risky decisions, whether these persons are other managers or only assistants or externals. Whereas the German and the French systems require that the main perpetrator effectively commit the offence, the English model allows for the punishment of the relevant actors even where this is not the case. It also includes possibilities to convict such persons for conspiring to commit the offence or for assisting where the main perpetrator has no required *mens rea*, as the *mens rea* of the assisting person may supplant it.

Finally, two of the above models, the English and the German, recently introduced provisions punishing excessively risky management of systemically important banking (and insurance) institutions.[103] Since there is no jurisprudence on these provisions and given their complex requirements, it is difficult to foresee how the new provisions will effectively influence the above models of criminalising excessive risk-taking by managers. Certainly, their application will be limited to the head management of systemically important companies of selected sectors. They will, however, include mismanagement committed by recklessness. What is certain so far is that these offences cannot be used to punish managers for mere excessive risk-taking per se, since both require the effective collapse of the institution. Therefore, these offences will rather be a reaction to effectively occurred failure and not to excessively risky management detected at an earlier stage.

[102] BGH (18 October 2006) NJW 2007, 1760, 1766.

[103] The punishment provided for the offence is imprisonment and a fine. The maximum level of imprisonment in the German law is five years, two years if the result was caused negligently. The English law provides for imprisonment up to seven years on conviction on indictment.

6

Criminalisation of Excessive Risk-Taking by Managers?

1. Introduction

The previous chapters focused on existing possibilities to punish managers for excessive risk-taking. The rest of the book will analyse whether it is ever justified and legitimate to criminalise excessive risk-taking by managers in companies and, if so, to examine the conditions and boundaries of such criminal liability.[1] This chapter will be divided into two parts having analogous structure. The first will present the criteria justifying the use of criminal law and principles limiting its use. Against this background, the second part will analyse the problems with criminalisation of excessive risk-taking. The outcome of this investigation should in turn allow to formulate (a) model(s) of criminalisation in the last chapter of the book.

While justifying a criminal provision, two perspectives need to be taken into account:

- Should the course of conduct be criminalised?
- Does the legislator have the right to do so?

The first question asks about the 'in principle justification' for criminalisation, which is based on criminal policy considerations. The second focuses on the limits of state power to issue criminal provisions (or to intervene at all) within a concrete system and in particular under constitutional law.[2] In other words, the first question concerns the legitimacy of a solution, the second one its legality. The analysis provided in this chapter and the model criminalisation presented in the following one, will not be limited to concrete legal orders, but is rather

[1] For analysis of the concept of legitimacy, see a compact summary provided at 'Political Legitimacy' in *Stanford Encyclopedia of Philosophy* (First published 29 April 2010), available at http://plato.stanford.edu/entries/legitimacy/; see also Ferry de Jong, 'A Reciprocal Turn in Criminal Justice? Shifting Conceptions of Legitimate Authority' (2013) 9(1) *Utrecht Law Review* 1–23. The term 'legitimate' is to be understood here as justified in a rational way. In this sense, the terms 'justified' and 'legitimate' are not given distinct meaning (see, eg A John Simmons, 'Justification and Legitimacy' (1999) 109(4) *Ethics* 739.

[2] AP Simester and Andreas von Hirsch, *Crimes, Harms, and Wrongs* (Oxford/Portland, OR: Hart Publishing, 2014) 31–32.

system-transcendent. Therefore, only the first perspective can be analysed in this chapter, since the second perspective is necessarily embedded in a concrete system. The aim of this analysis is to look for reasons and justifications for criminalising excessive risk-taking or refraining from doing so. The three legal orders analysed in the previous chapters will serve as inspiration, but the analysis will not be conducted only within the limits of these systems. This chapter's aim is to prepare a panorama of arguments for a responsible legislator[3] to decide whether and how to criminalise excessive risk-taking, be it a national legislator or potentially also the European one, if tackling managerial misconduct or countering excessively risky management proves 'essential to ensure the effective implementation of a Union policy' (Article 83(2) of the Treaty on the Functioning of the European Union (TFEU)).[4]

The starting point for an analysis on whether a certain type of conduct should be criminalised is that criminal law should be used with parsimony and that 'offences should be created only when absolutely necessary'.[5] Criminal law is a tool which possesses a very strong regulatory power, but also involves significant drawbacks, because of the limitations on personal liberties it may cause, through both the prohibitions it stipulates and the methods of enforcement it uses.[6] It is the most intrusive of the tools which are available to the legislator.[7]

Criminal law, and in particular punishment, are generally justified by reference to a 'deserved response to culpable wrongdoing and as a necessary institution to deter such wrongdoing',[8] as well as by reference to its communicative function.[9]

[3] It has been argued in the literature that in a liberal state there exists a kind of right not to be punished, which means that the justification for criminalisation must be provided by the legislator; see Douglas Husak, *Overcriminalization: The Limits of the Criminal Law* (Oxford University Press, 2008) 122 et seq; Andrew Ashworth, *Principles of Criminal Law*, 6th edn (Oxford University Press, 2009) 22.

[4] However, the chapter will not examine whether it is desirable to regulate the problem of risk-taking, in particular by stipulating criminal sanctions, at the EU level. This problem would require a separate study analysing different aspects of the EU legal system. See also Markus Kotzur, 'TFEU Article 83' in Rudolf Geiger, Daniel-Erasmus Khan and Markus Kotzur, *European Union Treaties, A Commentary* (Munich/Oxford/Portland, OR: CH Beck/Hart Publishing, 2015) 450; Paul Craig and Gráinne de Búrca, *EU Law: Text, Cases, and Materials*, 5th edn (Oxford University Press, 2011) 941–42. See also Katalin Ligeti, 'Approximation of Substantive Criminal Law and the Establishment of the European Public Prosecutor's Office' in Francesca Galli and Anne Weyembergh, *Approximation of Substantive Criminal Law in the EU: The Way Forward* (Editions de l'Université de Bruxelles, 2013) 73–83; John AE Vervaele, 'The European Union and Harmonization of the Criminal Law Enforcement of Union Policies: In Search of a Criminal Law Policy?' in Magnus Ulväng and Iain Cameron, *Essays on Criminalization and Sanction* (Iustus, 2014) 185–225.

[5] Per Lord Williams of Mostyn, HL Deb, vol 602, col WA 58, 18 June 1999, cited in AP Simester, JR Spencer, GR Sullivan and GJ Virgo, *Simester and Sullivan's Criminal Law: Theory and Doctrine*, 5th edn (Oxford/Portland, OR: Hart Publishing, 2013) 643.

[6] Simester and von Hirsch, *Crimes, Harms, and Wrongs* (n 2) 18.

[7] Simester et al, *Simester and Sullivan's Criminal Law* (n 5) 643.

[8] Ashworth, *Principles of Criminal Law* (n 3) 17.

[9] Klaus Günther, 'Criminal Law, Crime and Punishment as Communication' in AP Simester, Anthe du Bois-Pedain and Ulfrid Neumann, *Liberal Criminal Theory: Essays for Andreas von Hirsch* (Oxford/Portland, OR: Hart Publishing, 2014) 123–39, at 126 et seq.

Subjecting a certain course of conduct to criminal sanction has two main features: preventive and deontological.[10] The preventive function consists of deterring people from performing the forbidden act by means of fear of criminal sanction or through incapacitation resulting from the imposed sanction (deprivation of liberty, professional prohibitions). As to the deontological aspect, it formulates a duty that persons concerned should abstain from the criminalised conduct. The breach of this duty justifies the response in the form of punishment.

Moreover, there is something special in declaring a course of conduct (or the causing of a particular result) to be criminal. This particular aspect lies first of all in primary criminalisation, where labelling something a criminal offence carries a message that it is wrong. Furthermore, this message is reinforced by secondary criminalisation, through the triggering of criminal procedure and the stigmatising effect of sentencing and of punishment.[11]

Therefore, an investigation of whether it is legitimate to criminalise certain courses of conduct should establish what is the moral wrong it should reprobate, as well as what is the goal the particular criminalisation should achieve. This analysis will start with the question of moral wrongfulness. It will be followed by the examination of the two key theories of justification for criminalisation: the harm theory and the theory of *Rechtsgut* (theory of legal goods), which constitute the most theoretically sophisticated justification theories developed in modern criminal law. The former stems from the common law, whereas the second continues to inspire the criminal law of continental tradition.[12]

Furthermore, since criminal law is the tool which limits personal liberty the most, as well as potentially triggering the use of very coercive powers, it must fulfil the requirements guaranteeing that it is used with parsimony, among which the crucial one is formulated by the principle of proportionality. Even if moral wrongfulness can be demonstrated and there exists legitimate justification for subjecting certain conduct to a criminal section, there may still be reasons not to criminalise certain conduct or to limit the scope of such criminalisation. Moreover, since criminal law is based on the assumption of citizens as rational agents capable of controlling their behaviour in order to avoid criminal sanction, it must also formulate its prohibitions in a way which allows them to understand what conduct they should abstain from in order to direct their actions accordingly.[13] In view of these considerations, the reasons justifying the use of criminal law will be supplemented by an analysis of the principles limiting its use: the *ultima ratio* principle and the principle of proportionality, as well as the legality principle and the fair warning principle.

[10] Simester and von Hirsch, *Crimes, Harms, and Wrongs* (n 2) 18.

[11] Ibid 5.

[12] See n 55 below.

[13] Hans-Heinrich Jescheck and Thomas Weigend, *Lehrbuch des Strafrechts* (Berlin: Duncker & Humblot, 1996) 128 et seq, 137.

Before embarking on this analysis, one last introductory remark should be made. The principles and criteria chosen for this examination are commonly accepted in different criminal law traditions. However, none of them is able to give a precise answer to the question whether certain courses of conduct ought to be criminalised. The final answer is to be given by the legislator in view of the policy that the state wants to pursue. In the context of companies, it is not only the criminal policy, but mainly the economic policy, which will be decisive. The rules and principles analysed here are indicative parameters as to the boundaries of criminal law intervention. They may also form a sort of common language to debate its use and form intelligible arguments, without, however, giving a precise answer as to the correct scope of criminalisation. Ultimately, it is the legislator who will have to make a decision, within the boundaries indicated by these rules and principles, on how to balance the interests at stake. This decision will necessarily take into account 'a number of conflicting social, political, and historical factors'.[14] Since this analysis is not embedded in a concrete legal system, it is impossible to describe and analyse all such factors, which may determine the legislator's choices as to criminal as well as economic policy and the enforcement of the latter through criminal law. Therefore, the analysis below will aim at setting these boundaries outside a concrete legal system, showing within which limits the legislator should be operating as to excessive risk-taking, and what may be the consequences of his choices. If this analysis is to be used, it needs to be adapted to a concrete legal culture, as well as to concrete economic and criminal policy.

2. Justification for Use of Criminal Law and its Limits

2.1. Moral Wrongfulness

'A system of law that imposed punishment on people who were not at fault, or did so in a way that was disproportionate to their fault, would be unjust.'[15] This view is particularly relevant for the retributivist approach to criminal law, the core of which, regardless of its version, provides that punishment is deserved when offenders are morally at fault.[16] However, the requirement of moral fault is not limited to retributivism. The utilitarian approach (whether oriented towards individual prevention, thus seeking incapacitation, or general prevention, seeking deterrence)

[14] Ashworth, *Principles of Criminal Law* (n 3) 17.

[15] Stuart P Green, *Lying, Cheating, and Stealing: A Moral Theory of White-Collar Crime* (Oxford University Press, 2006/2010) 22.

[16] Ibid 21 et seq.

still requires a justification for using criminalisation (instead or together with the use of other legal or non-legal tools). These perspectives converge, as many legal systems and most of the contemporary scholars follow a mixed approach, which combines the utilitarian function of the punishment and retribution.[17]

In the words of Simester and von Hirsch:

> [B]y criminalising the activity of ϕing, the state declares that ϕing is morally wrongful; it instructs citizens not to ϕ; it warns them that, if they ϕ, they are liable to be convicted and punished within specified ranges (the levels of which signal the seriousness with which ϕing is regarded); and, further, the state undertakes that, on proof of D's ϕing, it will impose an appropriate measure of punishment, within the specified range, that reflects the blameworthiness of D's conduct.[18]

Jareborg formulates a comparable view: 'the threat of punishment is not only a conditional threat of a painful sanction. It is also an expression of *how* negatively different kinds of action or omission are judged'.[19] Weigend in his introductory chapter to the commentary to the German Penal Code (Strafgesetzbuch, StGB) expresses a very similar idea.[20]

Therefore, criminal law has a specific communicative function.[21] This aspect of criminal law is clearly visible in comparison to civil law. Whereas criminal law convictions and sanctions speak 'with a distinctively moral voice',[22] civil law does not convey this aspect:

> [Criminal law] does not only coerce; it also makes a moral appeal to citizens to desist. Its sanctions are not merely instrumental; they also express disapproval of the offender's conduct.[23]

This paradigm is more obvious as regards the classical offences (murder, rape, theft) as they have the 'moral resonance' typically associated with criminal law.[24] They were traditionally called *malum in se* offences. The counterpart category is

[17] Simester et al, *Simester and Sullivan's Criminal Law* (n 5) 14–16; Jescheck and Weigend, *Lehrbuch des Strafrechts* (n 13) 78–79; Jean Pradel, *Droit pénal général*, 15th edn (Paris: Editions Cujas, 2004) 506–8. Differently, Roxin whose theory focuses on deterrence (general and special prevention): Claus Roxin, *Strafrecht. Allgemeiner Teil*, 4th edn (Munich: CH Beck, 2006) vol 1, 88–96. For 'pure' retributivism, see, eg Michael S Moore, *Placing Blame: A General Theory of Criminal Law* (Oxford University Press, 2010). See also HLA Hart, *Punishment and Responsibility* (Oxford University Press, 1968).

[18] Simester and von Hirsch, *Crimes, Harms, and Wrongs* (n 2) 6. The Greek symbol ϕ (phi) is used by these authors as a symbol of any kind of action.

[19] Nils Jareborg, 'The Coherence of the Penal System' in his *Essays in Criminal Law* (Uppsala: Iustus Förlag, 1988) 105–21, at 112 (emphasis in original).

[20] Thomas Weigend, 'Einleitung' in Heinrich Wilhelm Laufhütte, Ruth Rissing-van Saan and Klaus Tiedemann, *Strafgesetzbuch. Leipziger Kommentar*, vol 1, Einleitung, §§ 1 bis 31, 12th edn (Berlin/New York: De Gruyter, 2007) marginal no 1.

[21] Günther, 'Criminal Law, Crime and Punishment as Communication' (n 9) 123–39.

[22] Simester and von Hirsch, *Crimes, Harms, and Wrongs* (n 2) 4.

[23] Ibid 212.

[24] Ibid 7.

formed by *malum prohibitum* offences, which do not present such obvious negative moral content. As to this category, the wrong should be found in the breach of rule as such, provided that this rule is justified and created for good reasons. The rule must form part of a strategy aiming at preventing harm or safeguarding interests and for this reason it must not be violated.[25] However, this division encountered criticism[26] and is particularly difficult to apply as regards white-collar criminality, where the wrongfulness may be even less evident than in traditional areas of criminal law. For instance, what for one person may only be cunning marketing, for another may already constitute a fraud.[27]

The use of moral reasoning is not to be confused with the adherence to legal moralism.[28] The perspective taken here considers that for criminalisation, there is not only a requirement of achieving certain goals (prevention of harm or protection of legal interests), but also that the conduct must be morally wrong (ie reprehensible).[29] At the same time, this analysis is not a contribution to moral philosophy, but its focus is criminal law, thus what is relevant is moral wrong that has an impact on another person(s) and not a vice, which is a sign of potentially bad character (such as greed or lust).[30]

2.2. Harm Principle

The Anglo-Saxon debate on reasons for criminalisation focuses on several principles, out of which the harm principle is always the starting point.[31] This principle,

[25] Ibid 26–27. There exist different approaches to this problem among those scholars who consider that criminalisation requires that the prohibited conduct is wrongful. For example, Douglas Husak requires that the conduct is wrongful independently of the legal regulation, while Simester and von Hirsch claim that it can be assessed 'all things considered'. The normative gap between criminalisation and punishment in their view does not exist, since 'at the stage of punishment, the reasons not to ϕ are to be assessed post-legally, not pre-legally'. Simester and von Hirsch, *Crimes, Harms, and Wrongs* (n 2) 27.

[26] For the critical approach, see Klaus Lüderssen, 'Soziale Marktwirtschaft, Finanzmarktkrise und Wirtschaftsstrafrecht' in Eberhard Kempf, Klaus Lüderssen and Klaus Volk, *Die Handlungsfreiheit des Unternehmers* (De Gruyter, 2009) 21–26, at 21.

[27] Charlotte Schmitt-Leonardy, *Unternehmenskriminalität ohne Strafrecht?* (Heidelberg et al: CF Müller, 2013) 26 et seq.

[28] On that see, eg RA Duff, 'Towards a Modest Legal Moralism' in Ulväng and Cameron, *Essays on Criminalization* (n 4) 39–67.

[29] Luigi Ferrajoli, *Derecho y razón, Teoría del garantismo penal* (Madrid: Editorial Trotta, 1995) 459; Green, *Lying, Cheating, and Stealing* (n 15) 44.

[30] On the relationship between law and morality in the context of criminal law, also in historical perspective, see Ferrajoli, *Derecho y razón* (n 29) 218 et seq, 459 et seq.

[31] Ashworth, *Principles of Criminal Law* (n 3) 27. Although the harm theory is criticised for its over-inclusiveness as well as for being under-inclusive, it remains the main tool to discuss the justification for criminalisation in the common law-based criminal law. See also RA Duff, *Answering for Crime: Responsibility and Liability in the Criminal Law* (Oxford/Portland, OR: Hart Publishing, 2007) 126 et seq. See also Tatjana Hörnle, '"Rights of Others" in Criminalisation Theory' in Simester, du Bois-Pedain and Neumann, *Liberal Criminal Theory* (n 9) 169–85, at 170 et seq.

which is enshrined in the liberalist approach as to the function of the state, was first formulated by John Stuart Mill in *On Liberty*, where he famously said:[32]

> The principle is, that the sole end for which mankind are warranted, individually or collectively, in interfering with the liberty of action on any of their number is self-protection. That the only purpose for which power can rightfully be exercised over any member of a civilised community against his will is to prevent harm to others. His own good, either physical or moral, is not a sufficient warrant.[33]

This negative version of the harm principle provides for a criterion to decide when the legislator is not entitled to regulate.[34] The contemporary version of that principle formulated by Feinberg presents it in the form of a positive, although not sufficient, requirement for criminalisation:

> It is always a good reason in support of penal legislation that it would be effective in preventing (eliminating, reducing) harm to persons other than the actor (the one prohibited from acting) and there is no other means that is equally effective at no greater cost to other values.[35]

This difference in approach results in that, whereas for Mill the harm principle is the only one legitimising the use of repressive intervention of the state, for Feinberg other legitimate reasons might also exist.[36]

Feinberg analyses further principles which could potentially justify limiting liberty through criminalisation, in particular the offence principle and legal paternalism. According to the former, criminalisation may be justified if it is to prevent 'serious offence to persons other than the actor and would probably be an effective means to that end if enacted'.[37] Legal paternalism would consider justified 'a prohibition that … is probably necessary to prevent harm (physical, psychological, or economic) to the actor himself'.[38]

The application of these principles as justification is subject to debate, as is their precise scope, including attempts to justify certain cases which Feinberg analyses under legal paternalism by means of the harm principle.[39] Nonetheless, these debates will be less relevant here, since the problem of excessive risk-taking as approached in this book will not be criminalised for reasons such as that it constitutes 'an affront to the senses' or 'sensibilities' or because it produces

[32] Simester and von Hirsch, *Crimes, Harms, and Wrongs* (n 2) 35.

[33] John Stuart Mill, *On Liberty*, 3rd edn (London: Longman, Roberts & Green, 1864) 22.

[34] Simester and von Hirsch, *Crimes, Harms, and Wrongs* (n 2) 35.

[35] Joel Feinberg, *The Moral Limits of Criminal Law*, vol I, *Harm to Others* (Oxford University Press, 1984) 26.

[36] Nina Peršak, *Criminalising Harmful Conduct: The Harm Principle, its Limits and Continental Counterparts* (Springer, 2007) 13.

[37] Feinberg, *Harm to Others* (n 35) 26.

[38] Ibid 26–27. See also Nina Peršak, 'Paternalistic Interventions Through the Law on Regulatory Violations' in Magnus Ulväng and Iain Cameron, *Essays on Criminalization and Sanction* (Iustus, 2014) 125–42.

[39] Simester and von Hirsch, *Crimes, Harms, and Wrongs* (n 2) 161 et seq.

repugnance, although some managerial misconduct might evoke such feelings, which would trigger the application of the offence principle.[40] Neither will it be punished in order to prevent the manager from inflicting harm on himself. The analysis will concern risk of damage inflicted on property of other persons, and should thus be resolved by application of the harm principle.[41] As to the fragment of the principle concerning a lack of other equally effective means, this aspect will be analysed under the *ultima ratio* principle.

Within the harm principle, harms are understood as 'setbacks to interests'.[42] As Feinberg explains:

> These interests, or perhaps more accurately, the things these interests are in, are distinguishable components of a person's well-being: he flourishes or languishes as they flourish or languish. What promotes them is to his advantage or in his interest; what thwarts them is to his detriment or against his interest.[43]

Thus, in order to verify whether harm occurred it is necessary to verify if that interest 'is in a worse condition than it would otherwise have been in had the invasion not occurred at all'.[44]

In both approaches, that of Mill and of Feinberg, it is considered sufficient for the justification of criminalisation that harm is 'likely' to occur.[45] It is thus legitimate that the state prohibits conduct which causes harm or 'the unreasonable risk of such harm', in other words that criminalisation is justified not only by prevention of harm but also in order to avoid 'the unreasonable risk of such harm'.[46] This approach resulted in a debate on the extension of the principle in order to avoid its excessively far-reaching use.[47]

An important part of this debate relates to the analysis of remote harms, which concerns legislative decisions to criminalise acts based on generalisations about risky situations likely to cause harm based (ideally) on empirical evidence.[48] Classic examples of this discussion concern criminalisation of possession of

[40] Joel Feinberg, *The Moral Limits of Criminal Law*, vol II, *Offense to Others* (Oxford University Press, 1985) 14 et seq.

[41] Further on the offence principle, see, eg Feinberg, *Offense to Others* (n 40); Simester and von Hirsch, *Crimes, Harms, and Wrongs* (n 2) 91 et seq. On legal paternalism, see Joel Feinberg, *The Moral Limits of Criminal Law*, vol III, *Harm to Self* (Oxford University Press, 1989); Simester and von Hirsch, *Crimes, Harms, and Wrongs* (n 2) 141 et seq.

[42] Feinberg, *Harm to Others* (n 35) 31 et seq.

[43] Ibid 34.

[44] Ibid 34.

[45] Peršak, *Criminalising Harmful Conduct* (n 36) 41.

[46] Feinberg, *Harm to Others* (n 35) 11; Andrew von Hirsch, 'Der Rechtsgutsbegriff und das "Harm Principle"' in Roland Hefendehl, Andrew von Hirsch and Wolfgang Wohlers (eds), *Die Rechtgutstheorie: Legitimationsbasis des Strafrechts oder dogmatisches Glasperlenspiel?* (Baden-Baden: Nomos, 2003) 13–25, at 15.

[47] Peršak, *Criminalising Harmful Conduct* (n 36) 44; Simester and von Hirsch, *Crimes, Harms, and Wrongs* (n 2) 53; Husak, *Overcriminalization* (n 3) 38.

[48] Feinberg, *Harm to Others* (n 35) 190.

different possibly harmful items, for example weapons (without required permission), driving under the influence of alcohol or surpassing speed limits.[49] All these types of behaviour do not necessarily cause harm and on many occasions would remain harmless. Their criminalisation is based on the assessment of the gravity of the danger which they pose (that a weapon is used by a person who is inapt to use it and another person is shot or that a grave traffic accident occurs), and the likelihood of its materialisation.[50] In order to verify whether criminal legislation should be introduced in order to address a particular instance of remote harm, Andreas von Hirsch proposed the Standard Harm Analysis.[51] According to this three-step test, it is first necessary to analyse the gravity and the likelihood of the harm to occur; secondly, it is necessary to compare this analysis with the social value of the act, which would be criminalised, and the degree of limitation of liberty caused by such prohibition; thirdly, other side-constraints (side-effects) should be observed.[52]

Excessively risky decisions present certain qualities similar to remote harm. Being too daring in business decisions is in a sense akin to driving too dangerously, and setting a limit to it must take into account the same considerations, namely not to prevent economic activities from happening at all, similarly as it is necessary to allow effective traffic. At the same time, excessive risk, as will be demonstrated below, has aspects which mean that it approaches much closer to actual harm. It is thus possible to analyse the situations of excessive risk-taking under both categories: as actual materialised harm (including concrete risk of its occurrence), and situations of remote harm. One can imagine the legislator providing punishment for creating concrete danger to property, as well as prohibiting certain acts which, based on empirical generalisations, may be considered too risky and forbidden, including being subject to criminal punishment.

2.3. Theory of Legal Good (*Rechtsgut*)

The continental counterpart of the Anglo-Saxon theories is the theory of *Rechtsgut* (legal good).[53] The theory's beginnings are associated with the

[49] Simester and von Hirsch, *Crimes, Harms, and Wrongs* (n 2) 53 et seq; Feinberg, *Harm to Others* (n 35) 191.

[50] Feinberg, *Harm to Others* (n 35) 216. For discussion on problems related to overextension of the principle, see, eg Peršak, *Criminalising Harmful Conduct* (n 36) 41 et seq.

[51] Simester and von Hirsch, *Crimes, Harms, and Wrongs* (n 2) 54; Andrew von Hirsch, 'Extending the Harm Principle: "Remote" Harms and Fair Imputation' in AP Simester and ATH Smith (eds), *Harm and Culpability* (Oxford: Clarendon Press, 1996) 259–76, at 261.

[52] Simester and von Hirsch, *Crimes, Harms, and Wrongs* (n 2) 55.

[53] The translation of the term *Rechtsgut* is problematic (Carl Constantin Lauterwein, *The Limits of Criminal Law* (Ashgate, 2010) 6). The most common translation of this notion is 'legal good', while 'legal interest' or 'good-in-law' (Claus Roxin, 'The Legislation Critical Concept of Goods-in-law under Scrutiny' (2013) 3(1) *European Criminal Law Review* 3) can also be found in the literature. The expression 'legal good' is used here when referring to the German concept of *Rechtsgut* and the expression

nineteenth century German scholar Johann Michael Franz Birnbaum, and it was developed further by Karl Binding and generations of German scholars.[54] This theory spread into various countries whose penal systems developed under the influence of the German doctrine, for example, into Spain, Poland, as well as the Netherlands.[55] The account of the theory of legal good is presented here according to the German scholarship.

The theory of *Rechtsgut* is embedded in the theory of social contract and individual freedom.[56] According to this view, it is assumed that certain organs have the obligation to watch over the coexistence of members of a given society, the obligation granted by all members of this society by virtue of a contract (not in an historical but a conceptual sense). Their intervention should be limited to what is necessary to guarantee the positive coexistence of such members and respect their fundamental rights. Within this vision, the task of the criminal law is protecting legal goods.[57]

Whilst the German doctrine generally holds this to be the essential aim of criminal law, practically every other aspect of the theory is subject to debate, in particular the meaning of the term 'legal good'.[58] As to the understanding of this term, two main approaches can be distinguished, which are represented by two leading textbooks of German penal law: the positivist or descriptively-oriented approach, and the normative or critical approach.[59] The positivist (or descriptively-oriented) approach represented by the textbook of Jescheck and Weigend formulates the task of criminal law – protecting legal goods – and enumerates various of them, for instance: human life, bodily integrity, personal freedom of action and movement, but also property, assets, security of traffic,

'legal interest' when the analysis does not specifically refer to the German theory. For comparison of the two notions 'harm' and 'legal goods', see, eg Winfried Hassemer, 'The Harm Principle and the Protection of "Legal Goods" (*Rechtsgüterschutz*): A German Perspective' in AP Simester, Anthe du Bois-Pedain and Ulfrid Neumann, *Liberal Criminal Theory: Essays for Andreas von Hirsch* (Oxford/Portland, OR: Hart Publishing, 2014) 187–204.

[54] Markus Dirk Dubber, 'Theories of Crime and Punishment in German Criminal Law' (2005) 53(3) *American Journal of Comparative Law* 679, 686 et seq.

[55] Santiago Mir Puig, *Derecho Penal. Parte General*, 9th edn (Barcelona: Editorial Reppertor, 2011) 119; Włodzimierz Wróbel and Andrzej Zoll, *Polskie Prawo Karne. Część Ogólne* (Kraków: Znak, 2010) 40; Constantijn Kelk and Ferry de Jong, *Studieboek materieel strafrecht*, 5th edn (Deventer: Kluwer, 2013) 17 et seq. See also the analysis in Ferrajoli, *Derecho y razón* (n 29) 464 et seq.

[56] Roxin, *Strafrecht. Allgemeiner Teil* (n 17) 16 et seq.

[57] Ibid 16 et seq; see also Jescheck and Weigend, *Lehrbuch des Strafrechts* (n 13) 7.

[58] Ibid 7; Roxin, *Strafrecht. Allgemeiner Teil* (n 17) 14, 53; Lauterwein, *The Limits of Criminal Law* (n 53) 5; Dubber, 'Theories of Crime and Punishment in German Criminal Law' (n 54) 683. See also Armin Kaufmann, *Die Aufgabe des Strafrechts* (Westdeutscher Verlag, 1983) 5–21. For critical analysis of the common approach to legal goods, see Roxin, *Strafrecht. Allgemeiner Teil* (n 17) 47 et seq; Günther Jakobs, *Strafrecht. Allgemeiner Teil*, 2nd edn (Berlin/New York: Walter de Gruyter, 1993) 35 et seq; a thorough summary of the current discussion around the notion of legal good has been provided in Gerhard Seher, 'Prinzipiengestützte Strafnormlegitimation und der Rechtsgutsbegriff' in Roland Hefendehl, Andrew von Hirsch and Wolfgang Wohlers (eds), *Die Rechtgutstheorie: Legitimationsbasis des Strafrechts oder dogmatisches Glasperlenspiel?* (Baden-Baden: Nomos, 2003) 39–56.

[59] This differentiation after Dubber, 'Theories of Crime and Punishment in German Criminal Law' (n 54) 684 et seq, 688; Peršak, *Criminalising Harmful Conduct* (n 36) 107 et seq.

incorruptibility of public officials, etc.[60] The authors do not venture into providing a definition of legal good. The normative (or critical) approach is represented by Roxin.[61] Although he gives examples of legal goods, he also provides a definition of the term:

> Legal goods are conditions or chosen ends, which are essential either to the free development of the individual, the realisation of his fundamental rights and the functioning of the state system based on these objectives.[62]

The main difference between the two approaches concerns the source of existence and knowledge about the legal goods. The positivist approach deduces it from the text of the criminal law, while the normative approach looks for this source outside the criminal law text, for example, in the constitution (eg the German Basic Law).[63] This differentiation results in an unequal critical potential of the analysis of legal good(s) protected by concrete offences. The legal good extracted from the legal norm does not have any normative value in the sense that it cannot give any direction as to what criminalisation should be directed at, since it only deduces the intention of the legislator. Its application is limited to teleological interpretation of the norm[64] and to limited critical analysis of existing provisions. The latter analysis is based on the deduction of which legal good is protected by a given offence, and examines whether the offence is well designed to protect this legal good (eg if it is not too broad or the criminalised conduct is not sufficiently connected to the legal good it is supposed to protect), together with respecting other principles of criminal law (eg the *ultima ratio* principle).[65]

The approach of the normative school seems to offer more critical potential in this regard since it allows examining criminal law provisions from a perspective of legal goods enshrined outside the criminal law text. However, this perspective also encounters difficulties. Since the source of legal goods should be outside the criminal law, the main problem is where to look for them. If this is the constitution, then there may be a tendency to go beyond the text and look for them in its 'spirit' or similar less concrete concepts.[66] This might result in interpreting them from the law in general, thus limiting the critical potential of the notion.[67] Looking for *Rechtsgüter* in texts such as the constitution or international human rights

[60] Jescheck and Weigend, *Lehrbuch des Strafrechts* (n 13) 7.

[61] Dubber, 'Theories of Crime and Punishment in German Criminal Law' (n 54) 684.

[62] 'sind unter Rechtsgütern alle Gegebenheiten oder Zwecksetzungen zu verstehen, die für die freie Entfaltung des Einzelnen, die Verwirklichung seiner Grundrechte und das Funktionieren eines auf dieser Zielvorstellung aufbauenden staatlichen Systems notwendig sind.' Roxin, *Strafrecht. Allgemeiner Teil* (n 17) 16.

[63] Dubber, 'Theories of Crime and Punishment in German Criminal Law' (n 54) 688.

[64] Peršak, *Criminalising Harmful Conduct* (n 36) 107; Roxin, *Strafrecht. Allgemeiner Teil* (n 17) 15.

[65] Dubber, 'Theories of Crime and Punishment in German Criminal Law' (n 54) 691 et seq.

[66] Peršak, *Criminalising Harmful Conduct* (n 36) 108, who refers also to the criticism formulated in Claes Lernestedt, *Kriminalisering – Problem och Principer* [*Criminalisation – Problems and Principles*] (Uppsala: Iustus Förlag, 2003) 362 (cited in Peršak).

[67] Peršak, *Criminalising Harmful Conduct* (n 36) 108.

treaties carries the risk that some important legal goods are omitted in these sources, and that changes in social situation or perception are not incorporated therein as they emerge.[68]

Although it is the dominant view that the goal of criminal law is protecting legal goods, one of the greatest proponents of the *Rechtsgut* theory admits that their followers are on the defensive and that a general fatigue about this theory seems to be the overriding feeling.[69] Some authors prefer to speak about protected interests (*Interessen*) as more concrete, contrary to excessively abstract legal goods.[70] Also, the German Federal Constitutional Court, while examining the constitutionality of offences, prefers to concentrate on the principle of proportionality instead of analysing the protection of legal goods.[71] The problems of this theory were memorably summarised by Jareborg:

> Personally, I see the doctrines concerning Rechtsgüter as a blind alley; something must be wrong when almost 200 years of intensive intellectual activity seem to have resulted in more confusion than clarity.[72]

Despite these reservations, the theory of legal goods remains the main tool for the analysis and justification of criminalisation in Germany and other legal orders, which developed their penal law under this influence. Even if it cannot be treated as an apparatus that could solve all the problems of criminalisation, it still remains, depending on the approach adopted, a common platform to discuss the justification for using criminal law provisions, the scope of criminalisation or the interpretation of concrete provisions.[73]

Indeed, the theory is commonly used to interpret criminal provisions. The notion of legal good within the German doctrine is not only used to analyse the purposes of criminalisation, but also for analysing, inter alia, the following issues: interpretation of the scope of the offence; the problem of consent; self-defence; and the defence of necessity as justification.[74] Thus, the determination of the protected legal good has important consequences when defining the scope of liability for the offence. As to consent, it will determine whether it will have any effect on the criminal liability and who can grant it. For instance, if it is determined that the offence protects property, the owner may consent to acts detrimental to it. If, however, assets are protected (exclusively or also) for other reasons, as is the case regarding the offence of forgery (StGB, section 267), which aims at protecting a general (and not individual) legal good of purity of circulation of (documentary)

[68] Ibid 109.

[69] Roxin, *Strafrecht. Allgemeiner Teil* (n 17) 53.

[70] Weigend, 'Einleitung' (n 20) marginal nos 1–4, 7–8.

[71] Roxin, *Strafrecht. Allgemeiner Teil* (n 17) 40; Lauterwein, *The Limits of Criminal Law* (n 53) 21.

[72] Nils Jareborg, 'Criminalization as Last Resort (*Ultima Ratio*)' (2005) 2 *Ohio State Journal of Criminal Law* 521, 524.

[73] Lauterwein, *The Limits of Criminal Law* (n 53) 38 et seq; Dubber, 'Theories of Crime and Punishment in German Criminal Law' (n 54) 694 et seq.

[74] Lauterwein, *The Limits of Criminal Law* (n 53) 30 et seq.

evidence (*Reinheit des Beweisverkehrs*), the sole 'victim' of such an offence cannot give consent which would exculpate the perpetrator.[75] The choice of legal good also has procedural consequences as to the determination of who is the victim and thus of who is entitled to participate in the process as an aggrieved party.

Rechtsgüter can be divided into individual (*Individualrechtsgüter*) and universal (*Universalrechtsgüter*) or collective legal goods (*Kollektivrechtsgüter*).[76] Property is included into the first category.[77] The problem of this category is how far the protection of individual legal goods should go. As to collective legal goods, the category into which, for instance, the stability of the financial system would fall, the question whether legal goods can serve as limitations to excessive criminalisation is linked to the problem of the vagueness of said legal goods.[78] Roxin exemplifies this problem, referring to legal goods such as public health (*Volksgesundheit*) in cases of possession of drugs for private consumption and the efficiency of the insurance industry (*Leistungsfähigkeit des Versicherungswesens*) in cases of handing over of one's property with the intention of declaring it as stolen.[79] In fact, by one act of light drug consumption or because of one case of hiding property for the purposes of insurance abuse, neither public health nor the efficiency of the insurance industry is damaged or even endangered. Only a multitude of such acts can have this effect. Thus, some authors have proposed a category of *Kumulationsdelikte*, which would encompass criminalisation of acts which when perpetrated on a larger scale would affect the legal good.[80] This concept can, however, be criticised on the grounds that it criminalises acts '*ex iniuria tertii*'.[81]

In view of the goal of penal law, which according to this theory is safeguarding legal goods, a criminal provision may aim at punishing conduct that infringes certain legal good(s). It is also in agreement with this theory when the offence punishes only endangerment of a legal good. In this regard, there are two options. Either the offence punishes (concrete) endangerment of a legal good (*konkrete Gefährdungsdelikte*) or certain courses of conduct considered dangerous are forbidden although they do not mention the protected legal good, which stays

[75] Roxin, *Strafrecht. Allgemeiner Teil* (n 17) 556.

[76] Jescheck and Weigend, *Lehrbuch des Strafrechts* (n 13) 259; see also Roxin, *Strafrecht. Allgemeiner Teil* (n 17) 28 et seq.

[77] Jescheck and Weigend, *Lehrbuch des Strafrechts* (n 13) 259.

[78] Roxin, *Strafrecht. Allgemeiner Teil* (n 17) 37. One of the authors speaks about the 'dematerialisation of legal goods tendency': Matthias Krüger, *Die Entmaterialisierungstendenz beim Rechtsgutsbegriff* (Berlin: Duncker & Humblot, 2000).

[79] Roxin, *Strafrecht. Allgemeiner Teil* (n 17) 37.

[80] Lothar Kuhlen, 'Der Handlungserfolg der strafbaren Gewässerverunreinigung (§ 324 StGB)' (1986) *Goltdammer's Archiv für Strafrecht* 389; Wolfgang Wohlers, *Deliktstypen des Präventionsstrafrechts – zur Dogmatik "moderner" Gefährdungsdelikte* (Berlin: Duncker und Humblot, 2000), in particular 318. See also Roland Hefendehl, 'Das Rechtsgut als materialer Angelpunkt einer Strafnorm' in Roland Hefendehl, Andrew von Hirsch and Wolfgang Wohlers (eds), *Die Rechtgutstheorie: Legitimationsbasis des Strafrechts oder dogmatisches Glasperlenspiel?* (Baden-Baden: Nomos, 2003) 119–32, 126 and Roland Hefendehl, *Kollektive Rechtsgüter im Strafrecht* (Köln/Berlin/Bonn/Munich: Carl Heymanns Verlag, 2002).

[81] Roxin, *Strafrecht. Allgemeiner Teil* (n 17) 39.

in the background of criminalisation (*abstrakte Gefährdungsdelikte*).[82] This raises the question of how far the legislator can go in the criminal law protection of legal goods.

The discussion has related mainly to offences of abstract endangerment, where the nature of the protected legal good is not as such sharply formulated.[83] In certain constellations, the prohibited conduct may remain far from effectively attacking or endangering the protected legal good, as in the case of a drug dealer who promises to sell drugs but is unable to find a provider. In the opinion of Roxin, such use may not be justified in view of legal good theory,[84] as is also the case for courses of conduct criminalised in order to overcome difficulties of proof.[85]

New inspiration to the discussion came through the concept of 'risk society', analysed in particular by Ulrich Beck in his seminal work *Risikogesellschaft*.[86] Within the criminal law, this concept translated into the question of the extent to which the risk coming from different activities created by man (eg ecological, economic) can be prevented (or sanctioned) by means of criminal law. Some scholars claimed that it is difficult to combine prevention of such risks with the modern liberal criminal law based on the rule of law and it is rather more important to eliminate sources of risk.[87] While this might not always be possible, it is necessary to limit criminal law intervention to situations where the decision upon creation of a state of affairs, which entails the risk, can be attributed to an individual.[88] A more intense reaction to this phenomenon came from the scholars of the so-called Frankfurt school of criminal law, who suggested limiting the intervention of criminal law to the traditional core offences (focused on protecting individual legal interests) and leaving other problems to administrative or civil law.[89] This view was criticised from within the Frankfurt school in particular by Lüderssen, who objected to the above suggestions since it would create a true class criminal law ('*Klassensstrafrecht*'), where offenders of classical crimes such as

[82] Ibid 34 et seq.

[83] Ibid 35. The discussion is summarised in these two paragraphs according to Roxin's account.

[84] Ibid 35.

[85] Thomas Weigend, 'Bewältigung von Beweisschwierigkeiten durch Ausdehnung des materiellen Strafrechts?' in Kurt Schmoller (ed), *Festschrift für Otto Triffterer* (Vienna/New York: Springer, 1996) 695–712.

[86] Ulrich Beck, *Risikogesellschaft. Auf dem Weg in eine andere Moderne* (Frankfurt am Main: Suhrkamp, 1986); English version: *Risk Society: Towards a New Modernity* (Sage, 1992).

[87] Roxin, *Strafrecht. Allgemeiner Teil* (17) 36.

[88] Cornelius Prittwitz, *Strafrecht und Risiko* (Frankfurt am Main: Vittorio Klostermann, 1993) 384. One can imagine liability of the legal person if such individualisation is impossible, provided that the latter is not required in order to hold the company liable. As to the German law, see Klaus Tiedemann, *Wirtschaftstrafrecht. Einführung und Allgemeiner Teil mit wichtigen Rechtstexten*, 3rd edn (Carl Heymanns Verlag, 2010) 105 et seq.

[89] See, eg Winfried Hassemer, 'Kennzeichen und Krisen des modernen Strafrechts' (1992) *Zeitschrift für Rechtspolitik (ZRP)* 378, 381 et seq; Peter-Alexis Albrecht, 'Erosionen des rechtstaatlichen Strafrechts' (1993) 2 *Kritische Vierteljahresschrift für Gesetzgebung und Rechtswissenschaft (KritV)* 163, 180–82. See also Wolfgang Naucke, 'Schwerpunktverlagerung im Strafrecht' (1993) *KritV* 135.

theft would be punished by means of criminal law, and white-collar offences or crimes against the environment would be treated by less intrusive means.[90]

As part of the above-mentioned debate, some authors belonging to the Frankfurt school questioned the use of criminal law, in particular as regards white-collar offences.[91] Other authors, in particular Klaus Tiedemann and his circle, have defended the use of criminal law for this type of offences.[92]

2.4. Limits to Use of Criminal Law

2.4.1. Ultima Ratio *Principle and Principle of Proportionality*

The principle of *ultima ratio* (known also as *ultimum remedium* or last resort principle[93]) requires that, since criminal sanction is the most severe among the tools that the legislator has at its disposal, criminalisation should be used as the last resort in order to protect certain legal values or prevent certain conduct.[94] In practical terms, by virtue of this principle it needs to be verified whether criminal legislation is necessary to protect the legal interest in question, or whether it could be granted sufficient protection through civil or administrative law or other (even non-legal) means. It is one of the most 'classical' principles evoked abundantly in the textbooks and other criminal law literature,[95] although mainly of continental tradition.[96]

According to Ashworth, other mechanisms of social control ('morality, social convention, and peer pressure'), and within the law civil liability and administrative regulation should be prioritised before using criminal sanctions.[97] In Jareborg's

[90] Klaus Lüderssen, *Abschaffen des Strafens?* (Frankfurt am Main: Suhrkamp, 1995) 11. See also Roxin, *Strafrecht. Allgemeiner Teil* (n 17) 37.

[91] Michael Lindemann, *Voraussetzungen und Grenzen legitimen Wirtschaftsstrafrechts* (Tübingen: Mohr Siebeck, 2012) 19 et seq; Roxin, *Strafrecht. Allgemeiner Teil* (n 17) 36–37; Hassemer, 'Kennzeichen und Krisen' (n 89) 378.

[92] See, eg Tiedemann, *Wirtschaftstrafrecht. Einführung* (n 88) 17–18; Gerhard Dannecker, 'Der strafrechtliche Schutz des Wettbewerbs: Notwendigkeit und Grenzen einer Kriminalisierung von Kartellrechtsverstößen' (789–815) and Joachim Vogel, '"Vergabestrafrecht": Zur straf- und bußgeldrechtlichen Verantwortlichkeit öffentlicher Auftraggeber bei Verletzung des Vergaberechts' (817–36), both in Ulrich Sieber et al, *Strafrecht und Wirtschaftsstrafrecht – Dogmatik, Rechtsvergleich, Rechtstatsachen – Festschrift für Klaus Tiedemann zum 70. Geburtstag* (Köln: Carl Heymanns Verlag, 2008).

[93] Ashworth, *Principles of Criminal Law* (n 3) 32.

[94] Weigend, 'Einleitung' (n 20) marginal no 1; Nils Jareborg, 'Criminalization and the *Ultima Ratio* Principle' in Magnus Ulväng and Iain Cameron, *Essays on Criminalization and Sanction* (Iustus, 2014) 23–38, at 25.

[95] Ibid 26 (see abundant bibliographical references in note 3 of this article); Peršak, *Criminalising Harmful Conduct* (n 36) 121; Weigend, 'Einleitung' (n 20) marginal no 1; Georges Levasseur, 'Le problème de la dépénalisation' (1983) 6 *Archives de politique criminelle* 53, 53 et seq.

[96] Douglas Husak, 'Applying *Ultima Ratio*: A Skeptical Assessment' (2005) 2 *Ohio State Journal of Criminal Law* 535.

[97] Ashworth, *Principles of Criminal Law* (n 3) 32.

view, the point of departure is a presumption that the state should not intervene. If such intervention is considered necessary, it must first take the form of 'aid, support, care, insurance and license arrangements' followed, only where necessary, by coercive measures prioritising private law sanction, administrative sanctions and ultimately by using criminal sanctions.[98] In fact, such an approach to *ultima ratio* raises it to a general principle of legislation.[99]

The principle is also connected to other aspects of criminal law, namely its subsidiarity: it should play only a subsidiary role in protecting legal interests, ceding priority to other branches of law (civil or administrative);[100] and its 'fragmentary character', meaning that protection granted by criminal law is selective, sanctioning only the gravest infringements of the protected legal interests.[101] It should lead to efficient and parsimonious use of criminal law in order to avoid its excessiveness, but also that its impact does not suffer through inflation of criminal sanctions.[102] Its roots can be found in tendencies to make criminal law more humane and in utilitarianism.[103]

In some legal systems, the principle is interpreted from the rules of the constitution (Germany),[104] in some others it can be found in the criminal codes (Slovenia, Croatia).[105] It has been also evoked in the jurisprudence of the European Court of Human Rights.[106] The addressee of the principle is the

[98] Jareborg, 'Criminalization as Last Resort' (n 72) 524.

[99] Peršak, *Criminalising Harmful Conduct* (n 36) 123.

[100] Roxin, *Strafrecht. Allgemeiner Teil* (n 17) 45.

[101] Jescheck and Weigend, *Lehrbuch des Strafrechts* (n 13) 52; Jareborg, 'Criminalization as Last Resort' (n 72) 525.

[102] Weigend, 'Einleitung' (n 20) marginal no 1.

[103] Samuel Pufendorf, *De Jure Naturae et Gentium Libri Octo* (Translation of the 1688 ednby CH Oldfather and WA Oldfather (New York: Oceana Publications, 1964), Bk 8, ch III: on the power of supreme sovereignty over the lives and fortunes of citizens, which arises by reason of their crimes, see 1158–228 (marginal nos 790–838), in particular 1188 et seq (marginal no 811 et seq); Cesare Beccaria, *Über Verbrechen und Strafen* (Leipzig, Verlag von Wilhelm Engelmann, 1905) 67 et seq; Voltaire, *Commentaire sur le Livre des Délits et des Peines* (Genève, 1767) eg ch XIX ('Du Suicide'); Voltaire, *Prix de la Justice et de l'humanité* (London, 1777) eg art 1; Jeremy Bentham, *An Introduction to the Principles of Morals and Legislation* (Athlone Press, University of London, 1970) ch XIII ('Cases Unmeet for Punishment'), 158–64. See also Ferrajoli, *Derecho y razón* (n 29) 465 et seq, who talks about the principle of necessity '*principio de necesidad*'; Arthur Kaufmann, 'Subsidiaritätsprinzip und Strafrecht' in Claux Roxin et al (eds), *Grundfragen der Gesamten Strafrechtswissenschaft, Festschrift für Heinrich Henkel* (Berlin/New York: Walter de Gruyter, 1974) 89–107; Cornelius Prittwitz, 'Die deutsche Strafrecht: Fragmentarisch? Subsidiär? Ultima ratio?' in Institut für Kriminalwissenschaften Frankfurt am Main (eds), *Vom unmöglichen Zustand des Strafrechts* (Frankfurt am Main et al: Peter Lang, 1995) 387–405.

[104] BVerfGE (15 December 1965) NJW 1966, 243; Mike Wienbracke, 'Der Verhältnismäßigkeitsgrundsatz' (2003) *Zeitschrift für das Juristische Studium (ZJS)* 148.

[105] Peršak, *Criminalising Harmful Conduct* (n 36) 121. See also art VIII of the Declaration of the Rights of Man and of the Citizen (*Déclaration des Droits de l'Homme et du Citoyen*, 1789): 'La Loi ne doit établir que des peines *strictement et évidemment nécessaires*, et nul ne peut être puni qu'en vertu d'une Loi établie et promulguée antérieurement au délit, et légalement appliquée' (emphasis added).

[106] Peršak, *Criminalising Harmful Conduct* (n 36) 122.

legislator, and it can be called the 'principle of legislative ethics'.[107] The principle is also known in the common law tradition, although it is much less recognised.[108]

Within the German legal system, the Federal Constitutional Court recognises the principle of proportionality (*Verhältnismäßigkeitprinzip*),[109] which is not only used to analyse the constitutionality of criminal law legislation, but of any legislation. Since it is a constitutional principle, the Federal Constitutional Court can annul laws which do not fulfil its criteria.[110] The principle is rooted in the Rule of Law (*Rechtsstaatsprinzip*), interpreted from various provisions of the German Constitution (Basic Law), and the idea behind it is that the state should not use its power in an 'unlimited and arbitrary' manner.[111] Nevertheless, many authors consider that the principle of proportionality plays a rather limited role in restraining the legislator's leeway to enact criminal provisions.[112] This scepticism has been reinforced after the judgment of the Federal Constitutional Court confirming the constitutionality of the criminalisation of incest between siblings.[113] This feeling has been expressed by Prittwitz:

> The *Ultima ratio* character of criminal law is equally often normatively adjured by criminal law theory as it is empirically refuted by the criminal policy.[114]

In contrast with the continental tradition, in the common law countries *ultima ratio* does not have the value of principle, and it is also not put into practice in criminalisation.[115] Criminal law is used not only for the gravest attacks on

[107] Jareborg, 'Criminalization as Last Resort' (n 72) 521. The Manifesto on European Criminal Policy also recognised it as one of the principles that should govern the criminal law legislation of the European Union. European Criminal Policy Initiative, 'A Manifesto on European Criminal Policy' (2009) *Zeitschrift für Internationale Strafrechtsdogmatik (ZIS)* 707.

[108] Andrew Ashworth is one of the main supporters of the principle (within his proposed 'minimalist approach'), see Ashworth, *Principles of Criminal Law* (n 3) 31 et seq. Sometimes its requirements are incorporated without making reference to it as to a 'principle', as eg in Simester et al, *Simester and Sullivan's Criminal Law* (n 5) 658 et seq.

[109] BVerfGE (15 December 1965) NJW 1966, 243.

[110] Roxin, *Strafrecht. Allgemeiner Teil* (n 17) 47.

[111] Wienbracke, 'Der Verhältnismäßigkeitsgrundsatz' (n 104) 148; Michael Bohlander, *Principles of German Criminal Law* (Oxford/Portland, OR: Hart Publishing, 2009) 24.

[112] Roxin, *Strafrecht. Allgemeiner Teil* (n 17) 46 et seq.

[113] Wolfgang Joecks, 'Einleitung' in Bernd von Heintschel-Heinegg (ed), *Münchener Kommentar zum Strafgesetzbuch*, vol 1, §§ 1–37 StGB, 2nd edn (CH Beck, 2011) marginal no 22; Bettina Noltenius, 'Grenzenloser Spielraum des Gesetzesgebers im Strafrecht? Kritische Bemerkungen zur Inzestentscheidung des Bundesverfassungsgerichts vom 26. Februar 2008' (2009) *Zeitschrift für das Juristische Studium (ZJS)* 15.

[114] Cornelius Prittwitz, 'Strafrecht als Propria Ratio' in Manfred Heinrich, Christian Jäger, Bernd Schünemann et al (eds), *Strafrecht als Scientia Universalis Festschrift für Claus Roxin zum 80. Geburtstag am 15. Mai 2011* (De Gruyter, 2011) 23: 'Der *Ultima Ratio*-Charakter des Strafrechts ist ebenso oft von der Strafrechtswissensschaft normativ beschworen wie von der Kriminalpolitik *empirisch* widerlegt worden' (emphasis in original).

[115] Husak, 'Applying *Ultima Ratio*' (n 96) 535; Simester and von Hirsch, *Crimes, Harms, and Wrongs* (n 2) 18. For criticism of the principle in the German literature, see, eg Bernhard Haffke, 'Symbolische Gesetzgebung? Das Wirtschaftsstrafrecht in der Bundesrepublik Deutschland' (1991) *KritV* 165, and 439.

values or interests, but also for relatively minor infringements.[116] Critics point to at least two main reasons for denying the criminal law the status of *ultima ratio* and preferring (or adding) criminalisation to other methods of state intervention (eg administrative). First, criminal law has the stigmatisation aspect, which other branches of law do not provide (or at least not to the same degree). While this is often seen as an argument in favour of granting the criminal law the status of *ultima ratio*, one could argue that the legislator may deem stigmatisation necessary for regulating certain conduct, which only criminal law can provide.[117] Secondly, in the case of enforcement through public agencies or prosecution offices, it may be more practicable to use criminal law, for example, in cases where material damages may be too small for the victim to afford the costs of a civil procedure, or where there is either a lack of concrete victims, or a very large number of them.[118]

2.4.2. Legality Principle and Fair Warning Principle

The principle of legality provides that no course of conduct can be declared criminal or no punishment may be pronounced without a legal basis. It is expressed by the Latin sentence *nullum crimen sine lege* and is considered 'the most basic, the most classical, the most elementary criminal legal principle on the Continent'.[119] It is enshrined in Article 7 of the European Convention on Human Rights (ECHR), with abundant jurisprudence of the European Court of Human Rights (ECtHR).[120] The principle is composed of several requirements, *nullum crimen sine lege scripta, stricta, preavia, certa* and *nulla poena sine lege*,[121] out of which the requirement of certainty will be the most relevant for the purposes of this chapter.

In view of the jurisprudence on ECHR, Article 7(1), the '*nullum crimen sine lege certa*' requirement entails that: 'an offence must be clearly defined in law'. This condition is satisfied 'where the individual can know from the wording of the relevant provision and, if need be, with the assistance of the courts' interpretation of it, what acts and omissions will make him liable.'[122] It means that the precision

[116] Ashworth, *Principles of Criminal Law* (n 3) 17.

[117] Husak, 'Applying *Ultima Ratio*' (n 96) 538.

[118] Simester and von Hirsch, *Crimes, Harms, and Wrongs* (n 2) 197 et seq.

[119] Peršak, *Criminalising Harmful Conduct* (n 36) 119. See also Gerhard Dannecker, 'Nullum crimen, nulla poena sine lege und seine Geltung im Allgemeinen Teil des Strafrechts' in Gerhard Dannecker (et al), *Festschrift für Harro Otto* (Köln/Berlin/Munich: Carl Heymanns Verlag, 2007) 25–40, at 25, and Ferrajoli, *Derecho y razón* (n 29) 34, 93, 373. The latter author points out that the law should not be formulated in such an elastic and open way that it would allow so broad an interpretation of it as to attribute liability to any kind of act, which would demonstrate the perpetrator's 'bad character' (376); see also Markus Dirk Dubber, 'Comparative Criminal Law' in Mathias Reimann and Reinhard Zimmermann, *The Oxford Handbook of Comparative Law* (Oxford University Press, 2006/2008) 1287–325, at 1313–18.

[120] Christoph Grabenwarter, *European Convention on Human Rights: Commentary* (CH Beck/Hart/Nomos/Helbing Lichtenhahn Verlag, 2014) 171 et seq.

[121] Peršak, *Criminalising Harmful Conduct* (n 36) 119.

[122] *Kokkinakis v Greece*, Application no 14307/88, EctHR, Judgment of 25 May 1993, para [52].

of the provision is assessed also taking into account the relevant case-law.[123] 'Furthermore, a law may still satisfy the requirement of "foreseeability" where the person concerned has to take appropriate legal advice to assess, to a degree that is reasonable in the circumstances, the consequences which a given action may entail.'[124] This interpretation has recently been repeated in the case *Contrada v Italy*.[125] In view of ECHR, Article 7(1), criminal law provisions are to be 'understandable, predictable and not vague'.[126]

The principle is recognised by the legal orders of the countries which are party to the ECHR.[127] It is enshrined as part of the principle of legality in article 103(2) of the German Basic Law and StGB, section 1 (*Bestimmtheitsgebot*)[128] and follows from articles 34 and 37 of the French Constitution, together with article VIII of the Declaration of the Rights of Man and of the Citizen (1789) and French Penal Code, article 111-3.[129] In the Anglo-Saxon tradition it is known as the principle of maximum certainty[130] or as the rule of 'fair warning' (these terms will be used interchangeably).[131]

There are several reasons for the importance of this principle. First, it should guarantee that every individual is able to foresee what kind of conduct may lead to punishment and direct his behaviour in such a manner as to avoid criminal liability.[132] This necessarily implies that the legislator treats citizens as rational and autonomous individuals capable of steering their behaviour.[133] Secondly, it prevents law enforcement agencies from having too much discretion in interpreting the law and thus from having excessive power in enforcing criminal

[123] Similar approach can be also found in national legal orders, eg in Germany, see Gerhard Dannecker, '§1 Keine Strafe ohne Gesetz' in Heinrich Wilhelm Laufhütte, Ruth Rissing-van Saan and Klaus Tiedemann, *Strafgesetzbuch. Leipziger Kommentar*, vol 1, Einleitung; §§ 1 bis 31, 12th edn (Berlin/New York: De Gruyter, 2007) marginal no 201; Volker Krey, *Keine Strafe ohne Gesetz* (Berlin/New York: De Gruyter, 1983) 126 et seq.

[124] *Kafkaris v Cyprus*, Application no 21906/04, ECtHR, Judgment of 12 February 2008, para [140].

[125] *Contrada v Italy (No 3)*, Application no 66655/13, EctHR, Judgment of 14 April 2015, para [60].

[126] Simester and von Hirsch, *Crimes, Harms, and Wrongs* (n 2) 199.

[127] Similarly to the *ultima ratio* principle, the Manifesto on European Criminal Policy recommends also that the criminal law legislation of the European Union fulfil the requirement of legal certainty in such a way that 'criminal law provisions must define offences in a strict and unambiguous way': 'A Manifesto on European Criminal Policy' (n 107) 708.

[128] Roxin, *Strafrecht. Allgemeiner Teil* (n 17) 139.

[129] Pradel, *Droit pénal général* (n 17) 128.

[130] Ashworth, *Principles of Criminal Law* (n 3) 63.

[131] Simester and von Hirsch, *Crimes, Harms, and Wrongs* (n 2) 198; Simester et al, *Simester and Sullivan's Criminal Law* (n 5) 26. The rule is also known in the United States: US Supreme Court, *Kolender v Lawson*, 461 US 352 (1983) and in Canada: Supreme Court of Canada, *Re ss 193 and 195.1(1)(c) of the Criminal Code (Man)* [1990] 1 SCR 1123. See also US Supreme Court, *Connally v General Construction Co*, 269 US 385, 391 (1926): 'a statute which either forbids or requires the doing of an act in terms so vague that men of common intelligence must necessarily guess at its meaning and differ as to its application violates the first essential of due process of law'. These three cases and the quotation mentioned also in Ashworth, *Principles of Criminal Law* (n 3) 63, 66.

[132] Jescheck and Weigend, *Lehrbuch des Strafrechts* (n 13) 137; BVerfG (15 March 1978) NJW 1978, 1423, 1423.

[133] Ashworth, *Principles of Criminal Law* (n 3) 65.

law.[134] It follows also from the rules of the separation of powers and the principle of democracy, since it is the task of the legislative branch to enact criminal law provisions.[135]

The requirement of legal certainty concerns the limbs of *actus reus* as well as that of *mens rea*.[136] It is not absolute and requires the maximum possible precision, but a certain degree of imprecision may be necessary in order for the law to be workable.[137] It is sometimes necessary that the law use abstract terms. Otherwise it would become too casuistic and potentially unable to cover all kinds of behaviour targeted and adapt to changing conditions.[138] It would also result in provisions being very complicated, cumbersome and difficult to understand.[139] Technical or open-ended terms, although not sufficiently clear for the average citizen, may be clear for persons whom the offence targets, for example, as regards white-collar offences.[140] As to the use of evaluative terms (eg 'reasonable', 'dishonest', etc), the legislator should use them with moderation and avoid doing so whenever possible.[141] It is in particular acceptable where the term is merely part of a definition of an offence comprising several other sufficiently defining elements.[142] It does not mean, however, that such terms have no meaning, since they also provide certain indications as to the expected behaviour.[143]

A principle linked with the requirement of maximum certainty or fair warning is the requirement of fair labelling, which is demanded sometimes in the scholarship.[144] It consists in expecting from the legislator that the law reflect the differences in harms and wrongs and the type of wrongdoing according to general perceptions.[145] On the one hand, proper labelling and dividing into categories should allow for the provision of gradual punishment reflecting the degree of law-breaking.[146] On the other, it is important in connection with the communicative function of criminal law. Namely, if criminal law is to deliver the message, both to the offender and to the public, of 'what is wrong', this message ought to reflect precisely what it is that is wrong about a concrete course of conduct. This goal should be achieved also by differentiating between various types of criminal

[134] Ibid 65.

[135] Volker Krey and Robert Esser, *Deutsche Strafrecht. Allgemeiner Teil*, 4th edn (Stuttgart: Verlag W Kohlhammer, 2011) 41.

[136] Dannecker, '§1 Keine Strafe ohne Gesetz' (n 123) marginal no 197.

[137] Ibid marginal no 183; Grabenwarter, *European Convention on Human Rights* (n 120) 180; Simester and von Hirsch, *Crimes, Harms, and Wrongs* (n 2) 201.

[138] *Kokkinakis v Greece*, Application no 14307/88, EctHR, Judgment of 25 May 1993, para [40].

[139] Ashworth, *Principles of Criminal Law* (n 3) 66.

[140] Grabenwarter, *European Convention on Human Rights* (n 120) 180 et seq; *Soros v France*, Application no 50425/06, EctHR, Judgment of 6 October 2011, paras [53] and [59].

[141] Simester and von Hirsch, *Crimes, Harms, and Wrongs* (n 2) 200.

[142] *Hashman and Harrup v United Kingdom*, Application no 25594/94, EctHR, Judgment of 25 November 1999, para [39].

[143] Simester and von Hirsch, *Crimes, Harms, and Wrongs* (n 2) 200.

[144] Ashworth, *Principles of Criminal Law* (n 3) 78.

[145] Ibid 78.

[146] Ibid 78.

conduct and avoiding overly-broad or all-encompassing provisions, where the prohibited wrong would not be clearly identifiable.[147]

3. Criminalisation of Excessive Risk-Taking by Managers?

The starting point of the analysis is that limited liability companies (of different form, private and public) have their own assets, which belong to them and not to the shareholders. The original founders of the company equipped the company with certain property and capital, which is further developed (or lost) over the course of the life of the company. The property of the company is no longer the property of the shareholders, whose ownership is limited to the shares they have and the rights enjoyed through those shares. This is linked with a basic feature of modern companies: the division of management and ownership. Contrary to partnerships, which tend to be more a form of cooperation between two or more persons in pursuing their activities, companies are managed by professional managers, with the investors as shareholders not having direct influence on the daily management, except the rights executed at general meetings. It is not excluded that shareholders take functions in the management, but even in such cases, they manage the assets of the company and not their own.

Moreover, the liability of a company is necessarily limited to its assets and its members (shareholders) are limited to their investment. This means that creditors of every kind have an interest in its sound functioning, since, if it collapses, they can recover their debts only to a limited extent. The liability of shareholders is limited to their shares, but they may lose their investment in the event of bad management.

So, the first element of the picture is that companies are legal persons with their own assets, which are entrusted to the management. The counterpart of the fact that these assets are entrusted is that management has a duty to use these assets for the benefit of the company. The assets of the company and the right to make use of them (in legal terms or making 'physical' use), as well as making binding agreements in the name of the company, are given to them so that they use it for the company to profit.

The task of running the company is necessarily not limited to the head management, usually described by the provisions of company law. Their powers are delegated to other employees, who use the assets of the company in order to achieve its objectives. Some of these employees make only determined use, eg operating a machine. Others are given a certain discretion/liberty within which they can use the assets or make binding agreements for the company. These are middle or lower level managers, although they are not directly concerned with the rules of company law.

[147] Simester and von Hirsch, *Crimes, Harms, and Wrongs* (n 2) 202.

In all decisions these managers take, they should have the prosperity of the company in mind. In order to make the company profit, they need to take decisions as to the use of the assets and agreements they make in the name of the company, which necessarily entail a lower or higher element of risk as to success.[148] Before taking such decisions, a more or less complicated risk assessment must be carried out, depending on the type and context of the decision.[149] This quality of decisions will depend on many more or less measureable factors, including the capacities and talents of the manager.

Another aspect of the fact that managers can take decisions which have an impact on the assets of the company is that they have the ability to abuse such powers. Therefore, there is a potential conflict between the discretion/liberty the manager needs to be able to make the company thrive and the possibilities to misuse this discretion/liberty against the interests of the company. Furthermore, the manager may also disregard rules of due diligence or otherwise unintentionally expose the company to excessive risk.

There are two aspects of an excessively risky decision which may influence the decision on criminal liability. First, it is necessary to find criteria which determine whether a decision is indeed excessively risky. These will be laid down outside criminal law, in legal acts describing the manager's duties, standards, practices or any other sources applicable to determine how the manager should perform his duties. The second aspect concerns whether the manager actually knew that the decision was too risky, or was aware that it might be so.

Furthermore, an excessively risky decision may have an impact, besides the company, on different types of persons more or less connected with the company. These persons may be shareholders or stakeholders (creditors, employees, the state as the tax collector, clients). Finally, excessively risky decision(s) leading to a failure of a company on the greatest scale may even have an impact on the economy as a whole, even globally.

All these aspects may possibly influence the choice and details of different legal tools used to regulate the duties and powers of managers and their relationship towards the company and the stakeholders, from soft law and self-regulation to the use of the most serious, which is criminal law. It results also that different legal interests are at stake: individual (of the shareholders and the stakeholders) or collective (of the community in which the company operates, of the state or

[148] In company law, if the manager's decision turns out to be disadvantageous for the company, but was taken in its interest and according to certain standards, they are protected by the business judgment rule. See also in this context Markus Adick, *Organuntreue (§ 266 StGB) und Business Judgment. Die strafrechtliche Bewertung unternehmerischen Handelns unter Berücksichtigung von Verfahrensregeln* (Peter Lang, 2010) in particular 70–127.

[149] On risk management, see, eg Brian Coyle, *Risk Awareness and Corporate Governance* (Financial World Publishing, 2002); Paul Hopkin, *Fundamentals of Risk Management*, Institute of Risk Management (London/Philadelphia, PA/New Delhi: Kogan Page Ltd, 2010); Oliviero Roggi and Edward Altman (eds), *Managing and Measuring Risk: Emerging Global Standards and Regulation After the Financial Crisis* (Singapore: World Scientific Publishing, 2013).

the interest in the well-functioning economic system). Against this background, the following sections will analyse the features which will determine the scope of possible criminal liability in the context described above and on the basis of which such criminalisation will be proposed in the concluding chapter.

3.1. Moral Wrongfulness

3.1.1. *Applicable Wrongs*

This section is based on the highly influential analysis of moral wrongfulness[150] in white-collar offences carried out by Stuart P Green.[151] Although the categorisation used here comes from Green's book, the author remains fully responsible for the details of the ensuing analysis. Green tackles the question of moral wrong from a non-consequentialist or deontological perspective, ie looking for some violation of a moral duty as such, and not regarded merely by its consequences.[152] Among the moral wrongs he enumerates, the following seem to be the most relevant when discussing excessive risk-taking: cheating, disloyalty and the breaking of promises.[153]

Green understands cheating in the following way:

> in order … to say that X has cheated, X must (1) violate a fair and fairly enforced rule, (2) with the intent to obtain an advantage over a party with whom he is in a cooperative, rule-bound relationship.[154]

Rules should be fair, prescriptive (not merely depicting reality), mandatory, and part of a 'cooperative rule-governed relationship', whilst their breach must be intentional.[155]

This approach does not require that X acted covertly or with deception. Green rightly points out that one might cheat overtly, ie in a way that others can see that one is cheating. As to deception, he uses an example of a car driver who, instead of waiting in the line in traffic, uses the emergency lane, thus openly cheating the other drivers who wait according to the rules.[156] Whereas this argument is convincing as regards lack of secrecy, it might be doubted as regards deception. One might claim that the law-abiding drivers are deceived – in a sense misled, made to believe something which is not true – insofar as they believe that all other drivers will also obey the rule. Understood this way, cheating always involves an

[150] Wrongfulness is understood here as comprising both the conduct (and sometimes its result) and the perpetrator's state of mind. The problem of individual blameworthiness is not analysed here.

[151] Green, *Lying, Cheating, and Stealing* (n 15).

[152] Ibid 39.

[153] The others being: deception, stealing, coercion, exploitation and disobedience.

[154] Green, *Lying, Cheating, and Stealing* (n 15) 57.

[155] Ibid 63 et seq.

[156] Ibid 57.

element of deception. Hence, bearing this in mind, there is no need to change the above definition.

In order to verify if the problem of cheating applies to the cases of excessive risk-taking by managers in companies, three questions need to be asked. First, what kind of rule would they need to break in order to be considered cheats? Second, with whom are they in a 'cooperative rule-governed relationship'? And third, against whom do they want to gain an advantage?

As to the first question, the assumption of cheating is a situation of interaction between two or more actors who are also engaged in some form of competition with each other. In this sense, two sportsmen compete for one prize. But this competition need not take the form of a win-lose situation. Students compete for good marks, but the fact that one received them often does not diminish the other's chances. However, both should observe the rules of the exams and if one disregards them, he cheats. Similarly in a contract, two sides can make a fairly good bargain. In all these situations, the rules the parties observe are supposed to give them a common ground of equal chances of success, and curb, if necessary, tendencies to unbalance this relationship. The relationship between the managers and the company or the shareholders presents these features only to a certain extent. The managers do not compete with the company in the above sense, but they are supposed to act for its benefit. At the same time, however, the corporate environment provides opportunities to abuse such positions held by managers as regards the assets of the company, at the expense of the company, shareholders and stakeholders, and there are rules that should limit these tendencies.

As to the second question, the managers are at the same time in the stated relationship with different stakeholders: the company, shareholders, employees, creditors, the state, etc. With all these groups, their relationships are different, as are the possibilities of cheating. The question of managing the entrusted assets in a way which represents the interests of those by whom those assets were entrusted, and in particular does not expose them to excessive danger, is a question of the relationship with the company and its shareholders. Here, different rules on the duties of managers as regards the shareholders and the company, including their fiduciary duties and standards of care, prescribe how the former ought to act. When they start using the assets of the company against these rules and to their own benefit, they start to cheat the company and the shareholders. Besides these stakeholders, one can claim, that by entering the economic system, managers subscribe also to certain rules, which are supposed to guarantee the correct functioning of this system.

The third question, besides the considerations set out in the previous paragraph, requires reflecting whether cheating concerns also cheating for the benefit of the company or shareholders. Examples of such behaviour were already seen in the context of the national legal orders analysed in the previous chapters. The question here would be what is morally wrong in, for example, bribing a public official in order to obtain a contract for the company or avoiding taxes. First, it is rather unlikely that such acts are carried out without any private interest of the manager (salary increase, bonus, position within the company). On the contrary, if a person is pressured to perform such acts against his will, although up to a certain point it may be considered neglect of duties towards the company for convenience (eg not losing the job), heightened levels of duress may diminish (or negate entirely) that person's liability. Secondly, even if the company (and possibly the shareholders) is meant to profit, it is still exposed by such acts to risk to which it should not be exposed. If this is the case, then even by bringing profit to the company, the manager is breaking his duty of care, since managers are expected to make the company thrive according to the rules, without exposing it to abnormal risk, which, if materialised, may bring much graver consequences than the expected benefit (in terms of sanctions, loss or reputation, etc). Therefore, the manager is still gaining advantage at the expense of the company.

Another type of moral wrong to be considered here is disloyalty. Although it might be tempting to present disloyalty as a general feature of white-collar crime, it is to be understood in a particular context where someone (principal) entrusts (partly) to another (agent) his assets in the pursuit of his interests.[157] This situation results in a duty of loyalty, which 'creates in one a prima facie obligation to act *in the best interests* of a particular person or cause, even when doing so would be against one's own self-interest'.[158] Loyalty can be also described as a 'rejection of alternatives that undermine the principal bond'.[159] Disloyalty is thus when one neglects the interests of the principal by pursuing self-interest in choosing alternatives which are not in accordance with the principal bond.

A typical case of agent-principal relationship is the situation of managers, to whom the assets of the companies, and indirectly the investment of the shareholders, are entrusted. The trust, which is allocated to the person of the manager, is equalled by his duty of loyalty towards the company, in the sense that he must pursue the goals of the company and not his own, while managing in the interests of the company. Loyalty demands that even if a golden opportunity arises, he must abstain from pursuing it if it is at the cost of the company's interests.

The problem of acting contrary to the interests of the company may be analysed also under the moral issue of promise-breaking, since the manager would normally be bound by a contractual relationship with the company stipulating that he has to act to the company's benefit and to avoid harm. This relationship seems, however, to be sufficiently and better addressed by the problem of disloyalty. Simple promise-breaking might arguably be considered less morally wrong than disloyalty.[160]

The exact definition and delimitation of these moral categories of wrongdoing may be subject to debate. In this regard, two points need to be made. On the

[157] Susan P Shapiro, 'Collaring the Crime, Not the Criminal: Reconsidering the Concept of White-Collar Crime' (1990) 55(3) *American Sociological Review* 346, 350.

[158] Green, *Lying, Cheating, and Stealing* (n 15) 99.

[159] George P. Fletcher, *Loyalty: An Essay on the Morality of Relationships* (New York: Oxford University Press, 1993) 8.

[160] Green, *Lying, Cheating, and Stealing* (n 15) 110.

one hand, it might be tempting to reduce certain or all categories of moral wrong to one, for example, stealing or exploitation, which may, however, blur the image of wrongdoing, and prevent a proper assessment of the gravity of wrong and lose the subtleties of such an assessment.[161] On the other hand, the exact naming of certain categories of moral wrong is less relevant than grasping its core '*malum*'. And the above analysis points out two major elements: the breaking of a rule and making one's interests prevail over those of others.

One more issue which may be raised in the context of such analysis is whether not obeying the law is as such immoral. However, solving this complex issue cannot bring forward the analysis here for the following reasons. To consider that there is no moral obligation to obey the law would in any case result in the need to look for a moral justification for criminalisation, among other potential premises. If it is considered that a breach of law is as such immoral, it cannot give guidance on the scope of criminalisation, since it would lead to a conclusion that every breach of law ought to be a criminal offence. If, as it is assumed here, criminal law should contain a certain moral reprobation, it must go beyond simple breach of a legal rule.

In this context, it might be useful to examine the five cases which were presented in the introductory chapter and studied within the national systems. The first two cases consist in disrespecting the rules according to which the loans should be granted. In both cases, the wrongfulness consists in disloyalty towards the bank, since instead of acting in the best interests of the bank, the perpetrator grants the credit contrary to the rules. The fact that he hopes that it would eventually turn out to be beneficial for the bank is irrelevant inasmuch as he knows that the conditions of the loan are detrimental for the bank. In addition, in the way it is formulated in the second case, he pursues his own interest (a bonus), which aggravates the disloyalty and may also present a form of cheating.

Similarly, cases 3 and 4 will also constitute a form of disloyalty. The perpetrator is not acting in pursuit of (evident) personal interest. However, he is not acting in the best interests of the company, which he is supposed to do. In both cases, he exposes the company to a risk of loss to which it should not be exposed, either by using the money in an abnormal way (for this type of company), or by allowing a situation in which the company may suffer the costs of being forced to call back the cars for repairs.

As to the fifth case, it includes an act of bribery, which may be wrongful as such (however, the analysis of moral wrongfulness of corruption remains outwith the topic of this book). Although the perpetrator's act of corruption is meant to bring benefit to the company, it exposes it to an unnecessary risk of negative consequences if discovered, thereby constituting yet another case of disloyalty. It might also be a case of cheating, if the perpetrator acted in order to be rewarded for bringing a new contract to the company, if one could say that the rule is that

[161] Ibid 127–28.

managers should gain new contracts in legal ways only and that is what they are rewarded for. In this case, he breaches this rule in order to obtain his reward.

3.1.2. Wrongfulness in the Analysed Offences

The analysis in the previous section demonstrated that two types of moral wrongfulness would be relevant for excessive risk-taking in managing the company: cheating and disloyalty. Both of these aspects are reflected in the offences analysed in the chapters on national legal orders. Already the names of the offences reflect the moral wrongs, which underlie the criminalisation provided in these systems. Interestingly, the English system includes the offence of (fraud by) abuse of position in the Fraud Act 2006, which could be considered unusual from the point of view of the continental tradition, where fraud and abuse of trust tend to be separated (Germany, France, and also Poland, Spain). However, this terminology in fact reflects the double moral nature of the offence. Fraud reveals an aspect of cheating and whereas its most classical form (fraud by false representation) involves presenting untrue or misleading facts (so deception), other sections (Fraud Act 2006, sections 3 and 4) do not require that element. Section 4 requires that the person abuse the position: that he use this position in breach of certain rules stipulating how the position should be used and that he do so for his benefit. The problem concerns what is morally wrong with misusing the position of trust in order to cause loss or expose to the risk of loss, since the element of self-interest is less present. The answer is not in cheating (although certain scenarios would probably also allow admitting this), but in disloyalty. The position required in section 4 creates a relationship of trust, which is defined at its minimum by the act: 'to safeguard, or not to act against, the financial interests of another person'. Thus, a person is committing a moral wrong of disloyalty when he acts in breach of this obligation, regardless of whether he is motivated by self-interest or wants to damage the principal or expose his assets to a risk of loss.

Similarly to the definition of cheating presented above, the definition of fraud by abuse of position in the Fraud Act 2006 does not require a formal element of deception or that the person acted covertly, in spite of proposals to include such requirements.[162]

The French offence of abuse of company assets also combines both perspectives. On the one hand, misusing the company assets, ie using them in a wrong way, means that the use is against certain rules, broken intentionally and for the purpose of private interests, which the managers enumerated in the relevant provisions pursue by breaching the rules (abusing the assets, the position or the credit of the company). On the other hand, although the relevant provisions do not

[162] See the discussion in Law Commission, *Legislating the Criminal Code: Fraud and Deception*, Consultation Paper No 155 (1999); Law Commission, *Fraud: Report on a Reference under Section 3(1)(e) of the Law Commissions Act 1965*, Law Com No 276 (July 2002).

mention the relationship, but name the categories of managers, these managers listed there are in an agent-principal relationship, which requires loyalty in the sense of using the assets properly and for the benefit of the company, thus rejecting opportunities which would undermine this relationship.

While in both previous offences the provisions concentrate on the act and its motivation, the German provision requires a situation of trust, ie a duty of loyalty, a breach of such duty in form of a breach of a rule governing (an aspect of) this relationship, which resulted in negative consequences, either in the form of a loss or exposure to risk, which can be qualified as such. Although it can often be deduced from the facts of the case, there is no formal requirement that the person acted in his personal interest. The term denoting the offence is *Untreue*, meaning abuse of trust or unfaithfulness (in fact, the same word signifies marital infidelity), and the core of the offence is disloyalty, on the condition, however, that it brings detrimental results (attempt is not criminalised). What defines the moral value of the perpetrator's wrongdoing is the fact that he broke one of the rules that define his relationship with the principal that was supposed to define the agent's room for manoeuvre and which was supposed to protect the principal. At the same time, the agent intended or accepted that as a consequence the principal would suffer a loss.

One can also ask what is the moral wrongfulness in offences described in UK Financial Services (Banking Reform) Act 2013, section 36 and German Banking Act, section 54a. Both offences require that the manager bring about a state, which is either of concrete endangerment to the existence of the institution or its failure. This is combined with his breaching of certain rules on how to manage such an institution. The German provision requires that these rules be broken intentionally (including *dolus eventualis*), but that the perpetrator may be negligent as to the result of such intentional rule-breaking. The English provision requires awareness of the risk, while it seems not to require awareness that the management is below the required standard. Although these provisions do not fall into the categories proposed above, this does not mean, all the same, that they do not contain an element of moral wrong which could be considered reprehensible.

It is morally wrong to behave in a way which brings a risk of the collapse of the institution one is entrusted to manage, while knowing that the way one acts may bring about such a risk, or knowingly neglecting the duties which are supposed to prevent such risk from occurring. Not only does this form a case of disloyalty to one's institution and, if an element of personal intent is present, a case of cheating, one may also build an argument that leading an institution, whose collapse may have grave consequences both for the stakeholders and for the economic system, implies a moral duty to strive for its survival, whilst also avoiding acting in a way which may imperil the existence of the institution.

3.1.3. Wrongfulness in Excessive Risk-Taking

When it comes to management in the corporate environment, as noted above, it is unavoidable that the company is exposed to risk. To consider that to expose the company to risk should be forbidden (or even criminal) would mean that managers should take only the most obvious decisions concerning day-to-day affairs, if at all, and cannot venture not only into any more ambitious endeavour, but even possibly into activities which are the main business of their companies; for instance, banks would need to stop giving loans – the result would be absurd.

Now, the question is whether exposing the company to excessive risk can be considered morally wrong. Two approaches are possible. One is consequentialist and would consider the wrong to consist in causing the excessive risk. The excessiveness of risk would be defined, as is already done above, as being higher than normally expected in this situation by any kind of standard applicable to the situation. Such an approach would need to take into account any kind of exposure to excessive risk for which the manager is somehow responsible, thus including all kinds of intention and also reckless and even negligent cases. Whilst this would give extensive grounds for criminalisation, its scope may be further curtailed by other rules, in particular *ultima ratio*. Moreover, it could be completed by the reasoning presented above as regards Financial Services (Banking Reform) Act 2013, section 36 and German Banking Act, section 54a. This would formulate stronger duties as regards conduct which may lead to the collapse of an institution based on the impact which the collapse may have on the different groups of stakeholders, and potentially on the economic system.

The other approach to defining the moral wrongfulness in excessive risk-taking is deontological and requires that there be some moral wrong intrinsic to what the manager has done, irrespective of the consequences as such. The basis of the relationship between the manager and the company is trust. The manager is obliged to be loyal to the company in the sense that he should act for its benefit and not against its interests. Therefore, privileging personal interests over the interests of the company is morally wrong. However, this type of relationship is not modelled as a strict martyr-like bond, where a person must forsake all their interests for the benefit of the superior goal. The scope of obedience required is described by rules defining the relationship between the company and the manager. Certainly, breaching these rules and pursuing one's interests against the company's is a case of disloyalty. However, if one finds a situation in which it is possible to both stay within the given rules *and* act to the detriment of the company, one is also disloyal. So, in fact, the moral wrongfulness in such a relationship is in accepting to act to the detriment of the company, or in accepting that a course of action may be detrimental to the company – and pursuing that course of action. It follows that one ought not to place too much emphasis on the element of seeking personal interest, since disloyalty already resides in the fact that one acts in a way which may result in a loss to the company.

Yet another approach hinted at above requires an analysis of whether there may be moral wrong in a breach of one of the relevant rules, leading to exposure to excessive risk. The German approach in *Untreue* requires a breach of duty in the form of a breach of a rule, which is designed to protect the owner of the assets (the company) from loss. The question is, what kind of moral wrong there is in committing such a breach. One answer could be that a manager does so for some personal benefit, which is wrong not only since it breaches the rule, but also for favouring one's own interest and thus constituting cheating according to the terminology adopted above. If there is no personal interest at stake, then the only possible reason would be a certain type of carelessness, which can be understood as a form of disloyalty: instead of making efforts to act in the best interests of the company, a manager allows himself to disregard some of his duties. This could mean that every breach of such rules should be criminalised, whether committed intentionally (eg disregard of the rule because of laziness or bravado), recklessly or negligently, resulting in the criminalisation of any kind of mismanagement regardless of the type of *mens rea*. The need for criminalisation may be further nuanced, in view of the *ultima ratio* principle, since different breaches may present various degrees of moral wrongfulness, and also in view of different *mens rea*, using also the level of punishment to reflect these differences.

It is submitted here that exposing the company to excessive risk combines two elements of moral wrongfulness: cheating and disloyalty. The act of the manager constitutes cheating in view of the following reasoning. The manager is expected to be acting for the benefit of the company. Not only is this subject to certain rules (with or without legal consequences), but also the mere imperative of acting for the company's benefit is a general rule that should govern the manager's behaviour and which is expected by the other actors in this relationship (this important aspect will be returned to below). Thus, by intentionally breaking this rule in order to pursue his own interest, the manager acts immorally. The picture is supplemented by the rules on conflicts of interest, which, if followed, also ensure the avoidance of wrongdoing where the manager is unable to pursue this imperative.

The manager exposing the company to excessive risk is acting disloyally according to the following logic. By accepting the position of a manager, thus having been entrusted with assets and power in order to act in the name of the company, the manager commits to pursuing the interests of the company. He also undertakes to abstain from pursuing his own interests at the expense of those of the company. As regards the use of the company's assets and representing its interests, the manager must do so in a way which (in his view) best serves the company. Therefore, he ought to abstain from exploiting opportunities which would be beneficial for him, but which would hamper the company. In theory, a use of the company's assets for the benefit of the manager which would neither impact negatively on the company, nor bring it any benefit, is morally neutral. Nonetheless, it would be necessary to carefully assess whether this is really the case. For example, taking funds belonging to the company in order to help the manager pay an urgent debt puts the company at abnormal risk that the manager would not be able to repay them.

It becomes problematic where the manager acts without intention to cause harm or expose to excessive risk, but only in a careless way. Here, it is possible to distinguish two types of situations. First, the manager may neglect his duties purposely. For example, in the process of verifying creditworthiness, a person may omit to verify certain aspects (knowing that they should be verified) not necessarily because of some vested interest (the client is the manager's brother or the manager needs to improve his statistics), but for instance because of laziness. This is certainly not cheating (to succumb to one's vice is not yet pursuing one's interest), but disloyalty, in the sense of a duty to make best efforts to pursue the company's interests and failing to fulfil it. It is disloyalty also, if the manager performs the creditworthiness check in a sloppy way and because of that he misses an important point, which results in granting an excessively risky loan, or according to the rules which would apply for less risky clients (eg with lower interest rates). By accepting the position the manager accepts to act according to a certain level of care and if he knowingly disregards it, he is disloyal to the company. However, one cannot say that it is disloyal to the company to fail to perform certain acts of care if he did not know that he was supposed to do so. He might be an incompetent manager, but not an immoral one. Secondly, a manager might not be able to meet a certain standard of care due to other conditions, which are not dependent on him, in particular if those conditions have been created by the company itself (eg all the elements of creditworthiness cannot be verified because the amount of applications to be dealt with within a certain space of time is too high). Similarly to the above, one cannot say that that manager is immoral. One could expect such a manager to raise a 'red flag' and inform the company that the duties cannot be performed. A work environment that would prevent the manager from doing so (eg expectations that managers perform as dictated, and/or a risk that the manager would suffer negative consequences if complaining) could serve as another justification for the manager's conduct, with the moral responsibility for the situation thus falling on those who had set up such arrangements.

Another question to be analysed is whether it can be considered immoral according to the standards adopted above to expose the company to excessive risk where managers act only for the benefit of the company. In other words, the manager acts in a way, which he knows is against the rules and in a way that makes the probability of loss higher than it should be or causes an abnormal risk (eg of criminal, if applicable, or administrative sanctions), but he hopes that the risk does not materialise and that eventually the company benefits. This might be considered cheating, if the manager were to pursue a personal interest alongside those of the company, eg in the form of a bonus or promotion. If he has no personal interest of this type however, the only possible moral wrongdoing to be considered is disloyalty. By being entrusted with the company's assets, the manager promises also to abide by certain rules and standards of care, which the person entrusting the assets trusts the manager will do. In other words, the assets are given to the manager in order that he manage them in a way which would not be considered excessively dangerous according to certain applicable standards. By intentionally disregarding these standards, the manager is disloyal to the person who entrusted the assets. One could also extend this reasoning to duties beyond the principal-agent relationship, as pointed out above, in particular as regards stakeholders who may also rightly expect that the company is managed in a more or less correct way, as well as to duties of avoiding the risk of collapse of the whole institution.

The moral wrongfulness of disloyalty does not explain the wrong in the setback to the interests of the stakeholders, as well as other actors, such as members of the society, if systemic interests are at stake. It was already demonstrated above that a consequentialist approach would focus on the reason for apportioning blame for acts detrimental to the interests of such actors. With the deontological approach, the notion of cheating would be applicable. The other stakeholders enter the (cooperative) relationship with the company and its managers in hope that the latter abide by the rules relevant for this relationship (including correct management of the company), and while knowingly exposing the company to excessive risk (against what the stakeholders expect), the manager may intend to gain an advantage in the sense that he intends to profit from the act (or make the company profit) whilst the stakeholder might be put at (higher than normal) risk of loss. Similar reasoning can be made for the systemic interests of the economic system, where the members of the society (participants in the economic system) function within it expecting that other actors do not breach rules in a way which would put at risk the functioning of the whole system.

3.2. Possible Harms

After having established possible moral wrongs linked with excessively risky decisions, it is necessary to reflect on the harm in which such decisions result or may result. The first question is what kind of harms are to be analysed. Managers, by using the company property in an excessively risky manner, can potentially cause harm to or endanger very different interests, not only including property, but also life, health, the environment, etc. Only the property interest is the subject of analysis here. A decision which is excessively risky may obviously finish in the materialisation of risk. This loss may be of differing natures: pecuniary, but also loss of opportunity, damage to reputation. In the context of the company, these other consequences translate also into economic consequences. Thus, in the context of the company, harm is understood as a negative consequence for the economic situation of the company either in the form of a loss or lack of gain. The question, for example, of whether companies have some kind of dignity which ought to be protected will be left out. Similarly, the psychological consequences of losing one's job will not be taken as a factor in the analysis below.

Secondly, the question is to whom the harm is done. It may be done to the company and its shareholders. The second circle of affected persons is constituted by stakeholders: employees, creditors, clients, the state as tax collector, etc. The third circle contains persons who may be affected by the deterioration of the company, but do not belong to the first two circles. For example, a closure of one of the company's sites may affect the region where it is situated. Finally, the economic system as such may also be harmed in certain circumstances.

The question whether exposing the company to a risk of loss would fulfil the criteria of the harm principle can be answered in two ways. First, the harm principle allows that a criminal provision punishes not only situations where harm occurs, but also where there is an unreasonable risk of harm.[163] Such risk is unreasonable by the applicable standards and it would be admissible to use criminal law to prevent and punish such risk. Secondly, under certain conditions, exposing the company to a risk of loss has an impact on the assets of the company in view of the accounting rules. A risk of loss may require that it be recognised as foreseeable loss, which influences the credit side of the balance and lowers the value of the assets.[164]

In conclusion, the criminalisation of exposing a company to excessive risk can fulfil the requirements of the harm principle because it may prevent harm to the company's property from occurring. Moreover, excessively dangerous management may lead to the deterioration of the company's condition (and eventually its collapse), which could lead to consequences for other circles of affected actors enumerated above (employees, creditors, the state or participants in the economic system). This will be treated in greater detail in the following section.

Besides these reasons, the legislature may wish also to prevent such harm by criminalising acts which do not necessarily create harm, but are generalisations of risky situations likely to cause such harm based on empirical evidence.[165] Such criminalisation may punish the use of certain concrete techniques which, although considered excessively risky, do not as such always create unreasonable risk (or any risk) or do not necessarily lead to a loss. For instance, it might be forbidden for a certain type of companies to invest in certain types of securities and the question would be whether a manager who violates this prohibition should also be held criminally liable. This is an example of a scenario of remote harm and in order to verify whether such acts should be subject to criminal sanction it is necessary, for each abstract type of act in question, to perform the Standard Harm Analysis. The latter is composed of an analysis of the gravity of the risk, the likelihood of it occurring, the balance to be struck between the social value protected and the degree of limitation of liberty, and a consideration of other aspects such as the practicability of such prohibition.[166]

From this analysis results a question as to which is better to use: a general criminalisation or the remote harm criminalisation, in other words punishing situations of concrete endangerment or providing for abstract endangerment offences. The added value of the first is that it encompasses only situations in which the actual harm occurred or a situation where excessive risk came into being. However, this approach can be criticised as it requires a constant judgement

[163] Feinberg, *Harm to Others* (n 35) 11, 105.

[164] See, eg German Commercial Code (Handelsgesetzbuch, HGB), s 253 I, IV; BVerfG (23 June 2010) NJW 2010, 3209, 3219, para [141].

[165] Feinberg, *Harm to Others* (n 35) 190.

[166] Simester and von Hirsch, *Crimes, Harms, and Wrongs* (n 2) 54.

(by the manager) as to the dangerousness of the decisions, which may be difficult in a dynamic situation. This shortcoming would, however, be curtailed by the *mens rea* requirement, if the offence is to be only intentional. On the other hand, concrete prohibitions (ie offences of abstract endangerment) may provide clearer indications as to required behaviour. In traffic offences, it is more practicable to say: 'do not drive above 90km/h', although driving above such a limit may in a concrete situation not be dangerous, than saying: 'do not drive dangerously'. The approach of the general prohibition may be defended by saying that managers are in any case required to assess the risks attached to their decisions, whether this obligation is reinforced by a criminal sanction or not. Moreover, the rules in the business environment seem to be much more dynamic and impossible to codify in contrast to the rules of road traffic. Finally, nothing precludes the use of both techniques, if they are well combined and justified in view of relevant considerations.

3.3. Possible Interests Worth Protecting

Another question to be asked is what kind of interest can and should be protected by criminalising excessive risk-taking, which corresponds to the question of what legal good is protected by means of criminalisation. The theory of legal goods requires, however, that the legal good be somehow embedded in the law, either within criminal provisions or in a legal source outside criminal law, eg the constitution. Since this chapter analyses the question irrespective of any single legal order, it will not refer to concrete legal goods, as perceived in the German doctrine, but to possible legal interests, which may be taken into account.

The interests which may be taken into account can be divided into the following categories:

- interests of the company;
- interests of the shareholders;
- interests of the stakeholders (employees, creditors, clients, the state as tax collector, etc);
- interests of persons who may be affected by the deterioration of the company, but do not belong to any of the above categories;
- systemic interests.[167]

First, the interests to be taken into account are those of the company, namely its property. The company has an interest in ensuring that its assets are maintained and used for its benefit. This feature has two sides: on the one hand, the company has an interest in its assets being used in the least risky way possible, so that it does not suffer loss. On the other hand, it also has an interest in these assets being used

[167] The nature of interests may be different (life, health, environment, etc), but only economic interests are taken into account in this analysis.

for endeavours which can bring profit to it, which necessarily exposes these assets to a risk of loss.

Secondly, shareholders have in principle a similar interest in the company's survival and prosperity. Another interest that could be protected by an offence is shareholders' trust, since shareholders entrust the assets of the company, and by that their investment in the company, to the managers. The problem with this legal interest is that it is questionable to claim that by establishing a criminal sanction, the trust of shareholders in the correct execution of managerial duties can be maintained or protected, similarly to other relationships of trust as legal goods, such as 'trust in the proper functioning of …' eg 'trust in non-corruptibility of public officials'.[168] Trust is a type of bond, which exists between the shareholders and the management (or any other two or more persons) not because of the existence of a criminal law provision, but because the shareholders have sufficient reasons to believe that the managers will fulfil their duties. This belief is not reinforced by a criminal sanction, but by (correct or incorrect) impressions of the personal and professional capacities of the managers. The function of criminal law is only to intervene if it turns out that the person in whom trust was vested has failed to fulfil expectations (eg not to mismanage, embezzle, etc) and not in order to reinforce that trust.

The shareholders may differ as to how they see the development of the company. In spite of individual differences, certain patterns have been observed. In particular, there is generally a difference in the approach between concentrated and dispersed shareholders.[169] In general, the block-owners (shareholders owning a large part of shares) tend to be more risk-averse, whereas small shareholders tend to accept more risk.[170] Against this backdrop, it is impossible to define the generally acceptable level of risk a manager should not surpass. The interest of the company may be a better criterion, in order to render the competition among different interests more objective. A criterion, which would set the limit by saying for instance 'no more than …', might not include the interests of shareholders who favour a riskier business strategy. A criminal provision aiming at protecting the interests of the shareholders by prohibiting taking excessive risks may result in a paradoxical situation, in which managers would avoid risk and, for precaution, choose less risky strategies. Managers, whose wealth is mainly dependent on the company's success, tend to be more risk averse than diversified shareholders.[171] A criminal law provision fostering risk aversion would thus promote the interests of managers, while neglecting those of (at least one category of) shareholders. It seems to be an incorrect result that a criminal provision aiming to protect shareholders' property from being exposed to excessive risk results in de facto

[168] Roxin, *Strafrecht. Allgemeiner Teil* (n 17) 39.

[169] Marcelo Donelli, Borja Larrain and Francisco Urzúa, 'Ownership Dynamics with Large Shareholders: An Empirical Analysis' (2013) 48(2) *Journal of Financial and Quantitative Analysis* 579.

[170] Peter O Mülbert, 'Corporate Governance of Banks' in Abol Jalivand and AG Malliaris (eds), *Risk Management and Corporate Governance* (New York/London: Routledge, 2012) 243–81, at 251 et seq.

[171] Ibid 252.

prohibiting the use they might be searching for. Of course, this does not exclude entirely excessive risk as a negative outcome of managers' acts, against which shareholders ought to be protected. Their interests do not seem, however, to be the best criterion in order to determine the scope of this protection.

Thirdly, deterioration of the company's condition may also infringe the interests of other stakeholders, in particular creditors, employees, the state (as the collector of taxes), etc, which may therefore have an interest in that it not be exposed to excessive risk. These interests may differ among these categories of actors. For example, whereas employees may tend to be more risk-averse in order to keep their jobs, they may be more risk-leaning if their salary is connected to the company's results.

Fourthly, deterioration of the company's condition may also affect different groups of persons who, although not formally linked to the company, may be affected by its economic condition. For instance, a larger group of persons (town, district, etc) together with entities operating within this community may have an interest in the well-being of the company affecting this community (because it is an important employer and contractor). These groups have an interest in the survival of the company (ie it should not risk its existence), but also that it should thrive (ie it must take the necessary risks). Similarly as is the case among the shareholders, the levels of risk which are in the best interests of the stakeholders and other actors may be different.

A different category of interests is linked to the economic system as such and its correct functioning. There might be systemic interests in that (certain) companies do not take too much risk or certain types of risk, because this may have an adverse influence on the market. This approach looks at the problem from a different angle. Here, the question is not whether the excessive risk is harmful for the company or other persons linked to it, but whether it is generally harmful to the economy as such, which may affect the society as a whole, ie all actors of an economic system. At the same time, there is undoubtedly a societal interest in companies venturing into innovations and enterprises that may sometimes bear a significant degree of risk. At this level as well, the question is how to balance these two aspects.

Because of this balancing act, all these interests may be in conflict. It is possible to draw lines of divergences between the groups of involved actors taking into account the interests they may have. In the first place, the company as an entity with legal personality has its own interests, from which results a desired policy on risk-taking. The managers may be required to adjust their policy according to these abstract interests of the company, ie in order to seek the best for the company, or according to the wishes of the shareholders. Moreover, the interests of other stakeholders and other actors may be divergent among themselves and with the interests of the shareholders or the company as a separate entity. Finally, all these interests may be in conflict with what the state perceives as a desirable risk-taking policy.

As to the interests of the company, shareholders, stakeholders and other interested actors, the common denominator which appears to strike the balance between them is the interests of the company, as the satisfaction of the interests of all these groups of actors is linked with the well-being of the company, which includes avoiding excessive risk. Moreover, stakeholders do not have a direct bond with the management in the sense that they do not influence the selection of the management and do not entrust their assets into their hands directly, but to the company. If the company functions correctly, their interests in general should be assured.

While focusing on company interests may constitute a fair compromise between different interests, it may contradict in particular the right of the shareholders – the ultimate owners of the company – to decide what to do with their company and its property. The basic line of conflict would be then between the interests of the company and the freedom of shareholders to use their property as they please. The solution to this problem is a question of economic policy. The legislator wishing to protect different categories of stakeholders and companies in general should prioritise the interests of the company. To the contrary, the legislator may want to pay more attention to the property of the shareholders, be it for political or philosophical reasons, or in order to allow them to freely use their assets, potentially venturing into innovative business but also potentially leading to bravado and failure. In this case, the legislation should focus on the interests of the shareholders. As regards criminal liability, that choice will in particular translate into the rules on consent. The shareholders should be protected against misuses committed by managers and a criminal law provision safeguarding the interests of the company would in principle protect their interests. By admitting exculpatory consent and depending on the scope of its application, the legislator may take more or less into account the interests of shareholders who wish to allow the managers to take risks beyond the level which would normally be allowed.

A general criminal provision cannot include all the nuances of the differences between various interests and has to concentrate on preserving the interests of the shareholders or of the company, thus safeguarding the 'average' interests of all the actors. It may be done, however, by other legal tools, as, for example, protection of minority shareholders in company law, or balancing of interests between different groups of creditors by insolvency law. These nuances may also be safeguarded by means of criminal provisions targeting specific acts which infringe the interests of certain groups, if a need for such a provision can be demonstrated (eg criminal provision as regards insolvency).

Although the state should protect the relevant actors against abuses of their property, it would be absurd to expect it to guarantee that all economic endeavours will finish in success. However, two considerations are called for here. First, exposing the company to excessive risk does not necessarily have to lead to its collapse. Moreover, even if the company collapses, this does not necessarily harm the economy (on the state or global level, whichever perspective is taken) in most cases, unless the company is particularly important to the economic system. Yet, such a phenomenon, when occurring on a large scale, can have systemic relevance, thus presenting the feature of what the theory of harm calls conjunctive harm.[172] In other words, if everybody is doing the same (in this case managing the company in an excessively risky way) it could pose a danger for the functioning of the economic system (eg investing in securities based on sub-prime mortgages).[173] This approach presents a similarity with pollution. Although one polluting enterprise may not create smog, several ones combined may create it.[174] The second argument is that although exposing the average company to a risk of loss, or even collapse, may not have relevance for the economic system, the collapse of certain companies ('too big to fail') or even their exposure to excessive risk may have a negative impact on the economy. For these reasons, there may be a systemic interest in limiting certain types of risk taken by companies in general or by certain type of companies deemed particularly systemically important.

All these aspects will need to be taken into account by the legislator and will be directly linked with criminal and mainly economic policy. On the one hand, the shareholders and management should have the freedom to decide how to pursue their business. The company belongs to the shareholders and they should be allowed to make use of it according to their wish. On the other hand, a company is interconnected with other actors, and its policy affects their interests. Finally, there might be systemic reasons to require that certain levels of risk are not exceeded or that certain protective measures are taken.

In order to protect these different, possibly conflicting, interests a plethora of tools can be applied, from soft law,[175] self-regulation and economic incentives, to legal tools of different degrees of intrusion: civil law, eg contractual or tort liability, or administrative law, eg concessions or administrative sanctions. According to the *ultima ratio* principle, criminal sanctions should be used only for those types of acts which cannot be effectively dealt with by the former tools.

3.4. Limits to Use of Criminal Law

*3.4.1. Extent of Criminalisation of Excessive Risk-Taking (*Ultima Ratio *Principle and Principle of Proportionality)*

The analysis in the previous sections demonstrated that there are reasons to curb excessive risk-taking committed by company management, possibly by means of criminal law intervention, in consideration of the interests of different groups of

[172] Simester and von Hirsch, *Crimes, Harms, and Wrongs* (n 2) 59. See also a more general discussion of this problem in Robert Nozick, *Anarchy, State, and Utopia* (Oxford/Cambridge, MA: Blackwell/Basic Books, 1974) 73–78 ('Risk').

[173] Simester and von Hirsch, *Crimes, Harms, and Wrongs* (n 2) 85 et seq.

[174] Ibid 87.

[175] See, eg Marloes van Rijsbergen, 'On the Enforceability of EU Agencies' Soft Law at the National Level: The Case of the European Securities and Markets Authority' (2014) 10(5) *Utrecht Law Review* 116.

relevant actors and in order to avoid harm or unreasonable risk of harm to these interests. Two areas of protection have been distinguished. The first one concerns protection of the financial interests of the company (thus protecting different groups of interested actors), where, depending on policy choices, the protection of the shareholders' interests is either made equal with the protection of the interests of other actors or given prevalence. The second area is linked to the protection against risks, which would endanger the economic system.

Criminal law is not the main tool to shape the economic policy of the state. It must be used with caution and only as the last resort. First of all, the criminal judge cannot be expected to act as an arbiter, either to assess the quality of management or to solve conflicts between different economic actors. Conflicts in this area should mainly be solved by civil law methods and not in a criminal court. Secondly, steering different aspects of the economy generally takes place through economic incentives and administrative law. As for economic incentives, these certainly are less intrusive tools than criminal procedure. On the other hand, the administrative regulation can be more effective in directing managers because such regulation is easier to enforce and it is more flexible in adapting to changing circumstances. Opening criminal proceedings for breach of every rule would be extremely burdensome and costly for the justice system, and for the managers and their companies, thereby suffocating the economy. Thirdly, taking risks is at the core of business activity. Therefore, criminal law intervention should not reach the point where business activities are no longer possible or become excessively unattractive. With this in mind, criminal law should only be used to counteract the gravest infringements, ones which the legislator deems cannot be dealt with better or at least equally efficiently by other tools of social control. Finally and as has already been shown, criminal law also contains an element of moral reprobation Thus, it should be limited to situations where it is possible to say that the perpetrator committed a moral wrong.

The major question in this regard is whether criminal law is suitable, necessary and adequate to effectively protect the interests described above or whether other tools should be used. Before embarking on answering this question, two remarks have to be made. First, this section will omit the general problem of the effectiveness of criminal law as a tool of social control and will limit itself only to problems relative to the topic of excessive risk-taking. Secondly, the problem of proportionality of criminal law interventions is also linked with the choice of punishment (its type and level). The choice of punishment is too deeply embedded in the particularities of a given legal systems, so this issue will not be given further consideration here. It is, however, worth recalling that while imprisonment, especially long term, could be considered in many cases disproportionate to the wrongdoing, fines and professional prohibitions might be equally or even more efficient in particular cases.

The first area to be analysed concerns the protection of financial interests of the company. These financial interests may be infringed by acts which are against the interests of the company and result in exposing the company to excessive risk, but obviously also in a loss. While the need to legally tackle the latter may be more evident, the above analysis of the moral wrong, possible harms and legal interests demonstrated that there are strong reasons to extend the scope of protection also taking into account excessive risk-taking. The process that the manager starts by his act or omission may immediately lead to a loss, or may pass through a stage where the company is exposed to excessive risk of such loss. The essence of the manager's wrongdoing is in the decision which exposes the company to excessive risk of loss, regardless of whether this risk materialises in an effective loss or not. It may be a question of sheer luck whether the loss occurs or not. If the same act may lead to loss or remain at the level of excessive risk, it does not seem fair to punish the unlucky manager who causes the loss, and leave unpunished the one who committed the same act, but was more fortunate. In view of the interlink between excessive risk and loss, the arguments for and against the use of criminal law will in some instances be valid for using criminal law against both loss and excessive risk, and in other instances will be risk specific only.

While from the perspective of harm and endangered or infringed legal interests the mental attitude of the manager while acting against the interests of the company is less relevant, it is crucial from the point of view of the act's wrongfulness (blameworthiness). This aspect is also highly important for the *ultima ratio* analysis. In this regard, three general categories of situations can be distinguished. They all consist in using the assets of the company or the powers granted to the managers in a way which exposes the company to excessive risk of loss (or causes that loss) and differ only as regards the manager's perception of the act, which will translate into the *mens rea* requirement.[176] The first category encompasses managers who either intentionally expose the company to excessive risk, or know that what they are doing may expose the company to excessive risk and accept this possibility (intentional mismanagement or misuse of the company's assets). The second category comprises managers who know that their act breaches certain rules or standards they should observe and that it might expose the company to excessive risk, however they are convinced that it will not be the case (reckless mismanagement). Finally, the third category encompasses managers who are not aware that by their act they are exposing the company to excessive risk. They are not aware of the fact that they are breaching some rule or standard (protecting the company against excessive risk), but they could and should have known this, or they are not aware of the rule or standard, but they could and should have been aware of it (negligent mismanagement).[177] While all these categories have to be taken into account in the analysis, the differences between them will translate into a different need to punish managers for excessive risk-taking.

[176] This abstract differentiation should not be understood in light of the doctrine on different categories of *mens rea* in any national system.

[177] What has been omitted from this list is the possibility to introduce criminal liability for breaching a concrete rule aimed at preventing excessive risk in the form of strict liability. This form of liability used in certain legal systems (eg England and Wales) is not accepted in others on the grounds of not respecting the *nullum crimen sine culpa* principle (eg Germany).

The property of the company (in economic terms owned by the shareholders) is entrusted to the managers, who have certain discretion in using it. Since the possibility of controlling that use is limited, the managers have the ability to abuse their rights to use the assets of the company. They can do it by representing the company in a way which is contrary to its interests, and possibly by using those assets for their own private purpose or any other which is not in accordance with the prosperity of the company and the interests of the shareholders. Hence, there is a need to create legal instruments compensating for that loss of control.

Abuses of the company cannot be fully contained by guidelines, soft law, ethics rules or peer pressure. Human nature, imperfect as it is, provides enough examples that among persons having access to assets of high or low value, there are those who cannot restrain themselves from making use of such assets contrary to the original purpose. The above analysis of moral wrong inherent in such conduct shows that criminal punishment, with its stigmatising effect, may be the necessary reaction to such acts and more appropriate than, for example, administrative sanctions.

Naturally there exist also civil law remedies, which will be in use in such cases. However, those remedies alone may not be sufficient, for the following reasons. First, imposing them does not involve stigmatisation of the perpetrator's wrongdoing. This is linked to the different purposes of civil and criminal justice. Secondly, if the assets were eventually lost (at least partially) they cannot be (at least fully) recovered and therefore civil law might not be able to offer a valuable remedy nor a meaningful consequence of one's act. Thirdly, the enforcement of civil law is generally left in the hands of the interested parties, whereas the enforcement of criminal law is in general entrusted in the state. Hence, there are major reasons to opt for criminal law enforcement. Shareholders, in particular minority ones, may be in a weaker position than managers. Moreover, they may not have access to all information if the managers withhold it, and even where the managers are obliged to disclose the information, they may still manipulate access to information and the information as such. For these same reasons, the shareholders may not even know that abuses are taking or have taken place. Criminal law works, in principle, irrespective of the victim's reaction, in contrast to tort law.[178] Moreover, where there is no effective loss, there may be no grounds to grant compensation for tort.[179] Hence, criminal justice with its instrumentarium can be more effective in investigating the misuses of entrusted assets and criminal law prohibition can be more effective in preventing abuses of which the shareholders may not be aware.

The reasoning concerning the criminal justice apparatus acquires an additional element, since the possibility to start investigations and discover abuses committed by management before the loss effectively happens is obviously beneficial for shareholders and all other stakeholders involved. Lack of criminalisation of

[178] Simester and von Hirsch, *Crimes, Harms, and Wrongs* (n 2) 17.
[179] Ibid 17, note 35.

excessive risk-taking (combined with no liability for attempts) would leave the investigative authority without grounds to open an investigation. While it has been claimed that some offences, for which courts rarely convict perpetrators, are provided for mainly in order to allow the investigating authorities to open criminal proceedings and potentially find evidence of the commission of more serious offences, mismanagement would not be one of such offences, as the harmfulness of the act which provides the reason to open the investigation has already been demonstrated.[180]

Another argument in favour of criminalising abuses of company assets entrusted to the managers by the shareholders is of a practical nature and focuses on situations where abuses are committed for a manager's benefit. Its point of departure is the trust which the shareholders should have in the managers, so that the latter may execute their functions in a system where management and ownership are divided. One of the arguments in favour of promoting trustworthiness is that it reduces costs.[181] In the case of managers, the more they can be trusted, the less instruments of control need to be implemented.[182] The necessary trust required between the agent (manager) and the owner of entrusted assets (the company and indirectly its shareholders) would need to assume that the manager would always take decisions that are (at least in their perception and according to their capacities) best for the company.[183] The question is whether such decisions would indeed have been taken even if 'golden opportunities arise for the decision maker to improve his own welfare at the trusting party's expense'.[184] Any theory of a rational agent responding to external incentives would struggle to explain how a rational manager, when presented with golden opportunities, would not pursue his own interest over the interests of the company.[185] Criminal law, at least if justified by general prevention, is based on the assumption that people make choices under the influence of disincentives in the form of the prospect of being subject to criminal sanctions. In this model, the possibility of a criminal sanction, together with other probable consequences of breaching trust, should balance the potential benefits of such golden opportunities with possible costs, which include criminal sanctions.

The communicative function of criminal law also speaks in favour of its use. While the harmfulness of loss is more evident, the harmfulness of excessive risk can be less apparent. By deciding that the exposure of company assets to excessive

[180] On the problem of so-called '*Türöffner*' (door opening) offences see, eg Michael Lindemann, *Vorasussetzungen und Grenzen legitimen Wirtschaftsstrafrechts* (Tübingen: Mohr Siebeck, 2012) 21.

[181] Shapiro, 'Collaring the Crime' (n 157) 348.

[182] Within this argument, trust is not understood in moral terms, but rather in economic ones. A criminal law provision cannot enhance the shareholders' trust in another person's goodwill, but can enhance their trust in that the circumstances discourage the managers from abusing their position.

[183] David C Rose, *The Moral Foundation of Economic Behavior* (Oxford University Press, 2011) 165 et seq.

[184] Ibid 166.

[185] Ibid 166.

risk by its managers should be an offence subject to punishment, the legislature sends a message that such conduct is wrong and should be avoided. Exposing the company to excessive risk does not need to be separated from causing loss, but if there is a reference to such an exposure and if the offence is properly defined, criminal law can perform its communicative function.

The criminalisation should also not be counter-productive, ie the outcome should not lead to a situation in which managers avoid taking risks at all for fear of criminal prosecution. Such an outcome would effectively paralyse business activity, which necessarily involves an element of risk, lower or higher depending on the type of activity. This is a strong argument against criminalising what was called above negligent mismanagement. It would effectively lead to a system where the criminal law judge becomes the ultimate arbiter of the quality of management. Not only would that be problematic for the development of the economy, if practically any wrong decision could be checked and potentially sentenced by a criminal law judge should he find that the manager acted negligently, it would also create the risk of saturating the criminal justice system. Eventually, any decision which somehow creates doubts as to its correctness could trigger the opening of a criminal procedure with all its weighty instruments. Moreover, there is less of a need to stigmatise a negligent manager as he is not failing in fulfilling his duty of loyalty to the company, but instead fails at being sufficiently diligent. While such diligence can certainly be required from a manager, it is also strongly linked to his talents and competencies, something which should remain outside of criminal justice assessment. The latter should be used for those who deliberately disregard the duty of loyalty.

In this regard, the case of reckless mismanagement is a borderline situation. A manager acting only for the company's benefit (as perceived by him) who, however, exposes the company to excessive risk and who knows that his decision breaches an applicable rule or standard, but is truly convinced that the company is not put at risk by his act, is merely an excessively daring manager. His acts may certainly be dangerous for the company, but the force which drives him is also precious to the company. It seems much more reasonable to contain its excesses by other tools, such as mechanisms of internal control, than to create a danger for such a manager that his too bold decisions, taken with good intentions, would lead him to a criminal investigation or trial. Furthermore, the argument of overly intense involvement of criminal law in business and oversaturation of criminal justice can be repeated. At the same time, it would create a climate which would incline managers to pursue very cautious policies for fear of triggering prosecution.

The assessment of a reckless manager should be different, if he is motivated by some personal benefits (be it for him or for another person). In such a scenario, he is disloyal to the company in that he does not fulfil his duty, not because of too optimistic interpretation of the situation, but by deliberately disregarding an applicable rule or standard in order to realise a personal gain. In order for these cases to be truly wrongful, it is necessary to take the requirement of personal benefit seriously. It is therefore insufficient for it to be fulfilled that the manager wanted to appear as a successful manager or wanted to realise his ambitions. These are the typical motivations of managers, which push them to achieve remarkable results for their companies. On the other hand, the requirement would be fulfilled if the manager wished to receive a bonus linked to the transaction, or acted in the interest of his close relative or friend.

In sum, the above analysis based on a combination of principled (moral) and practical arguments demonstrates that it is legitimate and proportionate to provide for a general offence criminalising intentional mismanagement, as well as reckless mismanagement, according to the above definitions, provided that the latter is committed for personal benefit. The latter modality will constitute a borderline situation and it would be a policy decision whether it should be criminalised or left unpunished and tolerated.

It should not, however, be forgotten that a manager's behaviour can also be steered by other (including non-legal) tools. Research institutes and universities can issue guidelines or propose standards. Regulatory institutions can also issue similar documents. Those standards and guidelines can provide information on what is too risky or how to correctly assess the prospects of success. Peer pressure or market forces can be instruments which enforce such guidelines, as well as high standards of management. Moreover, by making it known that certain policies are risky, it would be harder for a manager to claim that he was not aware of their dangerousness. Hence, if there is a lot of information suggesting that certain securities are extremely risky, even if many banks are investing in them, it cannot convincingly be claimed that it was not known that they were unsafe. Another technique which could be used is a system of obligations to inform. If a certain type of investment, deemed particularly risky, is being made, the company would have the obligation to make it public, giving the shareholders or (perhaps) stakeholders a possibility to react.

These actors – regulators, competent administrative enforcement agencies, academic institutions, the press, etc – are responsible for providing information on what is risky or too risky and how to assess it. Obviously, in view of the dynamic nature of the market, not everything can be known, and even by applying these methods, there will be space left for the managers' competence, intuition and talent. Inasmuch as only these factors are in place, but due diligence has been applied and standards respected, there can be no place for other sanctioning than dismissal.

On the other hand, the enforcement of detailed rules aiming at avoiding risk in concrete situations or providing techniques of risk assessment and avoidance ought to be mainly promoted by non-legal tools and enforced through administrative, company and civil law measures. Business is not like medicine, which should (except as regards experimental therapies) work according to detailed rules. There must be space for innovation, creativity and venturing. An offence which would generally sanction the non-observance of such rules could be counter-productive or useless. However, there may be reasons to consider that a particular rule is of special importance because, according to empirical generalisations, it often leads to grave consequences, which could potentially affect the economy as a whole.

The latter consideration leads to the second area of protection, which concerns the protection of systemic interests. It has been established that it may be justified (from the point of view of the harm analysis and the need to protect legal interests) either to provide for offences curbing excessive risk-taking within companies which are systemically important, or alternatively to enforce, through criminal law, certain concrete rules aiming at avoiding excessive risk. This results in two (not mutually exclusive) possibilities: establishing a general offence punishing for excessive risk taken by managers of systemically important companies, or/and providing for an offence punishing infringement of a concrete rule, which aims at preventing the excessive risk.

As to the first possibility, it is already comprised within the reflection on creating such an offence with respect to all companies. As to the particularities of systemically relevant companies, the question whether the risk was excessive or not will be answered in the context of a concrete company or a transaction in question. It may result in a context in which the threshold to consider the risk as too great is set lower or higher, depending on the type of the company. As the need for a general offence was denied in case of negligence or recklessness without personal interest, the question is whether it would be justified to extend criminalisation to those types of mental attitudes (translating into the *mens rea* requirements) in the case of systemically important companies. It appears, however, that the same arguments against criminalisation of negligence and recklessness without personal interest could be repeated here. In brief, if the managers of systemically important companies were at risk of criminal investigation and sentence even in relation to decisions where they were not even aware of the potential risks involved, it would make the criminal law judge a potential arbiter of the quality of any managerial decision within such companies, it would create a danger of paralysing the functioning of the companies, and it would also be highly burdensome for criminal justice. The problem of how to avoid the collapse of systemically important companies must be solved in the first place by means of other instruments, such as the Basel Accords in the banking industry.[186]

The other possibility concerns an offence (or offences) punishing for infringing a concrete rule (or rules). Such a rule would aim at preventing acts or requiring certain types of action, which, if not respected, could lead to excessive risk or loss of such gravity that it would endanger the economic system. Its justification would be based on empirical generalisation, which could demonstrate that, although the breach of such a rule does not always lead to excessive risk or to a loss, it may bring about this result if the rule is breached in many companies or in one or more systemically relevant companies, and thus may endanger the functioning of the economic system. An offence punishing for infringement of such rules would need to be justified by showing that the potential consequences are so grave that it

[186] Uwe Blaurock, 'Regelbildung und Grenzen des Rechts – Das Beispiel der Finanzkrise' (2012) 5 *JuristenZeitung (JZ)* 226.

is necessary to enforce the rule through criminal law, and that the possible drawbacks of criminalisation are less serious than the need to enforce the rule in this way. Such criminal offences could also potentially include liability even for negligence, if it proves necessary to combat breaches by perpetrators with this state of mind. The dangers of over-extensive influence of criminal law would be limited in this case, as it concerns a concrete rule that the managers should know they have to especially abide by.

3.4.2. Formulation of Criminalisation of Excessive Risk-Taking (Legality Principle and Fair Warning Principle)

The principle of legal certainty and the fair warning principle play a double role. First, the legal certainty imperative would require that, if the legislator decides to criminalise excessive risk-taking, this should be stated in the definition of the offence in such a way as to allow the potential perpetrator to modify his behaviour in order to avoid committing the offence. In this regard, the undesirable outcome would be that judges demonstrate a tendency to over-extend the elements of the offence so that excessive risk is punished, because they consider that it would be unjust to leave it out.

Moreover, the definition should not be so wide as to encompass such a large number of acts that many of them would be deemed unnecessary to prosecute, resulting in prosecuting authorities not initiating cases where the opportunity principle allows them to do so, or looking for ways to dispose of them in legal systems based on the legality principle. Indeed, a likely further drawback to a broadly-worded offence would be the saturation of the justice system due to a high volume of cases.

The principle of legal certainty requires the provision to be as precise as possible and, in particular, to clearly state what the targeted wrongdoing is. The provision may also refer to other legal acts or sources of duties, the breach of which can be part of the definition of the offence.

When criminalising excessive risk-taking by managers, four elements must be described with sufficient precision:

- Who is the perpetrator?
- What course of conduct is criminalised?
- Is there any requirement of result? And if so, what is it?
- What must be the perpetrator's state of mind so that he fulfils the *mens rea* requirement?

The problem of the definition of the perpetrator presents the same dilemmas as regards both types of offences, the general offence of excessive risk-taking and the offence(s) punishing an infringement of a concrete rule (protecting against excessive risk). In general, the perpetrator can be described using one of the two possible techniques: enumerating functions which the potential perpetrator would fulfil (eg the CEO, member of the management board, etc) and which would be described by other legal acts; or providing an abstract definition of the position which would make the person a perpetrator (eg a person supposed to safeguard the interests of another person).

Prima facie, the first option grants maximum legal certainty, however at the cost of not encompassing persons who may commit equally harmful and wrong acts with entrusted assets and remain unpunished. Criminal liability would depend here on a nomination, and could thus be deflected or avoided by formally nominating an individual (a 'straw man' in the German usage, or a 'fall guy' in colloquial English), through whom management is officially carried out, but who in reality is subject to the authority of another person or other persons: the de facto management. This result would not do justice. Therefore, the risk of applying this technique is that there may be a need to supplement it by adding certain categories of perpetrators, who would be considered equally responsible as the formally nominated individual, if their position can be aligned to the one required by the definition of the offence. In this way, however, some of the benefit of certainty is lost, without guaranteeing in return the equal treatment of all perpetrators deserving punishment. It is necessarily linked with how the additional categories are formulated. For these reasons the second technique seems more reasonable. It guarantees (at least to a greater extent) a more just application of the offence. It depends on the criteria which are chosen to describe the perpetrator, and in particular on how precise the definition will be. It will also be the role of jurisprudence to decide on whether the definition is fulfilled in borderline cases.

The analysis of the three other elements – conduct, result and *mens rea* – needs to be carried out separately for the two types of offences. Not too much can be said here about criminalising the infringement of particular rules, as the key to the fulfilment of the principles of certainty and fair warning is in a clear and precise description of the rule and its breach, as well as the required *mens rea*. This has to be verified for each potential offence, but it should be less problematic than in the case of a general offence of excessive risk-taking. The following reflection will concern the general offence.

As to the conduct, it can be described by using two techniques, either by some general terms such as abusing or misusing the position of a person entrusted with the assets and the rights to represent the company, or by reference to a set of rules describing the execution of duties related to this position, be those rules of a statutory or regulatory nature, or featuring in the manager's employment contract, where the breach of one or more of these rules exposes the company to excessive risk. The first technique gives more autonomy to the criminal law judge, who will have to interpret the provision, while the second requires him to verify whether the manager broke one of the rules stipulated outside criminal law. The difference between both approaches may be less significant in practice, for two reasons. In the first approach, the judge may tend to be inspired by the rules applicable to the execution of the managerial function in order to verify the abuse. This will depend on how autonomously this concept is interpreted. Within the second approach, certain general provisions requiring the manager to execute certain levels of diligence will also give the judge scope for appreciation. However, if these terms are borrowed from and rooted in eg company law, they will have to be interpreted according to the understanding given in this field.

Both approaches need to encompass exposing the company to excessive risk. The first one would need to focus the breach of rules not only on losses but also on excessive risk in defining the scope of the rules and the potential (or real) consequences of the breaches. The second one would require that abuse be understood not only as leading to a loss, but also as exposing the company to excessive risk of loss.

The two approaches have their own shortcomings as regards legal certainty. The first one gives less concrete indication as to what it means to misuse the assets because it refers to rules prescribed elsewhere; it can, however, be supplemented through explanations given by the law or jurisprudence. As to the second approach, it may be difficult to describe precisely which rules may lead to criminal liability. Moreover, criminal law ought not to be the way to enforce all the rules governing the execution of managerial activities. Not all the rules applicable to the management of a company necessarily aim at protecting its financial interests, so a lack of clarity in this regard may add uncertainty as to the scope of criminalisation. In any case, the offence should give precise enough indication which rules or at least which types of rules are concerned, so that the managers can modify their conduct in such a way as to avoid criminal liability.

The legislator may wish to limit the scope of criminalisation by requesting a proof of result, which would take the form of a situation where the company is exposed to excessive risk. The use of such a concept is not new to criminal law, at least in the criminal law systems influenced by the German approach, and is called concrete endangerment. The issue of the point at which a situation amounts to the concrete endangerment of the assets may be subject to some additional explanation by the legislator and interpretation in the doctrine. From the perspective of legal certainty, it is important that the offence clearly states whether it requires a proof of result and what kind of result fulfils its requirements.

The important difference between a definition requiring proof of result and a definition not requiring such proof is the perspective from which the exposure to excessive risk is assessed. The requirement of a result would entail that a situation of concrete excessive risk to the assets of the company is created at one point in time and that it can be connected, according to the rules of ascription of results in a concrete system of criminal law, to the act of the perpetrator. If there is no need for proof of result, then the exposure to excessive risk must necessarily be assessed *in abstracto* from the point in time when the act happened. In other words, did the perpetrator's actions lead, in a normal course of action, to exposing the company to excessive risk?

The remaining element of the definition of the offence is *mens rea*. The definition of the offence should precisely specify what kinds of *mens rea* requirements are necessary for criminal liability. This can be done in the definition of the offence or by means of general rules of criminal liability, depending on the national legal system. In the previous section, three categories of the perpetrator's mental attitude towards the offence have been distinguished: intention, recklessness and negligence. These categories have to be translated into the particularities of a concrete legal system and the legislator should sufficiently clearly provide for the respective requirements.

The *mens rea* requirement for the offence with or without the requirement of result will differ only subtly. Whereas in the latter option, the requirement would need to focus on the perpetrator's knowledge and intention as to the normal consequences of the act, in the former the *mens rea* would focus on the foreseen consequences of the act he was undertaking. The *mens rea* for the offence without the requirement of result would be as follows: the manager knew that what he was doing normally exposes the company to excessive risk and wanted to proceed with this act (*dolus directus*); or he knew that his act was such that in normal circumstances it would expose the company to excessive risk and accepted this possibility (*dolus eventualis*). For recklessness, the perpetrator would need to have the same degree of knowledge as for the latter form of *dolus*, but be convinced that the act would not be such, in normal circumstances, as to expose the company to excessive risk.

As regards intention for the offence containing the requirement of result, it would translate into requiring that the manager wanted his act to expose the company to excessive risk (*dolus directus*); knew that what he was doing would certainly expose the company to excessive risk (*dolus indirectus*); or knew that it might expose the company to excessive risk and accepted that possibility (*dolus eventualis*). As to recklessness, it would require the same degree of knowledge as for *dolus eventualis*, but the perpetrator did not want the company to be exposed to excessive risk and was convinced that it would not be exposed.

While the difference between the two approaches is theoretically relevant, it might in practice play a limited role. The requirement of *mens rea* will differ to a large extent depending whether the legislator chooses to define the conduct by general terms, such as abuse or misuse, or by requiring a breach of one or more rules. If the latter is the case, it is necessary also to define the degree of the required knowledge of the perpetrator as to the content of the rule and the details of its breach.

The definition of the offence should also be precise about the additional *mens rea* requirement of personal interest, if the legislator wishes to add it. According to the above analysis, it should form part of the liability for reckless mismanagement. While it has been argued that the requirement be taken seriously, the definition should ensure that the courts do not interpret it over-extensively by admitting any kind of motivation as its fulfilment.

Furthermore, the requirement of *mens rea* may play a certain role in adding certainty to the definition of the offence and remedy to some extent the shortcomings pointed out in the previous paragraphs as to the definition of the conduct. As noted above, both approaches to the description of the conduct present problems as to certainty, either in relation to the understanding of the abuse or to the rules that were broken. If the definition of conduct uses a reference to breach of rules, the perpetrator needs to have (at least some) knowledge about the rules in question and most importantly about the consequences of their breach. If the definition does not refer to the breach of rules, it still requires that the perpetrator understands the potential consequences of his act. The danger that the offence does not give him enough indication about what is wrong in his act is limited, as it requires him to understand that his act may (or will) expose the company to excessive risk.

The benefits of using *mens rea* to compensate for the lack of certainty may turn out to be limited by practical problems in proving the *mens rea*, namely, how to prove that the perpetrator knew or was aware or foresaw that the act exposed the company to excessive risk. Unless the manager is willing to admit it, the court would need to deduce his state of mind from other evidence (for instance, emails, witnesses, etc). In case such evidence is insufficient or unavailable, the judge may, depending on other aspects of a particular case, find it hard to believe that the manager was not aware of this aspect of his deeds. The particularities of the concrete legal systems will decide what needs to be proved in such cases. This aspect demonstrates the importance of raising awareness as to the dangerousness of certain types of investments, which was already mentioned in the previous section. If it is widely known that something is extremely risky, one may encounter difficulties in convincing the judge that it did not cross one's mind. In any case, if it is not possible to establish that the requirement of *mens rea* was fulfilled in a particular case according to the standards of the legal system in question, the manager should have the benefit of the doubt according to the maxim *in dubio pro reo*.

4. Outcome

The above analysis of whether criminalising excessive risk-taking by managers in companies is legitimate and proportionate can be summarised in the following points.

Since criminal law is also a tool of moral reprobation, an analysis of possible moral wrongdoing has been conducted, which led to the conclusion that excessive risk-taking by managers may present the features of cheating and disloyalty. In particular, the latter aspect can especially be present, since by exposing the company to excessive risk the manager breaches his duty of loyalty to the company and the shareholders, which is the counterpart of the fact that the care of the company's assets has been entrusted to him. Disloyalty is a characteristic of acts undertaken wilfully, but also of an act where the manager is aware of his duties and does not perform them correctly or neglects required acts of diligence. There is no need that the perpetrator acts in his personal interest, although the act is more wrongful if he does. As to cheating, it applies to the relationship with the stakeholders, who enter into the relationship with the company reasonably expecting that its managers act in the interests of this company and not against it, and to the relationship with the participants in the economic system generally, who may reasonably expect that managers do not undertake acts which would put this system in danger. Cheating requires that the perpetrator wants to obtain an advantage, which can be a benefit for himself or the company (if he acts under the conviction that the risk would not materialise and the company would profit).

From the point of view of the harm principle, excessive risk-taking by managers may be criminalised for several reasons. First, according to this principle, a criminal offence should aim at preventing harm or unreasonable risk of harm. Excessive risk of loss in fact represents both aspects. On the one hand, excessive risk-taking is unreasonable. On the other hand, excessive risk-taking may create an effective setback to the company interests due to book-keeping rules requiring the inclusion of foreseeable risks and costs related to the depreciation of the value of the endangered assets, resulting in an actual lowering of the value of company's assets. The harm or unreasonable risk of harm affects not only the company, but also the shareholders, stakeholders and other actors involved. Moreover, a prohibition of certain types of acts may fulfil the requirements of the harm principle according to the concept of remote harm, if it can be established that although those acts do not necessarily lead to a loss in every case, their consequences, if occurring in a large number of companies or in systemically important companies, may be so grave that they could endanger the whole economic system, thus justifying limiting, by means of criminal law, the liberty of managers to pursue business in that manner.

There may be a variety of interests worth protecting, which may be infringed by exposing the company to excessive risk. First, there are the inherent interests of the company as an entity, which has legal personality and its own property, as well as the interests of the shareholders. Secondly, stakeholders and other groups of actors also have interests in the prosperity of the company. The analysis has demonstrated that such interests as to the level of permitted risk can be very different between these groups or even between the shareholders. The interests of the company seem to be the best common denominator of the stakes held by these actors, as it can be assumed that they will all benefit from the company's prosperity. However, the legislator may give more prevalence to the interests of the shareholders through the rules of consent to acts of the management, without which consent the acts would be considered criminal. Thirdly, the protection of systemic interests in the well-functioning economy may require that certain acts, which may result in endangering the functioning of the economic system, should be prohibited and this prohibition may need to be enforced by means of criminal law. This concerns acts which, although as such do not always expose companies to excessive risk (or cause loss), if the risk materialises in a large number of companies or in systemically important companies, may lead to endangering the correct functioning of the economic system.

The analysis of the problem in view of the principle of *ultima ratio* and the principle of proportionality demonstrated that while generally other tools – legal or civil, of administrative or company law nature, or extra-legal methods – should be used in the first place in order to contain excessive risk-taking, there are a variety of arguments in favour of using criminal law to sanction acts that expose companies to such risks. It results that it is legitimate and proportionate to provide for a general offence of intentional mismanagement, including reckless mismanagement, if the latter is committed for personal interests (general offence of mismanagement punishing exposure of the company to excessive risk or causing a loss). However, it would be excessive to criminalise reckless mismanagement not perpetrated for such interest, or negligent mismanagement. Moreover, it was demonstrated that certain particular rules which are intended to prevent the exposure of the company to excessive risk (or prevent loss) may be deemed so important, and their breach so grave in terms of possible consequences for the economic system, that such breaches may be separately criminalised, even if committed negligently (offence(s) enforcing concrete risk-preventing rules). In each case, it must be verified whether other tools would not suffice to contain the breaches in question.

As to legal certainty and fair warning, if excessive risk-taking is to be criminalised, it must be made clear in such a way that managers can avoid criminal liability by abstaining from what is prohibited. It has been concluded that the description of the circle of potential perpetrators by enumeration of the potential functions those actors may fulfil does not necessarily add certainty. Indeed, this technique may turn out to be less just, and hence an abstract definition is to be preferred.

With regard to the first area of protection (interests of the company, including interests of the shareholders and stakeholders), as to the description of criminal conduct within the general offence of mismanagement, two techniques are possible: either by using general descriptions such as abusing or misusing the company assets or one's position (as a manager), or by referring to the breach of certain rules. The first technique would give more autonomy to the criminal law judge than the second and both present shortcomings as to legal certainty. In particular, the definition making reference to a set of rules should make it as precise as possible to which rules it refers and what kind of breach is sufficient for triggering criminal liability. By adding the requirement of result, the legislator may limit criminalisation to acts which effectively lead to concrete (excessive) endangerment of the company. Introducing this requirement may lead to unjust consequences, as it could be a question of sheer luck if an act, which in normal circumstances would expose the company to excessive risk, and thus should be avoided, does not in fact do so in a concrete case. It remains, however, a policy question whether to include this requirement in the definition of the offence or not. If the former is chosen, then the legislation should be clear about it. By including the requirement of result, the focus of the assessment of the manager's act changes, while without it the manager's act (abuse of the company) needs to be such that in normal circumstances it exposes the company to excessive risk. As to *mens rea*, the requirement would differ only slightly between the versions containing the requirement of result or omitting it. More important differences would result if the offence makes reference to a set of rules. In this case, it needs to be clarified how detailed the knowledge of the perpetrator as to these rules and what constitutes breach of them must be. Moreover, the offence should be precise in defining the requirement of personal interest, which is recommended for reckless mismanagement.

As to the second area of protection (systemic interests), criminalising breaches of concrete rules should present fewer difficulties with respect to legal certainty, provided that the rules and what constitutes breach of them are properly described and the offence includes a precise indication as to the required *mens rea*.

7

Conclusions

1. Introduction

Cicero considered it to be the gravest injustice when a person hides their falsity under a mask of good man.[1] Dante puts those who betray trust vested in them in the lowest circle of sinners.[2] Managers who act against the interests of their companies can easily find themselves at the centre of criticism from these two moralists. While the mask of serious and successful businessman and the attached prestige can hide their abuses, it qualifies their acts as the gravest injustice according to Cicero. Betraying the trust of those who entrusted their assets to them and the belief of the stakeholders that their behaviour is motivated only by the interest of the companies they represent deserve the greatest damnation in the eyes of Dante.

The previous chapter demonstrated that it is legitimate to criminalise excessive risk-taking by managers in companies and examined the conditions determining the scope of such criminalisation. It has been concluded that two types of criminal offences are legitimate and proportionate:

(1) a general offence of mismanagement punishing exposure of the company to excessive risk (or causing a loss);
(2) offence(s) enforcing concrete risk-preventing rules.

As to the first type of offence, it proved to be proportionate to criminalise mismanagement, if it was committed intentionally or recklessly, provided that for the

[1] 'Totius autem iniustitiae nulla capitalior quam eorum, qui tum, cum maxime fallunt, id agunt, ut viri boni esse videantur': Cicero, De Officiis, from the double language edition by Walter Miller (London: Heinemann, 1928) para [41]. There exist several translations of this book, besides the one mentioned, also: Cicero, On Obligations (Translated by PG Walsh, Oxford University Press, 2000) 17; Cicero, On Duties (Translated by MT Griffin, MT Griffin and EM Atkins (eds), Cambridge University Press, 1991). The version cited at the beginning of the book uses the translation quoted in Paul G Chevigny, 'From Betrayal to Violence: Dante's Inferno and the Social Construction of Crime' (2001) (26) 4 Law and Social Inquiry 787, 788.

[2] 'Per l'altro modo quell' amor s'oblia che fa natura, e quel ch'è poi aggiunto, di che la fede spezïal si cria; onde nel cerchio minore, ov' é 'l punto de l'universo in su che Dite siede, qualunque trade in etterno è consunto': Dante Alighieri, La Divina Commedia, Inferno (Giorgio Petrocchi (ed), Milan: A Mondadori Editore, 1966–67) canto 11, paras [61]–[66]. The English translation used at the beginning of this book provided by Robert Hollander and Jean Hollander, The Inferno (Doubleday/Anchor, 2000).

latter form the perpetrator acted from personal interests. Its aim is to protect the interests of the company, together with the interests of the shareholders as well as stakeholders. The question whether the interests of the shareholders (as owners of the company) should be given priority is a policy issue, which will mainly be reflected through the rules on the validity of consent to acts exposing the company to excessive risk. The second type of offences aims at protecting the interests of the economic system. Depending on the concrete rule in question, the gravity of potential consequences of its breach and other considerations, it may be legitimate to criminalise the breach even if committed negligently. The following section will delve more into the details of what should be the conditions and boundaries of criminalisation of excessive risk-taking, which variables the legislator may use in defining it, and what may be the consequences of particular choices.

2. How to Criminalise Excessive Risk-Taking by Managers?

The problem of excessive risk-taking by managers in companies cannot be tackled by criminal law alone. On the contrary, it primarily depends on the decisions as to what corporate and business culture should be promoted and expected, what kind of extra-legal tools the legislator can rely on, and how self-regulation and civil, company and administrative law instruments are used. In accordance with the principle of *ultima ratio*, criminal law should only complement the rules set out in these other domains. Even if one rejects this principle, from a practical point of view it remains reasonable that the criminal justice apparatus cannot be used in order to correct every aspect of the market economy. Therefore, the question to be answered in this section could also be formulated as: what is the role of criminal law as a tool when dealing with excessive risk-taking?

The previous chapter and this one examine criminalisation of excessive risk-taking in general, and not in a way which would be embedded in a concrete legal system. Some basic assumptions as to the features of such systems are made, as for instance a liberal approach to criminal law (eg criminal law as *ultima ratio*), the rule of law and the market economy, but otherwise none of the analysed systems or similar is borne in mind here. Such an approach has three consequences.

First, each legal tradition is embedded in a certain legal terminology, which encompasses certain legal traditions and the use of terms set by the legislator and by the jurisprudence. Therefore, the use of technical terms must accord with this terminology for systemic coherence. In view of that, this analysis necessarily uses the terms out of such context. It concentrates on the sense of the elements of which the definition of an offence is composed, and not on the connotations which particular expressions may have in different languages in view of traditions using these languages, in particular as to the English or common law tradition.

This chapter will only provide elements of such a definition; these elements can be expressed differently in different traditions.

Secondly, a concrete system of criminal law provides for a large set of rules, which in the continental tradition is described as the general part, eg rules on attempt or cooperation in the commission of the offence. Similarly, criminalisation in a concrete legal system takes into account the rules of criminal procedure and the organisation of the justice system. This analysis necessarily remains outside that context and cannot take into account such particularities. It therefore will not enter into details related to such aspects, which would need to be clarified in view of a concrete system. For instance, the analysis will suggest the scope of criminalisation, which in a concrete system could be achieved by describing the conduct in the definition of the offence or by rules of attempt. In other words, the analysis below gives an indication of what is crucial in the criminalisation of excessive risk-taking, what is the core wrongdoing, without translating it into a concrete legal text which would need to be adapted to the relevant legal tradition and context.

Thirdly, in view of the remarks on the principle of *ultima ratio*, an offence criminalising excessive risk-taking would necessarily be placed in a context of certain regulation encompassing different branches of law and extra-legal tools. It would be placed within a concrete economic and criminal policy. It is assumed here that criminal law is not the tool by which economic policy is decided. It is merely an auxiliary instrument, which may help, in respecting its basic principles, to achieve the goal of this policy. Hence, a study which focuses on criminal law cannot give general recommendations as to that policy. This proposal demonstrates what kinds of acts may deserve criminal punishment and what the reasons are to consider punishing them. However, the precise scope of criminalisation depends on choices linked mainly to economic policy and other social, political and historical factors.[3] Ultimately, it will also be the choice of the legislator as to what it considers necessary to subject to criminal punishment. Therefore, the proposal will show different variables the legislator may use to achieve its goals, and the possible consequences.

The two types of proposed offences – general offence of mismanagement and offence(s) enforcing concrete risk-preventing rules – will be analysed in turn. As both present the same dilemmas as to the definition of the perpetrator, this aspect will be analysed jointly. The ensuing analysis will study the possible scope of the general offence in the following order: definition of the perpetrator, conduct, result and *mens rea*. Then, the problems of defining the second type of offence will be discussed. The results of this analysis will be summarised and followed by some remarks on general aspects of criminal liability in the context of these offences. Finally, the analysis will close with an examination of the five model cases in light of the proposed scope and modalities of criminal liability.

[3] Andrew Ashworth, Principles of Criminal Law, 6th edn (Oxford University Press, 2009) 17.

2.1. Definition of the Perpetrator

It results from the analysis above that for reasons of certainty as well as in order to encompass all the necessary categories of potential perpetrators, it is preferable to define them by using an abstract definition. There is no need for the offence to be limited to companies or to the business context. It can very well encompass all types of situations where assets of other persons were entrusted to somebody. However, the analysis below will be limited to companies, as other categories of potential perpetrators (eg lawyers) would require a separate study.

Since the general provision criminalising excessive risk-taking should compensate for the loss of control of the assets by the owners, understood here as both the company and the shareholders, the perpetrator has to be a person to whom the assets were entrusted, giving him certain powers to make use of them for the benefit of the owner, thereby creating a duty of care. Moreover, it is better that the definition encompass the power to make binding decisions in the name of the company in order not to allow the exclusion of decisions that would not concern transfer of property. Such decisions would necessarily have a potential impact on the assets. The power to make use of the assets or represent the company's interests can come from different legal sources, be those a statute, a contract, or both combined, as well as decisions of competent organs (eg in case of insolvency procedure). Finally, the definition should also guarantee that if the legal basis for entrusting the assets is void or has terminated, but the perpetrator is executing the above rights, he can also be criminally liable. This would also allow the provision to encompass persons who execute these powers de facto, but hide behind persons executing these functions only on paper. Contrary to the situation of punishing de facto managers in a system which limits criminalisation to certain categories of enumerated persons, a system which encompasses all categories of persons who manage the assets of the company sends a clear message that abuses of such rights are considered criminal, regardless of the category of persons.

Of course, there are types of decisions which the manager cannot take alone, but the validity of which depends on two or more individuals concurring. If the decision is invalid (eg only one of the managers agrees to the excessively risky decision and the other refuses to concur with him), the company is not exposed to risk. The criminalisation of the act of the manager who agreed to the decision will be a policy decision and also largely depend on the approach to attempts in a concrete legal system.

A manager will usually be afforded some margin of discretion while using these powers. However, assets of the company can also be entrusted to a person without allowing them any margin of discretion as regards how to manage them, but in order to keep them or make certain use(s) thereof. An abuse of such assets is usually penalised by offences of misappropriation. Generally, these situations are characterised by more control over the use of the assets, whereas the managers in situations analysed in this book normally have much more discretion.

The main problem with using these offences is that the conceptual wrongdoing in question mainly concerns a person who is given something in order to use it in a certain, predetermined way and then uses it differently. The conceptual wrongdoing is different in the sense that in this offence, the perpetrator usurps the rights of the owner (to decide how to use the entrusted assets), while the situations discussed in this analysis concern a perpetrator who is granted the right to decide, within certain remits. The former scenario is not studied here, although usually criminalised in various legal orders (eg the French *abus de confiance*). It is a policy question whether to differentiate the gravity of these offences, eg by different level of punishment. The argument in favour would be that the element of discretion brings more possibilities to abuse the entrusted assets and less control over their use, which needs to be compensated by a stronger criminal law reaction.

This issue is linked to the problem of the scope of perpetrators of the offence to be decided here. If the scope of criminalisation is limited only to certain categories of managers (eg the most senior ones), there is a risk that other offences, in particular misappropriation, might be used, potentially resulting in overly broad interpretation and unjust legal solutions.

On the other hand, one may consider whether certain categories of managers should not be subject to stricter regulation, for example CEOs. As to the general provision, the main problem is that it would need to be justified why such individuals should be treated more severely and how to define the respective requirements. The differentiation could also be made on the level of punishment. Companies may differ as to their structure, in particular as to the practical aspects, and it is not necessarily the case that those at the top of the managerial hierarchy take the most relevant decisions, although the level of duties they have is the highest. Encompassing all categories of managers ensures the protection of companies without allowing some persons, despite their being able to take decisions that expose the company to excessive risk (or cause loss), to escape criminal liability or to be punished less severely than others purely for reasons of the company's structure, without there being any difference in their wrongdoing. Such gaps in the law could lead to impunity for certain categories of managers.

In sum, it has been argued here that the definition of the perpetrator should be made using abstract terms referring to his position as a person to whom company assets were entrusted, powers to make binding agreements in the name of the company were vested or who is obliged not to act against the company's interests. A certain margin of discretion should be presupposed. These rights and obligations can come from different sources and the provision should also allow for punishing managers who executed their function de facto (eg after the relationship has terminated). It remains, however, a policy question whether all categories of managers should be subject to criminal liability and whether all categories should be punished equally. Such decisions may result in overly broad interpretation of other provisions. Equal criminalisation of all types of managers is in particular recommended as to the general offence. However, this does not exclude the possibility to differentiate the punishment among the managers, taking into account their different powers and influence as regards the detrimental decision.

As to the special provisions punishing infringements of concrete risk-management rules, the scope of perpetrators will depend on the type of rule in question and on who is responsible for enforcing it. While the scope of perpetrators may be as wide as for the general offence, it is also conceivable that certain categories of persons, eg the CEO, the management board, etc, are made responsible for ensuring that certain concrete rules are observed and that failures to meet such obligation are subject to criminal sanction.

2.2. General Offence of Mismanagement

2.2.1. Conduct

As mentioned in the analysis above, while designing a general provision criminalising mismanagement including excessive risk-taking, the legislator may choose one of the two methods of describing the criminal conduct. The first one consists of making direct reference to a breach of specified rules which aim to protect the company's assets and prosperity, which breach may expose the company to excessive risk, and are embedded in one or more (or even all) of the following sources: statutes or other legal acts; administrative or judicial decisions; the manager's contract and its annexes; any other applicable guidelines and standards. The second technique would use such terms as abusing or misusing the company's assets or the right to make binding statements in the name of the company, misrepresenting the company's interests or acting against them, or breaching duties of loyalty or care. While the first technique makes criminal law rely more on the analysis of non-criminal law rules, the second would favour criminal law autonomy.

It has been demonstrated that, paradoxically, the reference to the concrete rules does not provide legal certainty, but may create confusion as to which rules trigger criminal liability and which do not. This problem is also linked to the question of the extent to which a rule must be broken. A breach of rule may be of lesser importance and insufficient to justify criminal liability. However, from the point of view of the first technique it would trigger criminal liability, while under the second approach it might not qualify as an abuse. Moreover, it may also result in a situation where criminal law is used to enforce civil liability. This problem may result in a tendency to add some qualifying terms to the breach, as was attempted in Germany by adding the term '*gravierend*' (rough meaning: severely). Such a solution would not necessarily enhance legal certainty. On the other hand, there may be situations where the manager misuses his powers and, while not in breach of any rules defining criminal liability, is nonetheless in breach of his duty of care, which although for some reason is not inscribed in the catalogue of rules, yet in the case at hand would undoubtedly be applicable. The question of whether this problem may occur depends on the catalogue of the applicable sources of rules.

Unless these problems can be remedied in a satisfying manner, preference should be given to the second method.

Describing the conduct by using the second method is also not flawless from the point of view of legal certainty, as it uses general terms such as abuse or misuse. Nevertheless, the shortcoming of this technique can be remedied and it can be in conformity with the European Court of Human Rights (ECtHR)'s take on the limitations set out in ECHR, Article 7, in particular if the case-law clarifies the doubts which are created by the abstract language of the provision.[4] The decision on the choice of technique will, however, be linked to the legislator's view as to how autonomous a criminal judge ought to be in analysing the acts detrimental to the company. It will also be linked to the approach to subsidiarity in a concrete legal system, ie whether it is required that the perpetrator's act is unlawful in view of other than criminal law provisions. If the legislator opts for the first method, the deficiencies described above should also be remedied. In particular, it should be made clear which breaches of which rules trigger criminal liability, ie whether every breach would trigger such liability or if there should be some qualifying threshold.

Whichever of the two methods is chosen, it must be ensured that various different types of acts which managers may perform and which would excessively endanger the company (or cause loss) are covered, including: legal acts, such as making binding agreements (those transferring the company's property as well as those creating obligations for the company); factual uses of the company's assets; and acts which may trigger consequences as to the company's interests (eg bribing a public official with private money but in order to get a contract for the company). It should include decisions which have immediate influence on the company's interests, as well as strategic decisions which will influence the company's interests only once implemented by other employees. As to legal acts, it ought to include both acts which are valid and those that are void (since the manager had no right to perform them, or no longer had the right to perform them due to rules of procedure having been violated) but may have some influence on the company's interests (eg are valid as to a third party involved).

The last aspect to be considered when designing the criminal conduct of the offence of mismanagement concerns the justificatory effect of consent to managers' acts given by the shareholders. Necessarily, consent can be envisaged only in the context of 'intentional' and 'reckless mismanagement', since the specific offence would protect systemic interests and not those of the company or shareholders. The problem and its solution are deeply embedded in the approach as to what constitutes a company in a concrete system, and as regards the position of the manager as a person managing the entrusted assets. As to the first aspect, the company may predominantly be considered as in the ownership of its shareholders, with

[4] See Chapter 6, 2.4.2.

the primary goal to serve their interests; or it may be seen as a legal entity having its own interests independent from shareholders' caprices. The first approach will naturally favour the interests of the shareholders, while the second approach would safeguard also the interests of the stakeholders and give preference to them, in situations where the shareholders wish to allow an act which exposes the company to excessive risk. The choice as to which interests should prevail will impact on the question of the function of the consent of the shareholders. The exculpating function of consent can be supported by the following arguments. The shareholders own the company and they have the right to make use of their property as they see fit. Moreover, the interests of other stakeholders should be safeguarded in different ways, since mismanagement is mainly about loyalty to the company, and thus to the shareholders. However, this reasoning is contradicted if the company is considered an independent entity with its own interests (making a profit, being successful, etc) and the legislator wishes to grant more protection to stakeholders and other interested actors, as well as to systemic interests in the correct functioning of companies, thus limiting shareholders' potential influence. In such a configuration, the managers' duty of loyalty would be strictly referred to the company as such and not to the shareholders. All of these choices are to be made within company law and criminal law should be applied accordingly in a subsidiary way.

Depending on these decisions, there are three possible outcomes as to the impact of consent on liability for criminal mismanagement. It may have no impact at all, or it may fully exculpate the managers, but the legislator may also provide that consent exculpates the managers to a certain extent, eg excluding the exculpatory effect of consent if the decision may endanger the existence of the company. If full or limited consent is accepted, the rules for valid consent should also be clarified, which is in turn linked to the problem of the protection of minority shareholders.

2.2.2. Result

The detrimental aspects of the conduct will be described by its result, either potential or real. The result (exposing the company to excessive risk of loss) may appear in different forms in the definition of the offence. There are three possibilities of including result into the definition of the offence. According to the first model, it is required as a potential result. According to this model, it must be verified whether what the perpetrator did could cause the required result, so the result is part of the conduct description. The second model requires a proof of actual result as it occurred. In this model, the result must be proved independently of the conduct and then connected with the latter (eg according to the rules of objective ascription). The third model concentrates on the intended result, so it is placed within the analysis of *mens rea*. The first two models, potential result and effective result,of course also require that the result be reflected in the *mens rea*. The third model would in fact differ in comparison to the two others in that it would include situations where the conduct was completely harmless, although performed with bad intentions. It is a question for particular legal systems whether this type of conduct is criminalised (eg *untauglicher Versuch*), which could be also achieved through the law on attempts. Hence, the ensuing analysis will concentrate on the first two models.

The relevant result here consists in exposure to excessive risk of loss. It should, of course, also include an effective loss. The main difference between the first and the second model, out of the three enumerated above, is the moment at which the detrimental result will be assessed. According to the model of potential result, the conduct will be considered detrimental because it potentially causes a loss or exposes the company to excessive risk of loss. In this model, it is not necessary to verify whether such loss occurred, or whether a concrete situation of exposure to excessive risk (concrete endangerment) has been created, but whether the conduct as such was of such a nature that in the normal course of action it would lead to such a result.

According to the model of effective result, it must be proved that the conduct effectively caused a result: a loss, or a state in which the company is exposed to excessive risk (concrete endangerment). Except those situations in which it can be claimed that the exposure to risk constitutes a loss (according to the book-keeping rules), it is necessary that the legislator expressly provide that criminalisation includes a result in the form of mere exposure to excessive risk. It is also possible to criminalise the exposure to excessive risk through attempt.

It is submitted here that exposure to excessive risk may be a detrimental consequence of the manager's act, which should be criminalised as such together with causing a loss. According to the reasoning presented in the previous chapters and here, it is the manager's act which is more relevant than its eventual consequences. Naturally, the occurrence of result may have an influence on the evidentiary process. However, the manager should abstain from decisions exposing the company to a risk to which it should not be exposed or at a level which should not be reached. By taking such a decision, he breaches his duty of loyalty or care and such acts are worthy of criminal punishment, regardless of whether the company is effectively exposed to risk, or loss eventually occurs. The consequences are to a certain extent a question of luck, in particular in such a dynamic, fast-changing environment as business activities may be. The margin of risk that the manager is allowed to take may be wide, but in any case, he should stay within these margins. If a manager gambles with the assets of the company (*nach Art eines Spielers*),[5] what is criminal is not so much the fact that the assets are eventually lost, but that he manages them improperly. It is not a just result that by performing the same act of mismanagement, one manager incurs criminal liability and another does not because of factors they cannot control. Such injustice may result in attempts to extend the understanding of loss in order to look for ways to penalise courses

[5] BGH (27 February 1975) NJW 1975, 1234, 1236.

of conduct which are deemed worthy of punishment. This does not mean that the punishment may not reflect the difference in harm caused by these acts. Another aspect, which reinforces this claim, refers to the *mens rea* and will be explained in the following section.

The question of choosing one of the methods of including result (potential or effectively occurred) will depend on which aspects the legislator decides to focus on, and also on the tradition as to criminalisation of attempts. By using the method of effective result, it is necessary that the legislator expressly provide that creating a state of concrete excessive endangerment is criminalised. Otherwise, there is a risk of over-extensive interpretation. Moreover, the question of criminal liability should not be dependent only on book-keeping rules, which might be the case were the exposure to excessive risk to be interpreted through the concept of loss. The problem which may be difficult to solve according to this method is at what point in time the state of excessive risk is to be assessed. It requires the verification of possibly complex chains of causality. The choice of method to reflect the result will also have to be echoed in the *mens rea* requirements.

The main difference in scope of criminalisation resulting from use of the technique of potential result is that it can also encompass situations which in the normal course of action would expose the company to excessive risk of loss (or cause a loss), but where due to an abnormal course of events a state of endangerment did not emerge. According to the philosophy presented here, even such acts ought to be criminalised, since it is the excessively risky decision which should be sanctioned and not the detrimental result, which failed to occur due to reasons beyond the control of the manager. For all these reasons, the technique of potential loss is preferred here.

Irrespective of the preferred method of including risk in the definition of the offence, the risk must be excessive according to the standards applicable in a given situation. Its excessiveness may come from the fact that the company must not be exposed to certain types of risk or that its level is too high. As to the first one, it is, for example, abnormal to expose the company to a risk of criminal or administrative sanctions (if applicable) for bribing a public official in order to obtain a benefit for the company. Similarly, for certain types of companies it will be abnormal to invest in highly risky derivatives, while it may be in the normal course of business for others. As to the second possibility, it is normal for banks to be exposed to a risk that a client will be unable to repay a loan. The risk becomes abnormal if the guarantees for the loan do not meet the standard applicable in the case.

Criminal law should not become a tool for sanctioning minor infringements in managing the company's assets, but serious breaches of one's duties of loyalty and care. Therefore, such cases as, for example, granting a loan where guarantees are only very slightly insufficient should not be penalised. This can be ensured either by prosecutorial discretion and adequately formulated guidelines, or by setting a threshold which would exclude criminalisation, if risk is minimally excessive.

2.2.3. Mens Rea

(i) Categories

Neither exposure to risk, even excessive, nor causing loss is abnormal in business activities and as such should not lead per se to criminal liability. The defining element is the perpetrator's mind-set, which will differentiate an act of simple mismanagement (be it due to the manager's bad luck, lack of intuition, incompetence, etc) from criminal mismanagement, which consists in the breach of his relationship of trust and duty of care. Whereas the first category of conduct may trigger different types of reaction, from dismissal to civil liability, it is justified that (only) the second leads to criminal conviction. Therefore, it is to a large extent the *mens rea* which will transform the act of 'simple' mismanagement into criminal mismanagement.

In the previous chapter, three general types of mental attitude of the perpetrator towards his act have been differentiated: 'intentional mismanagement or misuse of the company'; 'reckless mismanagement'; and 'negligent mismanagement'.[6] The purpose of this section is to analyse how these categories would translate into more concrete *mens rea* requirements. As has been said, the terms used in this chapter may evoke different concepts in concrete legal systems, so they should be taken here only in the meaning described below.[7]

These are the general possibilities to analyse *mens rea*:

(a) *Dolus directus* (direct intention): the perpetrator wants to bring about a certain result or perform an act of certain qualities.

(b) *Dolus indirectus* (indirect intention): the perpetrator does not want to bring about the result or to perform an act of certain qualities, but is 100 per cent or almost sure that what he is doing will do so.

(c) *Dolus eventualis*: the perpetrator does not want to bring about the result or to perform an act of certain qualities, but is aware that this may be the case and accepts this possibility.

(d) Recklessness (or conscious negligence): the perpetrator is aware that what he is doing may bring about the result or may be an act of certain qualities, however, he is convinced that it would not be the case.

(e) Negligence: the perpetrator does not foresee that what he is doing may bring about the result or be an act of certain qualities, however, it was possible for him to foresee it, a reasonable person would have done so and he was supposed to do so (and act accordingly).

[6] See Chapter 6, 3.4.1.

[7] Since national systems differ as to details of these categories (eg how to differentiate between recklessness and dolus eventualis), their understanding is defined here for the purpose of this analysis. See, eg the analysis of differences in understanding the terms 'recklessness', 'conscious negligence' and 'luxuria' in Jeroen Blomsma, Mens Rea and Defences in European Criminal Law (Intersentia, 2012) 134 et seq, see also 60 et seq.

In the context analysed here, the result may be a situation of exposure of the company to excessive risk of loss (concrete endangerment) or a loss. As to the act of certain qualities, it is an act which in normal circumstances exposes the company to excessive risk or causes a loss.

The analysis in the previous chapter showed that it is justified to legislate for an offence punishing mismanagement if committed intentionally or recklessly, provided that in the latter case the manager was motivated by personal interests. These two modalities of *mens rea*, intention and recklessness with personal interest, will be analysed in turn. This section will further elaborate on the findings of the previous chapter, which demonstrated that it is not proportionate to criminalise mismanagement (in a general manner) when committed negligently.

(ii) Intentional Mismanagement

Depending on which of the ways to describe the criminal conduct is chosen, the intention can be directed at different aspects of the offence: the potential detrimental results of the act (exposure to excessive risk or loss); the effective results of the act; as well as also on the breach of the rules or standards (to variable extent), if such breach is included in the definition of the offence. The consequences of making the choices as to the definition of the conduct for the definition of the *mens rea* as regards all three forms of *dolus* and their formulations have been sketched out in the previous chapter.[8] It is a question of legal tradition how the *mens rea* will be formulated, especially in relation to the general part of criminal law, if the system in question provides for one. Taking into account that the offence will encompass both possibilities (exposure to excessive risk of loss, as well as an effective loss), when designing it, the following reasoning may be taken into consideration.

Defining the *mens rea* as *dolus eventualis* towards exposing the company to a loss may be seen as equivalent to describing it as *dolus eventualis* towards exposing the company to an effective loss. If a manager of a bank deciding on a loan grants it knowing that it may not be sufficiently guaranteed (eg because he has doubts as to the value of the house given in mortgage, although he does not check it), which would expose the company to an abnormal risk of loss, but hoping that the debtor would repay the credit, he in fact accepts the possibility of loss (*dolus eventualis* towards a loss). It does not matter that he hopes that, even if the guarantee is insufficient, the client will be able to repay the loan anyway. Hence, an offence criminalising *dolus eventualis* towards an effective loss does not need to refer to excessive risk.

The *mens rea* of 'intentional mismanagement' will be constituted by two pairs. The first pair consists of intention (direct and indirect) and *dolus eventualis* towards bringing about a loss to the company. The second pair consists of intention (direct and indirect) and *dolus eventualis* to expose the company to excessive risk

[8] See Chapter 6, 3.4.2.

of such loss. The latter alternative does not mean that the perpetrator must intend the risk to be excessive, but he must want to create a certain situation which he knows may or will excessively endanger the company. The intention does not need to refer to all the details of the act in question, but it is necessary for the manager to know that the act in normal circumstances or in these concrete circumstances will lead to a situation of excessive risk to the company.

(iii) Reckless Mismanagement

As it is understood here, recklessness (advertent or conscious negligence) is distinguishable from intentional mismanagement in that the perpetrator would not want to cause loss to the company, nor would he accept the possibility that the company is exposed to excessive risk of loss. However, the perpetrator would know that his act is such that, in normal circumstances, it would expose the company to excessive risk of loss, or would know that it might expose the company to such risk, but he was convinced that it would not be the case (depending whether the offence is defined without or with the requirement of result). For example, while granting a loan the manager does not perform a correct analysis of the credit-worthiness of the client allowing him to foresee that it may be insufficient (or suspecting that it is so), but believing that the client will be able to repay the loan. He is not aware of the fact which would normally lead him to believe that the creditworthiness is insufficient, but he is generally aware that a lack of proper analysis may lead to the granting of credit to a person to whom it should not be granted, thereby exposing the bank to excessive risk that the credit would not be paid back.

As was demonstrated above, the criminal law should not be used as a tool to discipline sloppy managers. It would both render impossible pursuing business activities and saturate the criminal justice system, if the prosecuting services and criminal judges were responsible for verifying and sanctioning breaches of all possible rules applicable to managers. However, the legislator may choose to criminalise such behaviour if it constitutes disloyalty to the company, which arisies when managers behave carelessly because they are pursuing personal interests. This may not only protect the interests of the company and the shareholders, but also of stakeholders and other parties who have an interest in the company being run correctly (ie that managers care about its good standing and do not favour their own interests) and also act with the expectation that it will be run correctly.

However, liability for reckless mismanagement should not be determined too easily. It should comprise situations where the manager places his own interests ahead of the interests of the company. This does not mean that in cases which were qualified as intentional mismanagement, managers may not pursue a personal agenda. On the contrary, in most cases they would do so. However, it was shown that it is unnecessary to demonstrate this in order to justify criminalisation of such behaviour. Reckless mismanagement would become criminal only where managers disregard some rules or standards which they know they should observe, in order to attempt to obtain some personal advantage. They foresee that by disregarding these rules or standards they may create a situation which might turn out to be excessively risky for the company, but they hope that it will not materialise (neither the situation, nor the risk).

On the other hand, if the manager knowingly breaches the rule or the standard, but considers that he is acting for the benefit of the company and hopes that the company will actually benefit, and without seeking personal benefit (except perhaps the realisation of some personal ambition), criminalisation seems an excessive response. Such acts would come very close to situations of managerial creativity, which as such, must not be thwarted by the prospect of criminal sanctions. The sole fact of breaching a rule, even whilst foreseeing that it may endanger the company, can best be remedied by other legal or extra-legal methods. Engaging the criminal justice apparatus in assessing in fact only whether the perpetrator knowingly breached the rule or the standard and foresaw its potential detrimental consequences may result in the criminal process focusing only on aspects of civil, company or administrative law (or those provided by other applicable sources), and transform the criminal law judge into the arbiter of management quality. Furthermore, there would be no clear wrongdoing which could be sanctioned by the criminal conviction. This wrongfulness lies in the fact that the manager pursued his own interest at the expense of the company.

In order to guarantee that such an offence would not criminalise all cases of careless management, the requirement of personal interest should be taken seriously and be strictly interpreted. This requirement is not about punishing vice. Personal ambitions or (even) covetousness are natural motivators in the business world, and it might be counter-productive to constrain them. Moreover, this requirement ought not to be understood in such a way as to render it obsolete. To accept as personal intent such motivations as not losing one's job, strengthening one's position within the company or seeking prestige might result in the requirement being fulfilled in all imaginable cases.

The requirement of personal interest should ensure that criminalisation is limited to situations in which managers, instead of acting in the interests of the company, start using it as a vehicle to achieve their own goals. These goals may concern them directly, eg higher remuneration, obtaining a bonus or making a gain through another company, which benefits at the expense of the company in question. The requirement would also be fulfilled where a person seeks to increase his bonus through short-term gains, while the excessive risk taken might materialise in a longer perspective. Managers often have shares in the company they manage, so they profit when the share-value increases. Seeking to increase the value of these shares should be deemed to fulfil the requirement of personal interest only in cases where the manager acts mainly in order to fulfil this goal (eg achieve a short-term hike) whilst disregarding the interests of the company.

The personal interest does not need to be directly linked to the perpetrator. It may concern his family, friends, business partners or companies in which he has an interest.

(iv) Excluding Negligent Mismanagement

According to the same philosophy of not using criminal law to sanction careless or sloppy managers, criminal liability for negligence as regards the general criminalisation of excessive risk-taking should be excluded.

In view of the possibilities to design the offence elaborated above, the manager could be negligent in the four following forms: (a) he might not know that his act would be such that in normal circumstances it would expose the company to excessive risk, but he could have and should have foreseen that (modality of abuse without result); (b) he did not foresee that his act would expose the company to excessive risk, but he could have and should have foreseen that (modality requiring a result); (c) he did not foresee that his act would breach some applicable rule or standard or he did not know about the rule or the standards, but he could have and should have known that; (d) the breach of the rule or the standard is such that in normal circumstances it would expose the company to excessive risk (modality of breach of rules without result) or it effectively exposed the company to excessive risk (modality of breach of rules requiring a result), however, in all these situations the manager was unaware of the potential detrimental results of his acts.

The argument against general liability for negligent mismanagement would be very similar to the reasoning as stated above in respect of recklessness without seeking personal interest. Although one can say that the manager's negligence is wrong in the sense that he knew that he is supposed to abide by certain rules or he knew that he is supposed to acquaint himself with a set of rules and he disregarded these obligations, but the wrongdoing is less significant in comparison to a situation where the manager acts knowing that what he is doing may be against the company's interests. The need to stigmatise such behaviour is much less significant. Moreover, such criminalisation may be counter-productive as it risks paralysing business affairs. It would make the judge a general arbiter of the quality of business decisions and an adjudicator of all possible breaches of applicable rules or standards. Whether this might be justified for some particularly important rules with systemic relevance, it is disproportionate in general. It might create a climate of very conservative management.

It could be conceivable to criminalise negligent mismanagement as described above, adding the requirement of personal interest. It would encompass situations in which the perpetrator breached a rule or standard, without even foreseeing that it might expose the company to excessive risk, but in order to satisfy some personal goal. The wrongdoing of such act is more significant, as it would encompass behaviour where the manager uses the company for his own purposes, but completely ignoring potentially detrimental consequences. Although there may be moral grounds for blaming such a manager, as he is cheating the shareholders (and other actors) by breaching the rules he is expected to respect and he is doing so for his personal interest, such an act is certainly less wrongful than in all previous situations, where the manager was acting at least with an awareness of the detrimental character of this act.

If the manager is convinced that the company cannot be harmed or exposed to abnormal risk by his act, it is impossible to say that he is trying to attain his personal goals at the expense of the company. These two objectives are not irreconcilable. It is normal that the company profits from the manager's energy to attain personal goals, for example, by linking his bonus to performance through his ownership of some of the company's shares. Managers may differ as to their attitude towards risk, however in general they are rather risk-leaning persons. Looking for innovation and finding new ways of dealing with problems or new concepts are dispositions that the companies profit from. Such an attitude may lead them to breach some rules of conduct, which they are supposed to safeguard. If necessary, this can be dealt with by civil or administrative law, through best practices or guidelines. Adding criminal liability may unnecessarily thwart their initiative, as well as unnecessarily burden the criminal justice system, or otherwise leave such a provision a dead letter.

In particular, criminal law should not be made a tool which would serve to cure all damages done after certain practices turn out to be detrimental or riskier than expected, eg after a financial crisis erupts and reveals these aspects. If the manager was convinced that certain decisions are beneficial for the company because they are widespread and considered a normal tool for pursuing certain business activities, he cannot be criminally blamed if these decisions are later revealed to have been detrimental to the company's interests. Naturally, the question of whether such a manager truly ignored the excessive risk of such activity must be answered. This aspect is linked to what was described above as a crucial function of actors in business environments whose goal is to propagate knowledge, which on the one hand, will allow managers to avoid excessively risky policies, and on the other, deprive them of excuses and make it easier to prove the fact that they foresaw the excessive risk.

In response, it is possible to add the following to the argument presented above. There is not and there cannot be a guarantee of success in business activities. The main arbiter of managers' success is the market. Other branches of law may deal with breaches of rules, if that is necessary according to their standards and values. The comparison with road traffic offences or medical malpractice highlights the different character of business activity. First of all, it is *par excellence* about innovation, whereas medical practice should primarily follow the rules, and only exceptionally consist in experimenting, which is subject to certain conditions. As to road traffic, innovation does not play a role. Moreover, the protected interests at stake are different. While health and life are the main concern in road traffic offences and medical malpractice, mismanagement concerns safeguarding financial interests. Not only are health and life more important interests to protect, but damages to them may often be irremediable. The case may be similar with environmental catastrophes. This does not mean that damages to property may not have a grave impact on victims' interests. However, the protection they require need not be as intense as in the case of the former interests.

2.3. Offence(s) Enforcing Concrete Risk-Preventing Rules

As part of the general criminalisation of excessive risk-taking analysed above, it was demonstrated that it may be legitimate to criminalise breaches of concrete rules, which might, according to empirical generalisations, expose companies to excessive risk of loss. The legislator may decide to single out particular rules or groups of rules, which are deemed of such relevance (in one, several or all business areas) that their breach needs to be criminalised. The justification for this offence(s) would be that it should prevent potentially dramatic results for the economic system as a whole. It is necessary for each such rule to demonstrate that the potentially detrimental result and the probability of its occurrence justify the need to enforce it by means of criminal law.

As to the description of conduct, it should describe the breach of the rule in question as well as the breaches triggering criminal liability, in the most precise possible way. As to the requirement of result, there will be none. This type of provision criminalises abstract endangerment of assets, ie where the breach of that (or those) rule(s) may cause detrimental results, but it is not always the case. The justification for the offence is based only on the hypothetical result: if the risk materialises in a great number of companies or in a systemically important company, the economic system might be in danger.

While such breaches will naturally be penalised if committed intentionally, it is conceivable that the legislator might find it necessary to punish even negligent breaches of some of these rules, if there are strong reasons for such a solution, in particular taking into account the relevance of observing such rules or the detrimental consequences that breach may cause. For example, it may require that in certain cases there is a need to maintain a reserve of a certain amount of money. If deemed of such crucial importance, the legislator may sanction managers who were responsible for maintaining such a reserve, even if they were not aware that the relevant amount had not been maintained, but they were able to verify the state of the reserve and were aware of their responsibility to do so.

2.4. Summing-up

The above analysis showed that the following two categories of offences are legitimate and proportionate:

(1) A general offence of mismanagement punishing exposure of the company to excessive risk (or causing a loss) in the form of:

  (a) 'Intentional mismanagement', which would be an offence committed by a manager who intentionally performs an act, which in the normal course of action would cause a loss to his company or exposes it to excessive risk of such loss or an act which effectively leads to one of these results.

Depending on the decision of the legislator, it may require a breach of defined applicable rules of standards and relevant *mens rea* towards it. This offence would aim at protecting mainly the company's interests, and in this way also the general interests of shareholders, stakeholders and other actors' interests in the correct functioning of the company. The offence would not aim directly at protecting the interests of the economic system and society as a whole, but it would be generally beneficial for the economic system and society that managers abstain from such acts. The legislator may give more or less importance to the interests of the shareholders or the stakeholders, depending on the rules on justificatory shareholders' consent.

(b) 'Reckless mismanagement', which would be an offence committed by a manager who knows that what he is doing is such an act that in normal circumstances would expose the company to excessive risk or cause a loss, or may effectively expose the company to excessive risk or cause a loss, but is convinced that it would not be the case. Similarly to the above, it may require a breach of defined applicable rules or standards and relevant *mens rea* towards it. Moreover, it is required that the perpetrator acted in their personal interest. As to the protection of legal interests, it would protect the same ones as 'intentional mismanagement'.

A general offence of negligently exposing the company to excessive risk was shown not to be legitimate.

(2) Offence(s) enforcing concrete risk-preventing rules:

(c) Specific provisions, which consist in breaking particular rules, if it can be proved (by the legislator) that they are of such grave importance in view of their relevance for the economic system that their enforcement ought to be reinforced by criminal sanction and other regulatory tools cannot be equally efficient. This breach could be penalised not only when intentional, but also if committed recklessly or negligently. The aim of this offence would be mainly to protect the interests of the economic system and of society. Naturally, it would protect also companies, shareholders and other interested actors, but this would not be the main aim.

As to the relationship between the proposed offences when applied to the same conduct, the offences under (a) and (b) are mutually exclusive, since the perpetrator's *mens rea* will be of one the other nature. As to the relationship of these two offences ('intentional' and 'reckless mismanagement') and the specific offence, it may be more complicated and would need verification depending on how the specific offence is designed, and on the rules solving these types of conflicts. In any case, the relationship does not need to be the one of *lex generalis* and *lex specialis*, since they follow different aims as regards protected interests. Thus, the application of both to one conduct could be possible, unless it is not allowed in a concrete legal system.

Three additional remarks need to be made.

First, it should be ensured that these offences are not used in cases of a minor nature. This follows from the reflection on the *ultima ratio* aspect of criminalisation, ie that criminal law should not be used to solve any conflict the company may have with the manager or to tackle any breach of its interests. For example, it might be claimed that by smashing his smartphone against the wall, the manager exposes the company to excessive risk that it would suffer the loss of its value, or even causes this loss, depending on the power of the throw. Although the manager might be obliged to reimburse the value of the phone, it would be excessive to prosecute him. Elimination of minor cases can be achieved in different ways, depending on the tools available in a concrete legal system. For example, in a system based on the opportunity principle, it can be achieved by issuing prosecutorial guidelines (and in general trusting the choices made by the prosecutors). Systems based on legality may need to add a formal threshold, for example, of a certain value of loss or potential loss if the risk materialises, at a sufficient level to eliminate negligible cases.

Secondly, the model offences proposed above have been designed outside of the context of a concrete legal system, and in translating these findings into concrete law, the legislator must include all the particularities of that system, as explained in the introduction to this section. In view of this, the legislator may decide to use different available variables to narrow or broaden criminal liability according to what can be achieved through other available tools and to the goals of its economic policy. These variables can be the definition of the perpetrator (broader or narrower circle); the description of the conduct (whether it is limited to criminalising particular rules or uses a general clause); and the requirement of result (focusing on the act analysed in its potential harmfulness or on the actual endangerment or harm). Finally, the legislator may decide to limit criminal liability to intentional mismanagement or enlarge it to recklessness. Depending on these choices and in combination with other regulatory tools, the legislator will set the legal framework for more or less space for risk in business decisions and therefore for more or less innovative management, combined with more or less security and prevention of the risk of harm.

Finally, the question of choice of penalty also depends largely on the traditions of the legal system in question and therefore is not debated in this analysis. However, in view of the paradigm of restrained use of criminal law, which stems from the rules described above, it must be borne in mind that prison sentences do not need to be the only response to criminal misconduct. Such sanctions as fines or professional disqualification can be equally or more efficient and deemed more adequate to at least some of the types of wrongdoing described in this chapter.

2.5. General Aspects of Criminal Liability

As to liability for attempts to commit offences proposed in the previous section, the decision on their penalisation depends rather on choices of concrete legal systems concerning the punishment of attempts in general, along with the criminal enforcement of economic policy. As to the first issue, whereas in some legal systems attempts are traditionally criminalised in general (eg Poland), in other jurisdictions attempts are punished only in cases where this is provided for a concrete offence (eg Germany, France). In countries where attempts are criminalised only for enumerated offences, the legislator would need to decide whether to add the offences described above to the list of such offences, which is closely linked to the second factor, namely, choices as to how much criminal law should be the tool to implement the economic policy of the country. Depending on the criteria determining when the perpetrator's act amounts to an attempt, it may involve criminalising situations where the detrimental act is about to be undertaken (as exposing to loss is already included in the offence). By criminalising such attempts, the legislator gives the investigating authorities a ground to start investigating at a much earlier stage, which may be an unnecessary burden on companies, in particular in cases where the risk of loss implied by the decision is not straightforward. On the other hand, it may also give more protection to companies, by allowing for the punishment of decisions which may have detrimental results for those companies, although undertaking them was stopped or the exposure to risk was prevented (if the legislator opted for including result into the definition of the offence).

Similarly, the solution to the issue of how extensively cooperation in the offences of mismanagement should be criminalised will depend on the general rules on different forms of participation in the offence provided by concrete legal systems. Since mismanagement is an offence with a limited circle of potential perpetrators, the main question of policy is whether persons who do not fulfil the criteria for liability as principal offenders could be held liable as accomplices of a different type if they participate in, help or encourage the commission of these offences. Moreover, the legislator must decide if it is necessary to criminalise certain acts of general encouragement to take excessively risky decisions knowing that they may be detrimental to companies. Such a prohibition may be in conflict with freedom of speech and would require a separate study to verify if it is at all legitimate.

The question of what factors may justify or provide a defence to managers will also be embedded in concrete legal systems providing grounds for excluding criminal liability, so only limited remarks may be made here. In the chapters on national legal systems, three possible factors which might exclude the liability of managers were examined (not necessarily technically justifications or defences). As to situations where the decision of the perpetrator was based on an expert opinion to the effect that the decision to be taken does not exceed permissible levels of risk, it may preclude the fulfilment of the *mens rea* requirement of knowing that the decision may be too dangerous. However, if the decision is based on a dubious opinion or the manager is normally supposed to gather more information and advice, and if he is aware of the fact that the insufficiency of this process may expose the company to excessive risk, he cannot defend himself this way. As to orders of superiors, they may have the same effect as expert opinions, unless the perpetrator (a junior manager) is aware of the detrimental character of the decision. Whether such a manager has to carry out the order or refuse to execute it must be decided by company law and other sources describing duties of the managers. If the manager behaves according to such rules, his criminal liability must be excluded. The third exculpatory reason is shareholders' consent, which was already discussed in relation to the design of the criminal conduct.

2.6. Solutions to the Five Cases

The above model of criminalisation will be tested in this section in view of the five cases that were studied in relation to each of the legal systems analysed.[9] As it was specified above, two types of offences can come into play: mismanagement (intentional or reckless), and one or more specific offences aiming at preventing and punishing breaches of concrete excessive-risk-preventing rules. Whether the second category could be applied depends on concrete rules, which were not elaborated, since they depend on the economic and criminal policy of the concrete legal system in question. Therefore, the following analysis will concentrate on the offence of mismanagement.

The first question to be asked is whether a person in all these cases can be considered a manager. It would necessarily depend on the system adopted out of the two proposed above. It was demonstrated that preference should be given to the model of abstract definition, which makes reference to having been entrusted with assets of the company and the right to make decisions in the name of the company. The perpetrators in all five cases should meet such a definition, in particular since they have a certain independence in deciding how they are going to use the entrusted assets and should do so according to the company's interests.

The perpetrator's conduct in the proposed offence of 'intentional mismanagement' consists in intentionally performing an act which in the normal course of action would cause a loss to his company or expose it to excessive risk of such loss, or effectively causes one of these results (depending on the chosen model). The definition of the offence may also contain the requirement of breaching a standard or a rule, but as these will necessarily be embedded in concrete legal systems, their analysis has to be omitted here. For all of the five cases, the requirement of conduct will be fulfilled.

Granting credit which is not sufficiently secured exposes the company to excessive risk of loss, since the company should either be compensated for taking more risk (eg by higher interest rates) or should not grant credit in such circumstances. It will be similar in the second case and there should normally be no need to have recourse to rules, eg of principals by proxy, since the act of instructing the lower-tier managers to grant the credit under such circumstances fulfils the definition of the offence.

[9] For the hypotheses of the cases and explanations, see Chapter 1, section 4.

A decision to gamble on the stock exchange with the assets of the company, if this is not part of the normal activities of the company, and especially with the assets which the company will need for its vital interests, certainly constitutes an act exposing the company to unnecessary risk of loss. Of course, the result would be different if the nature of the company were such that gambling on the stock exchange is its normal business, thus the risk would not be unnecessary.

The act of the perpetrator in the fourth case consists in concealing the information about technical problems of the new car model. Although allowing production of the new car does not immediately bring a risk of damage, the probability is higher than normal that at some point the cars will be returned by disappointed buyers and eventually the company will have to call back the whole series and perform necessary repairs. The act of confirming the car as ready for production, which (in this case) was the responsibility of the perpetrator, was taken under circumstances which exposed the company to unnecessary risk of loss in form of the costs of repairs. This was so because by not disclosing the problems he did not allow the company to calculate these costs. Had he informed the other managers, the overall costs might have been calculated taking into account possible claims and the decision on introducing the car to the market could perhaps have been considered as bearing normal risk.

As to the fifth case, the perpetrator's act would normally lead to liability for corruption. It would be a question of criminal policy whether liability for the act detrimental to the company should also be considered. If so, the rules on multiple qualifications would decide how it would be treated. If the company may be subject to negative consequences, eg in the form of criminal or administrative sanctions, due to the fact that it obtained the contract through an act of corruption, the risk of such sanctions may be considered abnormal and therefore excessive.

If the legislator chooses to require a proof of result, it would be necessary in all these cases to demonstrate that a state of concrete endangerment to company assets occurred, which should not be problematic at stages when: the credit has been granted; the money has been invested on the stock exchange; the car was allowed for production and sale; the bribe was paid or promised. If a result is not required, it needs to be demonstrated that the perpetrator's act was of such a character that in the normal course of action it would expose those assets to an excessive risk of loss (potential result), allowing such a judgement to be made already from the point of view of the perpetrator's mere act.

In all of the five cases, it is necessary that the perpetrator fulfil the *mens rea* requirement, either in the form of intention to expose the company to excessive risk or in the form of recklessness with personal intention. In all five cases, the perpetrators are aware that the acts they undertake expose their companies to excessive risk, ie they intentionally create an abnormal situation in which the probability of suffering loss is higher than normal, and in cases 3 and 5 the source of risk is also of a kind to which the company should not be exposed. Therefore, there should be no particular problem in proving that in all the cases the perpetrators acted at least with *dolus eventualis*. The requirement of personal interest would not be necessary for intentional mismanagement. If necessary, it could be proved in case 2 only, in view of the strict approach to this requirement proposed here.

The negligence version of the five cases will not lead to criminal liability as this form of *mens rea* was excluded. In order for the manager who acts without intention to fall into the scope of the proposed offences, it is necessary that he acts at least recklessly and with personal intention.

3. Evaluation of the Three National Legal Systems

3.1. General Remarks

The analysis concluded in the preceding sections of this chapter demonstrated that excessive risk is harmful and should be criminalised, although the borders of criminal law intervention may depend on policy considerations. In this regard, all the three legal systems merit positive evaluation for including risk into their respective offences: fraud by abuse of position (among others),[10] abuse of company assets[11] and *Untreue*.[12] The requirements of these offences allow judges to convict managers who intentionally expose their companies to excessive risk and in general (minority views aside) it is sufficient that the intention is directed at excessive risk and the effective loss. Moreover, as it is recommended here, all three legal systems exclude liability for (inadvertent) negligence.

However, all the systems have their limitations, which create obstacles to punishing the wrongdoing to the full extent. These aspects will be discussed separately for each system below. Before embarking on this analysis, some preliminary remarks are in order.

In view of the detrimental consequences of excessive risk-taking, it is important that the law send a message that excessive risk-taking is not accepted. In this sense, if a law punishes such conduct, it should be clear about it. None of the three legal systems expressly informs that it criminalises excessive risk-taking. The English legal system interprets it from the term 'abusing one's position' or from elements of the offences of conspiracy to defraud or even theft. The requirement of acting against the company's interests in the French offence of abuse of company assets may be interpreted as acting in a way to cause loss or expose the company to abnormal risk of loss. These formulations may be influenced by legal tradition and as long as there is no doubt about including excessive risk, there is no ground for criticism. It is more problematic when excessive risk is hidden under terms which may suggest that criminalisation is limited to effective losses. This is the case for

[10] English Fraud Act 2006, in particular s 4.

[11] Provided mainly by French Commercial Code (Code de commerce), arts L241-3 4° and 5°, as well as L242-6 3° and 4°.

[12] German Penal Code (Strafgesetzbuch, StGB), s 266.

Germany, where only jurisprudential interpretation extended the understanding of the term 'damage' to include excessive risk by using the concept of 'risk-damage'. The details of this interpretation have changed considerably over time from a more extensive approach to a new, stricter one.[13] The extension from the requirement of damage to excessive risk demonstrates a need for criminalising excessive risk-taking by managers, and it shows that the judges may feel compelled to provide for it by extending the interpretation of the terms of available offences. The evaluation of the interpretation of the notion of 'risk-damage' demonstrates, however, how detrimental this approach is from the point of view of legal certainty.

As regards the legal interests protected by the analysed offences, these focus on protecting property or financial interests of the company and (more or less directly) of the shareholders. They differ as to the consideration given to the stakeholders, who are protected to the greatest extent by the French legislation and to the least extent by the English one, while the German legal system represents a middle way position. This is in accordance with the findings of this examination, because the question of balance of protection between these circles of actors is a policy question.

The analysed offences do not address the protection of systemic economic interests. However, the offences criminalising excessive risk-taking in companies indirectly play the function of protecting the economic system, because by safeguarding the companies from abuses of its assets, they should contribute (at least in theory) to the prosperity of the economy. This aim is reached under the condition that the abuses are punishable despite the shareholders' consent to acts which are detrimental for the company. This is the case for France and to a limited extent for Germany. Furthermore, two legal systems introduced provisions which incriminate excessively risky management of systemically important banking (and in the case of Germany insurance) institutions.

3.2. England

The English legal system provides for a plethora of offences, which, at least in theory, may be used to punish managers taking excessively risky decisions as regards the assets of their companies. All these offences provide for liability only if they are committed intentionally. Hence, the liability for recklessness, recommended in this study, is excluded. While the latter choice of the legislator may be accepted, as recklessness is considered here a borderline case, the abundance of legislation may be questioned. In particular, the existence of various inchoate offences punishing possession of items that may be used for committing fraud (eg in the form of exposing the company to excessive risk) might lead to liability for

[13] For details, see the analysis in Chapter 4, 3.5.2.

acts posing slight, if not nonexistent danger. The threat of such unjust solutions is tempered by prosecutorial discretion, and so far no cases where the necessity of conviction could be called into question have been identified.

The seemingly vast criminalisation offered by the English system is limited by the requirement of dishonesty. This requirement, which is the core feature of the English provisions analysed in this book, will affect the understanding of both the *actus reus* and the *mens rea*. It includes into the definition of the offence a sort of moral judgement. In cases where the jury acts as the tribunal of facts, the question of dishonesty will be decided by this body, ie a group of 12 laymen, most probably without experience in business affairs, and based only on a formal test. Moreover, juries do not give reasons for their findings.

Dishonesty is an element of definitions of many other offences in the English legal system (eg theft, false accounting) and has a long tradition. It would go beyond the scope of this book to examine the pros and cons of this requirement,[14] or of the jury system in general. However, some limited observations can be made. The analysis of the offences offered by the English legal system showed that despite providing for various requirements, eventually the whole wrongdoing was explained by this limb. One could wonder whether all offences analysed in the English chapter could not in fact be replaced by one criminalising 'acting dishonestly' in business. Dishonesty can be interpreted differently by different persons, but also have divergent meanings within various groups of people. Whilst it may be reasonable not to let the managers be detached from the moral standards of normal (reasonable and honest) people, the absence of a body of jurisprudence caused by the lack of justification for juries' decisions impedes better understanding of this limb as applied to concrete cases. Due to all these factors, such a solution does not contribute to legal certainty and it also fails to send a clear signal to potential perpetrators as to what types of acts or omissions should be avoided. The use of such imprecise terms to define the core of the offence requires significant trust in the functioning of the justice system. It cannot be excluded that investigative authorities would open proceedings for any, even slightly doubtful, act. While such an approach may give correct results within a concrete legal system, it cannot be recommended as a model in general.

The examination of the English system showed that the use of the requirement of dishonesty also has two consequences for the liability for excessive risk-taking. The impossibility of foreseeing the result of a jury trial limits cases for fraud or conspiracy to defraud to those where dishonesty is not very problematic. It results that the offence contains additional requirements, not defined in the offence, elevating the threshold of criminal liability: the manager must either behave in a way which would compromise his integrity or act in personal interest. This study

[14] The requirement of dishonesty is subject to debate in the English literature, see, eg Ashworth, Principles of Criminal Law (n 3) 65; Richard Tur, 'Dishonesty and the Jury: A Case Study in the Moral Content of Law' (1984) 18 Philosophy and Practice 75.

does not call for such requirements, although it cannot be excluded that on many occasions they will anyway be fulfilled. A very limited number of identified cases leave doubts as to whether in practice the system penalises the wrongdoing in question in this book.

Another aspect of the English legal system is that it contains a common law offence of conspiracy to defraud. As mentioned in Chapter 2, the use of this offence, and in general of the common law offence, has been subject to debate. The shortcomings of this offence are in line with the comments above: problems of the requirement of dishonesty and the overly extensive scope, encompassing acts which create only a very slight risk of harm.

Recently, the English legal system has also included an offence punishing banking managers for decisions which fall far below what could reasonably be expected from a person in the manager's position and taken while being aware that the implementation of the decision they took or failed to prevent carries a risk of causing the failure of the entire institution.[15] The aim of this offence is mainly the protection of the economic system. This formulation of the requirement of conduct comprises excessive risk-taking. However, it deserves criticism for its vague language. Moreover, this offence contains the requirement that the implementation of the manager's decision caused the failure of the bank. This requirement not only limits the application of the offence to those unlucky managers whose institutions effectively collapsed, but it renders the offence toothless, as it may be very difficult to prove that a concrete decision effectively caused the collapse of the institution. Furthermore, it limits its application also to the senior management. In effect, it can only be a reaction to an already occurred catastrophe, and only if liability can be clearly attributed. The fact that the offence opens criminal liability to recklessness, as it is recommended here, does not compensate for the mentioned shortcomings. Since the law provided for the offence has only recently entered into force, it is necessary to wait and see how the practice will react to these limitations.

3.3. France

The assessment of the French legal system points to several positive aspects of the French solution and to its major shortcomings. The French offence of abuse of company assets is based around the notion of acting against the company's interests. An act (including an omission) is interpreted as being against the company's interests, if it is of such character that in normal circumstances it would cause loss or expose the company to an abnormal (ie excessive) risk of loss. This approach is very much in line with the one recommended in this study, which demonstrated

[15] Financial Services (Banking Reform) Act 2013, s 36.

that these two aspects of mismanagement should be taken into account by the criminal provision. The lack of requirement of result, but assessing the detrimental character of the manager's act on the basis of its potential results in normal circumstances, is also in accordance with the philosophy argued for above. Such an approach does not leave criminal liability in the hands of fortune, but addresses all serious misdealings. At the same time, it avoids punishing managers whose acts, although not fully in compliance with some standards, were not of such gravity as to create abnormal risk of loss, where the loss occurred due to sheer bad luck. The offence sends quite a clear message as to what kind of activity should be avoided.

Although the scope of criminalisation created by the definition of conduct is well designed, two limitations inherent in the offence merit criticism. First of all, it is applicable only to a very limited circle of perpetrators, namely, the senior management of companies. This solution is doubtful as it excludes from its scope a large group of persons who may act against the interests of their companies and merit punishment in the same way as the senior management. This concerns, in particular, bigger companies with more sophisticated management structures. As a result of this limitation, other solutions have to be used in order to bring to justice managers who abused their position. One solution is to use the rules on complicity, which, however, requires that the main offence was committed by a senior manager. The second solution is to use the offence of abuse of trust. In order to apply this offence to mismanagement, it requires a broad interpretation of the requirement that the perpetrator misappropriated the assets of the company. Therefore, the application of this offence is limited as regards cases of excessive risk-taking (a problem well exemplified by the *Kerviel* case).

Secondly, the application of the offence of abuse of company assets is limited by the requirement that the senior manager acted in his personal interest. It was demonstrated above that such a limitation is only necessary as regards liability for recklessness, which as such is not provided for at all in the French system. Adding this requirement is a policy choice, which excludes from the scope of the offence situations where the perpetrator knowingly exposed the company to excessive risk, but without looking for personal benefit. Such a choice may be justified by the fact that acting in personal interest, at the expense of the company, adds a layer of wrongfulness to an act of mismanagement. However, as abundant jurisprudence demonstrates, the judges, when confronted with an act which gravely infringes the interests of the company, exhibit a tendency to interpret the requirement broadly, thus negating its real meaning for the definition of the offence. Such an extensive interpretation, where 'diluted' personal interest is sufficient, has not yet been applied in cases of excessive risk-taking. The possibility of its future application, however, cannot be excluded. In sum, while the limitation of the requirement of personal interest unnecessarily limits criminal liability as regards acts exposing companies to excessive risk, the potential use of the concept of 'diluted' personal interest does not contribute to legal certainty as regards the precise scope of the offence.

3.4. Germany

The German solution can be praised for including a wide scope of perpetrators. It is described in an abstract way, allowing the judges to apply the offence to managers of all levels of company hierarchy. What merits criticism is the design of the requirements of conduct and result and, to a limited extent, uncertainty as regards *mens rea*.

The distinctive characteristic of the German model is that for criminal liability, it requires that the manager breach a rule aimed at protecting the financial interests of the company. As such, this technique is not questionable and it could contribute to legal certainty if the catalogue of rules is well defined. The consequence of using this method is that it leaves less scope of appreciation in the hands of the judge, who has to rely on interpretation based in another domain of law. It is important that he does not become just a mouthpiece providing for a punishment for breaches of rules defined in other domains of law. In theory, such a risk does not exist in the German system, as the offence also contains further requirements describing the perpetrator's wrongdoing, including the condition that the breach should be severe. Furthermore, in practice the outcome will not differ much from the other examined legal systems, where the acts of the perpetrator will often breach an applicable rule or standard. However, the application of this method creates the risk that it is impossible to punish a manager who clearly and deliberately acted against his company's interests, but for some nuanced reason he did not infringe the rules. In order to avoid this danger in the system, it is necessary that the set of applicable rules is tight enough to avoid such loopholes.

In contrast to the advantages of the analysed technique as enumerated above, the application of the requirement of a rule breach within the offence of *Untreue* has created some unnecessary confusion. The imposition of the requirement of severity created some confusion. While it may be justified by the principle of subsidiarity to increase the threshold for criminal liability, in comparison with eg civil liability, this has resulted in losing the benefit of certainty. Not only is the requirement not part of the definition of the offence, but it was also unclear what 'severely' means. Furthermore, the decision to limit the catalogue of breaches to those which aim at protecting the financial interests of the company, may also raise doubts. A manager may expose the company to excessive risk or cause a loss by breaching rules describing the duties towards the administration. It is not so much a question of a catalogue of rules, but a question of whether a manager knowingly acts against the company's interest. The wrongfulness is not so much in the breach of rules, but in the manager's awareness that he is acting against the company's interests.

As already mentioned, the offence of *Untreue* as interpreted in the jurisprudence, includes the result in the form of excessive endangerment of the company through the notion of 'risk-damage', while the text of the offence provides only the result in the form of damage. It is probable that the attempts of the German jurisprudence to extend the concept of damage to encompass excessive risk are testament to frustration that the offence omits something which is wrong and should be included into the scope of *Untreue*. At the same time, criminal law should not be subject to overly broad interpretation, and recent efforts of the jurisprudence to limit the application of the concept of 'risk-damage' should be understood in this sense. However, it creates a situation, where criminal liability depends on accountancy rules and opinions of experts as to whether the risk can be quantified or not. The logic of this solution is understandable in light of the offence. It risks, however, drawing the line in a way which may not correspond with justice and fairness. While neither the old approach nor the new one is satisfactory, it is recommendable to clearly state in the offence that it encompasses excessive risk.

The last element of the offence of *Untreue* which has created doubts as to its scope is *mens rea*, as it was uncertain whether the perpetrator who created the result in the form of 'risk-damage' should have also foreseen that his act may cause an effective loss. Such a solution merits criticism, with which it was met in the German literature, as summarised in Chapter 4. So far, however, this approach does not seem to have gained wide acceptance.

In a development similar to those observed in the English legal system, the German legislator recently introduced special offences punishing the excessively risky management of banking and insurance institutions.[16] The offence allows judges to punish managers who breach one of the enumerated risk-preventive measures, which as such would stay in line with the approach proposed above (provided that the punishment is in proportion to the infringement). However, the offence requires an effective collapse of the institution and a causal link between the manager's failure and this result. The same remarks about the difficulty of proving especially the latter requirement, which were formulated as regards the English system, can be repeated here. Yet again, the circle of potential perpetrators is limited to senior managers. Moreover, the manager needs to be warned by the competent Financial Supervisory Authority about the failure of the institution to have an enumerated risk-preventive measure in place and he has to be requested to remedy this situation. Only a failure to execute this request may lead to criminal liability, and provided that it leads to the effective collapse of the institution. In view of these requirements, the fact that the offence comprises liability for negligence (as regards the detrimental result) does not alleviate much of the scepticism about the practical application of the said offences. If they are to be used at all, they will only be applicable to managers who knowingly failed at least twice to implement risk-preventive measures and effectively led to the collapse of a systemically important institution. While this may satisfy some need for justice, it is hard to foresee how this solution would effectively contribute to the protection of economic systems.

[16] Banking Act (Gesetz über das Kreditwesen, KWG), s 54a and Insurance Supervision Act (Gesetz über die Beaufsichtigung der Versicherungsunternehmen, VAG), s 142.

4. Final Conclusion

Breaching the trust of shareholders and stakeholders by acting against the entrusted interests of the company does deserve a criminal response. Most commonly, such acts of the managers cause loss and the visibility of the detrimental results makes the need for a criminal law reaction less debatable. The objective of this book was to analyse criminal response to the less obvious modality, which is exposing companies to excessive risk. This book thoroughly and critically examined the state of the art in three selected legal orders – England, France and Germany – as well as whether it is legitimate and proportionate to provide for such criminalisation and how this ought to be done.

It was demonstrated that all three legal systems feature provisions encompassing excessive risk-taking by managers. However, as regards all these systems, important shortcomings have been identified, which limit their practical use for cases deserving criminal law response. The analysis revealed also that in situations where excessive risk-taking is not directly targeted by a criminal law provision, the jurisprudence has a tendency to extend the understanding of the requirements of available offences in order to punish such acts.

The normative part of this book showed that it is indeed legitimate and proportionate to criminalise excessive risk-taking. It has explored conditions for such a criminalisation, suggesting the provision of offences of intentional and reckless mismanagement. The detailed design of these offences has been discussed and criminalisation of its negligence modality has been excluded. While these model offences aim at protecting the interests of companies, shareholders and, to variable extent, stakeholders, there may also be a need to subject to criminal liability breaches of certain rules aimed at safeguarding the interests of the economic system. The book examined also the general conditions of this type of offences, which could potentially extend even to acts committed negligently.

In sum, criminal law has been and should be used to contain abuses of companies consisting in exposing them to excessive risk. While the last financial crisis (2007–2008) showed the dangers of excessive risk in business, the importance of the issue goes beyond times of economic difficulties and must be seriously addressed by legislators. As cited cases indicate, the question of risk is an increasingly important factor in assessing criminal liability regarding business decisions, which also needs to be reflected in the law.

Punishing excessive risk does not necessarily mean that criminal law liability should be extended to the preparatory stage of wrongdoing. The act of the perpetrator takes place in any case and it is sometimes a question of sheer luck if it causes a loss, exposes the company to a risk of loss, or passes without any detrimental consequences. Although risk is certainly a less precise category than effective damage, this does not mean that it cannot be grasped and proven. And if it cannot be demonstrated with the required certainty, the perpetrator must benefit from the *in dubio pro reo* rule.

On the other hand, legislators should avoid the tendency of attempting to cure all problems by using criminal law. Criminalisation should be justified, observe basic principles and be limited to that which is truly necessary. The economy should not be thwarted by unnecessarily burdensome criminalisation, and enough space should be left for human creativity. Risk is an inherent part of business. In order for it to thrive, it must also embrace failure. Criminal law should not be used to punish a scapegoat after a failed project, or managers whose creativity led them to breach some standards or resulted in losses but where they did not betray the trust vested in them. Only those who effectively abuse their rights to manage the company should be the focus of criminal law provisions.

BIBLIOGRAPHY*

England

Official Documents

Attorney General, *Guidelines for Prosecutors on the Use of the Common Law Offence of Conspiracy to Defraud* (2007, updated version 29 November 2012)
Auld, Lord Justice Robert E, *Review of the Criminal Courts of England and Wales* (London: Stationery Office, 2001)
Crown Prosecution Service, *The Fraud Act 2006: Legal Guidance*, available at www.cps.gov.uk/legal/d_to_g/fraud_act/
Home Office, *Fraud Act 2006: Explanatory Notes* (8 November 2006)
Law Commission, *Criminal Law: Conspiracy to Defraud*, Working Paper No 56 (1974)
—— *Report on Conspiracy and Criminal Law Reform* (Law Com No 76, 1976)
—— *Conspiracy to Defraud*, Working Paper No 104 (1987)
—— *Criminal Law: Conspiracy to Defraud* (Law Com No 228, 1994)
—— *Legislating the Criminal Code: Fraud and Deception*, Consultation Paper No 155 (1999)
—— *Fraud: Report on a Reference under section 3(1)(e) of the Law Commissions Act 1965* (Law Com No 276, July 2002)
Parliamentary Commission on Banking Standards, *Changing Banking for Good*, vol I, HL Paper 27-I, HC 175-I (June 2013)
—— *Changing Banking for Good*, vol II, HL Paper 27-II, HC 175-II (June 2013)
Peck, Miriam, *The Fraud (Trials Without a Jury) Bill 2006–07*, House of Commons Research Paper 06/57 (23 November 2006)
Roskill Committee (Fraud Trials Committee), *Fraud Trials Committee Report* (London: HMSO, 1986)
Sentencing Council, *Sentencing for Fraud: Statutory Offences: Definitive Guideline* (October 2009)
—— *Fraud, Bribery and Money Laundering Offences: Definitive Guideline* (1 October 2014), available at www.sentencingcouncil.org.uk/wp-content/uploads/Fraud_bribery_and_money_laundering_offences_-_Definitive_guideline.pdf
Serious Fraud Office, Press Release, *Libor Investigation: Further Charge* (28 October 2014), available at https://www.sfo.gov.uk/2014/10/28/libor-investigation-further-charge/

Books, Journal Articles and Other Publications

Ashworth, Andrew, *Principles of Criminal Law*, 6th edn (Oxford University Press, 2009)
Ashworth, Andrew and Redmayne, Mike, *The Criminal Process*, 4th edn (Oxford University Press, 2010)
Brown, Lesley (e.), *The New Shorter Oxford English Dictionary on Historical Principles* (Oxford: Clarendon Press, 1993) vol 1, A–M

*Some references appear in the national bibliographies and also in the general bibliography (especially major criminal law textbooks). The separation of the bibliographies is intended to provide the reader with an overview of the sources used for different parts of the book.

Cambell, Kenneth, 'The Fraud Act 2006' (2007) 18 *King's Law Journal* 337

Coltart, Christopher, 'Banking Act is a Paper Tiger', *Law Society Gazette*, 3 February 2014

Devlin, Lord Patrick A, 'Trial by Jury for Fraud' (1986) *Oxford Journal of Legal Studies* 311

Du Bois-Pedain, Antje, 'Die Strafbarkeit untreueartigen Verhaltens im englischen Recht: "Fraud by abuse of position" und andere einschlägige Strafvorschriften' (2010) 122(2) *Zeitschrift für die gesamte Strafrechtswissenschaft* 325

Farrell, Simon, Yeo, Nicholas and Ladenburg, Guy, *Blackstone's Guide to the Fraud Act 2006* (Oxford University Press, 2007)

Levi, Michael, 'The Roskill Fraud Commission Revisited: An Assessment' (2003) 11(1) *Journal of Financial Crime* (July) 38

Montgomery, Clare and Ormerod, David (eds), *Montgomery and Ormerod on Fraud: Criminal Law and Procedure*, Release 9 (Oxford University Press, 2012)

Moran, Mayo, *Rethinking the Reasonable Person: An Egalitarian Reconstruction of the Objective Standard* (Oxford University Press, 2003)

Norre, Alan W, 'After Woollin' (1999) *Criminal Law Review* 532

Ormerod, David, 'The Fraud Act 2006: Criminalising Lying?' (2007) *Criminal Law Review* 193

Ormerod, David and Hooper, Anthony (gen eds), *Blackstone's Criminal Practice 2013* (Oxford University Press, 2012)

Ormerod, David and Williams, David H, *Smith's Law of Theft*, 9th edn (Oxford University Press, 2007)

Parry, Jacques, Arlidge, Anthony, Hacking, Joanne and Jacobson, Josepha, *Arlidge and Parry on Fraud*, 3rd edn (London: Sweet & Maxwell, 2007)

Sanders, Andrew, Young, Richard and Burton, Mandy, *Criminal Justice*, 4th edn (Oxford University Press, 2010)

Simester, AP, Spencer, JR, Sullivan, GR and Virgo, GJ, *Simester and Sullivan's Criminal Law: Theory and Doctrine*, 5th edn (Oxford/Portland, OR: Hart Publishing, 2013)

Smith, John, *Smith and Hogan Criminal Law*, 6th edn (Lexis Law Publishing, 1988)

Spencer, John, 'The Victim and the Prosecutor' in Anthony Bottoms and Julian V Roberts (eds), *Hearing the Victim: Adversarial Justice, Crime Victims and the State* (Cullompton: Willan Publishing, 2010) 141–62

Stafford, Andrew and Ritchie, Stuart, *Fiduciary Duties: Directors and Employees* (Bristol: Jordans, 2008)

France

Official Documents

Conseil National du Patronat Français (CNPF) and Association Française des Entreprises Privées (AFEP), *Le conseil d'administration des sociétés cotées* (July 1995) (Rapport Viénot), available at www.ecgi.org/codes/documents/vienot1_fr.pdf

Groupe de travail présidé par Jean-Marie Coulon, *La dépénalisation de la vie des affaires, Rapport au garde des Sceaux* (Ministre de la Justice, January 2008)

Books, Journal Articles and Other Publications

'L'abus de biens sociaux. Le particularisme français à l'épreuve de l'Europe', Materials of the Conference held at the École supérieure de commerce de Paris (ESCP-EAP) on 2 April 2003 (2004) *Gazette du Palais* (November–December) 3516

Brouillaud, Jean-Pierre, 'Faut-il supprimer la notion d'intérêt personnel dans la définition de l'abus de biens sociaux?' (2008) 6 *Receuil Dalloz* (7 February) 375

Caramalli, Delphine, 'Comment to the Judgment: Cass crim, 3 juin 2004, Bull crim, no 152' (2004) 44 *Receuil Dalloz* 3213

Cohen, Claude, 'L'abus de biens sociaux, délit imprescriptible?' (2002) *Gazette du Palais* (September–October) 1300

Conte, Philippe, Giraud-van Gaver, Chantal, Robert, Jacques-Henri and Saint-Paul, Jean-Christophe, *Le risque pénal dans l'entreprise* (Paris: Litec, 2003)

Dekeuwer, Alain, 'Les intérêts protégées en cas d'abus de biens sociaux', 43 *La Semaine Juridique Entreprise et Affaires*, 26 October 1995, 500

Delmas-Marty, Mirelle and Giudicelli-Delage, Geneviève (eds), *Droit pénal des affaires*, 4th edn (Paris: Pr Univ de France, 2000)

Desportes, Frédéric and Le Gunehec, Francis, *Droit Pénal Général*, 14 edn (Paris: Economica, 2007)

Dobkine, Michel, 'Réflexions itératives à propos de l'abus de biens sociaux' (1997) 37 *Recueil Dalloz*, Chronique, 323

Donnedieu de Vabres, Henri, 'IV. Crimes et délits contre les biens' (1938) *Revue de Science Criminelle et Droit Pénal Comparé* 716

Elliott, Catherine, *French Criminal Law* (Cullompton: Willan Publishing, 2001)

Jeandidier, Wilfrid, 'L'Elément matériel des infractions d'affaires où la prédilection pour l'inconsistance' in *Mélange offerts à Raymond Gassin* (Aix-Marseille: Presses Universitaires d'Aix-Marseille, 2007) 245–63

—— *Abus de confiance* (JurisClasseur Pénal, date du fascicule: 1 February2015, date de la dernière mise à jour: 1 September 2017)

—— *Abus des biens, du crédit, des pouvoirs ou des voix* (JurisClasseur Sociétés Traité, date du fascicule: 7 February 2017, date de la dernière mise à jour: 7 February 2017)

Joly, Eva and Joly-Baumgartner, Caroline, *L'abus de biens sociaux. Á l'épreuve de la pratique* (Paris: Economica, 2002)

Larguier, Jean and Conte, Philippe, *Droit pénal des affaires*, 11th edn (Armand Colin, 2004)

Lepage, Agathe, Maistre du Chambon, Patrick and Salomon, Renaud, *Droit pénal des affaires*, 2nd edn, (Paris: LexiNexis Litec, 2010)

Lucas de Leyssac, Marie-Paule and Mihman, Alexis, *Droit pénal des affaires, Manuel théorique et pratique* (Paris: Economica, 2009)

Mascala, Corinne, *Abus de confiance*, Répertoire de droit pénal et de procédure pénale (Dalloz, October 2003)

Mathieu, Gilles, 'L'acte contraire à l'intérêt social en matière d'abus de biens sociaux' (2002) *Gazette du Palais* (July–August) 1045

Matsopoulou, Haritini, 'Le retour en grâce de l'intérêt personnel dans l'abus de biens sociaux' (2005) 30 *Recueil Dalloz* 2075

Médina, Annie, *Abus de biens sociaux. Prévention - Détection - Poursuite* (Paris: Dalloz, 2001)

Muller, Yvonne, 'L'abus réprimé: la correction par le juge' 353 *Gazette du Palais*, 19 December 2009, 30

—— 'Le droit pénal des conflits d'intérêts' (2012) 1 *Droit pénal* (January)étude 1

Patin, Maurice and Rousselet, Marcel, 'Délits et sanctions dans les sociétés par actions' (1938) 292 *Sirey* 221

Rebut, Didier, *Abus de biens sociaux*, Répertoire de droit pénal et de procédure pénale, (Dalloz, January 2010, (dernière mise à jour: February 2017)

Renucci, Jean-François, 'Infractions d'affaires et prescription de l'action publique' (1997) *Recueil Dalloz* 23

Renucci, Jean-François and Mehdi, Houria, 'L'Actualité de l'abus de biens sociaux' (2002) 1 *Revue Pénitentiaire et de Droit Pénal* (April) 27

Robert, Jacques-Henri and Matsopoulou, Haritini, *Traité de droit pénal des affaites* (Presses Universitaires de France, 2004)

Stasiak, Frédéric, *Droit pénal des affaires*, 2nd edn (Paris: LGDJ, 2009)

Tchernoff, Iouda, *Traité de droit pénal financier* (Dalloz, 1937)

Urban, Quentin, 'De la difficulté pour le juge de caractériser l'abus de biens sociaux', 37 *La semaine juridique - édition générale*, 14 September 2005), 1619

Véron, Michel, *Droit pénal des affaires*, 9th edn (Dalloz, 2011)

Vitu, André and Beauvais, Didier, *Participation à une association de malfaiteurs*, Fasc 20 (JurisClasseur Pénal Code, mise à jour: 20 December 2016)

Germany

Official Documents

Deutscher Bundestag, *Drucksache 17/12601* (4 March 2013)

Books, Journal Articles and Other Publications

Andenas, Mads and Wooldridge, Frank, *European Comparative Company Law* (Cambridge University Press, 2009)
Beukelmann, Stephan, '§ 263 Betrug' in Bernd von Heintschel-Heinegg (ed), *Beck'scher Online-Kommentar StGB*, 27th edn (Munich: CH Beck, 2015), available at www.beck-online.beck.de
Bohlander, Michael, *Principles of German Criminal Law* (Oxford/Portland, OR: Hart Publishing, 2009)
Cichy, Patrick, Cziupka, Johannes and Wiersch, Rachid René, 'Voraussetzungen der Strafbarkeit der Geschäftsleiter von Kreditinstituten nach § 54 a KWG n. F.' (2013) *Neue Zeitschrift für Gesellschaftsrecht (NZG)* 846
Dahm, Georg, 'Untreue' in Franz Gürtner, *Das kommende deutsche Strafrecht, Besonderer Teil*, 2nd edn (Berlin: Verlag Franz Vahlen, 1936)
Dierlamm, Alfred, 'Der faktische Geschäftsführer im Strafrecht – ein Phantom?', *NStZ* 1996, 153
—— 'Untreue – ein Auffangtatbestand?', *NStZ* 1997, 534
—— '§ 266 Untreue' in Roland Hefendehl and Olaf Hohmann (eds), *Münchener Kommentar zum Strafgesetzbuch*, vol 5, *§§ 263–358 StGB*, 2nd edn (Munich: CH Beck, 2014)
Dunkel, Wolfgang, 'Nochmals: Der Scheckkartenmißbrauch in strafrechtlicher Sicht' (1977) *Goltdammer's Archiv für Strafrecht* 329
Fischer, Thomas, 'Die strafrechtliche Bewältigung der Finanzkrise am Beispiel der Untreue – Finanzkrise und Strafrecht' (2011) 123 *ZStW* 816
—— 'Untreue § 266' in *Strafgesetzbuch*, 61th edn (Munich: CH Beck, 2014)
Gerkau, Frank H, *Untreue und objektive Zurechnung* (Hamburg: Kovač, 2008)
Groß, Bernd, *Die strafrechtliche Verantwortlichkeit faktischer Vertretungsorgane bei Kapitalgesellschaften* (Berlin: Duncker & Humblot, 2007)
Günther, Hans-Ludwig, 'Die Untreue im Wirtschaftsrecht' in Bernd Heinrich et al (eds), *Festschrift für Ulrich Weber* (Bielefeld: Verlag Ernst und Werner Gieseking, 2004) 311–17
Häberle, Peter, 'KWG 54a Strafvorschriften' in Georg Erbs, Max Kohlhaas and Friedrich Ambs, *Strafrechtliche Nebengesetze, Loseblattausgabe*, 199th edn (Munich: CH Beck, 2014)
Hamm, Rainer and Richter, Thomas, 'Symbolisches und hypertrophes Strafrecht im Entwurf eines "Trennbankengesetzes"' (2013) 19(67) *Zeitschrift für Wirtschafts- und Bankrecht*, 865
Hefendehl, Roland, Andrew von Hirsch and Wolfgang Wohlers, *Die Rechtsgutstheorie. Legitimationsbasis des Strafrechts oder dogmatisches Glasperlenspiel?* (Baden Baden: Nomos, 2003)
Heger, Martin, '§ 266 StGB Untreue' in Kristian Kühl and Martin Heger, *Strafgezetzbuch Kommentar* (Lackner/ Kühl), 28th edn (Munich: CH Beck, 2014)
Heine, Günter and Weißer, Bettina, '§ 26 Anstiftung' in Adolf Schönke, Horst Schröder and Albin Eser et al (eds), *Strafgesetzbuch Kommentar*, 29th edn (Munich: CH Beck, 2014)
—— '§ 27 Beihilfe' in Adolf Schönke, Horst Schröder and Albin Eser et al (eds), *Strafgesetzbuch Kommentar*, 29th edn (Munich: CH Beck, 2014)
Hillenkamp, Thomas, 'Risikogeschäft und Untreue', *NStZ* 1981, 161
Jahn, Matthias, 'Untreue durch die Führung "schwarzer Kassen" – Fall Siemens/ENEL' (2009) *Juristische Schulung (JuS)* 173
Jakobs, Günther, 'LG Düsseldorf: *Untreue*-Vorwurf wegen Verletzung gesellschaftsrechtlicher Sonderpflichten – Mannesmann/Vodafone', *NStZ* 2005, 276
—— *Strafrecht. Allgemeiner Teil*, 2nd edn (Berlin/New York: Walter de Gruyter, 1993)
Jescheck, Hans-Heinrich and Weigend, Thomas, *Lehrbuch des Strafrechts* (Berlin: Duncker & Humblot, 1996)
Joecks, Wolfgang, '§ 27 Beihilfe' in Bernd von Heintschel-Heinegg (ed), *Münchener Kommentar zum Strafgesetzbuch*, vol 1: §§ 1–37 StGB, 2nd edn (Munich: CH Beck, 2011)

Kindhäuser, Urs, *Strafrecht. Besonderer Teil II*, 4th edn (Baden Baden: Nomos, 2005)
—— *Strafrecht. Allgemeiner Teil*, 4th edn (Baden Baden: Nomos, 2009)
—— '§ 266 Untreue' in Urs Kindhäuser, Ulfrid Neumann and Hans-Ullrich Paeffgen (eds), *Strafgesetzbuch*, 4th edn (Baden-Baden: Nomos, 2013)
Lüderssen, Klaus, 'Gesellschaftsrechtliche Grenzen der strafrechtlichen Haftung des Aufsichtsrats' in Dieter Dölling, *Jus Humanum. Grundlagen des Rechts und Strafrechts, Festschrift für Ernst-Joachim Lampe* (Berling: Duncker & Humblot, 2003) 727–42
—— 'Primäre oder sekundäre Zuständigkeit des Strafrechts?' in *Menschengerechtes Strafrecht, Festschrift für Albin Eser* (Munich: CH Beck, 2005) 163–80
Martin, Susanne, *Bankuntreue* (Berlin: Duncker & Humblot, 2000)
Maurach, Reihart, Friedrich-Christian Schroeder and Manfred Maiwald, *Strafrecht Besonderer Teil*, Teilband 1, Straftate gegen Persönlichkeits- und Vermögenswerte, 9th edn (Heidelberg: CF Müller Verlag, 2003)
Mayer, Hellmuth, 'Die Untreue' in *Materialien zur Strafrechtsreform*, vol 1, *Gutachten der Strafrechtslehrer* (Bonn, 1954) 333–56
Meyer, Dieter, 'Nochmals: Ist die Begebung ungedeckter Schecks mittels Scheckkarte durch ihren berechtigten Inhaber strafbar?' (1971) 11 *Monatschrift für Deutsches Recht (MDR)* 893
Murmann, Uwe, *Grundkurs Strafrecht* (Munich: CH Beck, 2015)
Nattkemper, Kristina, *Die Untreuestrafbarkeit des Vorstands einer Aktiengesellschaft* (Berlin: Duncker & Humblot, 2013)
Perron, Walter, 'Probleme und Perspectiven des Untreuetatbestandes' (2009) *Goltdammer's Archiv für Strafrecht* 219
—— '§ 266 Untreue' in Adolf Schönke, Horst Schröder and Albin Eser et al (eds), *Strafgesetzbuch Kommentar*, 29th edn (Munich: CH Beck, 2014)
Ransiek, Andreas, 'Risiko als Problem des Untreuetatbestandes' (2004) 116(3) *ZStW* 634
—— 'Anerkennungsprämien und Untreue – Das "Mannesmann" – Urteil des BGH', *NJW* 2006, 814
—— '"Verstecktes" Parteivermögen und *Untreue*', *NJW* 2007, 1727
Richter, Thomas, 'The New German Ringfencing Act Establishing Criminal Liability of Banking and Insurance Executives for Failures in Risk Management' (2013) 6(4) *Journal of Risk Management in Financial Institutions* 433
Roxin, Claus, *Strafrecht. Allgemeiner Teil*, 4th edn (Munich: CH Beck, 2006) vol 1
—— 'The Legislation Critical Concept of Goods-in-Law under Scrutiny' (2013) 3(1) *European Criminal Law Review* 3
Saliger, Frank, 'Wider die Ausweitung des Untreuetatbestandes' (2000) 112(3) *Zeitschrift für die gesamte Strafrechtswissenschaft (ZStW)* 563
—— '§ 266 Untreue' in Helmut Satzger, Wilhelm Schluckebier and Gunter Widmaier (eds), *StGB Strafgesetzbuch Kommentar*, 2nd edn (Carl Heymanns Verlag, 2014)
Schäfer, Ernst, 'Gesetz zur Abänderung strafrechtlicher Vorschriften vom 26. Mai' (1933) *Deutsche Juristenzeitung (DJZ)* 788
Schilling, Daniel, *Fragmentarisch oder umfassend?* (Frankfurt: Peter Lang, 2009)
Schmid, Wolfgang, '§31 Treupflichtverletzungen' in Christian Müller-Gugenberger and Klaus Bieneck, *Wirtschaftsstrafrecht. Handbuch des Wirtschaftsstraf- und – ordnungswidrigkeitenrechts*, 5th edn (Köln: Dr Otto Schmidt, 2011)
Schork, Alexander and Reichling, Tilman, 'Der strafrechtliche Schutz des Risikomanagements durch das sog. Trennbankengesetz' (2013) *Corporate Compliance Zeitschrift (CCZ)* 269
Schramm, Edward, *Untreue und Konsens* (Berlin: Duncker & Humblot, 2005)
—— 'Untreue, § 266 StGB' in Carsten Momsen and Thomas Grützner, *Wirtschaftsstrafrecht. Handbuch für die Unternehmens- und Anwaltspraxis* (Munich: CH Beck, 2013)
Schröder, Christian, 'Die strafrechtliche Bewältigung der Finanzkrise am Beispiel der Untreue' (2011) 123 *ZStW* 771
Schünemann, Bernd, 'Die "gravierende Pflichtverletzung" bei der Untreue: dogmatischer Zauberhut oder taube Nuss?', *NStZ* 2005, 473
—— 'Zur Quadratur des Kreises in der Dogmatik des Gefährdungsschadens', *NStZ* 2008, 430

—— '§ 266 Untreue' in Heinrich Wilhelm Laufhütte, Ruth Rissing-van Saan and Klaus Tiedemann (eds), *Strafgesetzbuch. Leipziger Kommentar*, vol 9/1, §§ 263–266b, 12th edn (Berlin: de Gruyter, 2012)

Seher, Gerhard, 'Grundfälle zur Mittäterschaft' (2009) *Juristische Schulung (JuS)* 304

Seier, Jürgen, 'Untreue' in Hans Achenbach and Andreas Ransiek (eds), *Handbuch Wirtschaftsstrafrecht*, 3rd edn (Heidelberg et al: CF Müller, 2012)

Szebrowski, Nickel, *Kick-Back* (Köln/Berlin/Munich: Heymanns, 2005)

Vogel, Joachim, *Einflüsse des Nationalsozialismus auf das Strafrecht* (Berlin: Berliner Wissenschafts-Verlag, 2004)

Waßmer, Martin Paul, *Untreue bei Risikogeschäften* (Heidelberg: CF Müller, 1997)

—— '§ 266 Untreue' in Jürgen Peter Graf, Markus Jäger and Petra Wittig (eds), *Wirtschafts- und Steuerstrafrecht* (Munich: CH Beck, 2011)

Wessels, Johannes and Hillenkamp, Thomas, *Strafrecht. Besonderer Teil 2, Straftaten gegen Vermögenswerte*, 36th edn (Heidelberg et al: CF Müller, 2013)

Wetzell, Richard F, 'Introduction. Crime and Criminal Justice in Modern Germany' in Richard F Wetzell (ed), *Crime and Criminal Justice in Modern Germany* (New York/Oxford: Berghahn Books, 2014) 1–30

Wittig, Petra, *Wirtschafsstrafrecht* (Munich: CH Beck, 2010)

—— '§ 266 Untreue' in Bernd von Heintschel-Heinegg (ed), *Beck'scher Online-Kommentar StGB*, 38th edn (Munich: CH Beck, 2018), available at www.beck-online.beck.de

Wohlers, Wolfgang, 'Die strafrechtliche Bewältigung der Finanzkrise am Beispiel der Strafbarkeit wegen Untreue' (2011) 123 *ZStW* 791

Wohlers, Wolfgang and Gaede, Karsten, '§ 13 Begehen durch Unterlassen' in Urs Kindhäuser, Ulfrid Neumann and Hans-Ullrich Paeffgen (eds), *Strafgesetzbuch*, 4th edn (Baden-Baden: Nomos, 2013)

General

Official Documents

Association of Chartered Certified Accountants (ACCA), *Corporate Governance and the Credit Crunch*, Discussion Paper (London: ACCA, 2008), available at www.accaglobal.com/gb/en/technical-activities/technical-resources-search/2008/november/corporate-governance-and-the-credit-crunch.html

DG Economic and Financial Affairs, 'Economic Crisis in Europe: Causes, Consequences and Responses' (2009) 7 *European Economy*, available at http://ec.europa.eu/economy_finance/publications/pages/publication15887_en.pdf

—— *Why Did the Crisis Happen?*, available at http://ec.europa.eu/economy_finance/explained/the_financial_and_economic_crisis/why_did_the_crisis_happen/index_en.htm

European Criminal Policy Initiative, 'A Manifesto on European Criminal Policy' (2009) *Zeitschrift für Internationale Strafrechtsdogmatik (ZIS)* 707

International Organisation of Supreme Audit Institutions (INTOSAI), *The Causes of the Global Financial Crisis and Their Implications for Supreme Audit Institutions* (INTOSAI, October 2010), available at www.intosai.org/uploads/gaohq4709242v1finalsubgroup1paper.pdf

Mack, John J, Chairman, *Written Submission of Morgan Stanley to the Financial Crisis Inquiry Commission* (January 2010), available at http://fcic-static.law.stanford.edu/cdn_media/fcic-testimony/2010-0113-Mack.pdf

Turner, Adair, *The Turner Review: A Regulatory Response to the Global Banking Crisis* (Financial Services Authority, March 2009), available at /www.fsa.gov.uk/pubs/other/turner_review.pdf

US National Commission, *The Financial Crisis Inquiry, Final Report of the National Commission on the Causes of the Financial and Economic Crisis in the United States* (January 2011), available at http://fcic.law.stanford.edu/report

Books, Journal Articles and Other Publications

Acharya, Viral, Philippon, Thomas, Richardson, Matthew and Roubini, Nouriel, 'The Financial Crisis of 2007–2009: Causes and Remedies' (2009) 18(2) *Financial Markets, Institutions and Instruments* 89

Adams, Maurice and Griffiths, John, 'Against "Comparative Method"' in Maurice Adams and Jacco Bomhoff (eds), *Practice and Theory in Comparative Law* (Cambridge University Press, 2012)

Adick, Markus, *Organuntreue (§ 266 StGB) und Business Judgment. Die strafrechtliche Bewertung unternehmerischen Handelns unter Berücksichtigung von Verfahrensregeln* (Peter Lang, 2010)

Albrecht, Peter-Alexis, 'Erosionen des rechtstaatlichen Strafrechts' (1993) 2 *Kritische Vierteljahresschrift für Gesetzgebung und Rechtswissenschaft (KritV)* 163

Andenas, Mads and Wooldridge, Frank, *European Comparative Company Law* (Cambridge University Press, 2009)

Ashby, Simon, *The 2007–09 Financial Crisis: Learning the Risk Management Lessons, Centre for Risk, Banking and Financial Services*, University of Nottingham Research Report (January 2010), available at www.nottingham.ac.uk/business/businesscentres/crbfs/research/researchreports.aspx

Ashworth, Andrew, *Principles of Criminal Law*, 6th edn (Oxford University Press, 2009)

Balthazar, Laurent, *From Basel 1 to Basel 3: The Integration of State of the Art Risk Modelling in Banking Regulation* (Palgrave Macmillan, 2006)

Beccaria, Cesare, *Über Verbrechen und Strafen* (Leipzig: Verlag von Wilhelm Engelmann, 1905)

Beck, Ulrich, *Risikogesellschaft. Auf dem Weg in eine andere Moderne* (Frankfurt: Suhrkamp, 1986) [English version: *Risk Society: Towards a New Modernity* (Sage, 1992)]

Bentham, Jeremy, *An Introduction to the Principles of Morals and Legislation* (Athlone Press, University of London, 1970)

Bernhard, Haffke, 'Symbolische Gesetzgebung? Das Wirtschaftsstrafrecht in der Bundesrepublik Deutschland' (1991) *KritV* 165

Blaurock, Uwe, 'Regelbildung und Grenzen des Rechts – Das Beispiel der Finanzkrise' (2012) 5 *JuristenZeitung (JZ)* 226

Blomsma, Jeroen, *Mens Rea and Defences in European Criminal Law* (Intersentia, 2012)

Bohlander, Michael, *Principles of German Criminal Law* (Oxford/Portland, OR: Hart Publishing, 2009)

Buder, Matthäus, Lienemeyer, Max, Magnus, Marcel, Smits, Bert and Soukup, Karl, 'The Rescue and Restructuring of Hypo Real Estate' (2011) 3 *Competition Policy Newsletter* 41

Cahn, Andreas and Donald, David C, *Comparative Company Law* (Cambridge University Press, 2010)

Chevigny, Paul G, 'From Betrayal to Violence: Dante's Inferno and the Social Construction of Crime' (2001) 26(4) *Law and Social Inquiry* 787

Cicero, *De Officiis* (London: Heinemann, 1928) [Translations: *On Obligations* (PG Walsh (trans), Oxford University Press, 2000); *On Duties* (MT Griffin (trans), MT Griffin and EM Atkins (eds), Cambridge University Press, 1991)]

Claessens, Stijn, Kose, M Ayhan, Laeven, Luc and Valencia, Fabián (eds), *Financial Crises: Causes, Consequences, and Policy Responses* (International Monetary Fund, 2014)

Coen, Mark and Doak, Jonathan, 'Embedding Explained Jury Verdicts in the English Criminal Trial' (2017) 37(4) *Legal Studies* 786

Coleman, Les, *Why Managers and Companies Take Risks* (Heidelberg: Physica-Verlag, 2006)

Coyle, Brian, *Risk Awareness and Corporate Governance* (Financial World Publishing, 2002)

Craig, Paul and de Búrca, Gráinne, *EU Law: Text, Cases, and Materials*, 5th edn (Oxford University Press, 2011) 941–42

Daly, Gillian, 'Jury Secrecy: R v Mirza; R v Connor and Rollock' (2004) 186(8) *International Journal of Evidence and Proof* 186

Dannecker, Gerhard, '§1 Keine Strafe ohne Gesetz' in Heinrich Wilhelm Laufhütte, Ruth Rissing-van Saan and Klaus Tiedemann, *Strafgesetzbuch. Leipziger Kommentar*, vol 1, *Einleitung: §§ 1 bis 31*, 12th edn (Berlin/New York: De Gruyter, 2007)

—— 'Nullum crimen, nulla poena sine lege und seine Geltung im Allgemeinen Teil des Strafrechts' in Gerhard Dannecker (et al), *Festschrift für Harro Otto* (Köln/Berlin/Munich: Carl Heymanns Verlag, 2007) 25–40

—— 'Der strafrechtliche Schutz des Wettbewerbs: Notwendigkeit und Grenzen einer Kriminalisierung von Kartellrechtsverstößen' in Ulrich Sieber, Gerhard Dannecker, Urs Kindhäuser, Joachim Vogel and Tonio Walter, *Strafrecht und Wirtschaftsstrafrecht - Dogmatik, Rechtsvergleich, Rechtstatsachen - Festschrift für Klaus Tiedemann zum 70. Geburtstag* (Köln: Carl Heymanns Verlag, 2008) 789–815

Dante Alighieri, *La Divina Commedia, Inferno* (Giorgio Petrocchi (ed), Milan: A Mondadori Editore, 1966–67) [English version: Robert Hollander and Jean Hollander, *The Inferno* (Doubleday/Anchor, 2000)

Donelli, Marcelo, Larrain, Borja and Urzúa, Francisco, 'Ownership Dynamics with Large Shareholders: An Empirical Analysis' (2013) 48(2) *Journal of Financial and Quantitative Analysis* 579

Drucker, Peter F, *Management: Tasks, Responsibilities, Practices* (Oxford et al: Butterworth-Heinemann, 1974, reprint 1999)

Dubber, Markus Dirk, 'Theories of Crime and Punishment in German Criminal Law' (2005) 53(3) *American Journal of Comparative Law* 679

—— 'Comparative Criminal Law' in Mathias Reimann and Reinhard Zimmermann, *The Oxford Handbook of Comparative Law* (Oxford University Press, 2006/2008) 1287–325

Duff, RA, *Answering for Crime: Responsibility and Liability in the Criminal Law* (Oxford/Portland: Hart Publishing, 2007)

—— 'Towards a Modest Legal Moralism' in Magnus Ulväng and Iain Cameron, *Essays on Criminalization and Sanction* (Iustus, 2014) 39–67

Feinberg, Joel, *The Moral Limits of Criminal Law*, vol I, *Harm to Others* (Oxford University Press, 1984)

—— *The Moral Limits of Criminal Law*, vol II, *Offense to Others* (Oxford University Press, 1985)

—— *The Moral Limits of Criminal Law*, vol III: *Harm to Self* (Oxford University Press, 1989)

Ferrajoli, Luigi, *Derecho y razón, Teoría del garantismo penal* (Madrid: Editorial Trotta, 1995)

Fletcher, George P, *Loyalty: An Essay on the Morality of Relationships* (Oxford University Press, 1993)

Giddens, Anthony, 'Risk and Responsibility' (1999) 62(1) *Modern Law Review* 1

Grabenwarter, Christoph, *European Convention on Human Rights: Commentary* (CH Beck/Hart Publishing/Nomos/Helbing Lichtenhahn Verlag, 2014)

Green, Stuart P, *Lying, Cheating, and Stealing: A Moral Theory of White-Collar Crime* (Oxford University Press, 2006/2010)

Griffith-Jones, Stephany, Ocampo, José Antonio and Stiglitz, Joseph E (eds), *Time for a Visible Hand: Lessons from the 2008 World Financial Crisis* (Oxford University Press, 2010)

Günther, Klaus, 'Criminal Law, Crime and Punishment as Communication' in AP Simester, Anthe du Bois-Pedain and Ulfrid Neumann, *Liberal Criminal Theory, Essays for Andreas von Hirsch* (Oxford/Portland, OR: Hart Publishing 2014) 123–39

Haldane, Andrew G and May, Robert M, 'Systemic Risk in Banking Ecosystems' 469 *Nature*, 20 January 2011, 351

Hart, HLA, *Punishment and Responsibility* (Oxford University Press, 1968)

Hassemer, Winfried, 'Kennzeichen und Krisen des modernen Strafrechts' (1992) *Zeitschrift für Rechtspolitik (ZRP)* 378

—— 'The Harm Principle and the Protection of "Legal Goods" (Rechtsgüterschutz): A German Perspective' in AP Simester, Anthe du Bois-Pedain and Ulfrid Neumann, *Liberal Criminal Theory, Essays for Andreas von Hirsch* (Oxford/Portland, OR: Hart Publishing, 2014) 187–204

Hefendehl, Roland, *Kollektive Rechtsgüter im Strafrecht* (Köln et al: Carl Heymanns Verlag, 2002)

—— 'Das Rechtsgut als materialer Angelpunkt einer Strafnorm' in Roland Hefendehl, Andrew von Hirsch and Wolfgang Wohlers (eds), *Die Rechtgutstheorie: Legitimationsbasis des Strafrechts oder dogmatisches Glasperlenspiel?* (Baden-Baden: Nomos, 2003) 119

Hellwig, Martin F, 'Systemic Risk in the Financial Sector: An Analysis of the Subprime-Mortgage Financial Crisis' (2009) 157(2) *De Economist* 129

Hopkin, Paul, *Fundamentals of Risk Management*, Institute of Risk Management (London/Philadelphia, PA/New Delhi: Kogan Page Ltd, 2010)

Hörnle, Tatjana, '"Rights of Others" in Criminalisation Theory' in AP Simester, Anthe du Bois-Pedain and Ulfrid Neumann, *Liberal Criminal Theory, Essays for Andreas von Hirsch* (Oxford/Portland, OR: Hart Publishing, 2014) 169–85.

Husak, Douglas, 'Applying *Ultima Ratio*: A Skeptical Assessment' (2005) 2 *Ohio State Journal of Criminal Law* 535

—— *Overcriminalization: The Limits of the Criminal Law* (Oxford University Press, 2008)

Jakobs, Günther, *Strafrecht. Allgemeiner Teil*, 2nd edn (Berlin/New York: Walter de Gruyter, 1993)

Jareborg, Nils, *Essays in Criminal Law* (Uppsala: Iustus Förlag, 1988)

—— 'Criminalization as Last Resort (*Ultima Ratio*)' (2005) 2 *Ohio State Law Journal* 521

—— 'Criminalization and the *Ultima Ratio* Principle' in Magnus Ulväng and Iain Cameron, *Essays on Criminalization and Sanction* (Iustus, 2014) 23–38

Jescheck, Hans-Heinrich and Weigend, Thomas, *Lehrbuch des Strafrechts* (Berlin: Duncker & Humblot, 1996)

Jickling, Mark, *Causes of the Financial Crisis*, Report for Congress (Congressional Research Service, 29 January 2009)

Joecks, Wolfgang, 'Einleitung' in Bernd von Heintschel-Heinegg (ed), *Münchener Kommentar zum Strafgesetzbuch*, vol 1, *§§ 1–37 StGB*, 2nd edn (Munich: CH Beck, 2011)

Jong, Ferry de, 'A Reciprocal Turn in Criminal Justice? Shifting Conceptions of Legitimate Authority' (2013) 9(1) *Utrecht Law Review*

Kaufmann, Armin, *Die Aufgabe des Strafrechts* (Westdeutscher Verlag, 1983)

Kaufmann, Arthur, 'Subsidiaritätsprinzip und Strafrecht' in Claux Roxin et al (eds), *Grundfragen der Gesamten Strafrechtswissenschaft, Festschrift für Heinrich Henkel* (Berlin/New York: Walter de Gruyter, 1974) 89–107

Keiler, Johannes, *Actus Reus and Participation in European Criminal Law* (Intersentia, 2013)

Kelk, Constantijn and de Jong, Ferry, *Studieboek materieel strafrecht*, 5th edn (Deventer: Kluwer, 2013)

Kim, Jongho, 'From Vanilla Swaps to Exotic Credit Derivatives: How to Approach the Interpretation of Credit Events' (2008) 13(5) *Fordham Journal of Corporate and Financial Law* 705

Kotzur, Markus, 'TFEU Article 83' in Rudolf Geiger, Daniel-Erasmus Khan and Markus Kotzur, *European Union Treaties: A Commentary* (Munich/Oxford/Portland, OR: CH Beck/Hart Publishing, 2015) 450

Krey, Volker, *Keine Strafe ohne Gesetz* (Berlin/New York: De Gruyter, 1983)

Krey, Volker and Esser, Robert, *Deutsche Strafrecht. Allgemeiner Teil*, 4th edn (Stuttgart: Verlag W Kohlhammer, 2011)

Krüger, Matthias, *Die Entmaterialisierungstendenz beim* Rechtsguts*begriff* (Berlin: Duncker & Humblot, 2000)

Kuhlen, Lothar, 'Der Handlungserfolg der strafbaren Gewässerverunreinigung (§ 324 StGB)' (1986) *Goltdammer's Archiv für Strafrecht* 389

Lauterwein, Carl Constantin, *The Limits of Criminal Law* (Ashgate, 2010)

Lemmens, Koen, 'Comparative Law as an Act of Modesty' in Maurice Adams and Jacco Bomhoff (eds), *Practice and Theory in Comparative Law* (Cambridge University Press, 2012)

Lernestedt, Claes, *Kriminalisering - Problem och Principer* [*Criminalisation - Problems and Principles*] (Uppsala: Iustus Förlag, 2003)

Levasseur, Georges, 'Le problème de la dépénalisation' (1983) 6 *Archives de politique criminelle* 53

Ligeti, Katalin, 'Approximation of Substantive Criminal Law and the Establishment of the European Public Prosecutor's Office' in Francesca Galli and Anne Weyembergh, *Approximation of Substantive Criminal Law in the EU: The Way Forward* (Editions de l'Université de Bruxelles, 2013) 73–83

Lindemann, Michael, *Vorasussetzungen und Grenzen legitimen Wirtschaftsstrafrechts* (Tübingen: Mohr Siebeck, 2012)

Lüderssen, Klaus, *Abschaffen des Strafens?* (Frankfurt am Main: Suhrkamp, 1995)

—— 'Soziale Marktwirtschaft, Finanzmarktkrise und Wirtschaftsstrafrecht' in Eberhard Kempf, Klaus Lüderssen and Klaus Volk, *Die Handlungsfreiheit des Unternehmers* (De Gruyter, 2009) 21–26

Márai, Sándor, 'Three Swans' in *Magia* (Warsaw: Czytelnik, 2008) 103–13

Mill, John Stuart, *On Liberty*, 3rd edn (London: Longman, Roberts & Green, 1864)

Mir Puig, Santiago, *Derecho Penal. Parte General*, 9th edn (Barcelona: Editorial Reppertor, 2011)

Moore, Michael S, *Placing Blame: A General Theory of Criminal Law* (Oxford University Press, 2010)

Mülbert, Peter O, 'Corporate Governance of Banks' in Abol Jalivand and AG Malliaris (eds), *Risk Management and Corporate Governance* (New York/London: Routledge, 2012) 243–81

Naucke, Wolfgang, 'Schwerpunktverlagerung im Strafrecht' (1993) *KritV* 135

Noltenius, Bettina, 'Grenzenloser Spielraum des Gesetzesgebers im Strafrecht? Kritische Bemerkungen zur Inzestentscheidung des Bundesverfassungsgerichts vom 26. Februar 2008' (2009) *Zeitschrift für das Juristische Studium (ZJS)* 15

Nozick, Robert, *Anarchy, State, and Utopia* (Oxford/Cambridge, MA: Blackwell/Basic Books, 1974)

Peršak, Nina, *Criminalising Harmful Conduct: The Harm Principle, its Limits and Continental Counterparts* (Springer, 2007)

—— 'Paternalistic Interventions Through the Law on Regulatory Violations' in Magnus Ulväng and Iain Cameron, *Essays on Criminalization and Sanction* (Iustus, 2014) 125–42

'Political Legitimacy', *Stanford Encyclopedia of Philosophy* (first published 29 April 2010), available at http://plato.stanford.edu/entries/legitimacy/

Pradel, Jean, *Droit pénal général*, 15th edn (Paris: Editions Cujas, 2004)

Prittwitz, Cornelius, *Strafrecht und Risiko* (Frankfurt am Main: Vittorio Klostermann, 1993)

—— 'Die deutsche Strafrecht: Fragmentarisch? Subsidiär? *Ultima ratio*?' in Institut für Kriminalwissenschaften Frankfurt am Main (eds), *Vom unmöglichen Zustand des Strafrechts* (Frankfurt am Main et al: Peter Lang, 1995) 387–405

—— 'Strafrecht als Propria Ratio' in Manfred Heinrich, Christian Jäger, Bernd Schünemann et al (eds), *Strafrecht als Scientia Universalis Festschrift für Claus Roxin zum 80. Geburtstag am 15. Mai 2011* (De Gruyter, 2011) 23–38

Pufendorf, Samuel, *De Jure Naturae et Gentium Libri Octo* (CH Oldfather and WA Oldfather (trans), New York: Oceana Publications, 1964 [1688])

Reimann, Mathias and Zimmermann, Reinhard (eds), *The Oxford Handbook of Comparative Law* (Oxford University Press, 2006/2008)

Reinhart, Carmen M and Rogoff, Kenneth S, *This Time is Different: Eight Centuries of Financial Folly* (Princeton University Press, 2009)

'Risk', *Stanford Encyclopedia of Philosophy* (first published 13 March 2007; substantive revision 11 August 2011), available at http://plato.stanford.edu/entries/risk/

Roggi, Oliviero and Altman, Edward (eds), *Managing and Measuring Risk: Emerging Global Standards and Regulation After the Financial Crisis* (Singapore: World Scientific Publishing, 2013)

Rose, David C, *The Moral Foundation of Economic Behavior* (Oxford University Press, 2011)

Rötheli, Tobias F, 'Causes of the Financial Crisis: Risk Misperception, Policy Mistakes, and Banks' Bounded Rationality' (2010) 39 *Journal of Socio-Economics* 119

Roxin, Claus, *Strafrecht. Allgemeiner Teil*, 4th edn (Munich: CH Beck, 2006) vol 1

—— 'The Legislation Critical Concept of Goods-in-Law under Scrutiny' (2013) 3(1) *European Criminal Law Review* 3

Schmitt-Leonardy, Charlotte, *Unternehmenskriminalität ohne Strafrecht?* (Heidelberg et al: CF Müller, 2013)

Seher, Gerhard, 'Prinzipiengestützte Strafnormlegitimation und der Rechtsgutsbegriff' in Roland Hefendehl, Andrew von Hirsch and Wolfgang Wohlers (eds), *Die Rechtgutstheorie: Legitimationsbasis des Strafrechts oder dogmatisches Glasperlenspiel?* (Baden-Baden: Nomos 2003) 39–56

Shapiro, Susan P, 'Collaring the Crime, Not the Criminal: Reconsidering the Concept of White-Collar Crime' (1990) 55(3) *American Sociological Review* 346

Simester, AP, Spencer, JR, Sullivan, GR and Virgo, GJ, *Simester and Sullivan's Criminal Law: Theory and Doctrine*, 5th edn (Oxford/Portland, OR: Hart Publishing, 2013)

Simester, AP and von Hirsch, Andreas, *Crimes, Harms, and Wrongs* (Oxford/Portland, OR: Hart Publishing, 2014)

Simmons, A John, 'Justification and Legitimacy' (1999) 109(4) *Ethics* 739

Skidelsky, Robert, 'What the Wolves of Wall Street can teach us about risk', Project Syndicate, *The Guardian*, 24 March 2014, available at www.theguardian.com

Tiedemann, Klaus, *Wirtschaftstrafrecht. Einführung und Allgemeiner Teil mit wichtigen Rechtstexten*, 3rd edn (Carl Heymanns Verlag, 2010)

Tosza, Stanisław, 'La responsabilidad por los actos riesgosos de gestión en las sociedades de capital: Un estudio de derecho comparado' (2010) 26 *La Revista Penal* 177

Tur, Richard, 'Dishonesty and the Jury: A Case Study in the Moral Content of Law' (1984) 18 *Philosophy and Practice* 75

Van Rijsbergen, Marloes, 'On the Enforceability of EU Agencies' Soft Law at the National Level: The Case of the European Securities and Markets Authority' (2014) 10(5) *Utrecht Law Review* 116

Vervaele, John AE, 'The European Union and Harmonization of the Criminal Law Enforcement of Union Policies: In Search of a Criminal Law Policy?' in Magnus Ulväng and Iain Cameron, *Essays on Criminalization and Sanction* (Iustus, 2014) 185–225

Viscusi, W Kip, 'How Do Judges Think about Risk?' (1999) 1(1) *American Law and Economics Review* 26

—— 'Corporate Risk Analysis: A Reckless Act?' (1999–2000) 52 *Stanford Law Review* 547

Vogel, Joachim, '"Vergabestrafrecht": Zur straf- und bußgeldrechtlichen Verantwortlichkeit öffentlicher Auftraggeber bei Verletzung des Vergaberechts' in Ulrich Sieber, Gerhard Dannecker, Urs Kindhäuser, Joachim Vogel and Tonio Walter, *Strafrecht und Wirtschaftsstrafrecht - Dogmatik, Rechtsvergleich, Rechtstatsachen - Festschrift für Klaus Tiedemann zum 70. Geburtstag* (Köln: Carl Heymanns Verlag, 2008) 817–36

Voltaire, *Commentaire sur le Livre des Délits et des Peines* (Genève, 1767)

—— *Prix de la Justice et de l'humanité* (London, 1777)

Von Hirsch, Andrew, 'Extending the Harm Principle: "Remote" Harms and Fair Imputation' in AP Simester and ATH Smith (eds), *Harm and Culpability* (Oxford: Clarendon Press, 1996) 259–76

—— 'Der Rechtsgutsbegriff und das "Harm Principle"' in Roland Hefendehl, Andrew von Hirsch and Wolfgang Wohlers (eds), *Die Rechtgutstheorie: Legitimationsbasis des Strafrechts oder dogmatisches Glasperlenspiel?* (Baden-Baden: Nomos, 2003) 13–25

—— 'Der Rechtsgutsbegriff und das "Harm Principle"' in Roland Hefendehl, Andrew von Hirsch and Wolfgang Wohlers (eds), *Die Rechtgutstheorie: Legitimationsbasis des Strafrechts oder dogmatisches Glasperlenspiel?* (Baden-Baden: Nomos, 2003) 13–25

Weigend, Thomas, 'Bewältigung von Beweisschwierigkeiten durch Ausdehnung des materiellen Strafrechts?' in Kurt Schmoller (ed), *Festschrift für Otto Triffterer* (Vienna/New York: Springer, 1996) 695–712

—— 'Einleitung' in Heinrich Wilhelm Laufhütte, Ruth Rissing-van Saan and Klaus Tiedemann, *Strafgesetzbuch. Leipziger Kommentar*, vol 1, *Einleitung: §§ 1 bis 31*, 12th edn (Berlin/New York: De Gruyter, 2007)

Wienbracke, Mike, 'Der Verhältnismäßigkeitsgrundsatz' (2003) *Zeitschrift für das Juristische Studium (ZJS)* 148

Wohlers, Wolfgang, *Deliktstypen des Präventionsstrafrechts – zur Dogmatik "moderner" Gefährdungsdelikte* (Berlin: Duncker & Humblot, 2000)

Wróbel, Włodzimierz and Zoll, Andrzej, *Polskie Prawo Karne. Część Ogólne* (Kraków: Znak, 2010)

Zweigert, Konrad and Kötz, Hein, *An Introduction to Comparative Law*, 3rd edn (Oxford: Clarendon Press, 1998)

INDEX

CPSIA information can be obtained
at www.ICGtesting.com
Printed in the USA
LVHW020713101122
732764LV00009B/282

9 781509 944958